Lecture Notes in Computer Science 13402

More information about this series at https://link.springer.com/bookseries/558

Bastien Chopard · Stefania Bandini ·
Alberto Dennunzio · Mira Arabi Haddad (Eds.)

Cellular Automata

15th International Conference on Cellular Automata
for Research and Industry, ACRI 2022
Geneva, Switzerland, September 12–15, 2022
Proceedings

 Springer

Editors
Bastien Chopard ⓘ
University of Geneva
Geneva, Switzerland

Alberto Dennunzio ⓘ
University of Milano-Bicocca
Milan, Italy

Stefania Bandini ⓘ
University of Milano-Bicocca
Milan, Italy

Mira Arabi Haddad
University of Geneva
Geneva, Switzerland

ISSN 0302-9743   ISSN 1611-3349 (electronic)
Lecture Notes in Computer Science
ISBN 978-3-031-14925-2   ISBN 978-3-031-14926-9 (eBook)
https://doi.org/10.1007/978-3-031-14926-9

This Springer imprint is published by the registered company Springer Nature Switzerland AG
The registered company address is: Gewerbestrasse 11, 6330 Cham, Switzerland

Preface

This volume contains a collection of original papers covering both applications and theoretical results on cellular automata, which were selected for presentation at the 15th International Conference on Cellular Automata for Research and Industry, ACRI 2022, held in Geneva, Switzerland, from September 12 to September 15, 2022. The event was organized by the Computer Science Department of the Faculty of Sciences at the University of Geneva.

The primary goal of the conference was to bring together researchers coming from many different scientific fields in order to favor and foster international collaborations on cellular automata as well as to spread scientific knowledge among the experts in several scientific areas: computer science, pure and applied mathematics, physics, biology, etc.

Cellular automata are powerful computational models used for studying complex phenomena characterized by simple local interactions. They are discrete (both in space and time) models that have been successfully applied in many different scientific fields for dealing with complex systems. Starting from their introduction in the middle of the 20th century, cellular automata have generated more and more interest in both the theoretical aspects and the practical applications.

The ACRI conference series was first organized in Italy, namely, ACRI 1994 in Rende, ACRI 1996 in Milan, and ACRI 1998 in Trieste, which were followed by ACRI 2000 in Karlsruhe (Germany), ACRI 2002 in Geneva (Switzerland), ACRI 2004 in Amsterdam (The Netherlands), ACRI 2006 in Perpignan (France), ACRI 2008 in Yokohama (Japan), ACRI 2010 in Ascoli Piceno (Italy), ACRI 2012 in Santorini (Greece), ACRI 2014 in Kraków (Poland), ACRI 2016 in Fez (Morocco), ACRI 2018 in Como (Italy), and ACRI 2020 in Łódź (Poland).

This 15th edition of ACRI aimed at enlarging the traditional topics to include other areas related to or extending cellular automata. This allowed a larger community to have the opportunity to discuss their work in various related fields like, for example, complex networks, games, cryptography, lattice gas and lattice Boltzmann models, agent-based models, etc.

Each paper inside this volume was reviewed by at least two Program Committee members. Following the initial, tutorial-related, paper, the remainder of the volume is divided into five parts, which collate the papers relating to different topic areas: Theory; Modelling and Simulation of Physical Systems and Phenomena; Cellular Automata and Spreading Dynamics; Crowds, Pedestrians, and Traffic Dynamics; and Other Studies on Cellular Automata.

We would like to express our sincere thanks to the invited speakers who kindly accepted our invitation to give plenary lecture at ACRI 2022: Michel Milinkovitch, Katsuhiro Nishinari, and Pablo Arrighi.

Moreover, we are grateful to the Program Committee and all the additional reviewers for their contribution in selecting the papers. We are also grateful for the financial and logistic support from CUI (Centre Universitaire d'Informatique) and the Computer Science Department of the University of Geneva. Finally, we acknowledge the excellent cooperation from the Lecture Notes in Computer Science team of Springer for their help in producing this volume in time for the conference.

July 2022

Bastien Chopard
Stefania Bandini
Alberto Dennunzio
Mira Arabi Haddad

Organization

Program Committee Chair

Bastien Chopard — University of Geneva, Switzerland

Program Committee

Andy Adamatzky	University of the West of England, UK
Jan Baetens	Ghent University, Belgium
Franco Bagnoli	University of Florence, Italy
Pedro Balbi de Oliveira	Universidade Presbiteriana Mackenzie, Brazil
Stefania Bandini	University of Milano-Bicocca, Italy
Bastien Chopard	University of Geneva, Switzerland
Bernard De Baets	Ghent University, Belgium
Alberto Dennunzio	University of Milano-Bicocca, Italy
Andreas Deutsch	TU Dresden, Germany
Salvatore Di Gregorio	University of Calabria, Italy
Samira El Yacoubi	Université de Perpignan, France
Jean-Luc Falcone	University of Geneva, Switzerland
Nazim Fates	Loria, Inria Nancy, France
Enrico Formenti	University of Nice Sophia Antipolis, France
Ioakeim Georgoudas	Democritus University of Thrace, Greece
Rolf Hoffmann	TU Darmstadt, Germany
Krzysztof Kułakowski	AGH University of Science and Technology, Poland
Martin Kutrib	Universität Giessen, Germany
Anna T. Lawniczak	University of Guelph, Canada
Laurent Lefevre	LCIS, Université Grenoble Alpes, France
Luca Mariot	Radboud University, The Netherlands
Genaro J. Martínez	National Polytechnic Institute, Mexico
Katsuhiro Nishinari	University of Tokyo, Japan
Dipanwita Roy Chowdhury	Indian Institute of Technology Kharagpur, India
Andreas Schadschneider	University of Cologne, Germany
Biplab K. Sikdar	Indian Institute of Engineering Science and Technology, India
Georgios Ch. Sirakoulis	Democritus University of Thrace, Greece
Pawel Topa	AGH University of Science and Technology, Poland

Hiroshi Umeo	University of Osaka Electro-Communication, Japan
Giuseppe Vizzari	University of Milano-Bicocca, Italy
Barbara Wolnik	University of Gdańsk, Poland
Thomas Worsch	Karlsruhe Institute of Technology, Germany
Radouane Yafia	Ibn Zohr University, Morocco

Steering Committee

Stefania Bandini	University of Milano-Bicocca, Italy
Bastien Chopard	University of Geneva, Switzerland
Samira El Yacoubi	University of Perpignan, France
Giancarlo Mauri	University of Milano-Bicocca, Italy
Katsuhiro Nishinari	University of Tokyo, Japan
Georgios Ch. Sirakoulis	Democritus University of Thrace, Greece
Hiroshi Umeo	Osaka Electro-Communication University, Japan
Thomas Worsch	Karlsruhe Institute of Technology, Germany

Organizing Committee

Bastien Chopard (Chair)	University of Geneva, Switzerland
Stefania Bandini	University of Milano-Bicocca, Italy
Alberto Dennunzio	University of Milano-Bicocca, Italy
Mira Arabi Haddad	University of Geneva, Switzerland

Organizing Institution

Faculté des Sciences
Université de Genève

Contents

Modelling and Simulation of Physical Systems and Phenomena

Cellular Automata and Spreading Dynamics

Crowds, Pedestrian, and Traffic Dynamics

Other Studies on Cellular Automata

Cellular Automata Tutoring

Cellular Automata Application on Chemical Computing Logic Circuits

Michail-Antisthenis Tsompanas[1]([✉])[iD],
Theodoros Panagiotis Chatzinikolaou[2][iD], and Georgios Ch. Sirakoulis[2][iD]

[1] Unconventional Computing Laboratory, University of the West of England,
Bristol BS16 1QY, UK
Antisthenis.Tsompanas@uwe.ac.uk

[2] Department of Electrical and Computer Engineering, Democritus University
of Thrace, Xanthi, Greece

Abstract. Cellular Automata (CAs) have been proved to be a robust tool for mimicking a plethora of biological, physical and chemical systems. CAs can be used as an alternative to partial differential equations, in order to illustrate the evolution in time of the aforementioned systems. However, CAs are preferred due to their formulation simplicity and their ability to portray the emerging of complex dynamics. Their simplicity is attributed to the fact that they are composed by simple elementary components, whereas their complexity capacities are the result of emerging behaviors from the local interactions of these elementary components. Here, the utilization of CAs on mimicking of physio-chemical reactions is presented. In specific, the implementation of chemical-based logic circuits with the use of the Belousov-Zhabotinsky (BZ) class reactions was illustrated. The BZ reaction can demonstrate non-linear oscillations that have been utilized in different scenarios as a computational substrate, whereas its photo-sensitivity have been exploited as an additional factor of manipulating the computations. A common method to mathematically represent the BZ dynamics is the Oregonator equations, which are a set of PDEs. In this work the approximation of the Oregonator equations is performed with CAs to simulate logic circuits (from classic logic gates like AND to combinatorial ones). The proposed tool has been proved to be in agreement with results produced in the lab from the actual chemical reactions. Moreover, the tool is used to design novel computing architectures in a trivial manner, without the need of specialized knowledge on chemistry, without the need to handle dangerous chemicals and alleviating unnecessary costs for equipment and consumables. The main advantage of this method can be summarized as the acceleration achieved in current implementations (serial computers), but also towards potential future implementations in massively parallel computational systems (like Field-Programmable Gate Array hardware and mainly nano-neuromorphic circuits) that have been proved to be good substrates for accelerating the implemented CA models.

Keywords: Cellular automata · Belousov-Zabotinsky reaction · Unconventional computing · Chemical computing

B. Chopard et al. (Eds.): ACRI 2022, LNCS 13402, pp. 3–14, 2022.
https://doi.org/10.1007/978-3-031-14926-9_1

1   Introduction

Limitations of silicon based computing, like Moore's Law and environmental reasons for higher integration of green computing have refueled the interest and effort put in the field of unconventional computing. Namely, specific features of physical, chemical and living systems are exploited to perform some types of computations [1]. The use of material in the liquid state for building computing systems is not a new concept, however, it still sounds alien to most of computer scientists [5]. Despite that, there are plenty prototypes build in laboratories that employ liquids to perform computations. The use of the liquids can be to carry signals, accommodate chemical reactions or actuate mechanical parts as an element of the calculations [5].

A well established medium that is utilized in several laboratory based experiments is the Belousov-Zhabotinsky (BZ) reaction [53,54]. This class of reactions is characterized by non-equilibrium thermodynamics that are the result of interactions between the activating and inhibiting species within the liquid solution [11]. Because of these dynamics, the reactions are ideal for use as a computational substrate. One of the first experiments to prove the suitability of BZ as a computational substrate was the successful replication of the diode on the medium [7]. Moreover, more complicated architectures were developed, like counters [24] and logic gates [45]. While, these experiments proved the concept that BZ medium can be utilized as the building block of a massively parallel computational medium, some other experiments targeted on computation beyond the use of classical von Neumann architectures. For instance, the use of a light-sensitive variant of the BZ solution to perform image processing [36] and more recently, the use of mechanical parts to build an array of programmable BZ cells that have achieved in memory computation, performing pattern recognition as a chemical auto-encoder [40].

The robustness of these unconventional computing machines is attributed to the fact that they are comprised by several elementary units that can be affected by and interchange signals internally or/and to their environment, in order to acquire, retain and process information [44]. This definition makes them ideal systems to be mimicked by Cellular Automata (CAs). CAs are models of physical systems that incorporate localized interactions, whereas space and time are defined in a discrete form [52]. In order to define a CA, the simulated plane is divided in a grid of cells, where each cell is described by an ensemble of parameters, namely its state, and a local rule that determines how the state of each cell is updated based on the neighboring cells' states. Usually the rule is the same for all the cells in the grid and they update their states in a synchronous manner [17,35], although, spatial inhomogeneity in the rule can be inserted and asynchronous updating of the local rule. The process of using CAs to simulate physical systems is in agreement with the present concept of unified space and time, as well as implementing the cutting-edge notion of in-memory computation. This is conceived by representing the memory as the state of the CA cell and the processing unit as the local rule of the grid [8].

There are numerous examples of successful explanation and simulation of real world phenomena by CAs [17, 26]. For instance, they were utilized as robust tools to extensively analyze and effortlessly imitate the dynamical wave propagation in chemical media [18, 27, 37, 38, 51]. These models enabled the analysis of the dispersion and curvature of wave patterns [22], the wave dynamics associated with turbulence [27] and anisotropic media [41]. Nonetheless, CAs are suitable tools to approximate the solution of partial differential equations (PDEs) and it has been established that they can easily represent high complexity in the initialization, constrains and anisotropies of PDEs [43, 47].

This study investigates the transformation of the Oregonator equations used to simulate light-sensitive BZ reactions into a local rule for CAs. In particular, the Oregonator is a very simple model of chemical dynamics of the BZ reaction oscillations [20, 25, 53, 54]. It was developed by Field and Noise [21] at the University of Oregon and consists of five elementary chemical stoichiometries. This network was obtained by reconstructing BZ's complex chemical reaction mechanism while the reduction is carried out using standard methods of chemical dynamics, in particular the approximation of the step ratio. The successful corresponding CA tool is then utilized to inform the development of light masks that can be used so that the reservoir performs the desired logic functionality. As examples here, the classic AND logic gate and a combinatorial one were demonstrated.

2 Methods for Simulation of Chemical Gates

The dynamics of the BZ reaction that is affected by light intensity can be determined by the Oregonator equation set with two variables [10, 21]. These two variables represent the concentrations of excitation (u) and refractory (v) components in the chemical solution. Namely, the equations are:

$$
\begin{aligned}
\frac{\partial u}{\partial t} &= \frac{1}{\epsilon}\left(u - u^2 - (fv + \phi)\frac{u-q}{u+q}\right) + D_u \nabla^2 u \\
\frac{\partial v}{\partial t} &= u - v
\end{aligned}
\tag{1}
$$

where u and v as mentioned previously are the activating/excitation and the inhibiting/refractory ingredients of BZ reaction, respectively. The time scale for the conversion of u to v is expressed as the ϵ parameter. The stoichiometric coefficient of the reaction is expressed as f, whereas, the proportional modulation between activation and inhibition of the ingredients is expressed by the parameter q. Also, the development of the inhibiting ingredient can be affected by the ϕ parameter, a fact that is employed to represent the photo-sensitivity of the BZ. Namely, the parameter ϕ can be associated with the illumination intensity of the specific area and, as a result, alter the speed of the inhibiting ingredient development. More specifically, the lower the parameter ϕ is, the lower the speed of the inhibiting ingredient is developed and, as a result, the BZ medium becomes more excitable.

The use of CAs for the numerical approximation of differential equations was studied and confirmed [16, 28, 30, 47, 48] as a powerful technique in order to provide significant speed up. Given the fact that CAs are viable alternatives of solving PDEs, the Oregonator equations were expressed in a CA format to study a photo-sensitive BZ medium and its application in unconventional computations.

This CA model has been developed and tested previously [15, 49, 50], and proved to replicate the results of previous models and actual chemical experiments with appropriate accuracy. It is based on a discrete grid that divides the area of interest in identical cells. These cells are characterized by a specific state each, which are updated in a synchronous fashion based on a local rule. The local rule takes into account the states of the current cell and all the cells in its neighborhood. From the two most renown neighborhoods for CAs in two dimensions, the von Neumann was utilized here. Namely, the center, north, south, east and west adjacent cells form a group that informs the updating of the local rule.

The cells that represent the laboratory area are defined by the following state:

$$ST_{i,j}^t = \{AA_{i,j}, U_{i,j}^t, V_{i,j}^t, \Phi_{i,j}\} \tag{2}$$

where $AA_{i,j}$ is a constant parameter that symbolizes the sectors that can be accessed by the chemical waves, i.e. sets the barriers of the computing architecture. Also, parameters $U_{i,j}^t$ and $V_{i,j}^t$ symbolize the aggregation of the excitation and refractory ingredients, respectively, of the simulated sector as the (i, j) cell on the time interval t. The final parameter of the state, defined as Φ, symbolizes the intensity of light in the appropriate cell (i, j) that affects the speed of development of the refractory ingredient, which is similar to the parameter ϕ used in Eq. (1).

Utilizing the technique of the three point central difference approximation:

$$\frac{d^2g}{dx^2}\bigg|_x = \frac{g(x + \Delta x) - 2g(x) + g(x - \Delta x)}{\Delta x^2} \tag{3}$$

and the set of the Oregonator equations (Eq. 1), the local rule is obtained as in the following:

$$U_{i,j}^{t+1} = \frac{\Delta t}{\epsilon}(U_{i,j}^t - U_{i,j}^t{}^2 - (fV_{i,j}^t + \Phi_{i,j})\frac{U_{i,j}^t - q}{U_{i,j}^t + q})$$
$$+ \frac{\Delta t D_u}{\Delta x^2}(U_{i-1,j}^t + U_{i+1,j}^t + U_{i,j-1}^t + U_{i,j+1}^t - 4 * U_{i,j}^t)) + U_{i,j}^t$$
$$V_{i,j}^{t+1} = \Delta t[U_{i,j}^t - V_{i,j}^t] + V_{i,j}^t \tag{4}$$

To initialize the architecture of the chemical gate and set its functionality, each parameter of the state of the CA cells were set to the following values for $t = 0$. For the area availability parameter, $AA_{i,j} = 1$ represents a section where the chemical waves can not reach, whereas $AA_{i,j} = 0$ represents a section that is part that is accessible by the chemicals. To express the inputs of the chemical gates, in these specific areas where logic values are considered *HIGH* the concentration of the excitation ingredient is set to the maximum values, namely $U_{i,j}^{t=0} = 1$. For the rest of the areas, the concentration of both ingredients are set to zero. Finally, the parameter that expresses the controllability by light intensity, $\Phi_{i,j}$ is equal with 0.088 for sections simulating excitable areas, whereas equal with 0.091 for sections simulating sub-excitable areas.

The aforementioned values of excitability control were based on previous works [4,50] where the simulations provided similar results to actual experiments. The traversing of the chemical waves in the simulated area for a sub-excitable and an excitable medium are compared in Fig. 1. This example is performed on a 100×100 cells grid, where the available area is illustrated with white color, whereas the unavailable area with grey color. An initial source of the wave fronts is defined as an ensemble of cells (here defined as an area of 5×1 cells) that were set with an initial parameter $U_{i,j}^{t=0} = 1$ and indicated by a black arrow. The difference of the traverse of wave fronts on an excitable and a sub-excitable medium can be realized in Figs. 1(b) and (c), respectively. The advance of the wave fronts in Fig. 1(b) and (c) is depicted in grey scale, whereas the unavailable area in black color. In the case of the excitable medium (Fig. 1(b)) it is apparent that the wave front is inflated around the whole available area after reaching a wider channel. On the other hand, in the case of the sub-excitable medium (Fig. 1(c)), the formation of the waves on the wider channel resembles the formation of the narrow channel where it was initiated. This can imitate

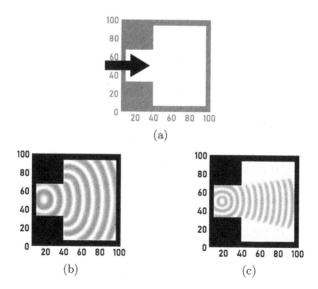

Fig. 1. (a) Chemical medium representation. wave front evolution for (b) excitable and (c) sub-excitable medium.

the ballistic features of entities used in collision based computing [2,3]. Thus, a similar approach is utilized to implement logic circuits.

3 Results

Having as main goal to simulate the potential computational capabilities of the chemical medium, two gates were demonstrated with the CA-based described earlier Oregonator model, namely a classic AND and one with combinatorial logic gate. For triggering the input signals, the $U_{i,j}^{t=0}$ ingredient was set to 1 for a column of 10×1 cells on the respective input channel. To provide a clear view of the wave front, the presented figures were considered as snapshots of every 500 time-steps of the simulation and not as the results on the final time-step of the simulation.

The AND gate was designed as depicted in Fig. 2(a) configuration, where the inputs, outputs and the light mask are properly illustrated. This is a two-input gate and only when both inputs are HIGH ("1"), the gate output requests to be HIGH, as can be realized in Fig. 2(d) through the merging of the two wave fronts that results to a unified one able to travel forward to the proper output channel. On the contrary, when only one of the proposed inputs is present, the wave front is not able to overcome the sub-excitable medium areas and, as a result, it is slowly decreasing till it dies out (Figs. 2(b) and (c)). Consequently, the light sensitive BZ logic gate acts as a constraint to the wave propagation. The truth table of AND gate is achieved in the experiments as shown in Fig. 2 owing to the topology of light illumination, given that the ("00") case is again omitted since no wave front would be propagated in the medium.

As next step, the emergence of increased complexity in logic functions, within the same grid of 200×500 cells used for the basic logic gate, was attempted. The presented gate of Fig. 3(a) is able to perform two logic functions at the same time, utilizing the illustrated light mask. The simulations for every input combinations were successfully performed (Figs. 3(b), (c) and (d)), verifying that the results comply with the theoretical background for the $F_U = \overline{A}B$ and $F_L = A\overline{B}$ functions of the upper and lower output channel, respectively.

In the aftermath, in case of cascading such gates, the formation of more complex functions can be achieved. For example, a XOR gate can be formed if both outputs of the combinatorial gate are connected to the inputs of an OR gate. Considering that XOR gate can be the "SUM" output of a half-adder, along with an AND gate representing the "CARRY" output, a complete computing system can be achieved.

In the view of the forgoing, there is a novel nano-electronic device suitable for the successful representation of CA models in hardware, and in particular for chemical logic gates, namely memristor device [46] able to perform effectively in-memory computations taking leverage of its inherent characteristics of non-volatility, high density and low power consumption. In more details, memristor is a two terminal nanoelectronic device with resistance controlled by an applied voltage signal across its terminals, and depended on its state's history [19]. It

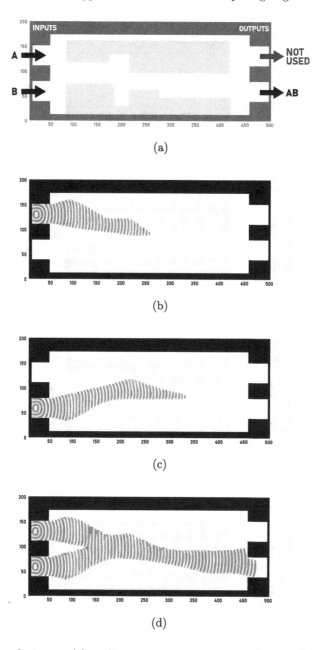

Fig. 2. AND logic gate (a) medium configuration and (b–d) simulation results.

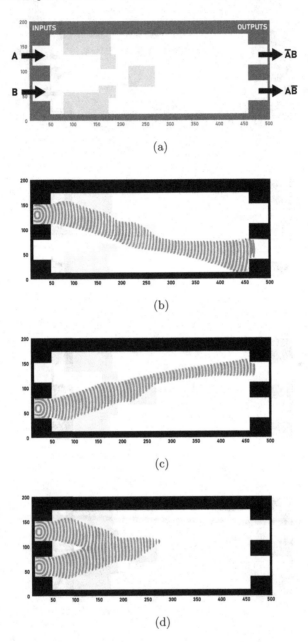

Fig. 3. Combinatorial logic gate (a) medium configuration and (b–d) simulation results.

presents certain similarities with the notion of unified memory and computation architecture in one physical unit like CAs while, at the same time, memristors are successfully implemented in a grid like manner as switching nodes on nano-crossbars. Moreover, memristors have been efficiently coupled with the CA notion resulting to the notion of memristive cellular automata [6,29,31–34,39,42]. Towards this path, memristors have been utilized for implementing a coupling between excitable elements [9,23] that are able to propagate wave fronts. Also, simplified MRLC and MRC circuits have been presented in literature that mimic the behaviour of the chemical waves propagation and interaction in order to perform logic computations [12–14]. The resulting unconventional logic gates as well as their nano-electronic representation through the memristors' oscillating networks in crossbar topologies incorporate basic principles of CA theory, like emergent computation, inherent parallelism, reprogrammability and neighborhood consideration.

Concerning the first approach, an implementation of a reaction-diffusion-based (RD-based) excitable medium is foreseen incorporating memristive devices into the nano-electronic circuit. These RD circuitries are able to perform CA-like computations of RD systems using nano-electronic elements that emulate chemical reactions. Having a rectangular or hexagonal grid of such RC cells coupled with each other through their neighboring connections via appropriate devices can result to a 2-D spatial chemical dissipation and wave propagation to the medium. The diffusion coupling of the RD-based excitable medium is modeled with the memristor nanodevices by changing their switching state when the excitable waves are propagating towards them. Both 1-D and 2-D RD models can be foreseen, showcasing the velocity change of the propagating excitable wave directly linked to the conductance change.

In the case of the latest approach, the wave propagation of a BZ membrane is presented thought the transmission-line-equivalent of appropriate nano-electronic circuits. A memristor is incorporated in these cells in order to expand the local non-linearity of BZ medium. The wave propagation is occurring through an applied voltage stimulus, which is transmitted to the neighboring cells of the proposed grid. In order to simplify the circuit, a corresponding memristor-based with elements unit can be utilized finally able to perform oscillations even with the inductor element is removed. Neighboring cells are connected using a power supply module that can activate their oscillation and effectively perform the wave propagation though the medium. Suitable simulations of chemical logic gates have been already presented in the corresponding literature for the successful evaluation of the discussed approaches enabling chemical computing with nano-electronic circuits.

4   Conclusions

In this work, chemical logic gates simulation was efficiently performed by utilizing the concept of CA in combination with the Oregonator model. In particular, chemical medium light sensitivity was taken into consideration and exploited to demonstrate various logic gates. Simulations for classic logic gate like the AND one, as well as for more complex and combinatorial functions were adequately delivered proving the correct functionality of the proposed model.

Acknowledgment. This work has been supported by the Hellenic Foundation for Research and Innovation (H.F.R.I.) under the "First Call for H.F.R.I. Research Projects to support Faculty members and Researchers and the procurement of high-cost research equipment grant" (Project Number: 3830).

References

1. Adamatzky, A. (ed.): Advances in Unconventional Computing: Volume 2: Prototypes, Models and Algorithms. ECC, vol. 23. Springer, Cham (2017). https://doi.org/10.1007/978-3-319-33921-4
2. Adamatzky, A.: Collision-based computing in Belousov-Zhabotinsky medium. Chaos, Solitons Fractals **21**(5), 1259–1264 (2004)
3. Adamatzky, A., Durand-Lose, J.: Collision-based computing. In: Rozenberg, G., Bäck, T., Kok, J.N. (eds.) Handbook of Natural Computing, pp. 1949–1978. Springer, Heidelberg (2012). https://doi.org/10.1007/978-3-540-92910-9_58
4. Adamatzky, A.: Fredkin and Toffoli gates implemented in Oregonator model of Belousov-Zhabotinsky medium. Int. J. Bifurcat. Chaos **27**(03), 1750041 (2017)
5. Adamatzky, A.: A brief history of liquid computers. Philos. Trans. R. Soc. B **374**(1774), 20180372 (2019)
6. Adamatzky, A., Chua, L.: Memristive excitable cellular automata. Int. J. Bifurcat Chaos **21**(11), 3083–3102 (2011)
7. Agladze, K., Aliev, R., Yamaguchi, T., Yoshikawa, K.: Chemical diode. J. Phys. Chem. **100**(33), 13895–13897 (1996)
8. Alonso-Sanz, R.: Cellular automata with memory. In: Meyers, R.A. (ed.) Encyclopedia of Complexity and Systems Science, pp. 823–848. Springer, New York (2009). https://doi.org/10.1007/978-0-387-30440-3_55
9. Asai, T.: Reaction-diffusion media with excitable Oregonators coupled by memristors. In: Chua, L., Sirakoulis, G.C., Adamatzky, A. (eds.) Handbook of Memristor Networks, pp. 1229–1239. Springer, Cham (2019). https://doi.org/10.1007/978-3-319-76375-0_44
10. Beato, V., Engel, H.: Pulse propagation in a model for the photosensitive Belousov-Zhabotinsky reaction with external noise. In: SPIE's 1st International Symposium on Fluctuations and Noise, pp. 353–362. International Society for Optics and Photonics (2003)
11. Cassani, A., Monteverde, A., Piumetti, M.: Belousov-Zhabotinsky type reactions: the non-linear behavior of chemical systems. J. Math. Chem. **59**(3), 792–826 (2021). https://doi.org/10.1007/s10910-021-01223-9
12. Chatzinikolaou, T.P., et al.: Margolus chemical wave logic gate with memristive oscillatory networks. In: 2021 28th IEEE International Conference on Electronics, Circuits, and Systems (ICECS), pp. 1–6 (2021)

13. Chatzinikolaou, T.P., et al.: Memristive oscillatory networks for computing: the chemical wave propagation paradigm. In: 2021 17th International Workshop on Cellular Nanoscale Networks and their Applications (CNNA), pp. 1–5 (2021)
14. Chatzinikolaou, T.P., et al.: Unconventional logic on memristor-based oscillatory medium. In: 2021 10th International Conference on Modern Circuits and Systems Technologies (MOCAST), pp. 1–4 (2021)
15. Chatzinikolaou, T.P., et al.: Chemical wave computing from labware to electrical systems. Electronics 11(11), 1683 (2022)
16. Chopard, B., Droz, M.: Cellular automata model for the diffusion equation. J. Stat. Phys. 64(3), 859–892 (1991)
17. Chopard, B., Droz, M.: Cellular Automata Modeling of Physical Systems. Collection Alea-Saclay: Monographs and Texts in Statistical Physics. Cambridge University Press, New York (1998)
18. Chopard, B., Luthi, P., Droz, M.: Reaction-diffusion cellular automata model for the formation of Leisegang patterns. Phys. Rev. Lett. 72, 1384–1387 (1994)
19. Chua, L.: Memristor-the missing circuit element. IEEE Trans. Circ. Theor. 18(5), 507–519 (1971)
20. Epstein, I.R., Pojman, J.A.: An Introduction to Nonlinear Chemical Dynamics: Oscillations, Waves, Patterns, and Chaos. Topics in Physical Chemistry. Oxford University Press (1998)
21. Field, R.J., Noyes, R.M.: Oscillations in chemical systems. IV. Limit cycle behavior in a model of a real chemical reaction. J. Chem. Phys. 60(5), 1877–1884 (1974)
22. Gerhardt, M., Schuster, H., Tyson, J.J.: A cellular automation model of excitable media including curvature and dispersion. Science 247(4950), 1563–1566 (1990)
23. Gong, X., Asai, T., Motomura, M.: Reaction-diffusion media with excitable Oregonators coupled by memristors. In: 2012 13th International Workshop on Cellular Nanoscale Networks and their Applications (CNNA), pp. 1–6. IEEE (2012)
24. Gorecki, J., Yoshikawa, K., Igarashi, Y.: On chemical reactors that can count. J. Phys. Chem. A 107(10), 1664–1669 (2003)
25. Gray, P., Scott, S.: Chemical Oscillations and Instabilities: Non-Linear Chemical Kinetics. International Series of Monographs on Chemistry. Clarendon Press (1994)
26. Cárdenas, R., Henares, K., Ruiz-Martín, C., Wainer, G.: ACRI 2020. LNCS, vol. 12599. Springer, Cham (2021). https://doi.org/10.1007/978-3-030-69480-7
27. Hartman, H., Tamayo, P.: Reversible cellular automata and chemical turbulence. Physica D Nonlinear Phenom. 45(1-3), 293–306 (1990)
28. Hu, R., Ruan, X.: Differential equation and cellular automata model. In: Proceedings of the 2003 IEEE International Conference on Robotics, Intelligent Systems and Signal Processing, vol. 2, pp. 1047–1051. IEEE (2003)
29. Itoh, M., Chua, L.O.: Memristor cellular automata and memristor discrete-time cellular neural networks. Int. J. Bifurcat. Chaos 19(11), 3605–3656 (2009)
30. Karafyllidis, I.: A model for the prediction of oil slick movement and spreading using cellular automata. Environ. Int. 23(6), 839–850 (1997)
31. Karamani, R.-E., et al.: Memristive learning cellular automata: theory and applications. In: 2020 9th International Conference on Modern Circuits and Systems Technologies (MOCAST), pp. 1–5 (2020)
32. Karamani, R.-E., Fyrigos, I.-A., Ntinas, V., Vourkas, I., Sirakoulis, G.C., Rubio, A.: Memristive cellular automata for modeling of epileptic brain activity. In: 2018 IEEE International Symposium on Circuits and Systems (ISCAS), pp. 1–5 (2018)
33. Karamani, R.-E., Fyrigos, I.-A., Tsakalos, K.-A., Ntinas, V., Tsompanas, M.-A., Sirakoulis, G.C.: Memristive learning cellular automata for edge detection. Chaos, Solitons Fractals 145, 110700 (2021)

34. Karamani, R.-E., Ntinas, V., Vourkas, I., Sirakoulis, G.C.: 1-D memristor-based cellular automaton for pseudo-random number generation. In: 2017 27th International Symposium on Power and Timing Modeling, Optimization and Simulation (PATMOS), pp. 1–6 (2017)
35. Kari, J.: Theory of cellular automata: a survey. Theoret. Comput. Sci. **334**(1–3), 3–33 (2005)
36. Kuhnert, L., Agladze, K., Krinsky, V.: Image processing using light-sensitive chemical waves. Nature **337**(6204), 244–247 (1989)
37. Markus, M., Hess, B.: Isotropic cellular automaton for modelling excitable media. Nature **347**(6288), 56–58 (1990)
38. Maselko, J., Showalter, K.: Chemical waves in inhomogeneous excitable media. Physica D **49**(1–2), 21–32 (1991)
39. Ntinas, V., Sirakoulis, G.C., Rubio, A.: Memristor-based probabilistic cellular automata. In: 2021 IEEE International Midwest Symposium on Circuits and Systems (MWSCAS), pp. 792–795 (2021)
40. Parrilla-Gutierrez, J.M., et al.: A programmable chemical computer with memory and pattern recognition. Nat. Commun. **11**(1), 1–8 (2020)
41. Schönfisch, B.: Anisotropy in cellular automata. Biosystems **41**(1), 29–41 (1997)
42. Secco, J., Farina, M., Demarchi, D., Corinto, F.: Memristor cellular automata through belief propagation inspired algorithm. In: 2015 International SoC Design Conference (ISOCC), pp. 211–212 (2015)
43. Sirakoulis, G.C., Adamatzky, A. (eds.): Robots and Lattice Automata. ECC, vol. 13. Springer, Cham (2015). https://doi.org/10.1007/978-3-319-10924-4
44. Solé, R., Moses, M., Forrest, S.: Liquid brains, solid brains. Philos. Trans. R. Soc. Lond. B Biol. Sci. **374** (1774), 20190040 (2019)
45. Steinbock, O., Kettunen, P., Showalter, K.: Chemical wave logic gates. J. Phys. Chem. **100**(49), 18970–18975 (1996)
46. Strukov, D.B., Snider, G.S., Stewart, D.R., Williams, R.S.: The missing memristor found. nature **453**(7191), 80–83 (2008)
47. Toffoli, T.: Cellular automata as an alternative to (rather than an approximation of) differential equations in modeling physics. Physica D **10**(1–2), 117–127 (1984)
48. Tsompanas, M.-A., Adamatzky, A., Ieropoulos, I., Phillips, N., Sirakoulis, G.C., Greenman, J.: Cellular non-linear network model of microbial fuel cell. Biosystems **156**, 53–62 (2017)
49. Tsompanas, M.A., Fyrigos, I.A., Ntinas, V., Adamatzky, A., Sirakoulis, G.C.: Cellular automata implementation of Oregonator simulating light-sensitive Belousov-Zhabotinsky medium. Nonlinear Dyn. **104**(4), 4103–4115 (2021)
50. Tsompanas, M.-A., Fyrigos, I.-A., Ntinas, V., Adamatzky, A., Sirakoulis, G.C.: Light sensitive Belousov-Zhabotinsky medium accommodates multiple logic gates. Biosystems **206**, 104447 (2021)
51. Weimar, J.R.: Three-dimensional cellular automata for reaction-diffusion systems. Fund. Inform. **52**(1–3), 277–284 (2002)
52. Wolfram, S.: A New Kind of Science, vol. 5. Wolfram Media, Champaign, IL (2002)
53. Zaikin, A., Zhabotinsky, A.: Concentration wave propagation in two-dimensional liquid-phase self-oscillating system. Nature **225**(5232), 535–537 (1970)
54. Zhabotinsky, A., Zaikin, A.: Autowave processes in a distributed chemical system. J. Theor. Biol. **40**(1), 45–61 (1973)

Theory

Exploring Lightweight S-boxes Using Cellular Automata and Reinforcement Learning

Tarun Ayyagari⬤, Anirudh Saji(✉)⬤, Anita John⬤, and Jimmy Jose⬤

National Institute of Technology Calicut, Kozhikode, India
{tarun_b180682cs,anirudh_b180387cs,anita_p170007cs,jimmy}@nitc.ac.in

Abstract. The most important elements of block ciphers are nonlinear functions known as substitution boxes (S-boxes). S-boxes with weak cryptographic properties are vulnerable to attacks by various cryptanalysis techniques. Cellular Automata has been used to design S-boxes with good cryptographic properties such as nonlinearity, differential uniformity, balancedness, etc. Cellular Automata based S-boxes also have low implementation cost due to their highly parallel nature. In this work, we explore an approach of using Cellular Automata based semi-bent Boolean functions to generate S-boxes. Genetic algorithms have been used extensively to generate CA based S-boxes. Here we explore the use of Reinforcement Learning algorithms that uses relatively well understood and mathematically grounded framework of Markov Decision Processes as an alternative to genetic programming.

Keywords: Lightweight S-boxes · Semi-bent Boolean functions · Cellular Automata · Reinforcement Learning · Block ciphers

1 Introduction

Cellular Automata (CA) have been proved to be quite useful in the field of cryptography, widely being used as keystream generators for stream ciphers due to their good pseudo-randomness. CAs have also been proved to be very useful in creating semi-bent functions with good cryptographic properties as proven in [1]. In this work, we expand on the work done by Mariot et al. in [1] and consider the different permutations of Boolean functions. Further, we implement these Boolean functions as the coordinate functions of an S-box. For finding a suitable subset of Boolean functions to use as coordinate functions, we will use Reinforcement Learning. By the end, we evolve a good set of functions which would result in an S-box with good cryptographic properties such as nonlinearity (NL) and differential uniformity (DU). In previous works [2], we have seen designs using genetic programming to create the S-boxes. Genetic programming is largely based on heuristics. Genetic programming's end goal is to evolve an unfit population of elements using various genetics inspired functions. Genetic programming has adapted concepts of crossover and mutation from genetics and

B. Chopard et al. (Eds.): ACRI 2022, LNCS 13402, pp. 17–28, 2022.
https://doi.org/10.1007/978-3-031-14926-9_2

implemented them in code. The crossover operation involves swapping random parts of selected pairs of parents (elements from the previous population) to produce new and different offspring that become part of the new generation. Mutation involves substitution of some random part of an element with some other random part of an element. Both these crossover and mutation functions are used on populations in the hope that the next population would create stronger off-springs (elements). This process will continue until the desired level of fitness is observed in a population. Our design involves using Reinforcement Learning (RL) instead of genetic programming to select the set of semi-bent Boolean functions that will be used to generate the S-boxes. Both Genetic Programming and Reinforcement Learning aim to maximize a defined reward signal. We aim to experiment with RL as it is based on the mathematically grounded framework of Markov Decision Processes (MDPs) and on initial analysis, can be seen to even speed up the convergence process of finding the set of functions that produce the strongest S-boxes. Reinforcement Learning is used to systematically explore the solution space to find the permutation of semi-bent Boolean functions which has the strongest cryptographic properties.

2   Cellular Automata

CA has been widely researched because of their low implementation cost and parallel computing nature. These properties of CA make them excellent high bandwidth cryptographic application solutions. A CA is a system of finite state automata (cells) which are arranged in a grid. The state of a cell at a timestep depends on the cell's state as well as the state of the cell's neighbours. Each cell has a local update rule which determines the state of the cell at the next timestep. The states of a cell in a CA are generally from the set $\{0,1\}$. In context of CAs, we consider both time and space to be discrete. In each timestep, each cell in the CA is updated according to the local rule of the cell. A local rule can be represented as a function

$$f : S^m \rightarrow S$$

where m represents the neighbourhood size considered in the update rule. For a 1D CA (where the cells are arranged in a 1-dimensional array), a neighbourhood size of m indicates that we consider $2m + 1$ states in the local update rule (m on each side and the state itself). For a 2D CA (where the cells are arranged as a 2-dimensional array), a neighbourhood of m considers $4m + 1$ states for the update rule (m on each side and the state itself). At the ends of the CA, the neighbourhood wraps around to the other end of the CA. Theoretically, a CA can be represented in any number of dimensions [3] but increasing the dimensionality also increases the computational cost for the CA. CA are mathematically complete and lightweight in most of their implementations, thus making them suitable for a wide range of applications. In our application, we will only be considering a 1D CA with a neighbourhood size of 1. The output for each combination can be succinctly represented by a single number called the CA's Wolfram Number [5]. An important aspect of the CA rule is that each CA rule can be represented in their *algebraic normal form (ANF)* in terms of the states of the cells considered. The ANF of a Boolean function f can be represented as

$$f(x_1, \ldots, x_n) = \bigoplus_{I \in 2^{[n]}} a_I x^I \tag{1}$$

where, $x^I = \prod_{i \in I} x_i$, $2^{[n]}$ is the power set of $[n] = \{1, 2, \ldots, n\}$ and $a_I = 0$ or 1. This is how the rules will be represented in code. The algebraic degree of the Boolean function f is the cardinality of the largest subset $I \in 2^{[n]}$ in its ANF, such that its coefficient $a_I \neq 0$.

3 Substitution Boxes (S-boxes)

S-boxes are an integral part of many encryption systems. An S-box can be represented as

$$F : \mathbb{F}_2^m \to \mathbb{F}_2^n$$

where n, m are two positive integers and $\mathbb{F}_2$ is the Galois Field of two elements. S-boxes are also referred to as (n, m) functions, where n and m correspond to number of inputs and outputs of the S-box respectively. The function F is also called a vectorial Boolean function. Function F can be decomposed into the vector $F = (f_1, f_2, \ldots, f_m)$ where each function f_i is a Boolean function $f_i : \mathbb{F}_2^n \to \mathbb{F}_2 \forall i$. The functions $f_i \forall i \in \{1, 2, \ldots, m\}$ are called the coordinate functions of S-boxes function F. Any non-trivial linear combination of the coordinate functions is called a component function of F. For an S-box to be cryptographically strong, there are a number of properties it must satisfy [7].

3.1 Nonlinearity

The *Walsh-Hadamard Transform* W_F of (n, m) function F is given by

$$W_F(u, v) = \sum_{x \in \mathbb{F}_2^n} (-1)^{v \cdot F(x) \oplus u \cdot x}, v \in \mathbb{F}_2^m, u \in \mathbb{F}_2^n \tag{2}$$

The nonlinearity N_F of function F is given by the equation:

$$N_F = 2^{n-1} - \frac{1}{2} \max_{u \in \mathbb{F}_2^n, v \in (\mathbb{F}_2^m)^*} |W_F(u, v)| \tag{3}$$

where $(\mathbb{F}_2^m)^* = \mathbb{F}_2^m \setminus \{0\}$. We aim to achieve maximum nonlinearity, i.e., reduce the linearity between the function F and its component functions. A high value for nonlinearity will make it harder to perform linear cryptanalysis on the S-boxes.

3.2   Differential Uniformity

For a given (n, m) function F, we can define a *difference distribution table* D_F as

$$D_F(a, b) = \{x \in \mathbb{F}_2^n : F(x) \oplus F(x \oplus a) = b\}, \ a \in \mathbb{F}_2^n, \ b \in \mathbb{F}_2^m$$

The value at (a,b) represents the cardinality of $D_F(a, b)$ denoted by $\delta(a, b)$. The differential uniformity of the function F, δ_F is given by

$$\delta_F = \max_{a \neq 0, b} \delta(a, b) \tag{4}$$

We aim to minimize the differential uniformity of an S-box. A low value of δ_F implies that the S-box can withstand differential cryptanalysis. The minimum attainable value for differential uniformity is 2 and S-boxes which achieve this value are called *almost perfect nonlinear (APN) functions*.

4   Semi-bent Boolean Functions

Consider a Boolean function f. From Eq. (3), it is evident that the maximum value of N_f is achieved when the max term in the equation evaluates to $2^{\frac{n}{2}}$, resulting in the bound: $N_f \leq 2^{n-1} - 2^{\frac{n}{2}-1}$. Functions that satisfy this bound are known as *bent functions*, but these functions only exist for even values of n [8]. Unfortunately, bent functions are not balanced, so they cannot be considered for use in cryptographic systems. A Boolean function is balanced if its truth table has equal number of 0's and 1's in its output, i.e., for an arbitrary input, it is equally likely to get a 0 or 1 as the output. The truth table of a Boolean function is the mapping of the input bits to the output bits for that Boolean function. Every Boolean function can be represented as a truth table. The quadratic bound for when n is odd is $N_F \leq 2^{n-1} - 2^{\frac{n+1}{2}-1}$. Any function of algebraic degree 2 can achieve this bound. In general, this bound is not tight when n is odd and $n > 7$. It is still an open problem to determine the true upper bound on the nonlinearity for that case. The Walsh transform for a Boolean function $f : \mathbb{F}_2^m \to \mathbb{F}_2$ is given by the equation

$$W_f(u) = \sum_{x \in \mathbb{F}_2^m} (-1)^{f(x) \oplus u \cdot x}, \ \forall u \in \mathbb{F}_2^m \tag{5}$$

The Walsh transform of a Boolean function measures the correlation between the function f and the linear function $u \cdot x$. It is therefore, used to calculate the nonlinearity of a Boolean function f. Semi-bent Boolean functions are Boolean functions whose Walsh transform can be defined as:

$$W_f(u) = \begin{cases} 2^{\frac{n+1}{2}} & \text{if } n \text{ is odd,} \\ 2^{\frac{n+2}{2}} & \text{if } n \text{ is even.} \end{cases} \tag{6}$$

These functions reach the bound on nonlinearity when n is odd. It is possible for these functions to be balanced, so we shall be considering these to use as coordinate functions in our construction of S-boxes. A Boolean function is balanced if its truth table has equal number of 0's and 1's in its output, i.e., for an arbitrary input, it is equally likely to get a 0 or 1 as the output.

5   Reinforcement Learning

Reinforcement Learning is the area of machine learning that deals with how intelligent agents interact within an environment to maximize a cumulative reward. RL is considered to be the 3rd machine learning paradigm alongside supervised learning and unsupervised learning and is sometimes semi-supervised in nature. The learner and decision maker is called the agent. The thing it interacts with, comprising everything outside the agent, is called the environment. RL agents interact with the environment, which can be classified as a set of states that can be both continuous or discrete, using a set of pre-defined actions. Each action in each state, also known as a state-action pair is associated with a reward signal. The goal of the agent is to maximize the cumulative sum of the reward signals. It does so by exploring the actions it has never taken before and exploiting the actions that have been taken and the agent has prior knowledge about. In almost all RL problems, there exists an exploration-exploitation dilemma. The dilemma is that the agent has to exploit what it already knows to obtain reward but the agent also has to explore in order to make better selections in the future. Generally, on knowing what actions are optimal in a state, the agent still chooses sub-optimal actions once in a while, in the hopes to achieve a greater cumulative sum of rewards by choosing a different sequence of actions and states. Apart from the actions and states, an RL problem has 4 more sub-elements: a policy, a reward signal, a value function and optionally a model of the environment [4]. The policy defines how the agent behaves in a state and what actions it chooses. In their book, Richard Sutton and Andrew Barto define a policy as a mapping from states to probabilities of selecting each possible action. A reward signal defines the goal of a reinforcement learning problem. The value function or the value of a state is the expectation of total reward it will accumulate over time. There also exists state action values, which is, the value of taking a particular action from a particular state. The reward signal, takes into account what is good as the immediate next step, whereas the value function is far sighted and looks into the total reward accumulated in the future. The last element is the model. This is something that mimics the behavior of the environment, or more generally, that allows inferences to be made about how the environment will behave. RL problems are usually formulated as a Markov Decision Processes. In [4], MDPs are defined as a mathematically idealized form of the reinforcement learning problem for which precise theoretical statements can be made. For a finite MDP, the states, actions and rewards have a well defined discrete probability. That is,

$$\sum_{s' \in S} \sum_{r \in \mathcal{R}} p\left(s', r \mid s, a\right) = 1, \forall s \in \mathcal{S}, a \in \mathcal{A}(s) , \tag{7}$$

where $\mathcal{S}$ is the set of all states, $\mathcal{A}(s)$ is the set of all actions available at the state s and r is the reward received when after transitioning to state s' from the state s on taking action a. In an MDP, the probabilities given by p completely characterize the environment's dynamics. That is, the probability of each possible value for S_t and R_t depends only on the immediately preceding state and action, S_{t-1} and A_{t-1}, and, given them, not at all on earlier states and actions [4]. The RL agent together with its policy and state action pairs make decisions to explore the environment, learning and exploiting data learnt through positive and negative reinforcements to maximize the reward signal.

6   Our Design

Our goal is to build an S-box with excellent cryptographic properties, i.e., high nonlinearity and low differential uniformity. To implement our goal, it has been formulated as a 3-part problem. The three parts include Boolean Functions, Substitution Box and Reinforcement Learning (Fig. 1 and 2).

6.1   Boolean Functions

Our design allows us to use a set of 2 or more semi-bent Boolean functions to generate the output array. We consider the CA as the input bits to the S-boxes. The CA length is 8 cells long, the state of each cell is given by the corresponding input bits. We consider the CA to have a periodic boundary, i.e., the neighbourhoods for the edge cells wrap around to the other end of the CA. In this work, we consider set sizes of 2 and 3 semi-bent Boolean functions to generate the output array from the set of input bits. Each Boolean function involves a set of 2 operations. The first operation is the application of a CA rule on the set of 8 input bits. After first step, an intermediary array is created whose bits are then XORed to get one bit. This is the second step. The size of this intermediary array depends on the size of the neighbourhood of the CA rule (Boolean function). In our design, the size of the intermediary array is always 6, as we are only work with CA rules of neighbourhood size 3 for both the set sizes of rules. Each intermediary array produces only one of the output bits. Hence, the process of creating the intermediary array is iterated 8 times in order to get the 8 output bits. During each of these iterations, the neighbourhood cells do not overlap with the initial cell. Hence, during each iteration to produce one output bit, it can be said that the boundary is fixed at 8 cells starting from the cell indexed at $start$ and ending at the cell indexed at $(start + nbr\_size)\%8$. Here, it is to be remarked that for periodic boundary conditions, the constructions from [1] does not work as it is not possible to prove that the resulting Boolean function has the same degree as the local rule [9]. The pseudocode for this has been given below in Algorithm 1. $rule$ is the CA rule which we will be applying on the input. nbr_size is the neighbourhood size on which the CA rule is applied. len is the size of the input CA (here 8). $start$ indicates the neighbourhood offset. 2 steps together make the semi-bent function. Semi-bent functions are known for

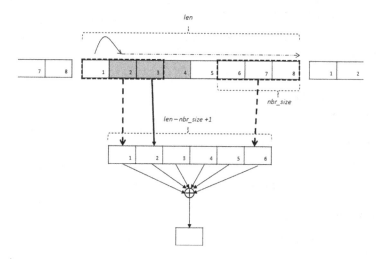

Fig. 1. First iteration of Algorithm 1 applying a CA rule of neighbourhood size nbr_size to a set of bits of length len generating $len - nbr\_size + 1$ output bits which are further XORed to get a single bit. Here, $start = 1$, and in our design $nbr\_size = 3$ bits and $len = 8$ bits.

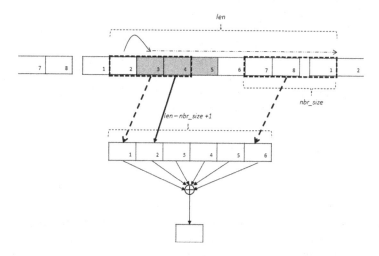

Fig. 2. Second iteration of Algorithm 1 applying a CA rule of neighbourhood size nbr_size to a set of bits of length len generating $len - nbr\_size + 1$ output bits which are further XORed to get a single bit. Here, $start = 2$, and in our design $nbr\_size = 3$ bits and $len = 8$ bits.

their high cryptographic standard, exhibiting properties of high nonlinearity and low differential uniformity. Mariot et al. [1] discovered several CA based semi-bent functions using varying neighbourhood sizes. For our use, we narrowed down to the 56 CA rules of neighbourhood size 3. We will use these rules in the construction of the S-boxes.

Algorithm 1

---

function RULE_OP(rule,nbr_size,len,start)
    $outputs \leftarrow \emptyset$
    $i \leftarrow start$
    $max\_iter \leftarrow start + len - nbr\_size + 1$
    while $i < max\_iter$ **do**
        $nbr \leftarrow \emptyset$
        $j \leftarrow 0$
        while $j < nbr\_size$ **do**
            $nbr.Append(CA[(i+j)\%len])$
        end while
        $outputs.Append(rule(nbr))$
        $i \leftarrow i + 1$
    end while
    return $\bigoplus_{bit \in outputs} bit$
end function

6.2 Substitution Box

Our design is implemented as a CA consisting of 8 cells. The CA rules are semi-bent functions as discussed in the previous section. In this work, we discuss 2 designs of S-boxes. In the first design, we use 2 CA rules, each generating 4 bits of the final output. In the second design, we use 3 CA rules, 2 of which generate 3 bits towards the final output and the last one generating only 2. The S-box pseudocode has been described in Algorithm 2. The S-box takes in the set of CA rules as parameter. *input_size* is the length of the CA (8 in our case) and *num_rules* represents the number of rules we are using in the design.

6.3 Reinforcement Learning

In this work, we will be using Reinforcement Learning to find suitable sets of semi-bent functions to use in our S-box design. To solve a problem using RL, it first has to be formulated as a Markov Decision Process. So we start by identifying our states, rewards and actions with respect to our design. We define the state space as all possible k-permutations of all semi-bent functions, where $k \in \{2, 3\}$. The number of permutations of k items from n objects is given by

$$^{n}P_k = \frac{n!}{(n-k)!} \tag{8}$$

where k is the number of rules selected and n is the total number of rules. The state space is discrete. Each permutation of the set of rules can be considered as a different state and hence, each state varies by at least one semi-bent function. When considering 2 semi-bent functions, the total space consists of $^{56}P_2 = 3080$ different states and in the 3 semi-bent functions design, we have $^{56}P_3 = 166320$ states. The set of actions are also discrete and can be considered as the swapping

---

Algorithm 2

---

function SBOX(rules)
    $outputs \leftarrow \emptyset$
    for each possible input ip **do**
        $output \leftarrow \emptyset$
        $start \leftarrow 0$
        $k \leftarrow ceil(input\_size/num\_rules)$
        for all rule in rules **do**
            $i \leftarrow 0$
            while $i < k$ **do**
                $op \leftarrow RULE\_OP(rule, 3, input\_size, ip, start)$
                $output.Append(op)$
                $start \leftarrow start + 1$
                $i \leftarrow i + 1$
            end while
        end for
        $outputs.Append(output[0 : 7])$ ▷ Only the first 8 bits of the output are taken
    end for
    return outputs
end function

---

of a rule for another rule. The reward for transitioning from one state to another is the cryptographic strength of the latter state given as

$$strength = (scaled\_NL + (100 - scaled\_DU))/2 \qquad (9)$$

where *strength* is the cryptographic strength of the current set of rules in the S-box. The scaled nonlinearity of the S-box denoted by *scaled_NL* is

$$scaled\_NL = (NL/112) * 100 \qquad (10)$$

scaled_DU is the scaled differential uniformity of the S-box.

$$scaled\_DU = ((DU - 4)/(128 - 4)) * 100 \qquad (11)$$

The scaling was done with respect to the values attained by the AES S-box [6]. The policy is chosen to be epsilon greedy, that is, with epsilon probability, the agent chooses a non greedy action. We talk about greedy/non-greedy with respect to the calculated state value or the state action value. We use the on-policy Sarsa algorithm [4] to calculate the state action value pairs from the information gathered during exploration. We use the concept of average reward in our Sarsa algorithm [4]. This is used in our problem as our problem deals with a continuous task. We chose to use the value-function approximation method [4], given the large state spaces. An Artificial Neural Network (ANN) was chosen to be the function approximator given the nonlinear relationship between the rules used and the strength of the state. The function approximator is used to approximate the value of a given state, given the input parameters from a given state. In our design, we give the rules used in that particular state as the parameters so as to calculate the value of the state using the rules used in that state. For each rule, the input array to the ANN is flattened, so as to achieve a distinct array for each distinct permutation of rules. In the 2 rule design, there are 2 positions for the rules and 56 rules can be inserted in each space. Hence the size of the input array to the ANN will be a binary array of length $2 * 56 = 112$.

We define the reward for transitioning from state s_1 to state s_2 as

$$reward = strength(s_2) \tag{12}$$

In other words, the immediate reward we get for transitioning to state s_2 from s_1 is the cryptographic strength of the state s_2. This indicates how good that particular transition is for us.

7   Results

We ran the experiment with set sizes of both 2 and 3 semi-bent Boolean functions. We ran the RL algorithm with each configuration 10 times, each time the algorithm traversed fifty unique states. The results obtained are summarized in Table 1. *Set Size* is the number of CA rules used in the S-box. The columns *DU*, *NL* and *Strength* represent the best values obtained for Differential Uniformity, Nonlinearity and Strength (computed using 9) by the particular design. $\overline{Strength}$ is the average strength of the S-boxes that were explored during the ten runs. $\sigma_{Strength}$ gives the standard deviation of the average strengths obtained by the S-boxes in the ten runs. The best possible properties obtained of the S-boxes created from the design consisting of 2 rules had a differential uniformity of 32 and nonlinearity of 96. There were multiple states that gave these properties. With the design consisting of 3 rules, the best S-box obtained had a nonlinearity of 96 and differential uniformity of 16. Again, there were multiple states that gave this result. The values obtained are on par with the values obtained using Genetic Programming. Furthermore, our design using 3 semi-bent functions was able to outperform the S-box obtained using genetic programming in both differential uniformity as well as nonlinearity. The genetic programming based S-box had a maximum differential uniformity and nonlinearity of 20 and 82 respectively [2].

Table 1. Summary of the results

Set Size	DU	NL	Strength	$\overline{Strength}$	$\sigma_{Strength}$
2	32	96	81.57	58.42	2.51
3	16	96	88.02	59.72	3.04

8   Conclusion and Future Work

It can be successfully concluded that not only genetic programming but reinforcement learning can also be used to generate S-boxes with strong cryptographic properties. The semi-bent Boolean function based S-boxes are relatively lightweight in their implementation as well.

Our work is heavily constrained by the computational resources and time. As Reinforcement Learning is a computationally intensive task, it requires very high performance computing machines. Certain computations such as the calculation of cryptographic properties is also a very compute intensive task. In our work, we only explored S-boxes created by 2 and 3 semi-bent functions. This work can be further expanded by increasing the number of rules used to 4, 5, etc. The manner of usage of rules can also be changed. In our work, the rules were used in an in-order manner. This can be changed to alternating rules, or randomly selecting rules from a subset of the rules. In the reinforcement learning part, a lot can be expanded and built on. Other control algorithms such as the off-policy Q-learning, or Expected Sarsa, can be used instead of the Sarsa algorithm used in our design. Other policies can also be implemented such as policy gradient methods instead of the epsilon greedy policy used in our design. The parameters to the function approximators (ANN) can be changed and experimented with. This work only focused on 8×8 S-boxes, we can also try to modify the design to work on different input and output sizes.

A   Appendix

The source code for the S-box design and RL implementation is available at https://github.com/tarunaygr/RL-based-S-boxes.

References

1. Mariot, L., Saletta, M., Leporati, A., et al.: Exploring semi-bent Boolean functions arising from cellular automata. In: Gwizdałła, T.M., Manzoni, L., Sirakoulis, G.C., Bandini, S., Podlaski, K. (eds.) Cellular Automata: 14th International Conference on Cellular Automata for Research and Industry, ACRI 2020, Lodz, Poland, December 2–4, 2020, Proceedings, vol. 12599, pp. 56–66. Springer, Cham (2021). https://doi.org/10.1007/978-3-030-69480-7_7
2. Picek, S., Mariot, L., Leporati, A., Jakobovic, D.: Evolving S-boxes based on cellular automata with genetic programming. In: Proceedings of the Genetic and Evolutionary Computation Conference Companion, GECCO 2017, pp. 251–252. Association for Computing Machinery, New York (2017). https://doi.org/10.1145/3067695.3076084
3. Kari, J.J.: Basic concepts of cellular automata. In: Rozenberg, G., Bäck, T., Kok, J.N. (eds.) Handbook of Natural Computing, pp. 3–24. Springer, Heidelberg (2012). https://doi.org/10.1007/978-3-540-92910-9_1
4. Sutton, R.S., Barto, A.G.: Reinforcement Learning: An Introduction, 2nd edn. The MIT Press, Cambridge, Massachusetts, London, England (2018)

5. Wolfram, S.: Statistical mechanics of cellular automata. Rev. Mod. Phys. **55**(3), 601 (1983)
6. afify, E., Khalil, A.T., El sobky, W.I., Alez, R.A.: Performance analysis of advanced encryption standard (AES) S-boxes. Int. J. Recent Technol. Eng. (IJRTE) **9**(1), 2214–2218 (2020). https://doi.org/10.35940/ijrte.F9712.059120
7. Mariot, L., Picek, S., Leporati, A., Jakobovic, D.: Cellular automata based S-boxes. Cryptogr. Commun. **11**(1), 41–62 (2018). https://doi.org/10.1007/s12095-018-0311-8
8. Carlet, C.: Boolean Functions for Cryptography and Coding Theory. Cambridge University Press, Cambridge (2021). https://doi.org/10.1017/9781108606806
9. Mariot, L., Saletta, M., Leporati, A., et al.: Heuristic search of (semi-)bent functions based on cellular automata. Nat. Comput. (2022). https://doi.org/10.1007/s11047-022-09885-3

Identification of Periodic Boundary SACA Rules Exploring NSRT Diagram

Baisakhi Das[1], Mousumi Saha[2], Nilanjana Das[3],
and Biplab K Sikdar[3](✉)

[1] Institute of Engineering Management, Kolkata, WB, India
[2] National Institute of Technology, Durgapur 713209, WB, India
mousumi.saha@cse.nitdgp.ac.in
[3] Indian Institute of Engineering Science and Technology, Howrah 711103, WB, India
biplab@cs.iiests.ac.in

Abstract. This work reports characterization of 1-dimensional periodic boundary cellular automata (PBCA) rules in 3-neighborhood for identification of CA rules that influence the formation of single length cycle attractors (fixed points). It targets the synthesis of CA with only one fixed point (SACA) for arbitrary length. The graph based tool NSRT diagram (NSRTD) provides the theoretical framework for this characterization. Schemes are developed to identify the SACA rules that form uniform SACA for all length.

Keywords: Cellular automata · Attractor · SACA · NSRTD

1 Introduction

A 3-neighborhood 2-state Cellular Automaton (CA) can be viewed as an autonomous finite state machine [15]. While characterizing such CA state space, the researchers identified a set of CA states, called attractors, towards which the neighboring states asymptotically approach during evolution [3]. A single length cycle attractor (fixed point) is one where the number of states in the attractor is one [3]. Characterization of this class of CA is yet to be formalized.

The synthesis of fixed point attractor CA in linear/additive domain [1,2,4,10] has been proposed in the literature [8,11]. The identification of attractors, specially for null-boundary, is explored in [3,14]. A tool called reachability tree is used in [13] to characterize and synthesize fixed point attractor CA in null-boundary. However, characterizations of fixed point PBCA, in non-linear domain, are yet to be explored. This motivates us to characterize the CA rules that can form fixed points in a PBCA state space. The NSRT Diagram (NSRTD) introduced in [12] is employed to explore existence of the multi-length cycle as well as the fixed points in a PBCA. It effectively identifies the SLCA (single length cycle attractor CA -that is, the CA with fixed point), specially, the class of SACA (single length cycle single attractor CA -that is, the CA with one and only one fixed point). It leads to the synthesis of uniform SACA of any length.

B. Chopard et al. (Eds.): ACRI 2022, LNCS 13402, pp. 29–39, 2022.
https://doi.org/10.1007/978-3-031-14926-9_3

2   Preliminaries of Cellular Automata

In 3-neighborhood (*self, left, right* neighbors) CA, the next state (NS) (at time
$t+1$) of the ith cell is
$$S_i^{t+1} = f_i(S_{i-1}^t, S_i^t, S_{i+1}^t)$$
where S_{i-1}^t, S_i^t and S_{i+1}^t are the present states (PSs) of its neighbors. The f_i is
the next state function. The collection of states $\mathcal{S}^t = (S_1^t, S_2^t, \cdots, S_n^t)$ of the n
cells at t is the state of CA at t. In a 2-state 3-neighborhood CA (ECA), there
are 256 next state functions called rules. Three such rules 184, 226, and 232 are
shown in Table 1. The first row lists the possible 2^3 (8) combinations of the PSs
of $(i-1)^{th}$, i^{th} and $(i+1)^{th}$ cells [7]. Such a combination is referred to as the
rule min term (RMT).

Table 1. Truth table for rule 184, 226, and 232

PS:	111	110	101	100	011	010	001	000	Rule
(RMT)	(7)	(6)	(5)	(4)	(3)	(2)	(1)	(0)	
(i) NS:	1	0	1	1	1	0	0	0	184
(ii) NS:	1	1	1	0	0	0	1	0	226
(iii) NS:	1	1	1	0	1	0	0	0	232

Figure 1 is the block diagram of an n-cell periodic boundary CA (PBCA). Its
left (right) neighbor of leftmost (rightmost) cell is the rightmost (leftmost) cell.

Fig. 1. Block diagram of an n-cell PBCA

The set of rules $<\mathcal{R}_1, \mathcal{R}_2, \cdots, \mathcal{R}_i, \cdots, \mathcal{R}_n>$ that configures the cells of a CA
is denoted as rule vector $\mathcal{RV}$. If $R_1 = R_2 = \cdots = R_n$, then the CA is uniform
(Fig. 2(c)) otherwise, it is a non-uniform/hybrid CA (Fig. 2(a)).

A set of states can form cycle $(0 \to 0, 10 \to 5 \to 10$ and $15 \to 15$ of Fig. 2(a))
and is called *attractor*. A self loop $(0 \to 0/15 \to 15)$ is called single length cycle
attractor or fixed point. Cycle involving multiple states $(10 \to 5 \to 10)$ is a multi-
length cycle attractor. An attractor forms a basin with the states that lead to
the attractor. For example, $(10 \to 5 \to 10)$-basin of Fig. 2(a) contains 4 states.

An RMT is represented as T(m), $m = \{0, 1, 2, 3, 4, 5, 6, 7\}$; and T$(m) \in$ T,
where T $= \{$T(0), T(1), ..., T(7)$\}$. The RMT for i^{th} cell based on which the cell
changes its state at t is denoted as T$_i^t(m)$. For example, T$_1^t(0)$ denotes at time
t cell 1 changes its state on RMT T(0). However, in the diagrams, an RMT is
represented only by corresponding decimal number (m) -that is, T$_i^t(0)$ is 0.

The RMT for which the next state is 0 (0-RMT), belongs to T/0 and that having next state as 1 (1-RMT) belongs to T/1, where T/0 ∩ T/1 = ∅ and T/0 ∪ T/1 = T. An RMT $x0y$ (respectively $x1y$), where x and y are the PSs of left and right neighbor in a rule $\mathcal{R}$ is called passive if it belongs to T/0 (respectively T/1). On the other hand, if an RMT $x0y$ (respectively $x1y$) belongs to T/1 (respectively T/0), it is active.

An RMT String (RS) is defined as a sequence of consecutive RMTs which appear in a state of CA. It is represented as $(T_1, T_2,...,T_n)$ for an n-cell CA, where $T_i \in$ T. For example, the state 1011 of a 4-cell CA can be represented by the RS $(T_1, T_2, T_3, T_4) = (T(6), T(5), T(3), T(7))$.

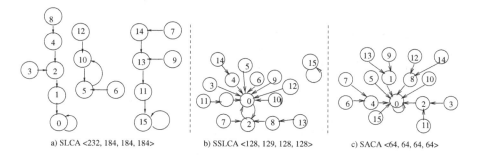

a) SLCA <232, 184, 184, 184>   b) SSLCA <128, 129, 128, 128>   c) SACA <64, 64, 64, 64>

Fig. 2. State transitions of CA

The CA having at least one fixed point attractor is the single length cycle attractor CA (SLCA). It can have multi-length cycle. The SLCA with only one fixed point is a single single length cycle attractor CA (SSLCA). Figure 2(b) is an SSLCA. The SLCA producing connected graph during its state transitions -that is, having one and only one fixed point attractor is called single length cycle single attractor CA (SACA). The rule that configures uniform SACA for all length is an SACA rule.

3 NSRTD

The NSRT diagram (NSRTD) is to characterize the 256 ECA rules to determine the presence of fixed points as well as multi-length cycles in a PBCA. The following terminologies are essential for describing the NSRTD [12].

If T_i^t is the RMT of ith-cell rule based on which the cell i changes its state at t^{th} time step, then the next cell RMTs (**NCRs**) of T_i^t are the RMTs $T_{i+1}^t = (2 \times T_i^t \bmod 8)$ and $((2 \times T_i^t + 1) \bmod 8)$ of $(i+1)^{th}$-cell rule based on which the $(i+1)^{th}$-cell can change its state at t^{th} time step. For example, if RMT of R_i is $T(1)$, then its NCRs are $T(2)$ (=$2 \times T(1) \bmod 8$) and $T(3)$ (=$(2 \times T(1)+1) \bmod 8$). The NCRs of all the 8 RMTs are shown in Table 2.

If T_i^t (respectively T_i^{t+1}) be the RMT of ith-cell rule R_i based on which cell i changes its state at time t (respectively at time $t+1$), then T_i^{t+1} is the Next

State RMT (**NSR**) of T_i^t for cell i. The sequence of NSRs based on which the ith-cell changes its state during the state transitions of the CA is called Next State RMT Sequence (**NSRS**). That is, an NSRS for the ith-cell (denoted as $NSRS_i$) is $T_i^0, T_i^1, ..., T_i^t, T_i^{t+1}, ...$, where T_i^{t+1} is the NSR of T_i^t.

For the ith-cell rule R_i of a CA, the all possible NSRSs can be represented by a directed graph G(V,E), called NSRS graph (**NSRS-G**), where all the T_i^ts $\in$ V and $e_i(T_i^t, T_i^{t+1}) \in$ E iff T_i^{t+1} is the NSR of T_i^t.

The NCR, NSR, NSRS and NSRS-G of a CA enable construction of the set of directed graphs, called NSRTD, as 2-dimensional arrangement of nodes. Each node is an RMT and each graph in NSRTD represents an attractor of the CA. The edge $(T_i^t, T_i^{t+1}) \in$ E, such that T_i^{t+1} is the NSR of T_i^t and also the edge $(T_i^t, T_{i+1}^t) \in$ E, such that T_{i+1}^t is the NCR of T_i^t. Further, the nodes T_i^t ($\forall t$) form an NSRS for i^{th}-cell.

The two NSRSs defined for i^{th} and $(i+1)^{th}$ cell ($NSRS_i$ and $NSRS_{i+1}$) are called **compatible** if j^{th} NSR of these two are related in the sense that j^{th} NSR of $NSRS_{i+1}$ is the NCR (Table 2) of jth NSR of $NSRS_i$.

Table 2. Relationship between T_i and T_{i+1} (NCR)

RMT T_i of ith rule	RMTs T_{i+1} of $(i+1)^{th}$ rule (NCR)
T(0)/T(4)	T(0), T(1)
T(1)/T(5)	T(2), T(3)
T(2)/T(6)	T(4), T(5)
T(3)/T(7)	T(6), T(7)

Figure 3 describes the computation of NSR of a cell of the uniform PBCA with rule 116. If the present RMT for i^{th} cell, based on which the cell changes its state, is xyz and l and r be the PSs of cell($i-2$) and cell($i+2$) respectively, then the NSR of cell i can be $d_l d d_r$, where RMT xyz of R_i (here 116) $T_i^t(xyz)$ is d and d_l = RMT lxy of R_{i-1} (here also 116) and d_r = RMT yzr of R_{i+1} (here is 116) - that is, $T_{i-1}^t(lxy) = d_l$ and $T_{i+1}^t(yzr) = d_r$. Now, if $xyz = 000$, then d_l = $T_{i-1}^t(l00)$, where l can be either 0 or 1. That is, $d_l = T_{i-1}^t(l00) = T_{i-1}^t(000)$ or $T_{i-1}^t(100)$. The T(0) and T(4) of rule 116 are 0 and 1 respectively (Fig. 3(a)). Therefore, d_l = 0 or 1. On the other hand, $d_r = T_{i-1}^t(yzr) = T_{i-1}^t(00r)$. That is, $d_r = T_{i+1}^t(000)$ or $T_{i+1}^t(001) = $ '0' (Fig. 3(a)). Therefore, the NSR of RMT 000 (T(0)) is 0 or 4. The NSRS-G of rule 116 -that is, of a uniform PBCA with rule 116, is shown in Fig. 4(a).

The cycles in the NSRS-G are $0 \rightarrow 0$, $1 \rightarrow 1$, $5 \rightarrow 6 \rightarrow 3 \rightarrow 5$, $4 \rightarrow 6 \rightarrow 3 \rightarrow 4$, $0 \rightarrow 4 \rightarrow 6 \rightarrow 3 \rightarrow 1 \rightarrow 0$, etc. Figure 4(b) shows the NSRTD of the uniform PBCA. It can be observed (in Fig. 4(bi)) that the NCR of cell i for T(5) is T(3). Now, the NSR of cell i in the NSRS ($5 \rightarrow 6 \rightarrow 3 \rightarrow 5$) is T(6). On the other hand, the NSR of T(3) at cell $i+1$ (also assuming the NSRS $5 \rightarrow 6 \rightarrow 3 \rightarrow 5$) is T(5) which is also the valid NCR of T(6) at cell i.

Similarly, it can be shown that if cell i follows NSRS $5 \rightarrow 6 \rightarrow 3 \rightarrow 5$ during its evolution, the cell $i+1$ follows NSRS $3 \rightarrow 5 \rightarrow 6 \rightarrow 3$. It can be noted from Fig. 4(bi) that all the cells of the PBCA of length $3n$ ($n = 1, 2, 3, ...$) can follow the NSRS of length 3 ($5 \rightarrow 6 \rightarrow 3 \rightarrow 5, 3 \rightarrow 5 \rightarrow 6 \rightarrow 3$) during evolution. It points to the fact that the PBCA with rule 116 forms a multi-length cycle attractor of length 3. On the other hand, the graph of Fig. 4(bii) corresponds to a fixed point attractor.

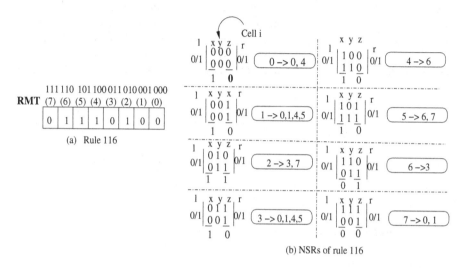

(a) Rule 116

(b) NSRs of rule 116

Fig. 3. Computation of NSRs for a uniform PBCA with rule 116

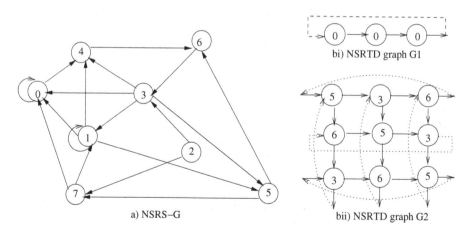

a) NSRS–G

bi) NSRTD graph G1

bii) NSRTD graph G2

Fig. 4. NSRTD of uniform PBCA with rule 116

The following properties [5] of NSRS-G and NSRTD guide the identification of CA rule ($\mathcal{R}$) that forms fixed point attractor PBCA.

Property 1. If there is no multi-length cycle in NSRS-G of rule R, then the uniform CA configured with rule R cannot have a multi-length cycle attractor.

Property 2. If there is no multi-length cycle in the NSRTD of a uniform PBCA, then the CA cannot have a multi-length cycle attractor in its state transitions.

Figure 5(a) shows the NSRS-G for rule 253. The self loops in the NSRS-G are $3 \rightarrow 3$ and $7 \rightarrow 7$. The NSRTD of the 4-cell uniform PBCA with rule 253 is shown in Fig. 5(b). It denotes 253 is an SACA rule. The NSRS-G of rule 116 in Fig. 4(a) points to the existence of multi-length cycles (for example, $3 \rightarrow 6 \rightarrow 5 \rightarrow 3, 4 \rightarrow 6 \rightarrow 3 \rightarrow 4$, etc.). The NSRTD (Graph G_1 of Fig. 4) denotes the multi-length cycle in uniform PBCA with rule 116. Following algorithm (Algorithm 1) checks whether an n-cell uniform PBCA with rule R is free from multi-length cycle.

Algorithm 1 COUNT_CYCLES_IN_PBCA (Rule R, length of CA (n), NCRs)
Input: Rule R, length of CA (n), NCRs for RMTs T(0), T(1), T(2), ..., T(7) forming the sets NCR0, NCR1, ..., NCR7
Output: Decision on multi-length cycles and number of fixed point attractors

1. *Find NSRSs for cell i for rule R*
2. *Construct NSRS-G*
3. *(a) Find self loops $SL = \{SL_j \mid$ where $j = 1, 2, ..., k$, k is the number of self loops in NSRS-G} and multi-length cycles $ML = \{ML_r,$ where $r = 1, 2, ..., p$, p is the number of multi-length cycles in NSRS-G};*
   (b) LP = SL, ML
4. *If the NSRS-G has only self-loops -that is, $ML = \emptyset$, then*
   */*There is no multi-length cycle attractor*/*
   Call FIND_SEQUENCES_NSRTD_IN_SL(R, n, NCRs, SL)
   else Call FIND_SEQUENCES_NSRTD_IN_GN(R, n, NCRs, LP)

Algorithm 2 FIND_SEQUENCES_IN_NSRTD_SL (Rule R, n, NCRs, SL)
Input: Rule R, CA length n, NCRs and SL
Output: Number of fixed point attractors (SLA)

1. *Find all unique sequences of RMTs (nodes) P_u of length n, where*
   $P_u = P_{1u} \rightarrow P_{2u} \rightarrow P_{3u} ... P_{(n-2)u} \rightarrow P_{(n-1)u} \rightarrow P_{nu}$,
   such that $P_{iu} \in SL \ \forall_i$ and P_{iu} is NCR of $P_{(i-1)u} \ \forall_{i \neq 1}$; P_{1u} is NCR of P_{nu};
2. *SLA = number of P_us (each of n-length);*
3. *return SLA*

Algorithm 3 FIND_SEQUENCES_NSRTD_IN_GN (Rule R, n, NCRs, LP)
Input: Rule R, CA length n, NCRs and LP
Output: Number of fixed point attractors (SLA) if there is no multi-length cycle

1. *Find compatibility class C among elements LP_1, LP_2, ...of LP, where*
   $C = \{C_j \mid C_j$ is compatible pair (LP_k, LP_l); LP_k and LP_l belong to L };
   /(LP_k, LP_l) is a compatible pair iff*

i) $LP_{lq} \in LP_l$ is the NCR of $LP_{kr} \in LP_k$, and

ii) $NSR(LP_{lq})$ is $NCR(NSR(LP_{kr}))$, $\forall_q$ */

2. Find all sequences of RMTs (nodes) P_u of length n, where
$P_u = P_{1u} \rightarrow P_{2u} \rightarrow P_{3u} \rightarrow P_{4u} \ldots P_{(n-2)u} \rightarrow P_{(n-1)u} \rightarrow P_{nu}$
such that

  a) for m=1 to n-1 {
    $P_{(m+1)u}$ is an NCR of P_{mu}, where $P_{mu} \in LP_o$, $P_{(m+1)u} \in LP_p$ for some
    o and p, and $(LP_o, LP_p) \in C$;
    $PLP_m = LP_o$;
    $LP_0 = LP_p$; }
  b) P_{1u} is an NCR of P_{nu} and $(PLP_n, PLP_1) \in C$;
    /*PLP_1 and PLP_n are resulted from (a)*/

3. $LPA_u = PLP_1, PLP_2, PLP_3, \ldots PLP_n$ selected in step 2;

4. Number of attractors = number of P_us (n-length)
  /*The length of an attractor is the maximum of cycle lengths of $PLP_h \in LPA_u$
  for a P_u;

5. if there exists an $PLP_h \in LPA_u$ without self-loop for a P_u, then
  /*that is, having multi-length cycle in the CA*/
  Exit (return 0); else {
  SLA = number of P_us; return SLA }

Example 1. Let us consider uniform PBCA with rule 116. Here, the NSRSs are
$0 \rightarrow 0$; $1 \rightarrow 1$; $1 \rightarrow 1 \rightarrow 0 \rightarrow$; $2 \rightarrow 7 \rightarrow 0 \rightarrow 0$; $2 \rightarrow 7 \rightarrow 1 \rightarrow 1$; $4 \rightarrow 6 \rightarrow 3 \rightarrow 4$;...
Its NSRS-G is shown in Fig. 4(a). The SL = $0 \rightarrow 0$, $1 \rightarrow 1$; and ML = $5 \rightarrow 6 \rightarrow$
$3 \rightarrow 5$, $0 \rightarrow 4 \rightarrow 3 \rightarrow 0$, ... (step 3(a) of Algorithm 1). That is, LP = $0 \rightarrow 0$, $1 \rightarrow 1$,
$5 \rightarrow 6 \rightarrow 3 \rightarrow 5$, $0 \rightarrow 4 \rightarrow 3 \rightarrow 0$, ... (step 3(b)). As there is multi-length cycle in
LP (ML$\neq\emptyset$), Algorithm 3 is called (step 4 of Algorithm 1).

As per step 1 of Algorithm 3, from the LP, the compatible pairs are $((0), (0))$;
$((0), (1))$; $((5, 6, 3, 5), (3, 5, 6, 3))$ and $((3, 5, 6, 3), (5, 6, 3, 5))$. The NSRTD
for the CA is shown in Fig. 4(b).

As per step 2 of Algorithm 3, the sequences of RMTs identified are
$P_1 = 0 \rightarrow 0 \rightarrow 0 \rightarrow 0$ ... that corresponds to graph G1 of Fig. 4(bi), and
$P_2 = 5 \rightarrow 3 \rightarrow 6 \rightarrow 5$ ... that corresponds to graph G2 of Fig. 4(bii).
Here, for P_1, the $PLP_1 = PLP_2 = \ldots PLP_n = 0 \rightarrow 0$.
For P_2, the $PLP_1 = 5 \rightarrow 6 \rightarrow 3 \rightarrow 5$, $PLP_2 = 3 \rightarrow 5 \rightarrow 6 \rightarrow 3$, $PLP_3 = 6 \rightarrow 3 \rightarrow$
$5 \rightarrow 6$, $PLP_4 = 5 \rightarrow 6 \rightarrow 3 \rightarrow 5$, ...

Now, the $LPA_1 = (0 \rightarrow 0)$, $(0 \rightarrow 0)$, $(0 \rightarrow 0)$ ...;
and $LPA_2 = (5 \rightarrow 6 \rightarrow 3 \rightarrow 5)$, $(3 \rightarrow 5 \rightarrow 6 \rightarrow 3)$, $(6 \rightarrow 3 \rightarrow 5 \rightarrow 6)$, ... (step 3).

As per step 4, the number of attractors in such a CA is 2. The cycles (PLP_h)
in LPA_2 are multi-length, therefore, Algorithm 3 exits (step 5).

The step 1 of Algorithm 1 finds NSRs and it requires constant time. In an
NSRS, the maximum number of nodes are 8 and the maximum out-degree of
a node is 4. Therefore, construction of NSRS-G (step 2) also requires constant
time. Now, the step 3 finds all possible Euler cycles from a graph of maximum

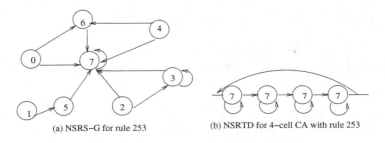

(a) NSRS–G for rule 253   (b) NSRTD for 4–cell CA with rule 253

Fig. 5. NSRS-G and NSRTD for rule 253

8 nodes, with maximum out-degree 4. The number of such cycles are of course finite and is independent of n (length of CA). Finding of all possible self-loops from the set of cycles is also independent of n (step 4).

Algorithm 2, finds all possible n-length sequence of RMTs following the condition mentioned in step 1. Extraction of each sequence is of $O(n)$ complexity. The total number of such sequences (number of graphs in NSRTD) depends on the rule. There can be 2^n-number of n-length sequences (corresponding to 2^n-number of fixed point attractors) in worst case. Hence, worst case running time of this algorithm is exponential. However, for most of the rules, the number of such sequences are $<<2^n$. The step 2 of Algorithm 2 counts the number of such sequences p in $O(p)$ time.

In step 1 of Algorithm 3, the time required to compute compatible classes depends on the maximum number of cycles in LP, and hence, it is independent of n. For a rule R, finding compatible classes is the one time cost. It is stored in a dictionary where against each rule there is the set C of compatible classes; and it is input to Algorithm 3. Extraction of sequences in step 2 has the same time complexity as that of step 1 of Algorithm 2. The steps 3, 4, and 5 count the number of cycles/sequences and have the same time complexity as that of step 2 of Algorithm 2.

4   SACA Rules

This section reports identification of SACA rules for PBCA out of the 256 ECA rules. The following properties are to reduce the search space.

Property 3 [9]. A rule R contributes to the formation of single length cycle attractor(s) if at least one of the RMTs T(0), T(1), T(4) or T(5) belongs to T/0 (that is, passive), or the RMT T(2), T(3), T(6) or T(7) belongs to T/1 (passive).

Based on this property, the 256 rules are classified in 9 groups (group 0–8) in [9]. The rule 207 (11001111) is in group 6 as it follows Property 3 for 6 RMTs (T(7), T(6), T(5), T(4), T(3), and T(2)).

Observation 1. *In PBCA, an SACA rule must be unbalanced.*

Observation 2. *An SACA rule belongs to either group 4 or group 5.*

The above properties reduce the number of candidate SACA rules to 89 [6].

Theorem 1. *In uniform periodic boundary SACA, there can be either all 0s fixed point attractor or all 1s fixed point attractor [6].*

Theorem 1 states that the even rules in between 128 and 254, and odd rules in between 1 and 127 cannot be the SACA rule. This reduces the number of candidate SACA rules from 89 to 52. The NSRTD for such 52 rules are constructed following Algorithm 4 and it identifies 6 SACA rules (Table 3) for $n \geq 3$.

Table 3. SACA rules for PBCA

Rule	Group	Fixed point	Property 3 Denial	Remarks
0	4	000000	7, 6, 3, 2	Unbalanced
8	5	000000	7, 6, 2	Unbalanced
64	5	000000	7, 3, 2	Unbalanced
239	5	111111	5, 1, 0	Unbalanced
253	5	111111	5, 4, 0	Unbalanced
255	4	111111	5, 4, 1, 0	Unbalanced

Algorithm 4. FIND_SACA_RULE_IN_PBCA (Rule R, NCRs)
Input: Rule R, NCRs for RMTs T(0), T(1), T(2), ..., T(7) forming the sets NCR0, NCR1, ..., NCR7
Output: Decision on SACA rule

1. *Find NSRSs of a cell for rule R*
2. *Construct NSRS-G*
3. *(a) Find self loops $SL = \{SL_j \mid$ where $j = 1, 2, ..., k$, k is the number of self loops in NSRS-G\} and multi-length cycles $ML = \{ML_r$, where $r = 1, 2, ..., p$, p is the number of multi-length cycles in NSRS-G\};*
   (b) $LP = SL, ML$
4. *If $ML = \emptyset$, then*
   /*There is no multi-length cycle attractor*/ \{
5. *Find all unique sequences of RMTs (nodes) P_u of length n, where*
   $P_u = P_{1u} \rightarrow P_{2u} \rightarrow P_{3u} ... P_{(n-2)u} \rightarrow P_{(n-1)u} \rightarrow P_{nu}$,
   such that $P_{iu} \in SL \,\forall_i$ and P_{iu} is NCR of $P_{(i-1)u} \,\forall_{i \neq 1}$; P_{1u} is NCR of P_{nu};
6. *$SLA =$ number of P_us;*
7. *if $SLA = 1$, then rule R is an SACA rule*
   else Exit (return 0) \} else \{

8. *Find compatibility class* C *among elements* LP_1, LP_2, *...of* LP, *where*
    $C = \{C_j \mid C_j$ *is compatible pair* $(LP_k, LP_l);$ LP_k *and* LP_l *belong to* L $\};$
    /*(LP_k, LP_l) *is a compatible pair iff*
    i) $LP_{lq} \in LP_l$ *is the NCR of* $LP_{kr} \in LP_k$, *and*
    ii) $NSR(LP_{lq})$ *is* $NCR(NSR(LP_{kr}))$, $\forall_q$ */
9. *Find all sequences of RMTs (nodes)* P_u *of length* n, *where*
    $P_u = P_{1u} \rightarrow P_{2u} \rightarrow P_{3u} \rightarrow P_{4u} \dots P_{(n-2)u} \rightarrow P_{(n-1)u} \rightarrow P_{nu}$ *such that*
    a) *for* $m=1$ *to* n-1 {
       $P_{(m+1)u}$ *is an NCR of* P_{mu}, *where* $P_{mu} \in LP_o$, $P_{(m+1)u} \in LP_p$ *for some*
       o *and* p, *and* $(LP_o, LP_p) \in C;$
       $PLP_m = LP_0;$ $LP_0 = LP_p;$ }
    b) P_{1u} *is an NCR of* P_{nu} *and* $(PLP_n, PLP_1) \in C;$
       /*PLP_1 *and* PLP_n *are resulted from (a)*/
10. $LPA_u = PLP_1, PLP_2, PLP_3, \dots PLP_n$ *selected in step 2;*
11. *Number of attractors = number of* $P_u s$ *(n-length)*
    /*The length of an attractor is the maximum of cycle lengths of
    $PLP_h \in LPA_u$ for a P_u;
12. *if there exists an* $PLP_h \in LPA_u$ *without self-loop for a* P_u, *then*
    /*that is, having multi-length cycle in the CA*/
    Exit (return 0); else { SLA = *number of* $P_u s;$
13. *if* SLA = 1, *then rule* R *is an SACA rule else Exit (return 0)* }

5   Conclusion

The property of fixed point attractor CA, is explored in this work. A special
class of irreversible CA, called SACA, has been introduced. The tool referred
to as the NSRTD provides the analytical foundations to synthesize fixed point
attractor CA having a single attractor (SACA).

References

1. Dennunzio, A., Formenti, E., Grinberg, D., Margara, L.: An efficiently computable
   characterization of stability and instability for linear cellular automata. J. Comput.
   Syst. Sci. **122**, 63–71 (2021)
2. Dennunzio, A., Formenti, E., Provillard, J.: Local rule distributions, language complexity and non-uniform cellular automata. Theoret. Comput. Sci. **504**, 38–51
   (2013)
3. Chaudhuri, P.P., Chowdhury, D.R., Nandi, S., Chatterjee, S.: Additive Cellular
   Automata - Theory and Applications, vol. 1. IEEE Computer Society Press, Cali-
   fornia, USA (1997)
4. Chopard, B.: Cellular automata and lattice Boltzmann modeling of physical systems. In: Rozenberg, G., Bäck, T., Kok, J.N. (eds.) Handbook of Natural Computing. Springer, Heidelberg (2012). https://doi.org/10.1007/978-3-540-92910-9_9
5. Dalui, M.: Theory and applications of cellular automata for CMPs cache system
   protocol design and verification, Ph.D. thesis, Indian Institute of Engineering Science and Technology (2014)

6. Das, B.: Design and evaluation of data migration policies for shared cache on chip multiprocessors, Ph.D. thesis, Indian Institute of Engineering Science and Technology (2017)

7. Das, B., Maiti, N.S., Das, S., Sikdar, B.K.: An efficient scheme for data block migration in tiled CMPs cache system. In: IEEE India INDICON, 13–15 December 2013, pp. 1–6 (2013)

8. Das, S., Mukherjee, S., Naskar, N., Sikdar, B.K.: Characterization of single cycle CA and its application in pattern classification. In: 15th International Workshop on Cellular Automata and Discrete Complex Systems, vol. 252, no. 1, pp. 181–203 (2009)

9. Das, S., Sikdar, B.K.: Characterization of 1-d periodic boundary reversible CA. Electron. Notes Theoret. Comput. Sci. **252**, 205–227 (2009)

10. Dennunzio, A., Formenti, E., Grinberg, D., Margara, L.: Decidable characterizations of dynamical properties for additive cellular automata over a finite abelian group with applications to data encryption. Inf. Sci. **563**, 183–195 (2021)

11. Ganguly, Niloy, Das, Arijit, Maji, Pradipta, Sikdar, Biplab K.., Pal Chaudhuri, P..: Evolving cellular automata based associative memory for pattern recognition. In: Monien, Burkhard, Prasanna, Viktor K.., Vajapeyam, Sriram (eds.) HiPC 2001. LNCS, vol. 2228, pp. 115–124. Springer, Heidelberg (2001). https://doi.org/10.1007/3-540-45307-5_11

12. Dalui, M., Chakraborty, B., Das, N., Sikdar, B.K.: NSRT diagram for identification of SACA and TACA rules in null-boundary. Int. J. Mod. Phys. C **33**(6), 2250071 (2022)

13. Kamilya, S., Adak, S., Das, S., Sikdar, B.K.: SACAs: (non-uniform) cellular automata that converge to a single fixed point. J. Cell. Automata **14**(1–2), 27–49 (2019)

14. Sutner, K.: De Bruijin graphs and linear cellular automata. Complex Syst. **5**(1), 19–30 (1991)

15. Wolfram, S.: Universality and complexity in cellular automata. Physica D **10**(1–2), 1–35 (1984)

A Cellular Automata Based Fault Resistant MICKEY-Like Stream Cipher

Anita John$^{(\boxtimes)}$ and Jimmy Jose

Department of Computer Science and Engineering, National Institute
of Technology Calicut, Kozhikode, India
{anita_p170007cs,jimmy}@nitc.ac.in

Abstract. In today's world of digital technology revolution, the need for
secure data transmission has become very crucial. Symmetric encryption
algorithms play a very vital role in securing data in almost every application. MICKEY is an efficient and compact synchronous stream cipher
designed to be used in resource constrained hardware applications. Even
though the mutual clocking mechanism made it resistant to statistical
attacks, the simple nature of the keystream generation algorithm made
it vulnerable to Differential Fault Attack. This paper proposes a Cellular Automata(CA) based MICKEY stream cipher which strengthens
the cipher against fault attacks. The proposed cipher is resistant to fault
attacks due to the inherent characteristic of CA and has enhanced cryptographic properties when compared to the original version of MICKEY.

Keywords: Stream cipher · Cellular Automata (CA) · Differential
Fault Attack (DFA) · 3-neighbourhood CA · Hybrid CA rules ·
Cryptography · MICKEY

1 Introduction

Nowadays, Internet is widely used in almost all sectors including banking, health
and business sectors. The need for secure data transmission and storage has
become inevitable to avoid cyber attacks. The Internet of Things (IoT) devices
which handle realtime data also needs security. Such devices have limited hardware resources and hence we need to implement cryptographic algorithms that
are fast and lightweight. Stream ciphers are found to be useful in resource -
constrained applications that need faster processing speed. Stream ciphers are
symmetric encryption algorithms that encrypt a bit or byte of plaintext at a time.
The historical stream ciphers were cryptanalysed and the need for the design of
new and secure stream ciphers emerged. eSTREAM [22], the ECRYPT stream
cipher project was intended to design efficient and compact stream ciphers. The
eSTREAM portfolio of stream ciphers are categorized into two profiles - Profile 1
(SW) and Profile 2 (HW). The profile-1 stream ciphers were suitable for software
applications and profile-2 stream ciphers were suitable for hardware applications
that have limited resources like internal storage and/or power consumption.

B. Chopard et al. (Eds.): ACRI 2022, LNCS 13402, pp. 40–51, 2022.
https://doi.org/10.1007/978-3-031-14926-9_4

MICKEY (Mutual Irregular Clocking KEYstream generator) [2], one of the finalists under profile-2, is a synchronous stream cipher. Several versions of MICKEY have emerged through the years. The new versions strengthened the cipher against cryptanlaytic attacks by increasing the size of key, Initialization Variable (IV) and registers. In this paper, we discuss about MICKEY 128 2.0 which takes 128-bit key and an IV whose length varies from 0 to 128 bits. The cipher uses a linear and nonlinear shift register each of length 160 bits. As the name says, MICKEY [2] follows an irregular clocking mechanism where the clocking of each register is controlled by the other register. This helps to prevent statistical attacks which was prevalent on stream ciphers that used variable clocking method. Later, Banik et al. [4] proposed a differential fault attack (DFA) on MICKEY and recovered the internal states of the cipher. This motivated us to find techniques to defend the fault attacks with the help of Cellular Automata (CA), a cryptographic primitive developed by Stephen Wolfram [23]. CA have been considered as an ideal primitive to prevent fault attacks on stream ciphers [15].

This work proposes a CA based variant of MICKEY which replaces the linear and nonlinear shift registers of MICKEY with 3-neighbourhood hybrid CA which makes MICKEY resistant to DFA. The paper is organized as follows, Sect. 2 gives an introduction to Cellular Automata and MICKEY stream cipher. Section 3 discusses the working of our proposed CA based MICKEY and Sect. 4 discusses the design rationale of the proposed cipher. In Sect. 5, we discuss about DFA and how CA has strengthened the cipher against fault attacks. Section 6 gives the implementation details and statistical analysis followed by the conclusion in Sect. 7.

2   Preliminaries

Here we give a brief description about the MICKEY 128 2.0 stream cipher, Cellular Automata and 3-neighbourhood linear and nonlinear CA rules.

2.1   MICKEY-Mutual Irregular Clocking KEYstream Generator

Stream ciphers have been widely used in many applications due to the ease in implementation, speed and limited error propagation. Most of the modern stream cipher designs have two phases:- the initialization phase and the keystream generation phase. During the initialization phase, the key and IV are loaded into the internal state of the cipher by invoking an updating function for sufficient number of rounds. This ensures the diffusion of the key and the IV bits. The keystream generation phase applies a keystream generator function which starts generating the keystream bits from these internal states. The updating function is invoked after the generation of each bit which ensures that the internal states are updated before the generation of the next bit. The design of the updating function and the keystream generation function plays an important role in the quality of the generated pseudorandom keystream.

The eSTREAM finalists Grain [10], Trivium [7] and MICKEY [2] made use of Linear and Nonlinear Feedback Shift Registers in their designs. Among them, MICKEY followed an irregular clocking mechanism to update the internal states of the cipher. The first version of MICKEY stream cipher was developed by Babbage and Dodd in 2005 [2] which was designed to be efficient in resource - constrained hardware environment. The cipher generates a maximum key length of 2^{40} bits from a single (key, IV) pair where the size of key is 80 bits and IV length varying between 0 and 80 bits. The same IV value must not be reused with the same key to ensure security.

Working of MICKEY. Here, we discuss about the basic working of MICKEY 128 2.0 [3]. It makes use of two registers R and S. R is a linear feedback shift register, where r_i $(0 \leq i \leq 159)$ denotes the ith cell of the R register and S is a nonlinear feedback shift register, where s_i $(0 \leq i \leq 159)$ denotes the ith cell of the S register. Initially, the registers are loaded with zeroes. During the initialization phase, the key and the IV bits are successively used to update the internal state registers by invoking the initialization function which clocks the registers.

The registers are clocked in two different ways based on a clock control bit which is set for each register. This is derived from the XOR of different pairs of state bits, one from each of the registers. The control bit of register R is $s_{54} \oplus r_{106}$ and that of register S is $s_{106} \oplus r_{53}$. The two registers are clocked based on the value of the control bit during each iteration. This is followed by a preclocking round which invokes the function for register updates 160 times. This ensures the diffusion of the key and IV bits at the end of initialization phase.

The initialization phase is followed by the keystream generation phase which outputs the keystream bit by taking the XOR of r_0 and s_0. After the generation of each clock bit, the registers are clocked based on the control bits. The involvement of cells from both the R and S registers makes the cipher secure against guess and determine attacks. The detailed working of MICKEY cipher is available in [3].

2.2   Cellular Automata - An Overview

Cellular Automata (CA) are a lattice of cells that evolve through discrete time steps. Each cell can be in a finite set of states. The change in state values in each cell takes place simultaneously based on a transition function or CA rule. The rules are defined on a neighbourhood N of a cell. The number of cells involved in the transition function decides the neighbourhood of CA. If the state of a cell gets updated with the values of its left neighbour, right neighbour and itself, it is called a 3-neighbourhood CA since the rule is based on the 3 neighbours of a cell including itself. CA have evolved as a good pseudorandom number generator [23] and hence a good cryptographic primitive in the design of stream ciphers. The state of each cell of a CA together at any instant t defines the current state of the CA. In 3-neighbourhood CA, the value of the cell after one clock cycle depends on one left neighbour, itself and one right neighbour. The next state of the ith cell of a 3-neighbourhood CA at any instant t is given by

$$S_i^{t+1} = f(S_{i-1}^t, S_i^t, S_{i+1}^t)$$

where f is the next state function or rule, S_i^{t+1} denotes the next state of the ith cell, S_{i-1}^t is the current state of left-neighbour, S_i^t is the current state of the cell to be updated, S_{i+1}^t is the current state of right-neighbour. The state of a CA at any time instance is based on the the the CA rules. These rules can be classified as linear and nonlinear rules based on the underlying logical operations used. The linear CA rules involve only XOR operation while the nonlinear CA rules involve AND/OR operations in addition to XOR. The number of cells n that participate in a CA cell update is given by $n = 2r + 1$, where r is the radius of the neighbourhood [5]. In a two-state, three-neighbourhood CA, there are $2^8 = 256$ possible rules. When all the cells in the CA use the same rule to update the state, the CA is called uniform CA while non-uniform CA or hybrid CA refers to the case where different cells update the state using different rules. Some of the cryptographically suitable 3-neighbourhood CA rules are rules 30, 90 and 150, where 90 and 150 are linear rules and 30 is a nonlinear rule.

3   Proposed Cipher - CA Based MICKEY

Here, we have proposed a CA based MICKEY which resembles the original MICKEY in all the functionalities. The following are the modifications that we have made in our design

1. We have replaced both the R and S shift registers of MICKEY with a hybrid $<30, 60, 90, 120, 150, 180, 210, 240>$ CA applied alternatively to all the cells. The combination of linear and nonlinear 3-neighbourhood CA rules used in this rule set have been suggested in [16] as "*Ruleset 5*". We have used two null-boundary hybrid CA R and S each having 160 cells. The rules in the rule set are applied such that r_0 works on rule 30, r_1 works on rule 60 and so on, where r_i denotes the ith cell of R. The same strategy is followed for the S register also.
2. In the original version of MICKEY, the nonlinearity was introduced into the cipher through the S register which makes use of two predefined sequences COMP0 and COMP1 [3]. In our proposed design, we have eliminated these sequences. The use of hybrid CA rule set which contains nonlinear CA rules helps to compensate for this loss without compromising the quality of the generated keystream.

The cipher proceeds through 2 phases - the initialization phase and the keystream generation phase. It accepts a 128-bit key and variable length IV, with the length varying between 0 and 128 bits.

Initialization Phase: Initially, the two CA will be loaded with zeroes. The key and the IV bits are taken successively and are loaded into the CA. During each iteration, the state of each cell in the CA gets updated based on its three neighbouring cells. The CA gets updated while each of the key and IV bits are loaded into the CA, i.e., for a total of $128 + <IVlength>$ cycles (128 is the length of the key and IV length denotes the length of the IV which is variable). Once the key and IV bits are fully loaded into the two CA, an additional *preclocking* round of 80 cycles is executed. This ensures the diffusion of key and IV bits at the end of the initialization phase.

The CA update function for both R and S CA which is invoked during the initialization phase make use of the clock control bits. These control bits are derived from the XOR of a pair of states of cells, one from each CA. The functionality of these bits remain the same as in the case of original MICKEY with the only difference that during each cycle, each of the cells involved in the control bits will be influenced by its three neighbouring cells.

Keystream Generation Phase: The output keystream bits are generated during this phase. The first bits of the R and S CA are XORed to get the output keystream bit z_i. i.e., $z_i = r_0 \oplus s_0$. After the generation of each keystream bit, the cells in both the CA will get updated depending on the state of its neighbours. The CA update function that was invoked during the initialization phase is used during the keystream generation phase also.

We have used the functions CLOCK_R_CA and CLOCK_S_CA which introduce the hybrid CA into the cipher. In the algorithms, $CA(x)$ refers to the output obtained in cell x when the corresponding rule in the hybrid rule set is applied and z_i is the ith output. The clock control bits CONTROLBIT_R and CONTROLBIT_S contain bits from both the R and S CA and it controls the clocking of the respective CA during each iteration. A detailed description of CLOCK_R_CA and CLOCK_S_CA are provided in Algorithms 1 and 2 given in Appendix. We follow the same steps as in the original MICKEY stream cipher [3] for all the other functionalities.

4 Design Rationale

This section discusses about the design rationale for the proposed CA based MICKEY stream cipher. MICKEY stream cipher was vulnerable to time/memory/data trade-off (TMD) attacks as suggested by Hong and Kim [13]. This occurs due to the limited updates in the internal state of the cipher before generating the next output bit. The cipher was also vulnerable to DFA. Inorder to thwart these attacks, we have suggested the inclusion of CA into the keystream generator function, so that after the generation of each output bit, each cell in the CA gets updated based on the state of its neighbouring cells. In addition, CA helps to diffuse the defects introduced in the cipher which prevents side channel attacks on the cipher [18].

4.1 Selection of Hybrid CA Rules

Choice of Rules: The choice of rules used in any CA based stream cipher plays an important role in the strength of the cipher against cryptanalytic attacks.

Some of the most commonly used elementary CA rules in cryptographic applications are rules 30, 90 and 150, where 90 and 150 are linear rules and 30 is a nonlinear rule. The linear rules provide randomness, but are susceptible to linear cryptanalysis. Nonlinear CA rules, on the other hand, do not have good pseudorandom properties, but have high algebraic degree making them resistant to linear cryptanalysis [6]. So, the construction of hybrid rule sets that contain both linear and nonlinear rules helps to utilize the good properties of each set of rules making them a strong primitive to be used in cryptographic applications. This was investigated in [16] through a newly developed statistical measure called d-monomial test which was introduced in [9]. Karmakar et al. applied this test to CA configurations to assess their pseudorandom properties in addition to other properties like nonlinearity, algebraic degree and resiliency. They have suggested 6 hybrid CA rule sets which contained rule 30 in all of them in addition to other linear and nonlinear rules. They conducted the d-monomial test on all these rulesets and the ruleset $<30, 60, 90, 120, 150, 180, 210, 240>$ was considered better than the others. The same ruleset have been used by them in the design of CAvium [17], a CA based variant of Trivium [7]. The ruleset was also found to be a good pseudorandom sequence generator in [18].

As a first step of the introduction of CA into the original MICKEY, we have restricted ourselves to the use of 3-neighbourhood CA to make it hardware efficient. We do not rule out the option of using higher radii CA where we can use the hybrid ruleset of radius-2 as selected in [14].

Choice of Number of Pre-clocking Cycles: During the initialization phase of the cipher, each key and IV bits are loaded into the CA successively. The CAs have executed for atleast 128 cycles to a maximum of 256 cycles, since the length of the key is 128 and IV length varies from 0 to 128 bits. Once the key and IV bits are loaded, both the CA are mixed through the pre-clocking round which runs for 80 cycles. Due to the inherent nature of CA, after t cycles, each CA cell depends on $2t + 1$ neighbouring cells if they exist. Moreover, the mutual clocking function invoked during each of these cycles enhance the diffusion of key and IV bits which is an important factor in the design of stream ciphers. From a theoretical standpoint, the key and IV loading, together with the preclocking round, blends the key and IV bits together at the end of initialization phase.

5   Security Analysis and Resistance of CA Based MICKEY to DFA

5.1   Differential Fault Attack on MICKEY

Differential Fault Attack (DFA) is a side channel attack in which the attacker has control on the hardware that implements the cryptosystem. The attacker tries to inject faults into the hardware and produce faulty output. The fault free output will also be available. The faulty and the fault free keystream bits produced are compared to extract the details about the internal state of the cipher which can be used to deduce information about the secret key used in the cipher. DFA have been implemented on all the profile-2 eSTREAM finalists Grain, Trivium and MICKEY [8,12,19]. MICKEY family of ciphers were found to be vulnerable to fault attacks [4,19]. Even though the mutual irregular clocking makes the attack more difficult when compared to the fault attacks on other eSTREAM candidates Grain and Trivium, the simple nature of the output function of MICKEY opens avenues for the attack.

The DFA on MICKEY cipher in [19] proceeds in two phases - The first phase is determining the position of fault. The output keystream bit z_i is dependent on r_0 and s_0. Since $r_0(i)$ is dependent on $r_{159}(i-1)$, the fault induced will propagate and give a different output. Due to the mutual clocking mechanism, the fault difference may not be a constant since the bit in the S register in the $CONTROL\_BIT\_R$ is also involved in the R register update. This is followed by obtaining and solving linear equations from the identifiable fault locations. The detailed description of the attack and the closed form of the equations are given in [19].

Role of CA to Resist DFA: CA have been considered effective in the prevention of fault attacks on stream ciphers [15]. It was found that the incorporation of CA into the cipher helps in faster diffusion of bits which makes the DFA computationally infeasible on the cipher. Here, we provide only a sketch of the proof, where we show the effect of CA by using the closed form of equations mentioned in [19], while a rigorous one is possible.

The equations of the state update function of R and S in CA based MICKEY can be expressed as follows

$$r_k(i) = (k > 0)CA(r_k(i-1)) + (k \in RTAPS)CA(r_{159}(i-1))$$
$$+ (CA(s_{54}(i-1)) + CA(r_{106}(i-1)))CA(r_k(i-1)) \quad (1)$$

$$s_k(i) = (k > 0)CA(s_k(i-1)) + (0 < k < 159)CA(s_{159}(i-1))FB0_k$$
$$+ CA(s_{159}CA(s_{106}))(FB0_kFB1_k) + CA(s_{159}(i-1))CA(r_{53}(i-1))(FB0_k + FB1_k) \quad (2)$$

$$z(i) = r_0(i) + s_0(i) \quad (3)$$

The output bit during the 2nd iteration of MICKEY is expressed as

$$z_1 = r_{159} \oplus r_0 \cdot s_{54} \oplus r_0 \cdot r_{106} \oplus s_{159} \quad (4)$$

The output bit during the 2nd iteration of CA based MICKEY can be expressed as

$$z_1 = CA(r_{159}) \oplus CA(r_0) \cdot CA(s_{54}) \oplus CA(r_0) \cdot CA(r_{106}) \oplus CA(s_{159}) \quad (5)$$

which can be expressed as

$$r_{158} \oplus r_0 \cdot r_{105} \cdot r_{107} \oplus r_1 \cdot r_{105} \cdot r_{107} \oplus s_{53} \cdot s_{55} \cdot r_{105} \cdot r_{107}$$
$$\oplus s_{55} \cdot r_{105} \cdot r_{107} \oplus s_{54} \cdot r_{105} \cdot r_{107} \oplus s_{158}$$

We can observe that during the 2nd iteration of our design, the number of bits involved in the output bit generation is more when compared to original MICKEY. In original MICKEY, only CLOCK_S function introduced nonlinearity, while CLOCK_R function updated the register linearly. This leads to slow growth of properties like algebraic degree and nonlinearity which are the essential cryptographic properties needed for a good stream cipher [24]. In CA based MICKEY, we have used hybrid rule set in both the update operations. This helps in faster growth of algebraic degree and nonlinearity during the initial iterations itself.

In the proposed design, the fault position determination will be difficult since the fault induced at one position will not be moving as in the case of a shift register. The fast diffusion property of CA thwarts the attempt to find the fault position. The effect of propagation will be affecting the control bits which inturn makes the task of fault position determination more difficult. When the fault position determination phase fails, the second phase of obtaining equations will also fail. Moreover, in our CA based MICKEY we are using hybrid rule set in both CLOCK_R_CA and CLOCK_S_CA functions. So, the underlying equations during these operations contain nonlinear terms which thwarts the attempt to solve the obtained equations and find the inner state of the cipher.

In CLOCK_S_CA function, we have avoided the predefined sequences COMP0 and COMP1 whose predefined values were utilized during the DFA. The replacement of these sequences with hybrid CA enhances the security, since after each iteration, the bits involved will be based on the CA rules applied on the state bits and this makes the task of obtaining equations through the already known sequences difficult.

6   Software Implementation and Results

The proposed cipher was implemented in C and compiled using gcc 7.5.0. The code was run on on an Intel(R) Core(TM)-i3 1005G1 CPU @ 1.20 Gz. The time for computing 1 million and 100 million keystreams were computed. We analysed the pseudorandom properties of the keystream generated using NIST test suite [1] developed by National Institute of Standards and Technology (NIST) for testing the randomness of the binary sequence of arbitrary length. This suite consists of a set of 15 tests which assess the quality of a bitstream. For these tests, each P-value is the probability that a perfect random number generator would have produced a sequence less random than the sequence that was tested, given the kind of non-randomness assessed by the test [1]. If the P-value for a test is determined to be equal to 1, then the sequence appears to have perfect randomness and a P-value of zero indicates the non-randomness of the cipher. We have given 10 million keystream bits generated by CA based MICKEY and the results show that the keystream generated is random which adds to the strength of the cipher against statistical attacks. Table 1 shows the NIST test suite results of our cipher.

Table 1. CA based MICKEY NIST TEST RESULTS

Sl. No.	Test name	P-value	Status
1	Frequency	0.514124	Pass
2	Block frequency	0.657933	Pass
3	Cumulative sums	0.637119	Pass
4	Runs	0.289667	Pass
5	Longest run	0.171867	Pass
6	Rank	0.401199	Pass
7	FFT	0.145326	Pass
8	Non overlapping template	0.595549	Pass
9	Overlapping template	0.366918	Pass
10	Universal	0.304126	Pass
11	Approximate entropy	0.723129	Pass
12	Random excursions	0.875539	Pass
13	Random excursions variant	0.474986	Pass
14	Serial	0.946308	Pass
15	Linear complexity	0.924076	Pass

Cryptographic Properties of CA Based MICKEY: Some of the most important cryptographic properties for Boolean functions are algebraic degree, balancedness, resiliency and nonlinearity. We have found the cryptographic properties of MICKEY and CA based MICKEY and are given in Table 2. Table 3 shows the comparison of parameters between MICKEY and CA based MICKEY.

Table 2. Comparison of cryptographic properties

Iteration	Balancedness	Nonlinearity	Algebraic degree	Resiliency
MICKEY				
1	Balanced	0	1	1
2	Balanced	8	2	1
CA based MICKEY				
1	Balanced	0	1	1
2	Balanced	64	4	1

Table 3. Comparison of MICKEY and CA based MICKEY

Cipher	Keysize	IV size	State size	Initialization cycles	Time taken in seconds		
					Initialization time	KeyGeneration time	
						10^6 bits	10^8 bits
MICKEY 128 2.0	128	0–128 bits	320	159	0.001465	3.914	266.656
CA based MICKEY	80	0–128 bits	320	80	0.002028	5.17	475.281

7   Conclusion and Future Work

This paper proposes a CA based MICKEY-like stream cipher. The cipher was one of the finalists of the eSTREAM project and is efficient as well as compact. But the simple nature of the cipher made it vulnerable to fault attacks. The intention of this work is to make the cipher strong against fault attacks by using the CA primitive. Here, we have incorporated 3-neighbourhood null-boundary hybrid CA replacing the shift registers of the original MICKEY cipher with lesser number of initialization cycles compared to original MICKEY. The addition of CA primitive has not only strengthened MICKEY against fault attacks, but has also strengthened the cryptographic properties like algebraic degree and nonlinearity. As a future work, we plan to explore the advantages of incorporating 5-neighbourhood CA into MICKEY. Another direction of research is in the use of asynchrony-immune CA [20,21] in the cipher which resists clock based fault attacks [11] on stream ciphers.

Appendix

Algorithm for CA Based MICKEY

Algorithm 1: CLOCK_R_CA(R, INPUT_BIT_R, CONTROL_BIT_R)

Let $r_0, r_1, \ldots, r_{159}$ be the state of the CA before clocking, and let $r_0', r_1', \ldots, r_{159}'$ be the state of the CA after clocking.

FEEDBACK_BIT $= r_{159} \oplus INPUT\_BIT\_R$

for $i \leftarrow 1$ **to** 159 **do**
    $r_i' = CA(r_i);$ // Addition of CA

for $i \leftarrow 0$ **to** 159 **do**
    if $i \in RTAPS$ **then**
        $r_i' = r_i' \oplus$ FEEDBACK_BIT

if $CONTROL\_BIT\_R = 1$ **then**
    for $i \leftarrow 0$ **to** 159 **do**
        $r_i' = r_i' \oplus r_i$

Algorithm 2: CLOCK_S_CA(S, INPUT_BIT_S, CONTROL_BIT_S)

Let $s_0, s_1, \dots , s_{159}$ be the state of the CA before clocking, and let $s_0', s_1', \dots , s_{159}'$ be the state of the CA after clocking. Let $s_0'', s_1'', \dots , s_{159}''$ denote the intermediate values

FEEDBACK_BIT $= s_{159} \oplus INPUT\_BIT\_S$

for $i \leftarrow 1$ **to** 159 **do**

   $s_i' = CA(s_i)$;   // Addition of CA

if $CONTROL\_BIT\_S = 0$ **then**

   for $i \leftarrow 0$ **to** 159 **do**

      $s_i' = s_i'' \oplus(FB0_i,$ FEEDBACK_BIT$)$

else

   if $CONTROL\_BIT\_S = 1$ **then**

      for $i \leftarrow 0$ **to** 159 **do**

         $s_i' = s_i'' \oplus(FB1_i,$ FEEDBACK_BIT$)$

References

1. NIST Statistical Test Suite. https://csrc.nist.gov/projects/random-bit-generation/documentation-and-software. Accessed 22 Mar 2022

2. Babbage, S., Dodd, M.: The stream cipher mickey (version 1) (May 2005)

3. Babbage, S., Dodd, M.: The MICKEY stream ciphers. In: Robshaw, M., Billet, O. (eds.) New Stream Cipher Designs. LNCS, vol. 4986, pp. 191–209. Springer, Heidelberg (2008). https://doi.org/10.1007/978-3-540-68351-3_15

4. Banik, S., Maitra, S.: A differential fault attack on MICKEY 2.0. In: Bertoni, G., Coron, J.-S. (eds.) CHES 2013. LNCS, vol. 8086, pp. 215–232. Springer, Heidelberg (2013). https://doi.org/10.1007/978-3-642-40349-1_13

5. Cattell, K., Muzio, J.C.: Synthesis of one-dimensional linear hybrid cellular automata. IEEE Trans. Comput. Aided Des. Integr. Circ. Syst. **15**(3), 325–335 (1996). https://ieeexplore.ieee.org/document/489103

6. Chakraborty, K., Chowdhury, D.R.: CSHR: selection of cryptographically suitable hybrid cellular automata rule. In: Sirakoulis, G.C., Bandini, S. (eds.) ACRI 2012. LNCS, vol. 7495, pp. 591–600. Springer, Heidelberg (2012). https://doi.org/10.1007/978-3-642-33350-7_61

7. Cannière, C.: TRIVIUM: a stream cipher construction inspired by block cipher design principles. In: Katsikas, S.K., López, J., Backes, M., Gritzalis, S., Preneel, B. (eds.) ISC 2006. LNCS, vol. 4176, pp. 171–186. Springer, Heidelberg (2006). https://doi.org/10.1007/11836810_13

8. Dey, P., Chakraborty, A., Adhikari, A., Mukhopadhyay, D.: Improved practical differential fault analysis of grain-128. In: 2015 Design, Automation Test in Europe Conference Exhibition (DATE), pp. 459–464 (2015). https://doi.org/10.7873/DATE.2015.0921

9. Filiol, E.: A new statistical testing for symmetric ciphers and hash functions. In: Deng, R., Bao, F., Zhou, J., Qing, S. (eds.) ICICS 2002. LNCS, vol. 2513, pp. 342–353. Springer, Heidelberg (2002). https://doi.org/10.1007/3-540-36159-6_29

10. Hell, M., Johansson, T., Maximov, A., Meier, W.: The grain family of stream ciphers. In: Robshaw, M., Billet, O. (eds.) New Stream Cipher Designs. LNCS, vol. 4986, pp. 179–190. Springer, Heidelberg (2008). https://doi.org/10.1007/978-3-540-68351-3_14

11. Hoch, J.J., Shamir, A.: Fault analysis of stream ciphers. In: Joye, M., Quisquater, J.-J. (eds.) CHES 2004. LNCS, vol. 3156, pp. 240–253. Springer, Heidelberg (2004). https://doi.org/10.1007/978-3-540-28632-5_18

12. Hojsík, M., Rudolf, B.: Differential fault analysis of Trivium. In: Nyberg, K. (ed.) FSE 2008. LNCS, vol. 5086, pp. 158–172. Springer, Heidelberg (2008). https://doi.org/10.1007/978-3-540-71039-4_10

13. Hong, J., Kim, W.-H.: TMD-tradeoff and state entropy loss considerations of streamcipher MICKEY. In: Maitra, S., Veni Madhavan, C.E., Venkatesan, R. (eds.) INDOCRYPT 2005. LNCS, vol. 3797, pp. 169–182. Springer, Heidelberg (2005). https://doi.org/10.1007/11596219_14

14. John, A., Nandu, B.C., Ajesh, A., Jose, J.: PENTAVIUM: potent Trivium-like stream cipher using higher radii cellular automata. In: Gwizdałła, T.M., Manzoni, L., Sirakoulis, G.C., Bandini, S., Podlaski, K. (eds.) Cellular Automata: 14th International Conference on Cellular Automata for Research and Industry, ACRI 2020, Lodz, Poland, December 2–4, 2020, Proceedings, pp. 90–100. Springer, Cham (2021). https://doi.org/10.1007/978-3-030-69480-7_10

15. Jose, J., Das, S., Roychowdhury, D.: Prevention of fault attacks in cellular automata based stream ciphers. J. Cell. Autom. **12**(1–2), 141–157 (2016)

16. Karmakar, S., Mukhopadhyay, D., Roy Chowdhury, D.: d-monomial tests of nonlinear cellular automata for cryptographic design. In: Bandini, S., Manzoni, S., Umeo, H., Vizzari, G. (eds.) ACRI 2010. LNCS, vol. 6350, pp. 261–270. Springer, Heidelberg (2010). https://doi.org/10.1007/978-3-642-15979-4_28

17. Karmakar, S., Mukhopadhyay, D., Roychowdhury, D.: Cavium - strengthening trivium stream cipher using cellular automata. J. Cellular Automata **7**(2), 179–197 (2012). http://www.oldcitypublishing.com/JCA/JCAabstracts/JCA7.2abstracts/JCAv7n2p179-197

18. Karmakar, S., Chowdhury, D.R.: Countermeasures of side channel attacks on symmetric key ciphers using cellular automata. In: Sirakoulis, G.C., Bandini, S. (eds.) ACRI 2012. LNCS, vol. 7495, pp. 623–632. Springer, Heidelberg (2012). https://doi.org/10.1007/978-3-642-33350-7_64

19. Karmakar, S., Roychowdhury, D.: Differential fault analysis of mickey-128 2.0. In: 2013 Workshop on Fault Diagnosis and Tolerance in Cryptography, pp. 52–59 (2013). https://doi.org/10.1109/FDTC.2013.8

20. Mariot, L.: Asynchrony immune cellular automata. In: El Yacoubi, S., Was, J., Bandini, S. (eds.) ACRI 2016. LNCS, vol. 9863, pp. 176–181. Springer, Cham (2016). https://doi.org/10.1007/978-3-319-44365-2_17

21. Mariot, L., Manzoni, L., Dennunzio, A.: Search space reduction of asynchrony immune cellular automata. Nat. Comput. **19**(2), 287–293 (2020). https://doi.org/10.1007/s11047-020-09788-1

22. Robshaw, M.: The eSTREAM project. In: Robshaw, M., Billet, O. (eds.) New Stream Cipher Designs. LNCS, vol. 4986, pp. 1–6. Springer, Heidelberg (2008). https://doi.org/10.1007/978-3-540-68351-3_1

23. Wolfram, S.: Random sequence generation by cellular automata. Adv. Appl. Math. **7**(2), 123–169 (1986). https://doi.org/10.1016/0196-8858(86)90028-X

24. Wu, C.-K., Feng, D.: Boolean Functions and Their Applications in Cryptography. ACST, Springer, Heidelberg (2016). https://doi.org/10.1007/978-3-662-48865-2

On the Linear Components Space of S-boxes Generated by Orthogonal Cellular Automata

Luca Mariot[1][✉] and Luca Manzoni[2]

[1] Digital Security Group, Radboud University,
PO Box 9010, Nijmegen, The Netherlands
luca.mariot@ru.nl
[2] Department of Mathematics and Geosciences,
University of Trieste, Via Valerio 12/1, Trieste, Italy
lmanzoni@units.it

Abstract. We investigate S-boxes defined by pairs of Orthogonal Cellular Automata (OCA), motivated by the fact that such CA always define bijective vectorial Boolean functions, and could thus be interesting for the design of block ciphers. In particular, we perform an exhaustive search of all nonlinear OCA pairs of diameter $d = 4$ and $d = 5$, which generate S-boxes of size 6×6 and 8×8, respectively. Surprisingly, all these S-boxes turn out to be linear, and thus they are not useful for the design of confusion layers in block ciphers. However, a closer inspection of these S-boxes reveals a very interesting structure. Indeed, we remark that the linear components space of the OCA-based S-boxes found by our exhaustive search are themselves the kernels of linear CA, or, equivalently, *polynomial codes*. We finally classify the polynomial codes of the S-boxes obtained in our exhaustive search and observe that, in most cases, they actually correspond to the cyclic code with generator polynomial $X^b + 1$, where $b = d - 1$. Although these findings rule out the possibility of using OCA to design good S-boxes in block ciphers, they give nonetheless some interesting insights for a theoretical characterization of nonlinear OCA pairs, which is still an open question in general.

Keywords: S-boxes · Boolean functions · Cellular automata · Orthogonal Latin squares · Polynomial codes · Cyclic codes

1 Introduction

Substitution Boxes (most often referred to as *S-boxes*) are mappings of the form $F : \{0,1\}^n \to \{0,1\}^m$, i.e. vectorial Boolean functions that evaluate n-bit vectors in input, and give m-bit vectors in output. S-boxes play a fundamental role in the design of *block ciphers*, most notably in the so-called *Substitution-Permutation Network* (SPN) paradigm [1]. There, S-boxes are used to implement the *confusion layer* of the cipher, whose role is to make the relationship between the ciphertext and the encryption key as "complicated" as possible. Typically, an

B. Chopard et al. (Eds.): ACRI 2022, LNCS 13402, pp. 52–62, 2022.
https://doi.org/10.1007/978-3-031-14926-9_5

SPN cipher uses an S-box with $n = m$, where n is much smaller than the block length. For instance, the RIJNDAEL cipher (standardized by the NIST as the AES encryption algorithm) is based on an 8×8 S-box which is evaluated in parallel over sub-blocks of a 128-bit plaintext block [2]. In particular, this S-box computes the multiplicative inverse of an element over the finite field $\mathbb{F}_{2^3}$. The 128-bit block resulting from this parallel application of the S-box is then fed to the *permutation layer*, which diffuses the information in a non-local way.

Other than the one used in RIJNDAEL, many other S-boxes of different sizes and defined by different operations have been considered in the literature. The choice of a specific S-box mainly depends on the security and efficiency requirements for a particular cipher. For example, *lightweight* ciphers such as PRESENT [3] and RECTANGLE [4] employ small 4×4 S-boxes, since they are designed for very efficient hardware implementations.

Among the different approaches used to define good S-boxes, *Cellular Automata* (CA) are one of the most interesting, since they can provide a good trade-off between security and efficiency. Indeed, CA can be seen as *shift-invariant* functions, where the same local rule is applied in each output coordinate function. This enables a simple and compact implementation both in hardware and software. The most notable example of a symmetric cryptographic primitive that uses a CA-based S-box is KECCAK [5], which has been selected by the NIST in 2012 as the new SHA-3 standard for cryptographic hash functions [6]. In particular, the confusion layer of KECCAK is a 5×5 S-box defined by the elementary CA χ, which corresponds to rule 210 in Wolfram's numbering convention. Beside their use in KECCAK, the body of research related to CA-based S-boxes is quite extensive. The common thread in these work is to consider a CA as a particular kind of vectorial Boolean function, which is then either iterated for multiple time steps as a dynamical system [7–11] or evaluated only once, as in KECCAK [12–14].

In this work, we consider a different approach to design S-boxes, namely leveraging on *orthogonal* CA (OCA). Two CA are called orthogonal if their Cayley tables define a pair of *orthogonal Latin squares* [15]. Beside defining an invertible transformation—which is necessary for decryption—the use of orthogonal Latin squares also ensures a certain amount of diffusion, since they are equivalent to $(2, 2)-multipermutations$ [16]. Therefore, S-boxes defined by orthogonal Latin squares can provide both good diffusion and confusion, provided that their nonlinearity is high enough. In this regard, while the theory of linear OCA is well developed [17], significantly less is known about nonlinear OCA [18].

Given a pair of OCA defined by two local rules of diameter d, we first give a formal description of the associated S-box of size $n \times n$, where $n = 2b = 2(d - 1)$. This basically amounts to use the output of the first (respectively, the second) CA as the left (respectively, right) b output bits of the S-box. Next, we perform an exhaustive search of all OCA of diameter $d = 4$ and $d = 5$, which correspond respectively to S-boxes of size 6×6 and 8×8, with the goal of finding those with the best nonlinearity. Quite surprisingly, we remark that *all these S-boxes are linear*, even if the respective OCA are defined by nonlinear local rules. Since the nonlinearity of an S-box is defined as the minimum nonlinearity of its component functions, it follows that the S-boxes found by our exhaustive search always have at least one linear component. It is a well-known fact that the set of linear components in a linear S-box is a vector space over the finite field $\mathbb{F}_2$. Therefore, we investigate the linear components spaces of the S-boxes generated in our experiments, and remark that they are polynomial codes. The interesting aspect of this finding is that the generator matrix of a polynomial code is the transition matrix of a linear CA. Equivalently, this means that *the linear components space of a linear S-box defined by a pair of nonlinear OCA is itself the kernel of a linear CA.* We conclude our investigation by classifying the OCA-based S-boxes generated in our exhaustive search experiments in terms of the generator polynomials of their linear components spaces. Interestingly, *for most S-boxes the linear components space is the cyclic code defined by the generator polynomial $X^b + 1$.* This corresponds to the situation where the two CA local rules share the same nonlinear terms in their algebraic normal form. Consequently, each component function that sums only the coordinates i and $i + b$ is linear, for all $1 \le i \le b$.

Overall, the experimental findings of this paper rule out the possibility of using OCA to design good S-boxes for symmetric primitives. Nonetheless, the coding-theoretic structure of the linear component spaces unveiled here could be useful to give a theoretical characterization of certain classes of nonlinear OCA pairs. To this end, we mention in the conclusions of this paper some directions and ideas that we plan to pursue for future research on this topic.

2   Basic Definitions

We start by introducing all necessary background definitions and results used throughout the paper. For a systematic treatment of the part on (vectorial) Boolean functions, we refer the reader to Carlet's recent book [19]. For orthogonal CA, we follow the notation in [17]. The recent chapter [20] gives a general overview of the applications of CA to cryptography.

2.1   Cryptographic Boolean Functions and S-boxes

In what follows, we denote by $\mathbb{F}_2 = \{0, 1\}$ the finite field with two elements, with sum and multiplication defined, respectively, as the XOR (denoted by $\oplus$) and logical AND (denoted by concatenation) of two elements. Given $n \in \mathbb{N}$, the n-dimensional vector space of all n-bit strings is denoted by $\mathbb{F}_2^n$. The sum between two vectors $x, y \in \mathbb{F}_2^n$ is defined as their bitwise XOR (and, slightly abusing notation, still denoted as $x \oplus y$), while multiplication of a vector $x \in \mathbb{F}_2^n$ by a scalar $a \in \mathbb{F}_2$ is the field multiplication of each coordinate of x by a. In particular, this implies that two vectors $x, y \in \mathbb{F}_2^n$ are linearly independent if and only if $x \ne y$. Further, the *dot product* of two vectors $x, y \in \mathbb{F}_2^n$ is defined as $x \cdot y = \bigoplus_{i=1}^{n} x_i y_i$, while their *Hamming distance* $d_H(x, y) = |\{i : x_i \ne y_i\}|$ is the number of coordinates where x and y disagree. The *Hamming weight* $w_H(x)$ of $x \in \mathbb{F}_2^n$ is the Hamming distance between x and the null vector $\underline{0}$, or, equivalently, the number of ones in x.

An n-variable *Boolean function* is a mapping $\mathbb{F}_2^n \rightarrow \mathbb{F}_2$. Since $\mathbb{F}_2^n$ is finite, the most obvious way to uniquely represent f is to specify its *truth table*, which is the 2^n-bit vector $\Omega_f = (f(0, \cdots, 0), \cdots, f(1, \cdots, 1))$. In other words, the truth table specifies the output value of f for each possible input vector, in lexicographic order. The function f is called *balanced* if and only if Ω_f has an equal number of zeros and ones, which is a basic property for Boolean functions used in cryptographic applications. A second common method to uniquely represent a Boolean function is the *algebraic normal form* (ANF). Remarking that $x^2 = x$ for all $x \in \mathbb{F}_2$, the ANF of f is the multivariate polynomial in the quotient ring $\mathbb{F}_2[x_1, \cdots, x_n]/[x_1^2 \oplus x_1, \cdots, x_n^2 \oplus x_n]$ defined as:

$$P_f(x) = \bigoplus_{u \in F_2^n} a_u x^u = \bigoplus_{u \in F_2^n} a_u x_1^{u_1} x_2^{u_2} \ldots x_n^{u_n} \ , \tag{1}$$

where $a_u \in \mathbb{F}_2$ for all $u \in \mathbb{F}_2^n$. The *algebraic degree* of f is formally defined as $deg(f) = \max_{u \in \mathbb{F}_2^n} \{w_H(u) : u \neq 0\}$. Intuitively, the degree of f is simply the size of the largest nonzero monomial in the ANF of f. Functions of degree 1 are also called *affine*, and an affine function is called *linear* if $a_{\underline{0}} = 0$ (i.e., the ANF of f does not have any constant term). Nonlinear functions are simply those of degree higher than 1. The nonlinearity of a Boolean function $f : \mathbb{F}_2^n \rightarrow \mathbb{F}_2$ corresponds to the minimum Hamming distance of its truth table from the set of truth tables of all n-variable affine functions. Formally, this can be determined in terms of the *Walsh transform* of f, which is the mapping $W_f : \mathbb{F}_2^n \rightarrow \mathbb{Z}$ defined as:

$$W_f(a) = \sum_{x \in F_2^n} (-1)^{f(x) \oplus a \cdot x}, \ , \tag{2}$$

for all $a \in F_2^n$. Then, the nonlinearity of f equals

$$nl(f) = 2^{n-1} - \frac{1}{2} \max_{a \in \mathbb{F}_2^n} \{|W_f(a)|\} \ . \tag{3}$$

As a cryptographic criterion, the nonlinearity of Boolean functions used in stream and block ciphers should be as high as possible to withstand fast-correlation attacks and linear cryptanalysis, respectively.

The treatment above is generalized to the vectorial case as follows. Given $n, m \in \mathbb{N}$, an (n, m)-*function* (or *S-box*) is a vectorial mapping $F : \mathbb{F}_2^n \rightarrow \mathbb{F}_2^m$, which is defined by the set of its *coordinate functions* $f_i : \mathbb{F}_2^n \rightarrow \mathbb{F}_2$ that represent the i-th output bit of F for all $i \in \{1, \cdots, m\}$. The *component functions* of F are the non-trivial linear combinations of its coordinate functions. A component function is defined by a vector $v \in \mathbb{F}_2^n \setminus \{\underline{0}\}$ as the dot product $v \cdot F(x)$ for all $x \in \mathbb{F}_2^n$. Many block ciphers employ S-boxes with an equal number of inputs and outputs, which is also the focus of this paper. When $n = m$, the concept analogous to balancedness in S-boxes is *bijectivity*: indeed, a (n, n)-function is bijective if and only if all its component functions are balanced. Bijective S-boxes are necessary for decryption in SPN ciphers. The algebraic degree of an S-box $F : \mathbb{F}_2^n \rightarrow \mathbb{F}_2^m$ is defined as the *maximum degree* of all its *coordinate functions*.

On the other hand, the nonlinearity of F is the *minimum nonlinearity* of all its *component functions*. Therefore, there can be S-boxes with degree higher than 1 which are nonetheless linear: it suffices that a single non-trivial linear combination of coordinates gives an affine function. It is also easy to see that the set $\mathcal{L}_F = \{v \in \mathbb{F}_2^m \setminus \{\underline{0}\} : nl(v \cdot F) = 0\}$ of all linear component functions of an S-box F is a subspace of $\mathbb{F}_2^m$. As a matter of fact, if two functions are affine, their sum must be affine too. We will call $\mathcal{L}_F$ the *linear components space* (LCS) of F.

2.2 Orthogonal CA

A *cellular automaton* (CA) is characterized by a regular lattice of *cells*, where the state of each cell is determined by the application of an update rule over the cell's neighborhood. Most of the research related to CA focuses on the long-term behavior of the dynamical system arising from the iteration of the update rule for multiple time steps. Here, on the other hand, we consider CA as a particular kind of vectorial Boolean functions, as per the following definition:

Definition 1. *Let $d, n \in \mathbb{N}$ such that $d \leq n$, and let $b = d - 1$. A no-boundary cellular automaton with local rule $f : \mathbb{F}_2^d \to \mathbb{F}_2$ of diameter d is a vectorial Boolean function $F : \mathbb{F}_2^n \to \mathbb{F}_2^{n-b}$ whose i-th coordinate is defined as:*

$$F(x_1, \cdots, x_n)_i = f(x_i, \cdots, x_{i+b}) \tag{4}$$

for all $i \in \{1, \cdots, n - b\}$ and $x \in \mathbb{F}_2^n$.

In other words, each output coordinate F_i corresponds to the local rule f applied to the i-th input cell and the b cells to its right. The "no-boundary" specification stems from the fact that we apply the local rule as long as we have enough right neighbors, that is until $i = n - b$. The fact that the cellular lattice "shrinks" after evaluating F does not pose an issue, since as mentioned above we are only interested in the one-shot application of a CA rather than on its dynamical behavior. Hence, we do not need to consider boundary conditions.

A *Latin square* of order $N \in \mathbb{N}$ is a $N \times N$ square matrix L where each rows and columns are permutation of $[N] = \{1, \cdots, N\}$. Two Latin squares L_1, L_2 of order N are said to be *orthogonal* if their *superposition* yields all possible pairs in the Cartesian product $[N] \times [N]$ exactly once. Orthogonal Latin squares are combinatorial designs with several applications in cryptography and coding theory, most notably secret sharing schemes and MDS codes [21]. Eloranta [22] and Mariot et al. [23] independently proved that a CA equipped with bipermutive local rule can be used to define a Latin square. A local rule $f : \mathbb{F}_2^d \to \mathbb{F}_2$ is called bipermutive if it can be written as the XOR of the leftmost and rightmost variables with a generating function of the $d - 2$ central ones, i.e. $f(x_1, \cdots, x_d) = x_1 \oplus g(x_2, \cdots, x_b) \oplus x_d$, with $g : \mathbb{F}_2^{d-2} \to \mathbb{F}_2$. Then, a CA $F : \mathbb{F}_2^{2b} \to \mathbb{F}_2^b$ equipped with such a local rule f corresponds to a Latin square of order $N = 2^b$. The idea is to use the left and right b input cells of F respectively to index the rows and the columns of a $2^b \times 2^b$ square, and then take the output of the CA as the entry of the square at those coordinates. A pair of *orthogonal CA* (OCA) is a pair of CA $F, G : \mathbb{F}_2^{2b} \to \mathbb{F}_2^b$ defined by bipermutive rules $f, g : \mathbb{F}_2^d \to \mathbb{F}_2$ such that the corresponding Latin squares of order 2^b are orthogonal. The authors of [23] that two CA with *linear* bipermutive local rules are orthogonal if and only if the associated polynomials are coprime. Following our notation above on Boolean functions, a linear bipermutive rule is defined by a vector $a = (1, a_2, \cdots, a_b, 1)$ as $f(x_1, \cdots, x_d) = x_1 \oplus a_2 x_2 \oplus \cdots \oplus a_b x_b \oplus x_d$ for all $x \in \mathbb{F}_2^d$. Then, the polynomial associated to f is the monic polynomial $P_f(X) \in \mathbb{F}_2[X]$ of degree b defined as $P_f(X) = 1 + a_2 X + \cdots + a_b X^{b-1} + X^b$. Stated otherwise, we use the coefficients of a as the coefficients of the increasing powers of the indeterminate X in $P_f(X)$.

The authors of [17] expanded on the previous results of [23] by further providing counting results for the number of linear OCA and an optimal construction of families of *mutually orthogonal CA* (MOCA), i.e. sets of CA that are pairwise orthogonal. The great amount of theory developed for linear OCA [17, 23–27] contrasts with what little is known about the nonlinear setting. From a theoretical point of view, only a necessary condition on the local rules of two nonlinear OCA is currently known [18], and an inversion algorithm for the configurations of nonlinear OCA has been proposed in [15]. The authors of [28] also used evolutionary algorithms to evolve pairs of nonlinear OCA. However, to date a theoretical characterization of nonlinear OCA similar to the linear case is still missing.

3   S-boxes Based on OCA

Given a bipermutive local rule $f : \mathbb{F}_2^d \to \mathbb{F}_2$ of diameter $d = b + 1$, one can interpret the corresponding CA $F : \mathbb{F}_2^{2b} \to \mathbb{F}_2^b$ both as a Latin square of order 2^b and as a $(2b, b)$-function. However, as we mentioned in Sect. 2.1 the S-boxes used in SPN ciphers need to have the same number of inputs and outputs. To this end, our approach is to define a (n, n)-function where $n = 2b$ by using two OCA $F, G : \mathbb{F}_2^{2b} \to \mathbb{F}_2^b$ respectively defined by two d-variable bipermutive local rules $f, g : \mathbb{F}_2^d \to \mathbb{F}_2$. In particular, we define the S-box $H : \mathbb{F}_2^n \to \mathbb{F}_2^n$ for all $x \in \mathbb{F}_2^n$ as $H(x) = F(x)||G(x)$, where $||$ denotes the concatenation of the two operands. In other words, we evaluate the input x both under the CA F and G, thereby obtaining two output vectors of length b each, and then we concatenate them to get an output of length $n = 2b$. The formal definition of $H(x)$ in full is thus:

$$H(x) = (f(x_1, \cdots, x_d), \cdots, f(x_b, \cdots, x_n), g(x_1, \cdots, x_d), \cdots, g(x_b, \cdots, x_n)) \ . \tag{5}$$

At this point, the reader might wonder why one would go to the trouble of defining an S-box in this way, instead of using a single CA with periodic boundary conditions, as done in most of the related literature (e.g., [2, 7, 13, 14]). Analogously to the work done in [26], where OCA are considered for the design of pseudorandom number generators, the motivation is twofold:

1. The fact that F and G are OCA means that the superposed Latin squares are orthogonal, or equivalently they define a permutation over the Cartesian product $[2^b] \times [2^b]$, which is isomorphic to $\mathbb{F}_2^b \times \mathbb{F}_2^b$. Hence, the S-box H in

Equation (5) is bijective, since it is simply the concatenation of the outputs of F and G, and $\mathbb{F}_2^n$ is in turn isomorphic to $\mathbb{F}_2^b \times \mathbb{F}_2^b$, as $n = 2b$. As we discussed before, bijectivity is necessary for decryption in SPN ciphers, and this condition is not guaranteed by generic S-boxes defined by single CA.

2. The bijection induced by two Orthogonal Latin squares L_1, L_2 (and thus by two OCA) have the peculiar property of being $(2, 2)$-*multipermutations*. As shown by Vaudenay [16], this provides an optimal amount of diffusion between 4-tuples formed by pairs of inputs and outputs. Concerning the OCA S-box H defined in Equation (5), this means that for all $x, x', y, y' \in \mathbb{F}_2^b$ such that $(x, y) \neq (x', y')$, the tuples $(x, y, F(x||y), G(x||y))$ and $(x', y', F(x'||y'), G(x'||'y))$ always disagree on at least 3 coordinates.

Clearly, the S-box H associated to two linear OCA is also linear: indeed, any linear combination of linear coordinates will always yield a linear component functions. Therefore, one cannot use the theoretical characterization in terms of coprime polynomials of [17] in order to get good S-boxes.

For this reason, we set out to investigate the nonlinearity of S-boxes of the form (5) defined by nonlinear OCA. We performed an exhaustive search of all distinct pairs of bipermutive local rules of diameters $d = 4$ and $d = 5$, which corresponds to S-boxes $H : \mathbb{F}_2^n \to \mathbb{F}_2^n$ with $n = 6$ and $n = 8$, respectively. Since the set of all bipermutive rules of diameter d is composed of $2^{2^{d-2}}$ elements, the sizes of the explored search spaces are respectively $(2^{2^2} \cdot (2^{2^2} - 1))/2 = 120$ for $d = 4$ and $(2^{2^3} \cdot (2^{2^3} - 1))/2 = 32640$ for $d = 5$. We did not consider higher diameters because the size of the search space grows super-exponentially in the diameter of the local rules, making an exhaustive search unfeasible already for $d \geq 7$. This leaves out the case of diameter $d = 6$ (i.e. $n = 10$), which we discarded anyway since S-boxes of sizes larger than $n = 8$ are seldom used in SPN ciphers [19]. Further, we did not consider diameter $d = 3$ ($n = 4$) since it is already known that there are only linear OCA pairs in that case [18].

For each pair $f, g : \mathbb{F}_2^d \to \mathbb{F}_2$ of bipermutive rules visited by our exhaustive search, we first computed their nonlinearity, discarding them if they were both linear. Otherwise, we generated the corresponding CA $F, G : \mathbb{F}_2^{2b} \to \mathbb{F}_2^b$ and checked if they were orthogonal. If so, we further defined the associated S-box $H : \mathbb{F}_2^n \to \mathbb{F}_2^n$ and determined its nonlinearity.

Much to our surprise, *all S-boxes obtained in this way turned out to be linear, both for diameter $d = 4$ and $d = 5$, even if we only considered nonlinear OCA pairs.* Hence, for each of these S-boxes there is at least one linear combination of coordinate functions which results in an affine function. Table 1 reports the classification of the obtained S-boxes for each diameter d, with $nl(f, g)$ denoting the nonlinearity of the underlying local rules f and g, $\#OCA$ the total number of nonlinear OCA pairs for that nonlinearity, dim the LCS dimension of the corresponding S-box H, and $\#dim$ the number of S-boxes whose LCS have that dimension. One can see from the table that for $d = 4$ all S-boxes have LCS dimension $d - 1$. The same happens also for S-boxes of diameter $d = 5$ defined by local rules with nonlinearity 4. For nonlinearity 8, there 704 out of 768 with LCS dimension $d - 1$, while the remaining 64 have LCS dimension $d - 2$.

Table 1. Classification of OCA-based S-boxes of diameter $d = 4$ and $d = 5$ in terms of the nonlinearity of their local rules and LCS dimensions.

d	$nl(f,g)$	#OCA	dim	#dim
4	$(4,4)$	32	3	32
5	$(4,4)$	768	4	768
	$(8,8)$	768	4	704
			3	64

4 Polynomial Codes from Linear Components Spaces

The results obtained so far clearly prevent the use of nonlinear OCA pairs to define good S-boxes up to size $n = 8$. Despite this negative result, we now analyze more closely the LCS of the S-boxes arising from our exhaustive search, unveiling an interesting coding-theoretic structure.

Recall that a (n,k) *binary code* $C \subseteq \mathbb{F}_2^n$ of length n and dimension k is a k-dimensional subspace of $\mathbb{F}_2^n$. Any set of k linearly independent vectors are a basis of the code C, and they form the rows of a $k \times n$ *generator matrix* G of C. The encoding of a message $m \in \mathbb{F}_2^k$ of length k is performed by the multiplication $c = mG$, which gives the *codeword* c of length n. The $n \times k$ *parity-check* matrix P is used in the decoding step: a received codeword $y \in \mathbb{F}_2^n$ is multiplied by P, and if the result $s = yP$ (also called the *syndrome*) is the null vector $\underline{0}$, then no errors were introduced by the channel during transmission. A *polynomial code* is a particular type of (n,k) code where the generator matrix can be compactly described by a *generator polynomial* $g(X) \in \mathbb{F}_2^n$ defined as $g(X) = a_1 + a_2 X + \cdots + X^t$, with $t < n$. Specifically, the generator matrix G is:

$$G = \begin{pmatrix} a_0 & \cdots & a_{t-1} & 1 & 0 & \cdots \cdots \cdots & \cdots & 0 \\ 0 & a_0 & \cdots & a_{t-1} & 1 & 0 & \cdots \cdots & \cdots & 0 \\ \vdots & \vdots & \vdots & \ddots & \vdots & \vdots & \vdots & \ddots & \vdots & \vdots \\ 0 & \cdots & \cdots & \cdots & \cdots & 0 & a_0 & \cdots & a_{t-1} & 1 \end{pmatrix}. \tag{6}$$

In other words, each subsequent row of the matrix is obtained by shifting one place to the right the coefficients of g. A polynomial code is *cyclic* if and only if its generator polynomial g divides $X^n + 1$. In that case, the resulting code is closed under *cyclic shifts*: shifting a codeword one place to the left (with the first coordinate becoming the last one) yields another valid codeword[1].

Interestingly, *the LCS of the OCA-based S-boxes found by our exhaustive search experiments are all polynomial codes of length* $n = 2b$. Referring to

---

[1] Notice that certain authors (see e.g. Kasami et al. [29]) use the term *polynomial code* to actually refer to a *subclass* of cyclic codes. Here, instead, we follow Gilbert and Nicholson's notation (see [30]), where a polynomial code is a generalization of a cyclic code (specifically, the generator polynomial does not have to divide $X^n + 1$).

Table 1, all the 32 LCS for diameter $d = 4$ and the 768 LCS for $d = 5$ and nonlinearity $(4, 4)$ are actually $(2b, b)$ cyclic codes with generator $g(X) = 1 + X^b$. For diameter $d = 5$ and nonlinearity $(8, 8)$, the 704 S-boxes with LCS of dimension 4 are again $(2b, b)$ cyclic codes with generator $1 + X^b$, while the remaining 64 are split in four classes, each of size 16, defined by the following generators:

$$g_1(X) = X + X^4 + X^5; \quad g_2(X) = 1 + X^4 + X^5;$$
$$g_3(X) = 1 + X + X^4; \quad g_4(X) = 1 + X + X^6.$$

$$(7)$$

We remark that the case of generator polynomial $1 + X^b$ (which accounts for the great majority of the LCS examined here) corresponds to the case where the local rules f and g *share the same nonlinear terms in their ANF*. Indeed, this is the only way how the linear components of the form $F_i \oplus G_i$ for $i \in \{1, \cdots b\}$ can give an affine function, since f and g are evaluated on the same neighborhood.

5　Conclusions

Although the findings of this paper are negative from the perspective of cryptographic applications (as all OCA-based S-boxes generated in our exhaustive search turned out to be linear), they prompt us nonetheless with new interesting venues for the theoretical study of nonlinear OCA. Indeed, the fact that the LCS of these S-boxes are all polynomial codes is particularly interesting, since *polynomial codes are simply linear CA under a coding-theoretic disguise*: as remarked for example in [31], the generator matrix of a polynomial code can be regarded as the *transition matrix* of a linear CA, where the coefficients of the generator polynomial are the coefficients of the linear local rule. In other words, the LCS of the S-boxes generated by the nonlinear OCA found in our exhaustive search are *themselves* the kernels of a linear CA. Whether this fact holds also for higher diameters is an interesting question that we plan to address in future research. In particular, we conjecture that if an OCA-based S-box is linear, then its LCS is *always* a polynomial code. More in general, it would also be interesting to extend the exhaustive search to higher diameters (in particular $d = 6$) to verify if the corresponding S-boxes are always linear as observed for $d = 4$ and $d = 5$. If this is the case, the coding-theoretic structure observed in this paper could help in finding a theoretical characterization of nonlinear OCA pairs.

Appendix: Source Code and Experimental Data

The source code and experimental data are available at https://github.com/rymoah/orthogonal-ca-sboxes.

References

1. Stinson, D.R., Paterson, M.: Cryptography: Theory and Practice. CRC Press (2018)
2. Daemen, J., Rijmen, V.: The Design of Rijndael - The Advanced Encryption Standard (AES). Information Security and Cryptography, 2nd edn. Springer, Heidelberg (2020). https://doi.org/10.1007/978-3-662-04722-4
3. Bogdanov, A., et al.: PRESENT: an ultra-lightweight block cipher. In: Paillier, P., Verbauwhede, I. (eds.) CHES 2007. LNCS, vol. 4727, pp. 450–466. Springer, Heidelberg (2007). https://doi.org/10.1007/978-3-540-74735-2_31
4. Zhang, W., Bao, Z., Lin, D., Rijmen, V., Yang, B., Verbauwhede, I.: RECTANGLE: a bit-slice lightweight block cipher suitable for multiple platforms. Sci. China Inf. Sci. **58**(12), 1–15 (2015)
5. Bertoni, G., Daemen, J., Peeters, M., Van Assche, G.: Keccak. In: Johansson, T., Nguyen, P.Q. (eds.) EUROCRYPT 2013. LNCS, vol. 7881, pp. 313–314. Springer, Heidelberg (2013). https://doi.org/10.1007/978-3-642-38348-9_19
6. Dworkin, M.J.: SHA-3 Standard: Permutation-Based Hash and Extendable-Output Functions. Federal Information Processing Standards (NIST FIPS), vol. 202, pp. 1–35 (2015)
7. Seredynski, F., Bouvry, P., Zomaya, A.Y.: Cellular automata computations and secret key cryptography. Parallel Comput. **30**(5–6), 753–766 (2004)
8. Seredynski, M., Bouvry, P.: Block encryption using reversible cellular automata. In: Sloot, P.M.A., Chopard, B., Hoekstra, A.G. (eds.) ACRI 2004. LNCS, vol. 3305, pp. 785–792. Springer, Heidelberg (2004). https://doi.org/10.1007/978-3-540-30479-1_81
9. Marconi, S., Chopard, B.: Discrete physics, cellular automata and cryptography. In: El Yacoubi, S., Chopard, B., Bandini, S. (eds.) ACRI 2006. LNCS, vol. 4173, pp. 617–626. Springer, Heidelberg (2006). https://doi.org/10.1007/11861201_72
10. Szaban, M., Seredynski, F.: Cryptographically strong s-boxes based on cellular automata. In: Umeo, H., Morishita, S., Nishinari, K., Komatsuzaki, T., Bandini, S. (eds.) ACRI 2008. LNCS, vol. 5191, pp. 478–485. Springer, Heidelberg (2008). https://doi.org/10.1007/978-3-540-79992-4_62
11. Oliveira, G.M.B., Martins, L.G.A., Alt, L.S., Ferreira, G.B.: Exhaustive evaluation of radius 2 toggle rules for a variable-length cryptographic cellular automata-based model. In: Bandini, S., Manzoni, S., Umeo, H., Vizzari, G. (eds.) ACRI 2010. LNCS, vol. 6350, pp. 275–286. Springer, Heidelberg (2010). https://doi.org/10.1007/978-3-642-15979-4_30
12. Bertoni, G., Daemen, J., Peeters, M., Assche, G.V.: Radiogatún, a belt-and-mill hash function. IACR Cryptology ePrint Archive, Paper 2006/369 (2006)
13. Picek, S., Mariot, L., Leporati, A., Jakobovic, D.: Evolving s-boxes based on cellular automata with genetic programming. In: Companion Material Proceedings of GECCO 2017, pp. 251–252. ACM (2017)
14. Mariot, L., Picek, S., Leporati, A., Jakobovic, D.: Cryptogr. Commun. Cellular automata based s-boxes **11**(1), 41–62 (2019)
15. Mariot, L., Leporati, A.: Inversion of mutually orthogonal cellular automata. In: Mauri, G., El Yacoubi, S., Dennunzio, A., Nishinari, K., Manzoni, L. (eds.) ACRI 2018. LNCS, vol. 11115, pp. 364–376. Springer, Cham (2018). https://doi.org/10.1007/978-3-319-99813-8_33
16. Vaudenay, S.: On the need for multipermutations: cryptanalysis of MD4 and SAFER. In: Preneel, B. (ed.) FSE 1994. LNCS, vol. 1008, pp. 286–297. Springer, Heidelberg (1995). https://doi.org/10.1007/3-540-60590-8_22

17. Mariot, L., Gadouleau, M., Formenti, E., Leporati, A.: Mutually orthogonal Latin squares based on cellular automata. Designs Codes Crypt. **88**(2), 391–411 (2019). https://doi.org/10.1007/s10623-019-00689-8
18. Mariot, L., Formenti, E., Leporati, A.: Enumerating orthogonal Latin squares generated by bipermutive cellular automata. In: Dennunzio, A., Formenti, E., Manzoni, L., Porreca, A.E. (eds.) AUTOMATA 2017. LNCS, vol. 10248, pp. 151–164. Springer, Cham (2017). https://doi.org/10.1007/978-3-319-58631-1_12
19. Carlet, C.: Boolean Functions for Cryptography and Coding Theory. Cambridge University Press (2021)
20. Mariot, L., Jakobovic, D., Bäck, T., Hernandez-Castro, J.: Artificial intelligence for the design of symmetric cryptographic primitives. In: Security and Artificial Intelligence, pp. 3–24 (2022)
21. Stinson, D.R.: Combinatorial Designs - Constructions and Analysis. Springer, Heidelberg (2004). https://doi.org/10.1007/b97564
22. Eloranta, K.: Partially permutive cellular automata. Nonlinearity **6**(6), 1009 (1993)
23. Mariot, L., Formenti, E., Leporati, A.: Constructing orthogonal Latin squares from linear cellular automata. CoRR abs/1610.00139 (2016)
24. Gadouleau, M., Mariot, L., Picek, S.: Bent functions from cellular automata. IACR Cryptology ePrint Archive, Paper 2020/1272 (2020)
25. Gadouleau, M., Mariot, L.: Latin hypercubes and cellular automata. In: Zenil, H. (ed.) AUTOMATA 2020. LNCS, vol. 12286, pp. 139–151. Springer, Cham (2020). https://doi.org/10.1007/978-3-030-61588-8_11
26. Mariot, L.: Hip to be (Latin) square: maximal period sequences from orthogonal cellular automata. In: Proceedings of CANDAR 2021, pp. 29–37. IEEE (2021)
27. Mariot, L.: Enumeration of maximal cycles generated by orthogonal cellular automata. CoRR abs/2203.02726 (2022)
28. Mariot, L., Picek, S., Jakobovic, D., Leporati, A.: Evolutionary algorithms for the design of orthogonal Latin squares based on cellular automata. In: Proceedings of GECCO 2017, pp. 306–313. ACM (2017)
29. Kasami, T., Lin, S., Peterson, W.W.: Polynomial codes. IEEE Trans. Inf. Theor. **14**(6), 807–814 (1968)
30. Gilbert, W.J., Nicholson, W.K.: Modern Algebra with Applications. Wiley (2004)
31. Mariot, L., Leporati, A.: A cryptographic and coding-theoretic perspective on the global rules of cellular automata. Nat. Comput. **17**(3), 487–498 (2018)

The Structure of Configurations in One-Dimensional Majority Cellular Automata: From Cell Stability to Configuration Periodicity

Yonatan Nakar$^{(\boxtimes)}$ and Dana Ron

Tel-Aviv University, Tel Aviv-Yafo, Israel
yonatannakar@mail.tau.ac.il, danaron@tau.ac.il

Abstract. We study the dynamics of (synchronous) one-dimensional cellular automata with cyclical boundary conditions that evolve according to the majority rule with radius r. We introduce a notion that we term *cell stability* with which we express the structure of the possible configurations that could emerge in this setting. Our main finding is that apart from the configurations of the form $(0^{r+1}0^* + 1^{r+1}1^*)^*$, which are always fixed-points, the other configurations that the automata could possibly converge to, which are known to be either fixed-points or 2-cycles, have a particular spatially periodic structure. Namely, each of these configurations is of the form s^* where s consists of $O(r^2)$ consecutive sequences of cells with the same state, each such sequence is of length at most r, and the total length of s is $O(r^2)$ as well. We show that an analogous result also holds for the minority rule.

1 Introduction

Dynamic processes that evolve according to the majority rule arise in various settings and as such have received wide attention in the past, primarily within the context of propagation of information or influence (e.g., [7,12,17]). Here we consider perhaps the most basic case, that of one-dimensional cellular automata, where our focus is on analyzing the structure of the configuration space. Specifically, we analyze the configuration space of one-dimensional cellular automata with cyclical boundary conditions that evolve according to the majority rule with radius r.

It is well-known [8,13] that these processes always converge to configurations that correspond to cycles either of length 1 (fixed-points) or of length 2 (period-2 cycles). In particular, it is easy to verify (see, e.g., [14]) that configurations in which each cell belongs to a consecutive sequence of at least $r+1$ cells with the same state[1] are fixed-points. Not much is currently understood, however, about the structure of the other fixed-point configurations or of configurations that correspond to cycles of length 2.

---

[1] In this work, a state is a value in $\{0,1\}$.

B. Chopard et al. (Eds.): ACRI 2022, LNCS 13402, pp. 63–72, 2022.
https://doi.org/10.1007/978-3-031-14926-9_6

The reason for this gap in understanding is largely due to the fact that most previous research has made assumptions about the mechanism producing the initial configuration. Namely, it is usually assumed that the state of each cell in the initial configuration is randomly chosen, independently from the other cells. See, for instance, the theoretical analysis in [14] and the experimental results in [15], both for one-dimensional majority cellular automata (and also the references within Sect. 5 for examples in other models). Under such assumptions, as shown in [14], these other configurations are indeed rarely encountered.

In this work, we tackle the problem of understanding the structure of the possible configurations without making assumptions about the mechanism behind the generation of the initial configuration. One of our main results (stated formally in Theorem 1) is that all period-2 configurations and all fixed-point configurations (other than those mentioned above) have a very special structure. Specifically, they have a "spatially" periodic structure with a period that is quadratic in the radius r. In the course of the proof of this result, we introduce several notions and prove several claims, which we believe are of interest in their own right as they shed light on the dynamics of the majority rule in cellular automata (and not only on the configurations they converge to).

1.1 Organization

In Sect. 2 we formally define the majority rule and other basic terms required for the formulation of our results. Then, in Sect. 3, we introduce the notion of cell stability and state Theorem 1, which is the main result of this paper. In Sect. 3.1, we illustrate Theorem 1 for the special cases of $r = 1, 2, 3$. In Sect. 4, we discuss some of the high-level ideas behind the proof of Theorem 1. Finally, in Sect. 5, we review related work.

2 Preliminaries

2.1 The Majority Rule with Radius r

In all that follows, when performing operations on cells $i \in \mathbb{Z}_n$, these operations are modulo n.

Definition 1 (cell interval). *For a pair of cells $i, j \in \mathbb{Z}_n$ we use $[i, j]$ to denote the sequence $i, i + 1, \ldots, j$ (so that it is possible that $j < i$), which we refer to as a cell interval.*

For an integer n, we refer to a function $\sigma : \mathbb{Z}_n \to \{0, 1\}$ as a *configuration* and view σ as a (cyclic) binary string of length n.

Definition 2 (neighborhood). *For a cell $i \in \mathbb{Z}_n$ and an integer r, the r-neighborhood of i, denoted $\Gamma_r(i)$, is the cell interval $[i - r, i + r]$. For a set of cells $I \subseteq \mathbb{Z}_n$, we let $\Gamma_r(I)$ denote the set of cells in the union of cell intervals $[i - r, i + r]$ taken over all $i \in I$.*

Given a state $\beta \in \{0, 1\}$, a configuration $\sigma : \mathbb{Z}_n \rightarrow \{0, 1\}$ and a cell interval $[i, j]$, we denote by $\#_\beta(\sigma[i, j])$ the number of cells $\ell \in [i, j]$ such that $\sigma(\ell) = \beta$.

Definition 3 (the majority rule). *Denote by MAJ_r majority rule with radius r. That is, for a configuration $\sigma : \mathbb{Z}_n \rightarrow \{0, 1\}$, $MAJ_r(\sigma)$ is the configuration σ' in which for each cell $i \in \mathbb{Z}_n$,*

$$\sigma'(i) = \begin{cases} 0 & \text{if } \#_0(\sigma[\Gamma_r(i)]) > \#_1(\sigma[\Gamma_r(i)]) \\ 1 & \text{otherwise} \end{cases}$$

For each $t \geq 0$, denote by $MAJ_r^t(\sigma)$ the result of repeatedly applying the majority rule with radius r, starting from the configuration σ. In particular, $MAJ_r^0(\sigma) = \sigma$ and $MAJ_r^1(\sigma) = MAJ_r(\sigma)$.

2.2   Temporal and Spatial Periodicity

Eventually, for every initial configuration, the majority rule, and, in fact, any rule, reaches a *cycle*: a periodic sequence of configurations. As mentioned earlier, in the case of the majority rule, that cycle is always either a *2-cycle* or a *fixed-point*.

Definition 4 (fixed-point). *We say that a configuration $\sigma : \mathbb{Z}_n \rightarrow \{0, 1\}$ is a fixed-point if $MAJ_r(\sigma) = \sigma$.*

Definition 5 (2-cycle). *We say that a pair of distinct configurations $\sigma, \sigma' : \mathbb{Z}_n \rightarrow \{0, 1\}$ is a 2 cycle if $MAJ_r(\sigma) = \sigma'$ and $MAJ_r(\sigma') = \sigma$.*

We refer to the *configurations* that constitute a cycle as temporally periodic configurations. That is,

Definition 6 (temporally periodic). *We say that a configuration $\sigma : \mathbb{Z}_n \rightarrow \{0, 1\}$ is temporally periodic if $MAJ_r^2(\sigma) = \sigma$.*

Note that if a configuration σ is temporally periodic, then it is either the case that $MAJ_r(\sigma) = \sigma$ (i.e., σ is a fixed-point), or $MAJ_r(\sigma) = \sigma'$ for $\sigma' \neq \sigma$, in which case σ and σ' constitute a 2 cycle.

Definition 7 (transient). *If a configuration $\sigma : \mathbb{Z}_n \rightarrow \{0, 1\}$ is not temporally periodic, we say that σ is transient.*

Definitions 4–7 are all related to the notion of *temporal* periodicity, i.e., periodicity that occurs over time. In this paper, we relate temporal periodicity to *spatial* periodicity, i.e., periodic behavior exhibited within individual configurations. Formally,

Definition 8 (spatial period). *We say that a configuration $\sigma : \mathbb{Z}_n \rightarrow \{0, 1\}$ has spatial period p if p is the minimum positive integer such that for every cell $i \in \mathbb{Z}_n$, $\sigma(i + p) = \sigma(i)$.*

Definition 9 (spatially periodic). *We say that a configuration $\sigma : \mathbb{Z}_n \rightarrow \{0, 1\}$ is spatially periodic if its spatial period p satisfies $p < n$.*

3 Our Main Result and the Notion of Cell Stability

In this section we state our main result, Theorem 1, whose proof can be found in the full version of the paper [10] and some the proof's high level ideas appear in Sect. 4. In order to state Theorem 1, we introduce the notion of a cell's stability within a configuration via Definitions 10–12 (illustrated in Fig. 1).

Definition 10 (unstable). *We say that a cell $i \in \mathbb{Z}_n$ is **unstable** with respect to a configuration $\sigma : \mathbb{Z}_n \to \{0,1\}$ if $\sigma(i) \neq \sigma''(i)$ where $\sigma'' = MAJ_r^2(\sigma)$.*

Recall that after a finite number of steps,[2] a one-dimensional cellular automaton that evolves according to the majority rule, reaches either a fixed-point or a 2 cycle. Thus, a configuration $\sigma : \mathbb{Z}_n \to \{0,1\}$ is transient if and only if it contains unstable cells.

As for the "stable" cells, we define two variants: strongly stable and weakly stable.

Definition 11 (strongly stable). *We say that a cell $i \in \mathbb{Z}_n$ is **strongly stable** with respect to a configuration $\sigma : \mathbb{Z}_n \to \{0,1\}$ if there exists a cell interval $[a,b]$ of length at least $r + 1$ such that $i \in [a,b]$ and for each $j \in [a,b]$, $\sigma(i) = \sigma(j)$.*

Definition 12 (weakly stable). *We say that a cell $i \in \mathbb{Z}_n$ is **weakly stable** with respect to a configuration $\sigma : \mathbb{Z}_n \to \{0,1\}$ if i is not strongly stable with respect to σ, but $\sigma(i) = \sigma''(i)$ where $\sigma'' = MAJ_r^2(\sigma)$.*

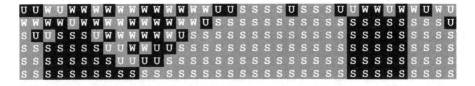

Fig. 1. The evolution under the majority rule with $r = 2$. Gray squares correspond to state-0 cells and dark squares correspond to state-1 cells. Each cell is labeled by a letter indicating the cell's *stability*, where S stands for *Strongly* stable, W for *Weakly* stable and U for *Unstable*.

The crucial property of the strongly stable cells is that their states, unlike the states of the weakly stable cells, cannot change in later configurations. In that sense, their stability is "stronger" than that of the weakly stable cells. It is worth noting, though, that if a cell lies within a long cell interval of weakly stable cells, then that cell remains weakly stable, alternating between the same pair of states, for a number of steps that depends on the cell interval length.

---

[2] Which can be shown to be at most linear in n [10].

Accordingly, given a configuration $\sigma : \mathbb{Z}_n \to \{0,1\}$, we say that a cell interval $[i,j]$ is strongly stable, weakly stable or unstable if all the cells in that cell interval are, respectively, strongly stable, weakly stable or unstable.

Considering complete configurations, observe that all the configurations of the form $(0^{r+1}0^* + 1^{r+1}1^*)^*$ contain only strongly stable cells. As noted previously and explained in the characterization provided in [14], these configurations are always fixed-points, which means that they are, in particular, also temporally periodic (with a period of 1). However, there are more forms of temporally periodic configurations, both period-1 and period-2, that contain only weakly stable cells and are not addressed by [14]'s characterization, as the authors of [14] were only interested in "typical" configurations, which are not of that kind.[3]

Theorem 1 complements [14]'s characterization by additionally specifying the structure of the remaining temporally periodic configurations. In addition to temporally periodic configurations, Theorem 1 also includes a property of the transient configurations that is related to the dynamics by which they eventually converge.

Theorem 1. *For any configuration $\sigma : \mathbb{Z}_n \to \{0,1\}$, exactly one of the following must hold:*

1. *The configuration σ is a temporally periodic configuration and it is either the case that:*
   (a) all the cells in σ are strongly stable, in which case σ is of the form $(0^{r+1}0^* + 1^{r+1}1^*)^*$), or
   (b) all the cells in σ are weakly stable, in which case σ is spatially periodic with spatial period at most $2r(r+1)$.
2. *The configuration σ is a transient configuration and the length of every unstable cell interval in σ is at most $2r$.*

In the full version [10] we show that an analog of Theorem 1 holds for the minority rule as well, with analogous variants of cell stability.

Under the assumption that r is a constant, Theorem 1 directly yields an output-sensitive algorithm that, given n, generates all the temporally periodic configurations of length n. The running-time of the algorithm is linear in the number of temporally periodic configurations.

Turning to transient configurations, recall that all transient configurations contain unstable cells, and the evolution of the transient configurations can be described using the notion of cell stability. Namely, the following can be shown regarding any transient configuration $\sigma : \mathbb{Z}_n \to \{0,1\}$ (see proofs in the full version [10]). First, the configuration $\mathrm{MAJ}_r(\sigma)$ contains strictly fewer unstable cells

---

[3] Indeed, it is shown in [14] that the probability that a randomly selected configuration of length n being transient approaches 1 as $n \longrightarrow \infty$. As such, the additional temporally periodic configurations that we address in this work are, in a sense, not "typical". We, in contrast to [14], make no assumption about the distribution of the configuration space, and are therefore interested in understanding the structure of *all* configurations, not only the "typical" ones.

than σ. Second, if σ contains strongly stable cells, then $\mathrm{MAJ}_r(\sigma)$ contains even more strongly stable cells than σ, and the automaton eventually converges to a fixed-point of the form defined in Case (1a). Third, if there are no strongly stable cells in σ, then there are cases in which the automaton eventually converges to a fixed-point of the form defined in Case (1a)[4] and there are also cases in which it eventually converges to a fixed-point or to a 2 cycle of the form defined in Case (1b)[5].

3.1   Illustrating Theorem 1 for $r = 1, 2, 3$

To get a feel for the nature of the statement in Theorem 1, we demonstrate some of its aspects for $r = 1, 2, 3$.

1. For $r = 1$, the temporally periodic configurations are either
   (a) of the form $(000^* + 111^*)^*$, or
   (b) of the form $(01)^*$.[6]
2. For $r = 2$, the temporally periodic configurations are either
   (a) of the form $(0000^* + 1111^*)^*$, or
   (b) of one of the following forms: $(01)^*$, $(0011)^*$, $(001101)^*$, $(001011)^*$.
3. For $r = 3$, the temporally periodic configurations are either
   (a) of the form $(00000^* + 11111^*)^*$, or
   (b) of the form s^*, where s belongs to the set:[7]

$$\left\{\begin{array}{l} 01, \\ 0011, \\ 010011, 010110, 001110, \\ 01011001, 10100101, 10100110, 01011100, 10010011, 00011101, 10110001, \\ 0011001110, 1000111001 \end{array}\right\}$$

An interesting observation about the patterns in Case (1b) in our demonstration is that the number of zeros in each of them equals the number of ones. This, in fact, holds in general, as we prove in the full version [10].

---

[4] e.g., for $r = 3$, the transient configuration 001001001001001001 converges after one step to the fixed-point configuration $(0)^*$.

[5] e.g., for $r = 4$, the transient configuration 00101100101100101100101100101100101011 converges after one step to the 2 cycle consisting of $(111000)^6$ and $(000111)^6$.

[6] Also $(10)^*$, but since the configurations are cyclic, the patterns $(01)^*$ and $(10)^*$ correspond to equivalent sets of configurations.

[7] The string s could also be the *mirror* or the *complement* of any of the specified patterns, which we omit for the sake of conciseness. For example, since we explicitly specified that s could be 010011, it means that s could also be 110010 (which is the mirror of 010011) or 101100 (which is the complement of 010011), even though these two are not explicitly specified.

4   The Alignment Mapping (High-Level Idea)

In proving Theorem 1, we define a number of notions and establish several claims, some of which we believe are valuable in and of themselves. We decided to focus in this section on a high-level description of only a few of the ideas underlying the proof of Theorem 1. The complete proof as well as the precise definitions of the notions we introduce in order to establish the proof can be found in the full version [10]. We have chosen to highlight the high-level idea behind one of the key tools we utilize, which is a *mapping* we introduce between *blocks* of consecutive configurations.

Given a configuration $\sigma : \mathbb{Z}_n \to \{0,1\}$, we say that a cell interval $[i,j]$ is a *maximal homogeneous block* in σ with value $\beta \in \{0,1\}$ if for every cell $\ell \in [i,j]$, $\sigma(\ell) = \beta$, and also $\sigma(i-1) = \sigma(j+1) \neq \beta$ if the length of $[i,j]$ is less than n.

We refer to this mapping, defined below (and illustrated in Fig. 2), as the alignment mapping. The alignment mapping, beyond being essential for the proof of Theorem 1, has several features that make it useful for reasoning about the dynamics of the majority rule, which is why we present its definition here.

Definition 13 (alignment mapping). *Let σ and σ' be a pair of configurations satisfying $MAJ_r(\sigma) = \sigma'$. Given a block $[i',j']$ in σ', let I be the block in σ that contains the cell $i + r$ and let J be the block in σ that contains the cell $j - r$. The* alignment mapping *maps the block $[i',j']$ (in σ') to the* middle[8] *block $[i,j]$ between I and J in σ.*

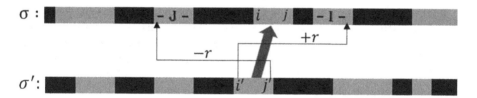

Fig. 2. *The alignment mapping.* The figure depicts a pair of configurations, σ and σ', where $\sigma' = MAJ_r(\sigma)$, and also a pair of blocks, $[i,j]$ in σ and $[i',j']$ in σ', where $[i',j']$ is mapped to $[i,j]$ by the alignment mapping. The block I in σ is the one that contains the cell $i' + r$, and the block J in σ is the one that contains the cell $j' - r$. The block $[i,j]$ in σ is the one right in the middle of the interval of five blocks in σ whose left and right ends are I and J. Hence, by Definition 13, the alignment mapping maps $[i',j']$ to $[i,j]$.

We stress that the alignment mapping, as defined in Definition 13, is a *backward* mapping, in the sense that, given a configuration σ', it maps all blocks in σ' into those of the configuration σ that *precedes* σ'. This naturally suggests

---

[8] The middle block is well defined, as it is shown in the full version [10] that the number of blocks between I and J must be odd.

defining the notion of *the forward alignment mapping* as the *inverse* function of the backward alignment mapping that would map the blocks of the configuration σ to those of the configuration σ' that *follows* σ (for example, in Fig. 2, the forward alignment mapping maps $[i, j]$ in σ to $[i', j']$ in σ').

However, while it can be shown that the backward alignment mapping is always one-to-one, it is not necessarily *onto* (unless we apply it within a pair of temporally periodic configurations). Hence, under our definition of the forward alignment mapping, not all blocks will be mapped forward.

Formally, let $\sigma_0, ...\sigma_m$ be a sequence of configurations where $\mathrm{MAJ}_r(\sigma_{t-1}) = \sigma_t$ for each $1 \leq t \leq m$. We define the step-t *forward alignment mapping*, denoted φ_t, as follows. Given a block $[i, j]$ in σ_t, if there is a block $[i', j']$ in σ_{t+1} such that the backward alignment mapping between the configuration pair σ_t, σ_{t+1} maps $[i', j']$ into $[i, j]$, then $\varphi_t([i, j]) = [i', j']$. Otherwise, $\varphi_t([i, j]) = \perp$. In the case in which $\varphi_t([i, j]) \neq \perp$, we also define $\varphi_t^2([i, j])$ as $\varphi_{t+1}(\varphi_t([i, j]))$.

One notable property of the forward alignment mapping is what we refer to as "identity preservation in stable intervals". Roughly speaking, consider any block $[i, j]$ residing in a sufficiently long weakly stable or strongly stable cell interval of σ_t. Then $\varphi_t([i, j]) \neq \perp$, and hence $\varphi_t^2([i, j])$ is defined and is equal to the same block $[i, j]$ we started with. In particular, for a pair of configurations comprising a 2 cycle, applying the forward alignment mapping *twice* essentially maps each block to itself.

In the proof of Theorem 1, we essentially use the forward alignment mapping and its properties to show that for a configuration in which all blocks are of length at most r, if the configuration is temporally periodic, then it is also spatially periodic. We achieve this through three steps.

In the first step, we employ the alignment mapping to express the length of each of the configuration's blocks in terms of the lengths of other $O(r)$ blocks in the preceding configuration. Specifically, given a pair of temporally periodic configurations σ_t and σ_{t+1}, we obtain a relationship between the length of each block $[i, j]$ in σ_t and the lengths of $O(r)$ consecutive blocks, belonging to a block sequence centered at the block $\varphi_t([i, j])$, in the configuration σ_{t+1}.

In the second step, we look at the *difference* between the length of each block $[i, j]$ and the lengths of the blocks at the two ends of the sequence mentioned above, and define *aligned difference vectors*, whose entries are these differences. We use the properties of the forward alignment mapping to establish that the aligned difference vectors (defined formally in the full version [10]) are spatially periodic with a spatial period that is *linear* in r.

In the third and final step, by applying the relationship between aligned difference vectors iteratively, we use the spatial periodicity of the aligned difference vectors to establish that the configurations themselves are spatially periodic as well, and that each configuration's spatial period must be quadratic in r.

5   Related Work

The main focus of most of the research on majority/minority (and more generally, threshold) cellular automata so far has been on the convergence time (e.g., [3,4,11]) and on the dominance problem[9] (e.g., [1,2,9]).

As mentioned earlier, most of the work on the problem of understanding the structure of the configuration space is based on the assumption that the initial configuration is random. For the one-dimensional case, the case with which the current paper is concerned, this includes the paper of Tosic and Agha [14]. In their paper, they distinguish between synchronous/sequential and finite/infinite majority cellular automata with radius r, and our work can be viewed as extending their result for the finite and synchronous case.

They show that whereas 2 cycles cannot emerge under the sequential model, in the synchronous model (the one we focus on in this paper), 2 cycles exist even for $r = 1$. They also show that a randomly picked configuration is a transient configuration (and, in particular, not a 2 cycle) with probability approaching 1 (both for finite and infinite configurations), and it can additionally be shown that the probability that such a random transient configuration eventually converges to a 2 cycle approaches 0. Finally, they characterize the "common" forms of fixed-point configurations (those that in our paper are described in Case (1a) of Theorem 1).

Their theoretical result is supplemented by a later experimental work [15], showing that in practice, convergence to these "common" fixed-point configurations occurs relatively quickly. Namely, the simulations in [15] demonstrate that convergence tends to occur in less than five steps for $n = 1000$ and $1 \leq r \leq 5$.

Additional work beyond the one-dimensional case includes [6] for two-dimensional majority cellular automata, [5] for majority in random regular graphs, [18] for majority in Erdos–Rényi graphs as well as expander graphs.

One notable work that does not rely on the assumption that the initial configuration is random is Turau's work [16] on characterizing all the temporally periodic configurations for majority and minority processes on trees. The characterization presented in [16] also yields an output-sensitive algorithm for generating these configurations.

References

1. Balogh, J., Bollobás, B., Duminil-Copin, H., Morris, R.: The sharp threshold for bootstrap percolation in all dimensions. Trans. Am. Math. Soc. **364**(5), 2667–2701 (2012)
2. Flocchini, P., Královič, R., Ružička, P., Roncato, A., Santoro, N.: On time versus size for monotone dynamic monopolies in regular topologies. J. Discrete Algorithms **1**(2), 129–150 (2003)
3. Fogelman, F., Goles, E., Weisbuch, G.: Transient length in sequential iteration of threshold functions. Discret. Appl. Math. **6**(1), 95–98 (1983)

---

[9] In the dominance problem, one asks how many cells must initially be at a certain state so that eventually all cells have the same state.

4. Frischknecht, S., Keller, B., Wattenhofer, R.: Convergence in (social) influence networks. In: Afek, Y. (ed.) DISC 2013. LNCS, vol. 8205, pp. 433–446. Springer, Heidelberg (2013). https://doi.org/10.1007/978-3-642-41527-2_30
5. Gärtner, B., Zehmakan, A.N.: Majority model on random regular graphs. In: Bender, M.A., Farach-Colton, M., Mosteiro, M.A. (eds.) LATIN 2018. LNCS, vol. 10807, pp. 572–583. Springer, Cham (2018). https://doi.org/10.1007/978-3-319-77404-6_42
6. Gärtner, B., Zehmakan, A.N.: Majority rule cellular automata. Theoret. Comput. Sci. **889**, 41–59 (2021)
7. Goles, E., Martinez, S.: Neural and Automata Networks: Dynamical Behavior and Applications, vol. 58. Springer, Cham (2013). https://doi.org/10.1007/978-94-009-0529-0
8. Goles, E., Olivos, J.: Comportement périodique des fonctions à seuil binaires et applications. Discret. Appl. Math. **3**(2), 93–105 (1981)
9. Mitsche, D., Pérez-Giménez, X., Prałat, P.: Strong-majority bootstrap percolation on regular graphs with low dissemination threshold. Stoch. Process. Their Appl. **127**(9), 3110–3134 (2017)
10. Nakar, Y., Ron, D.: The structure of configurations in one-dimensional majority cellular automata: from cell stability to configuration periodicity. arXiv preprint arXiv:2205.08972 (2022)
11. Papp, P.A., Wattenhofer, R.: Stabilization time in minority processes. arXiv preprint arXiv:1907.02131 (2019)
12. Peleg, D.: Local majorities, coalitions and monopolies in graphs: a review. Theor. Comput. Sci. **282**(2), 231–257 (2002)
13. Poljak, S., Sura, M.: On periodical behaviour in societies with symmetric influences. Combinatorica **3**(1), 119–121 (1983)
14. Tosic, P.T., Agha, G.A.: Characterizing configuration spaces of simple threshold cellular automata. In: Sloot, P.M.A., Chopard, B., Hoekstra, A.G. (eds.) ACRI 2004. LNCS, vol. 3305, pp. 861–870. Springer, Heidelberg (2004). https://doi.org/10.1007/978-3-540-30479-1_89
15. Tošic, P.T., Raju, S.N.: On convergence properties of one-dimensional cellular automata with majority cell update rule. In: Proceedings of International Conference on Scientific Computing, pp. 308–314 (2011)
16. Turau, V.: Fixed points and 2-cycles of synchronous dynamic coloring processes on trees. arXiv preprint arXiv:2202.01580 (2022)
17. Zehmakan, A.N.: On the spread of information through graphs. Ph.D. thesis, ETH Zurich (2019)
18. Zehmakan, A.N.: Opinion forming in Erdős-Rényi random graph and expanders. Discret. Appl. Math. **277**, 280–290 (2020)

Synchronisation of Elementary Cellular Automata with a Small Initial Error. Application to Rule 18

Théo Plénet[1]([✉]), Samira El Yacoubi[1], Clément Raïevsky[2], Laurent Lefèvre[2], and Franco Bagnoli[3]

[1] Images UMR Espace-Dev, University of Perpignan via Domitia, Perpignan, France
{theo.plenet,yacoubi}@univ-perp.fr
[2] Univ. Grenoble Alpes, Grenoble INP, LCIS, 26000 Valence, France
{clement.raievsky,laurent.lefevre}@lcis.grenoble-inp.fr
[3] Physics and Astronomy and CSDC, University of Florence, Florence, Italy
franco.bagnoli@unifi.it

Abstract. In this paper, we study how synchronization and state estimation are related in the context of elementary cellular automata. We first characterize the synchronization error between two 1D elementary cellular automata implementing Wolfram's 18th rule. Then we propose a simple approach to statistically model the transient phase of the synchronization error spread. We finally present a way to utilize this model of the error spread to place mobile sensors in order to reduce the overall synchronization error when the initial error is small.

Keywords: Cellular automata · Synchronization · Mobile sensors

1 Introduction

In control theory, monitoring physical systems which are distributed in space is based on the construction of an estimate from measurements and the dynamics of the system. Measurements which come from potentially mobile sensors. The problem of positioning these sensors is crucial to make it possible to estimate the state of the system. This state estimation problem is widely studied by classical control theory [5,7] and it follows from the verification of observability, a notion that ensures that the sensors are well placed. This notion of observability can be applied to cellular automata (CA) [3,4,6] (and by extension to Boolean networks [10] which can be seen as a generalization of CA) but its evaluation has proven to be extremely complicated when it comes to non-linear CA [6].

The synchronization problem consists in converging a system called replica to another one called driver by means of a unidirectional coupling between the two. In the case of CA, the state of some cells of the driver are copied to these same cells of the replica. The coupling between the two can be realized with a single cell [2], with fixed cells [8] or with cells chosen randomly at each time step [1]. In the first case, Dogaru et al. showed that a strong condition regarding

© The Author(s), under exclusive license to Springer Nature Switzerland AG 2022
B. Chopard et al. (Eds.): ACRI 2022, LNCS 13402, pp. 73–82, 2022.
https://doi.org/10.1007/978-3-031-14926-9_7

the chaoticity of the system is needed to synchronize the driver and the replica. In the second case, Urías et al. propose a necessary and sufficient condition concerning the cell position to ensure the synchronization of linear elementary cellular automata. Finally, Bagnoli and Rechtman propose a statistical approach to synchronization with a critical probability p_c that ensures synchronization.

The problem of synchronization of two CA can also be seen as a state estimation problem. Indeed, the driver can be seen as the system to be observed, the replica as the state estimator and the synchronized cells as sensors. For the purpose of monitoring physical systems, the conditions on the system imposed by Dogaru et al. (choaticity) and by Urías et al. (linearity) make it difficult to apply to this type of system. The approach of Bagnoli and Rechtman, on the contrary, is not based on a specific type of system. Moreover, it allows to include the notion of mobile sensor through the random choice of synchronized cells.

The main objective of this paper is to study a synchronized CA as a state estimator for the observation of distributed parameter system with spatio-temporal dynamics. We focus on synchronization with a small initial error because in some physical system monitoring, only a small portion of the system is unknown. For example, when monitoring forest fires spread, the topology of the forest is known but only the ignition points are unknown. Throughout this article, we focus on a single elementary rule that exhibits spatio-temporal dynamics so that the obtained results may be transferred to other CA and in particular to physical systems. Therefore, we chose to study the elementary rule 18 because it is the smallest chaotic, symmetric, and nonlinear rule [9].

The article starts by studying the differences in synchronization performance as a function of the initial synchronization error. Then, we model the spreading of the initial error within the CA using basic geometry. We finish by presenting an improvement of the synchronization algorithm for systems with a small initial error.

2   Influence of Initial Error on Synchronization

In order to study the impact of the initial error on the synchronization performance, we need to define the synchronization method but also to express it in terms of the initial error. For this purpose, we chose the definition proposed by Bagnoli and Rechtman [1] which expresses the synchronization of two 1D CA of N cells: x and y. The synchronisation of y with x is done by copying some of x cells' state in the matching cells in y, at each time step. A diagonal matrix P indicates which cells are coupled. A value of 1 in this matrix indicates that the corresponding cells are coupled. The position of the coupled cells are determined randomly at each time step with a probability p, called control strength. The expression for synchronization is:

$$\begin{cases} x_{t+1} = f(x_t) \\ y_{t+1} = (I - P) \cdot f(y_t) + P \cdot f(x_t) \\ e_{t+1} = x_{t+1} \oplus y_{t+1} \\ \epsilon_{t+1} = \frac{1}{N} \cdot \sum_i e_{t+1}^{(i)} \end{cases} \tag{1}$$

The synchronization error e_t is the difference between x_t and y_t, and ϵ_t its normalized mean error value. Since we are studying the influence of the initial error, we initialize x_0 and e_0 randomly and set $y_0 = x_0 \cdot e_0$. We will note e the proportion of cells in y_0 that are different from cells in x_0, in percentage.

In [1], Bagnoli and Rechtman discuss the notion of critical control strength p_c (determined statistically or analytically using maximum Liapunov exponents) which guarantees that the synchronization is total during a random synchronization. This critical parameter insures, for a state estimator, that the estimated state correctly corresponds to the state of the observed system. In Sect. 4, we present an improvement of this synchronization algorithm in order to reduce this critical power control for a total synchronization.

To get relevant results, we conducted a large number of simulations for each initial conditions. This is required by the fact that some initial conditions lead very quickly to a convergence that biases the results. More on this later.

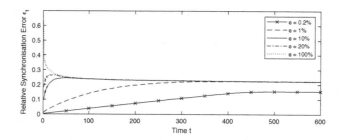

Fig. 1. Mean synchronization error as a function of time for different initial error ϵ_0.

Figure 1 presents mean synchronization error ϵ_t as a function of time for different initial error ϵ_0 values. These results were obtained by taking the mean of the synchronization error ϵ_t over 500 simulations for the elementary rule 18 with 500 cells and a control strength $p = 0.1$. The initial configuration x_0 was randomly initialized at each simulation, same for the initial unsynchronized cells, ϵ_0. Initial error has a clear impact on the performances of synchronization. Its first influence is on the speed of convergence towards the asymptote. Indeed, the 10% curve seems to converge faster than the 20% and 100% curves which converges earlier than the 1% and 0.2% curves. The second effect of the initial error is on the value of the asymptote when the error is small enough. For sufficiently large errors, all simulations converge towards the same asymptote value, around 0.23. But if ϵ_0 is sufficiently small, the reached asymptote is lower than this "generic" one.

To understand the difference in value between the two asymptotes, we studied the evolution of the error as a function of time for the particular case of a single cell of initial error ($e = 0.2\%$). As we can see on Fig. 2, there are two very different kind of evolution of the synchronization error e_t. On one hand, in Fig. 2a, the error spreads until it covers the whole CA and reaches the asymptotic non-zero value. On the other hand, in the very specific case depicted on

Fig. 2b, the synchronization quickly becomes total and the error reaches zero. Therefore, when we average these two cases, which we did for Fig. 1, we obtain a lower asymptotic value than the generic case will give. For the remaining of the study, we chose to dissociate the two cases and to not consider the fast total synchronization cases when we study the asymptotic value.

(a) Asymptotic Synchronization   (b) Total Synchronization

Fig. 2. Evolution of the synchronization error for elementary rule 18 with 500 cells from a single cell error ($e = 0.2\%$). The time is represented on the vertical axis. A black pixel is an erroneous cell in the synchronized CA.

To characterize the influence of the initial error ϵ_0 on the ability of the synchronized CA to be considered as a state estimate, we will only consider the mean of the asymptotic value of the synchronization error. Figure 3 represents this mean asymptotic synchronization error as a function of the initial error. First, if we consider only the asymptotic synchronization (without special cases of early complete synchronization), the value of the asymptote does not depend on the initial error. Second, the value from which the average error with and without total synchronization become different depends on the strength of the control p: the stronger it is, the more the chances of total synchronization increase.

3   Modeling of the Error Spreading Dynamics

In order to explain the dynamics of the evolution of the synchronization error, we will study how the error propagates within the CA as a function of the control strength. To do so, we will start by studying the propagation of the error with the simple case of a single erroneous cell, and then generalize these results.

Typical error propagation dynamics from one erroneous cell are depicted in Fig. 4. We adopted a triangle as a simple geometric model for these dynamics. It appears that the top angle of the triangle is inversely proportional to the control strength p.

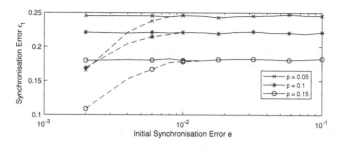

Fig. 3. The asymptotic value of the mean synchronization error as a function of initial error ϵ_0. This was obtained by taking the mean of the synchronization error ϵ_t as a function of time over 200 iterations. The continuous lines consider only the asymptotic synchronization while the dashed lines include both asymptotic and total synchronisation.

(a) $p = 0.0$ (b) $p = 0.05$ (c) $p = 0.10$ (d) $p = 0.15$

Fig. 4. Evolution of the error for elementary rule 18 with 500 cells from a single erroneous cell ($e = 0.2\%$). The time is represented on the vertical axis.

To describe how the synchronization error spreads, two parameters will be used: the first being the aperture angle of the propagation triangle, and the second being the shift angle between the altitude and the median of the triangle. Indeed, the median of the triangle seems to vary from one simulation to another. Figure 5 describes the geometry associated with these angles α and β which describe respectively the aperture angle and the shift angle.

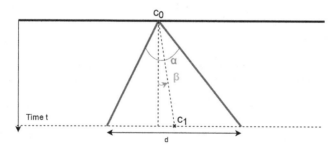

Fig. 5. Schematic of the theoretical spread of the synchronization error from a single initial error cell.

For the purpose of this article, we will not use directly the α and β angles but their tangents, which represents spread velocities. We will simply call α and β the velocities associated to the angles and not the angles themselves. Therefore, the **error spreading ratio** α represents the mean number of cells by which the triangle base increases at each time step and **error shift ratio** β the mean number of cell shift at each time step.

We can calculate the mean value of the error spreading ratio by measuring the area of the error at time T and divide by current time to obtain the tangent of α. Figure 6 describes the evolution of the average spread ratio as a function of the control strength. This one is a linear function of which we experimentally obtained the equation $\alpha = -8.23.p + 1.93$ using linear regression.

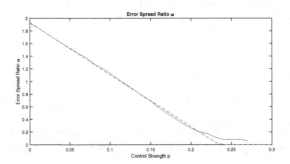

Fig. 6. The error propagation coefficient α as a function of control strength. The continuous curve is obtained by taking the mean of α over 1000 simulations. The dashed curve is the curve obtained by linear regression.

The error spreading ratio α has, for a given control strength, a normal distribution whose average is presented on Fig. 6. The standard deviation related to α can be calculated in order to have a better representation of α. The error shift ratio β also follows a normal distribution. Based on these two parameters, we can express the width and the center of the error at time T by $c_1 = c_0 + \beta \cdot T$ and $d = \alpha \cdot T$.

Corollary 1. *The synchronization error ϵ_t can be estimated from the parameter α as well as the value of the asymptote γ associated to the control strength p. Thus, the synchronization error ϵ_t is defined by:*

$$\epsilon_T = \frac{\gamma}{N} \cdot \max(\alpha \cdot T, N)$$

Indeed, $\alpha \cdot T$ gives the width of the error in number of cells. When dividing by N, we obtain the normalized error width and then multiplying by the asymptote γ, the value of ϵ_t when the error is present on the whole CA, we obtain the synchronization error ϵ_T.

Using the Corollary 1, we can make an example for $p = 0.1$. For this control strength, the error spreading ratio α follows a normal distribution with mean 1.127 and standard deviation 0.1376. On Fig. 7, the synchronization error ϵ_T is displayed as well as the estimated error with an α fixed at the mean and an α that follows the normal distribution. We quickly notice that the use of the normal distribution in the calculation of the error allows to explain the rounded curve when the error approaches the asymptote. However, the two theoretical curves have a difference with the real curve which is explained by a faster increase of the error during the first iterations which is caused by a higher α as the error is not yet detected, and therefore controlled, by the sensor.

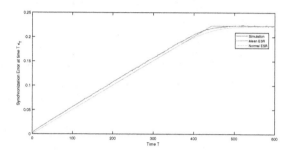

Fig. 7. Evolution of the average synchronization error as a function of time for the real case as well as the theoretical cases with the error spreading ratio which is constant and follows a normal distribution.

This method allows us to simply represent the propagation of the error in the case where a single cell is erroneous in the initial configuration. If we consider two or more erroneous cells then the modeling becomes more complex. Indeed, the two errors propagate independently until they *collide*, in this case we must consider that the errors merge in a single (larger) source of error. Thus, considering that the collision takes place at time t_1, we can consider that the error spreading ratio α is expressed as:

$$\alpha(t) = \begin{cases} \alpha_0 + \alpha_1 & , \text{ if } t \leq t_1 \\ \frac{(\alpha_0 - \beta_0 + \alpha_1 + \beta_1)}{2} & , \text{ if } t \geq t_1 \end{cases}$$

The time t_1 of the collision depends on the initial distance between the two initial errors, whose probability distribution depends on the boundary conditions used. Moreover, since each of these initial errors is subject to the total and fast synchronization (of probability τ), the model must include, with probability $2\tau(1 - \tau)$, a propagation with only one initial error using the model of Fig. 5. With more than two erroneous cells, the operation is the same but it is necessary to take into account several collisions at different times.

4   Optimization of Algorithm for a Single Erroneous Cell

If we consider that the synchronized cellular automaton has only a few errors at initialization, then it is possible to adapt the synchronization algorithm so as to concentrate the sensors only on the area that contains errors. To do this, we must first identify the areas that possibly contain errors and then distribute the sensors over those.

To identify the error area, a sensor must already detect an error. Then, with a method similar to the one shown in Fig. 5, it is possible to backpropagate the error measured at time t to obtain the possible error area $\hat{e}_0$ at time 0 which could lead to the initial error. Propagating an error from this initial estimate, we can obtain the possible current error area $\hat{e}_t$. Figure 8 represents the backpropagation of the error with a ratio α_{max} which corresponds to a ratio α large enough to include all (or a large part) of the possible spread ratios. The maximum ratio is 2 because it is not possible for the error to spread to more than one cell on each side (this results from the size of the neighbourhood) but if the strength of the control p is strong enough α_{max} can be chosen smaller. As α follows a normal distribution, a ratio $\alpha_{max} = \alpha_{mean} + 3\sigma$ encompasses 99.9% of the possible spreading ratios.

As new errors are detected, the initial error area can be refined using the intersection of all the initial error areas of all the errors detected by the sensors. In this way, it is possible to reduce the size of the error zone at time t but also to locate the position of the initial error.

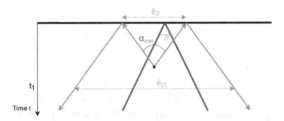

Fig. 8. Schematic of the backpropagation of the synchronization error to find the initial error area $\hat{e}_0$

Now that error area can be estimated, it remains to position the sensors. The method consists in placing the sensors only in the area where the error could be present. The number of sensors will remain the same but the control strength (the sensor density) of the error area will increase proportionally to the smallness of the error area resulting in a lower critical control strength p_c as shown in Fig. 9. The control strength in the error area is described by:

$$p_{error} = p \cdot \frac{N}{\hat{e}_t}$$

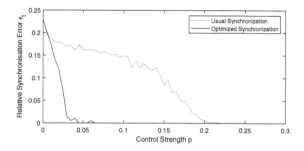

Fig. 9. Evolution of the average synchronization error as a function of control strength for a single cell error.

As shown in Fig. 9, the optimized synchronization performs better than the usual one with a critical control strength p_c at 0.05 instead of 0.21. However, when the control is too weak, the difference between the two is negligible because the first error cell is detected too late by the sensors and therefore the optimized control strength p_{error} is not sufficient to synchronize the two systems. In Fig. 10, we have compared these two synchronization methods on other elementary rules belonging to different classes [9]. The results obtained are minimal in that the error spreading ratio used for the backpropagation is $\alpha_{max} = 2$, smaller values according to the distribution of probability could have been chosen to further increase the performances. The optimized synchronization performs better but the difference between the two seems to depend on the class. Class 2 CA (presented by Wolfram as "filters") seem to exhibit lower error propagation coefficients α than class 3 and 4 CA. Without control, α is 0.048 for rule 37, 0.54 for rule 110 and 1.9 for rule 126. However, a systematic study on elementary CA would be necessary to confirm this conjecture.

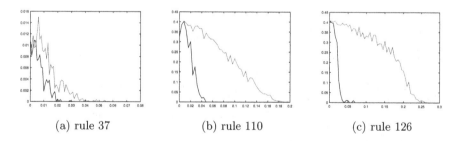

(a) rule 37   (b) rule 110   (c) rule 126

Fig. 10. Evolution of the average synchronization error as a function of control strength p for a single cell error for different rules. From left to right: rule 37 class 2; rule 110 class 4; and rule 126 class 3. Continuous line represents the optimized synchronization and dotted line the usual synchronization.

5   Conclusion and Perspectives

In this paper we studied how CA synchronization relates to state estimation of distributed parameter system in the context of Wolfram's 18th rule. In order to understand how a synchronized CA can be seen as an estimated state, we studied the dynamics of the synchronization error spreading. To do so we proposed a simple geometric model of this propagation. Finally, we present a sensors placement algorithm utilizing this geometric model in order to reduce the synchronization error and improve the accuracy of the synchronized CA as an estimate of the original CA representing the studied system. This optimized synchronization has been studied in the case of different elementary rules of classes 2, 3 and 4 whose performance increase in comparison to the usual synchronization is particularly important in the case of classes 3 and 4.

In the future, we will be able to adapt this algorithm to more than a single initial error cell. Furthermore, a systematic study on the elementary automata could be carried out in order to refine the algorithm of synchronization according to damage (error) spreading.

References

1. Bagnoli, F., Rechtman, R.: Synchronization and maximum Lyapunov exponents of cellular automata. Phys. Rev. E **59**(2), R1307 (1999)
2. Dogaru, R., Dogaru, I., Kim, H.: Binary chaos synchronization in elementary cellular automata. Int. J. Bifurc. Chaos **19**(09), 2871–2884 (2009)
3. Dridi, S., Bagnoli, F., Yacoubi, S.E.: Markov chains approach for regional controllability of deterministic cellular automata, via boundary actions. J. Cell. Autom. **14**(5/6), 479–498 (2019)
4. El Yacoubi, S., Plénet, T., Dridi, S., Bagnoli, F., Lefèvre, L., Raïevsky, C.: Some control and observation issues in cellular automata. Complex Syst. **30**(3), 391–413 (2021)
5. Kalman, R.E.: Mathematical description of linear dynamical systems. J. Soc. Ind. Appl. Math. Ser. A Control **1**(2), 152–192 (1963)
6. Plénet, T., El Yacoubi, S., Raïevsky, C., Lefèvre, L.: Observability and reconstructibility of bounded cellular automata. Int. J. Syst. Sci., 1–17 (2022). https://doi.org/10.1080/00207721.2022.2064556
7. Sarachik, P., Kreindler, E.: Controllability and observability of linear discrete-time systems. Int. J. Control **1**(5), 419–432 (1965)
8. Urias, J., Salazar, G., Ugalde, E.: Synchronization of cellular automaton pairs. Chaos Interdiscip. J. Nonlinear Sci. **8**(4), 814–818 (1998)
9. Wolfram, S.: Universality and complexity in cellular automata. Physica D **10**(1–2), 1–35 (1984)
10. Zhu, Q., Liu, Y., Lu, J., Cao, J.: Observability of Boolean control networks. Sci. China Inf. Sci. **61**(9), 1–12 (2018)

Millions of 5-State n^3-Real Time Sequence Generators via Local Simulations

Tien Thao Nguyen[1] and Luidnel Maignan[1,2(✉)]

[1] Univ Paris Est Creteil, LACL, 94000 Creteil, France
{tien.thao.nguyen,luidnel.maignan}@u-pec.fr
[2] Université Paris-Saclay, Inria, CNRS, ENS Paris-Saclay,
Laboratoire Méthodes Formelles, 91190 Gif-sur-Yvette, France

Abstract. In this paper, we come back on the notion of local simulation allowing to transform a cellular automaton into a closely related one with different local encoding of information. In a previous paper, we applied it to the Firing Squad Synchronization Problem. In this paper, we show that the approach is not tied to this problem by applying it to the class of Real-Time Sequence Generation problems. We improve in particular on the generation of n^3 sequence by using local mappings to obtain millions of 5-state solution, one of them using 58 transitions. It is based on the solution of Kamikawa and Umeo that uses 6 states and 74 transitions. Then, we explain in which sense even bigger classes of problems can be considered.

Keywords: Cellular automata · Automata minimization · Firing Squad Synchronization Problem · Real-Time Sequence Generation

1 Introduction

1.1 Local Mappings to Explore the Cellular Solution Space

This paper is about the formal concepts of *local mapping* and *local simulation* which found their firsts applications in the study of the so-called Firing Squad Synchronization Problem (FSSP) proposed by John Myhill in 1957. In the latter, the goal is to find a single cellular automaton (CA) such that any one-dimensional horizontal array of an arbitrary number of cells *synchronizes*, *i.e.* such that a special state is set for all the cells at the same time. As explained in [8], there was a race to obtain solutions with as few states as possible, leading in 1987 to a situation where it was established, for minimal-time time solutions, that there were no 4-state solutions, and only one solution had 6-state using a unique strategy. In 2018, a surprise came when 718 solutions were found using massive computing power, but a bigger surprise came in 2020 when many millions of solutions where discover using ordinary computer power. It is still not known whether there is a 5 state solution, but the concept used to generate the millions of solutions, local mappings and local simulation still have many things to tell, a story that is not tied to FSSP, but that may lead to some ideas about the famous 5-state FSSP open problem. More information can be found in [8,9].

B. Chopard et al. (Eds.): ACRI 2022, LNCS 13402, pp. 83–93, 2022.
https://doi.org/10.1007/978-3-031-14926-9_8

1.2   Real-Time Sequence Generation Problems

To show explicitly in which sense the approach can be applied to other problems, let us focus here on the so-called Real-Time Sequence Generation problems, or RTSG problems for short. In the latter, given a fixed sequence $S \subseteq \mathbb{N}$, the goal is to find a cellular automaton running on an one-dimensional horizontal array of cells such that the leftmost cell is in a special state exactly when the number of transition t from the beginning belongs to S. A formal description is given later. In the following, we write $f(n)$ to mean $S = \{f(n) \mid n \geq 1\}$.

The study of such problems began in 1965 for the sequence of prime numbers, with a description of a cellular automaton algorithm by Fischer [1]. In 1998, Korec [6] proposed a 9-state solution. Other sequences where considered in 2007 by Kamikawa and Umeo [7] who gave some different algorithms for the sequences 2^n, n^2, and 3^n using one-bit inter-cell-communication cellular automata. In 2012, Kamikawa and Umeo [3] described the sequence generation powers of CAs having a small number of states, focusing on the CAs with one (only one sequence n of all positive natural numbers), two, and three internal states, respectively. The authors enumerate all of the sequences generated by two-state CAs (linear sequences: $2n, 4n, 3n - 1, n, 3n - 2, 2n - 1, n + 1$; non-regular sequences: $2^{n+1} - 2, 2^n - 1$) and present several non-regular sequences like $2^n, n^2, 3^n$ that can be generated in real-time by three-state CAs, but not generated by any two-states CA. In 2016 [4], they gave a construction for the Fibonacci sequence using five-state, followed in 2019 [5] by two solutions of 8 states and 6 states for the sequence n^3. In these studies, much attention has been paid to the developments of *small-state* RTSG solutions for specific non-regular sequences. Other complexities are also studied such as the space, communication or state-change complexities.

Here we consider the sequence n^3 and provide millions of 5-state solutions using local mappings from the known 6-state solution. This reduction from 6 to 5 is reminiscent of the FSSP situation. The work presented here leaves open the question of the existence of solutions with 3 or 4 states for the n^3 sequence. Advances have been made since the writing of this paper as described in the conclusion. This doesn't impact the content of this paper, the goal here being simply to illustrate the generality of the local simulation approach.

1.3   Organization of the Content

In Sect. 2, we begin by defining formally cellular automata, local mappings, local simulations, RTSG solutions and related objects in a suitable way for this study. In Sect. 3, we explain how local mappings can be used firstly to obtain a first 5-state solution to the n^3-RTSG problem, and then to generate millions of other solutions. These other solutions are essentially the same, but differ in the way the local information is encoded, leading to different numbers of transitions for example. This is in direct comparison with compiler optimization where a program is optimized but stays essentially the same. We finish this section by making more precise the generality of the approach. We conclude in Sect. 4 with a discussion of some additional aspects of this investigation, in particular with the relation with some topological concepts.

2   Preliminaries

We summarize here the formal definitions of CA, local mappings solutions as defined in [8]. More detailed explanations can be found in [8,9]. We then define RTSG solutions in a formally relevant way for this framework. As for the other papers, the formal setting is presented for one dimensional CA with usual neighborhood $\{-1, 0, +1\}$, but is easily extended to any (non necessarily commutative) group and any (none necessarily fixed) neighborhood.

2.1   Cellular Automata, Local Mappings, and Local Simulations

The purpose of these following definitions is to describe CA with partial transition table first directly and then in terms of their deterministic family of space-time diagrams. With the latter representation, local mapping and local simulations are more easily understood. Non-deterministic families also play a role.

Definition 1. *A* cellular automaton *α consists of a finite set of states Σ_α, a set of* initial configurations *$I_\alpha \subseteq \Sigma_\alpha{}^{\mathbb{Z}}$ and a partial function $\delta_\alpha : \Sigma_\alpha{}^3 \rightharpoonup \Sigma_\alpha$ called the* local transition function *or* local transition table. *Elements of $\Sigma_\alpha{}^{\mathbb{Z}}$ are called* (global) configurations. *Those of $\Sigma_\alpha{}^3$ are called* local configurations. *For any $c \in I_\alpha$, its* space-time diagram *$D_\alpha(c) : \mathbb{N} \times \mathbb{Z} \rightarrow \Sigma_\alpha$ is defined as:*

$$
D_\alpha(c)(t, p) = \begin{cases} c(p) & \text{if } t = 0, \\ \delta_\alpha(c_{-1}, c_0, c_1) & \text{if } t > 0 \text{ with } c_i = D_\alpha(c)(t-1, p+i). \end{cases}
$$

The partial function δ_α is required to be such that all space-time diagrams are totally defined. When $D_\alpha(c)(t, p) = s$, we say that, for the cellular automaton α and initial configuration c, the cell at position p has state s at time t.

Definition 2. *A* family of space-time diagrams *D consists of a set of states Σ_D and a set $D \subseteq \Sigma_D{}^{\mathbb{N} \times \mathbb{Z}}$. The* local transition relation *$\delta_D \subseteq \Sigma_D{}^3 \times \Sigma_D$ of D is:*

$$
((c^0_{-1}, c^0_0, c^0_1), c^1_0) \in \delta_D : \iff \exists (d, t, p) \in D \times \mathbb{N} \times \mathbb{Z} \text{ s.t. } c^j_i = d(t + j, p + i).
$$

We call D a deterministic family *if its local transition relation is functional.*

Definition 3. *Given a deterministic family D, its* associated cellular automaton *Γ_D is defined with set of states $\Sigma_{\Gamma_D} = \Sigma_D$, set of initial configurations $I_{\Gamma_D} = \{d(0, -) \in \Sigma_\alpha{}^{\mathbb{Z}} \mid d \in D\}$, and local transition function $\delta_{\Gamma_D} = \delta_D$.*

Definition 4. *Given a cellular automaton α, its* associated family of space-time diagrams *(abusively denoted) D_α is defined as having the set of states $\Sigma_{D_\alpha} = \Sigma_\alpha$, and the set of space-time diagrams $\{D_\alpha(c) \mid c \in I_\alpha\}$ and is clearly deterministic.*

Definition 5. *A* local mapping *ℓ from a CA α to a finite set X consists of two functions $\ell_z : \{d(0, p) \mid (d, p) \in D_\alpha \times \mathbb{Z}\} \rightarrow X$ and $\ell_s : \text{dom}(\delta_\alpha) \rightarrow X$. We define its* associated family of diagrams *$\Phi_\ell = \{\ell(d) \mid d \in D_\alpha\}$ where:*

$$
\ell(d)(t, p) = \begin{cases} \ell_z(d(0, p)) & \text{if } t = 0, \\ \ell_s(d(t-1, p-1), d(t-1, p), d(t-1, p+1)) & \text{if } t > 0. \end{cases}
$$

If Φ_ℓ is deterministic, we say that ℓ is a local simulation *from CA α to CA Γ_{Φ_ℓ}.*

Q (Left State \ Right State)	Q	A	B	C	D	E
Q	Q	Q	B	C	D	D
A						
B	C					
C	Q					
D	Q					
E	Q					
★	Q	Q	B	E	E	E

A (Left State \ Right State)	Q	A	B	C	D	E
Q			Q	Q	Q	Q
A						
B						
C						
D						
E						
★			Q	Q		

B (Left State \ Right State)	Q	A	B	C	D	E
Q	B		B			
A			C	C		
B			B	B		
C			B	B		
D						
E						
★	A		A			

C (Left State \ Right State)	Q	A	B	C	D	E
Q			C	C	C	C
A	E		A	A	A	A
B	C					
C	C		C	C	C	C
D						
E			A	A	A	A
★						

D (Left State \ Right State)	Q	A	B	C	D	E
Q	D				D	D
A	B				C	C
B						
C	D				D	D
D	D				D	D
E	B				C	C
★						

E (Left State \ Right State)	Q	A	B	C	D	E
Q	E					
A	D					
B						
C	E					
D	E					
E	D					
★				Q	Q	Q

Fig. 1. Transition table of Kamikawa and Umeo's 6-state solution using 74 transitions.

2.2 Real-Time Sequence Generators

Definition 6. *A CA α is* RTSG-candidate *if there are $\star_\alpha, \mathtt{B}_\alpha, \mathtt{Q}_\alpha, \mathtt{S}_\alpha \in \Sigma_\alpha$ such that $\mathrm{I}_\alpha = \{\overrightarrow{\infty}_\alpha\}$ with $\overrightarrow{\infty}_\alpha$ the* RTSG right-infinite initial configuration, *i.e. $\overrightarrow{\infty}_\alpha(p) = \star_\alpha$, $\mathtt{B}_\alpha$ and $\mathtt{Q}_\alpha$ if, respectively, $p \leq 0$, $p = 1$ and $p \geq 2$. Moreover, $\star_\alpha$ must be the* outside state, i.e. $\forall (c_{-1}, c_0, c_1) \in \mathrm{dom}(\delta_\alpha), [\delta(c_{-1}, c_0, c_1) = \star_\alpha \Leftrightarrow c_0 = \star_\alpha]$*, and $\mathtt{Q}_\alpha$ must be* quiescent *so $\delta_\alpha(\mathtt{Q}_\alpha, \mathtt{Q}_\alpha, \mathtt{Q}_\alpha) = \delta_\alpha(\star_\alpha, \mathtt{Q}_\alpha, \mathtt{Q}_\alpha) = \mathtt{Q}_\alpha$.*

State $\star_\alpha$ is not counted as a state since it represents cells considered as non-existing. So an RTSP-candidate cellular automaton α will be said to have s states when $|\Sigma_\alpha \setminus \{\star_\alpha\}| = s$, and m transitions when $|\mathrm{dom}(\delta_\alpha) \setminus \Sigma_\alpha \times \{\star_\alpha\} \times \Sigma_\alpha| = m$.

Definition 7. *Given $S \subseteq \mathbb{N}$, a RTSG-candidate cellular automaton α is a S-*RTSG solution *if for any time t, $\mathrm{D}_\alpha(\overrightarrow{\infty}_\alpha)(t, 0) = \mathtt{S}_\alpha$ if and only if $t \in S$.*

Proposition 1. *There is a n^3-RTSG solution using 6 states and 74 transitions.*

Proof. Figure 1 shows Kamikawa and Umeo's solution, reproduced with the same format as their paper to ease comparison, that should be completed with obvious entries for the outside state $\star$. The proof of correction can be found in [5].

The corresponding diagram is shown on the left half of Fig. 2, where cell 0 has state A at time 1, 8, 27, and 64 as expected. In [5], the table of D wrongly has column C identical to column E, as the proofs and diagrams of [5] makes clear.

3 Exploring RTSG Solutions via Local Mappings

Let us now describe how to apply the same techniques used for the FSSP in [8] in order to first obtain a first optimization from 6-state to 5-state, and then use the exploration algorithm to generate millions of other 5-state solutions. The first step is to study those local mappings which *complies* with RTSG problems.

3.1 Compliant Local Mappings

Given two CA α and β, a local mapping between them associates to each triplet found in a space-time diagram d at position p and time t of α to the state found in the associated diagram d' at position p and time $t+1$. When both of these CA are RTSG solutions, this implies the following properties on the local mapping.

Definition 8. *A local mapping ℓ from an RTSG solution α to the states Σ_β of an RTSG-candidate CA β is said to be* RTSG-compliant *if it is such that (0) ℓ_z maps $\star_\alpha$, B_α, and Q_α respectively to $\star_\beta$, B_β, and Q_β, (1) $\ell_s(c_{-1}, c_0, c_1) = \star_\beta$ if and only if $\delta_\alpha(c_{-1}, c_0, c_1) = \star_\alpha$ (meaning simply $c_0 = \star_\alpha$), (2) $\ell_s(\star_\alpha, c_0, c_1) = S_\beta$ if and only if $\delta_\alpha(\star_\alpha, c_0, c_1) = S_\alpha$, and (3) $\ell_s(Q_\alpha, Q_\alpha, Q_\alpha) = \ell_s(\star_\alpha, Q_\alpha, Q_\alpha) = Q_\beta$.*

Proposition 2. *Given S, an S-RTSG solution α, a RTSG-candidate β and a local simulation ℓ from α to β, β is an S-RTSG solution iff. ℓ is RTSG-compliant.*

Proof. To see this, consider the diagram $d \in D_\alpha$ of the solution α. The special RTSG states appear at specific places and ℓ ensures or witnesses, depending on the direction of the implication considered, that these special states/places are conserved in $\ell(d) \in D_\beta$, (Definition 5). Indeed, condition (0) is just about the initial configuration, condition (1) is about the conservation of the outside state, condition (2) is about the conservation of the special generation state for the leftmost cell only and condition (3) about the conservation of the quiescent state behaviour. These conditions are sufficient to ensure and β is a solution, and clearly necessary since they perfectly match Definitions 6 and 7 of the problem.

Note that once α fixed, β can be reconstructed from ℓ, and ℓ from β. So local mappings are another representation of their generated RTSG-candidates (see Definition 5), but it is much easier to check compliance of the former than correctness the latter as an RTSG solution. This is the key feature justifying this application.

3.2   A Hand-Crafted Local Simulation

The first local mapping that we consider is the *identity local mapping id*, given by the local transition function of the 6-state solution of Proposition 1. The latter simply transforms this solution into itself. The point here is that we can now work with local mappings. However, the reader should be careful to clearly distinguish modifications made local mappings and the resulting modifications on transition tables. It is easier to think in terms of space-time diagram, since each modification in local mappings corresponds directly to a uniform set of modifications in the target diagram, which may thus become non-deterministic.

Let us now describe how the second, hand-crafted, local mapping is obtained, as we come back on the process itself later. It is build by noticing different features of the original space-time diagram on the left of Fig. 2. Firstly, the state A is not often used, so we can try to remove it entirely. This means changing every entry (x, y, z) of id_s such that $id_s(x, y, z) = A$. Since A is the special generating state, we can not replace it by B, Q or E as they appear in the evolution of the leftmost cell. So we are left with C or D. However, looking at time 1, we see changing A into C would lead to a CCQ local configuration, which is already used. So we heuristically choose D instead, to have DCQ at time 1, an unused local configuration. To summarize, for the leftmost cell we choose to change A by D, and for the other cells, we can choose any state *a priori*.

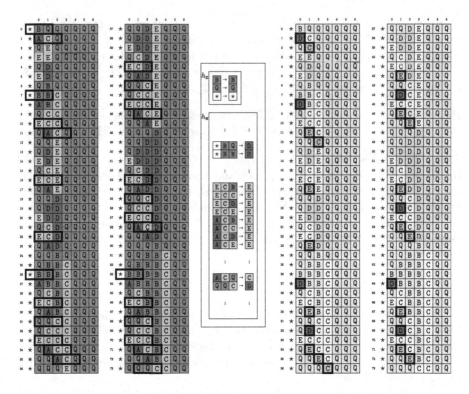

Fig. 2. 6-state diagram, hand-crafted local mapping and resulting 5-state diagram.

The second local mapping is thus obtained by taking every local configurations (x, y, z) of id_s such that $id_s(x, y, z) = A$, and setting them to D if $x = \star$, and to E otherwise. The result is not a deterministic space-time diagram, but this is easily corrected with two additional modifications for ACQ and QQC. The local mapping has the same entries as the transition table of Fig. 1 except for 12 entries as depicted in the center of Fig. 2 update. The space-time diagram on the right is obtained by applying the local mapping on the space-time on the left as indicated by the outlined local configuration on the left, and resulting state on the right, at the following timestep as dictated by Definition 5.

Proposition 3. *There is a n^3-RTSG solution using 5 states and 72 transitions.*

Proof. First note that the right space-time diagram is deterministic.[1] We can therefore extract the transition table given in Fig. 3 from it. All entries of this table actually appear in the part of the right space-time shown in Fig. 2. To prove this CA to be an n^3-RTSG solution, it is enough to check that the local

---

[1] The quickest way to convince oneself is to compute 10.000 transitions of the 6-state solution and notice that all quintuplets occur by timestep 237. So it is enough to check for non-determinism only up to timestep 237. See [9] for more information.

Q	Right State				
	Q	B	C	D	E
Q	Q	B	D	D	Q
B	C				
C	Q				
D	Q				
E	Q				
★	Q	B	E	E	Q

B	Right State				
	Q	B	C	D	E
Q	B	B			
B		B	B		
C		B	B		
D			C	C	
E			C	C	
★	D	D			

C	Right State				
	Q	B	C	D	E
Q	E	C	C	C	C
B	C				
C	C	C	C	C	C
D	C	C	C	C	C
E	C	E	E	E	E
★					

D	Right State				
	Q	B	C	D	E
Q	D		C	D	D
B					
C	D			D	D
D	D			D	D
E	B			C	C
★	Q	Q			

E	Right State				
	Q	B	C	D	E
Q		Q	Q	Q	Q
B					
C		E			
D		E			
E		D			
★			Q	Q	Q

Fig. 3. Transition table of the hand-crafted 5-state solution using 72 transitions.

mapping is RTSG-compliant. Note that the new solution has a different special accepting state (D instead of A) as allowed by Definition 8. Since the source CA is a solution, we can conclude using Proposition 2.

To ease the comparison of this 5-state solution with the original 6-state one, the transitions that are different, added or removed are highlighted in Fig. 3. All transition containing A should be considered as removed. Note that these differences do not correspond exactly to those described in the local mapping.

3.3 Optimizing Through Millions of Solutions

We are ready to generate millions of 5-state solutions. They are essentially the same, but can have fewer states or/and a different number of transitions. We briefly summarize of the algorithm (more details in [8]) then examine the results.

The Exploration Algorithm. The exploration algorithm is related to the hand-crafted process above. We start it with the identity local mapping of the hand-crafted 5-state solution. Then, only compliant modifications of the local mapping are considered. In fact, this is a graph exploration algorithm. The node of this graph are the compliant local mappings from the hand-crafted 5-state solution to a fixed set of 5 states (and an outside ★ state). The neighbors of a local mapping ℓ are all the local mapping obtained by exactly one compliant modification on ℓ. The identity local mapping is obviously a compliant local simulation, and the algorithm generates all its neighbors and add to the "remaining tasks" queue any neighbor that is also a compliant *simulation*. Continuing in this way with the content of the queue, the algorithm explores the complete connected component of compliant simulations. By Proposition 2, all these compliant local simulations are n^3-RTSG solutions. Let us describe two additional ingredients.

The first one is that there is an initialization step. To check that a local mapping ℓ is a local simulation, we need generate its local transition relation δ_{Φ_ℓ} to check if it is a function or not. This is easy to do for all the local mappings if we first collect all the *super-local transition* of the hand-crafted solution, *i.e.* all quintuplets of states with their resulting triplet of states appearing anywhere in the space-time diagram of the hand-crafted solution. From these data, and for any local mapping ℓ, it is enough to apply ℓ_s on all the super local transitions to generate the entries of associated local transition relation δ_{Φ_ℓ}.

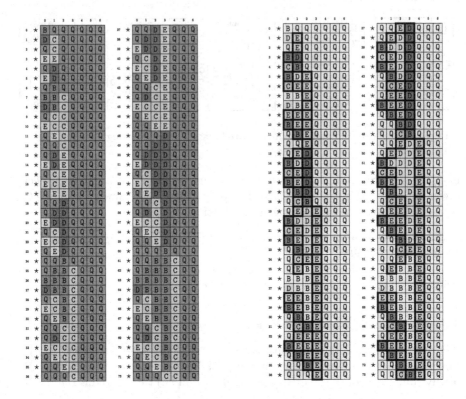

Fig. 4. Hand-crafted 5-state diagram and optimized 5-state/58-transition diagram.

The second ingredient is a parameter k allowing the discovery of more compliant simulation connected component. With $k = 0$, the algorithm is unchanged and a compliant local simulation is reached only if its modifications can be applied one at a time while leading to compliant local simulation all the way through. With $k \geq 1$, the algorithm randomly apply k additional modifications simultaneously on any given compliant local simulation. If fact, it is often the case that many modifications need to be applied simultaneously, for example the two last modifications described in the design of the hand-crafted solution (Fig. 4).

Generated Solutions and Optimizations. Running the algorithm on a 32 cores of 2.00 GHz machine having 126 Gb of memory, we obtain so many solutions that the algorithm stops because of memory overflow. The first time, we ran the algorithm with $k = 0$. The program actually uses 2 cores and about 43 Gb of memory. We did not optimize the program nor the configuration of the Java Virtual Machine of this Java implementation. The following data are not reproducible but gives a rough idea: after 1 days about 15 millions local simulations have been obtained, after 6 days about 85 millions, and after 20 days about 90 millions. The number of solutions found each day was steady for the 6 firsts days then dropped,

Q	Right State				
Left State	Q	B	C	D	E
Q	Q	Q	Q		E
B	E				
C					
D	Q				
E	Q				
★	Q	Q	Q		B

B	Right State				
Left State	Q	B	C	D	E
Q		C		C	Q
B		B			B
C	C	D	E		E
D		E			E
E		B			B
★	D	D		C	Q

C	Right State				
Left State	Q	B	C	D	E
Q		E			E
B	B				
C	C				
D	D				
E	E				
★		B			B

D	Right State				
Left State	Q	B	C	D	E
Q	Q				
B	B	B		E	E
C	C				
D	D	D		D	D
E	E	D		D	D
★		E			Q

E	Right State				
Left State	Q	B	C	D	E
Q		D	B		D	E
B	B	E	B		B	B
C	C				E	B
D	D	E			
E	E	E	E		E	E
★					B

Fig. 5. Transition table of the generated 5-state solution using 58 transitions.

presumably because of memory issues. Running concurrently the program with $k = 2$, it uses 2 cores and 36 Gb of memory before memory overflow: after 1 days about 15 millions found local simulations, after 6 days about 70 millions local simulations, after 20 days, about 74 millions. In fact, all solutions was kept in memory to keep track of the total number of generated solutions. Better strategies can be found if the goal is only to optimize the solution.

Proposition 4. *There are at least 90,000,000 n^3-RTSG solutions using 5 states.*

Among these millions of solutions, no 4-state solutions are found, but 32379 of them have fewer transitions. The following table indicate for each number of transitions (first line) the corresponding number of solutions (second line).

58	59	60	61	62	63	64	65	66	67	68	69	70	71
1	7	22	51	98	174	336	589	1044	1618	2696	4643	7671	13429

Proposition 5. *There is a n^3-RTSG solution using 5 states and 58 transitions.*

Proof. The transition table of the generated solution is shown in Fig. 5. The local mapping having 45 entries different from the identity local mapping, it is not practical to display it, but it can be reconstructed from both CA. It is then a matter of checking that it is compliant and apply Proposition 2 to conclude as before.

3.4 Beyond RTSG and FSSP Optimizations

It should be clear by now that the approach can be applied to a large class of problems. For example, the same algorithm used here for the n^3-RTSG problem is not particular to the n^3 sequence and can be used for any sequence S, as indicated in the definitions and propositions above. Also, the slightly differently parameterized algorithm for the minimal-time FSSP is not particular to minimal-time solutions and can be used for any synchronization time, without specifying this synchronization time to the algorithm. The difference in the parameters only reflects the slightly different notion of compliance for RTSG problems and FSSP. The notion of compliance being the only changing factor, the approach can readily be adapted to any class of problem for which an appropriate notion of compliance can be designed. As exemplified here, and in the FSSP case described in [8], the compliance property is a direct translate of the problem.

4   Conclusion

There are still many components of this work to communicate properly, including how local mappings compose and relate to each other and how the integration of non-deterministic family of space-time diagrams can allow to explore even more (deterministic) solutions, and this conclusion is not the place to start these discussions. Let us nonetheless comment on two other aspects.

Firstly, the notion of local mapping appears to be a bridge between a common practice and a topological tool. On the practical side, it is common to work directly at the level of space-time diagrams, and this is this practice that is partly captured formally and automatized by local mappings. On the topological side, a question was raised about the relation with conjugacy classes, a standard notion in the CA and symbolic dynamics literature [2]. In fact, the concept of local mapping appears to be an adaptation of the notion of shift-equivariant homomorphism between two cellular automaton. Such homomorphisms are usually described on total transition functions, with any configuration being a valid initial configuration. This is a dynamical system point of view not necessarily aligned with the more algorithmic point of view of FSSP and RTSG problems. Local mappings augment the notion of homomorphism by including the partiality of the transition functions and the temporal aspect of the space-time diagrams, essential for the very specification of many algorithmic problem. Forming a bridge between the algorithmic and dynamical points of view might be the reason of their effectiveness.

Secondly, more results have been obtained since the writing of this paper and we now have 4-state and 3-state solutions, but the details of these news results still need to be worked out. The 4-state solution is obtained by running again the exploration from the solution of Proposition 5. Running again the exploration from it gives no additional local simulation. The 3-state solutions are obtained by a brute force exploration in a particular order to maximize pruning. This gives optimal-state solutions for the n^3-RTSG problem, and more data to deepen our understanding of the local mapping landscape, with possible applications to the famous 5-state FSSP problem.

References

1. Fischer, P.C.: Generation of primes by a one-dimensional real-time iterative array. J. ACM **12**(3), 388–394 (1965). https://doi.org/10.1145/321281.321290
2. Jalonen, J., Kari, J.: On the conjugacy problem of cellular automata. Inf. Comput. **274**, 104531 (2020). https://doi.org/10.1016/j.ic.2020.104531

3. Kamikawa, N., Umeo, H.: A study on sequence generation powers of small cellular automata. SICE J. Control Meas. Syst. Integr. **5**(4), 191–199 (2012). https://doi.org/10.9746/jcmsi.5.191

4. Kamikawa, N., Umeo, H.: A construction of five-state real-time Fibonacci sequence generator. Artif. Life Robot. **21**(4), 531–539 (2016). https://doi.org/10.1007/s10015-016-0309-2

5. Kamikawa, N., Umeo, H.: Two implementations of real-time sequence generator for $\{n^3 \mid n = 1, 2, 3, ... \}$ and their comparison. Int. J. Netw. Comput. **9**(2), 257–275 (2019). http://www.ijnc.org/index.php/ijnc/article/view/209

6. Korec, I.: Real-time generation of primes by a one-dimensional cellular automaton with 9-states. In: Margenstern, M. (ed.) International Colloquium Universal Machines and Computations, MCU 1998, Proceedings, Metz, France, 23–27 March 1998, vol. II, pp. 101–116. IUT Metz (1998)

7. Kamikawa, N., Umeo, H.: Some algorithms for real-time generation of non-regular sequences on one-bit inter-cell-communication cellular automata. In: SICE Annual Conference 2007, pp. 953–958 (2007). https://doi.org/10.1109/SICE.2007.4421122

8. Nguyen, T.T., Maignan, L.: Exploring millions of 6-state FSSP solutions: the formal notion of local CA simulation. In: Zenil, H. (ed.) AUTOMATA 2020. LNCS, vol. 12286, pp. 1–13. Springer, Cham (2020). https://doi.org/10.1007/978-3-030-61588-8_1

9. Nguyen, T.T., Maignan, L.: Some cellular fields interrelations and optimizations in FSSP solutions. J. Cell. Autom. **15**(1–2), 131–146 (2020). https://www.oldcitypublishing.com/journals/jca-home/jca-issue-contents/jca-volume-15-number-1-2-2020/jca-15-1-2-p-131-146/

System Reduction: An Approach Based on Probabilistic Cellular Automata

Pierre-Alain Toupance[1,2]([✉]), Bastien Chopard[1], and Laurent Lefèvre[2][iD]

[1] University of Geneva, Geneva, Switzerland
bastien.chopard@unige.ch
[2] Univ. Grenoble Alpes, Grenoble INP, LCIS, Valence, France
pierre-alain.toupance@grenoble-inp.fr,
laurent.lefevre@lcis.grenoble-inp.fr

Abstract. The problem of cellular automata coarse-graining is considered. The case of 1D boolean cellular automata (CA) is investigated. Probabilistic rules for 1D CA are parameterized. Then the coarse-graining procedure and the reduced probabilistic CA are defined in the general case. The reduction procedure is illustrated on the example of the Wolfram CA deterministic rule 30. It is then analyzed on the example of a 1D ring probabilistic voter model. The coarse-grained transition rule is improved by making use of the network adjacency matrix. Results obtained for the original and the coarse-grained models are compared, both in the uncontrolled and controlled cases.

Keywords: Cellular automata · Coarse-graining · Projection · Dynamical systems · Probabilistic dynamics · Voter model

1 Introduction

Many systems of interest to scientists are made of a large number of interacting constituents whose detailed behavior may not be of great interest when observing the system at a larger scale. For instance a fluid is made of many molecules but such a fine grain description is not tractable if one is interested in local macroscopic properties such as pressure, velocity or temperature.

In the realm of complex systems, it is an interesting question to understand when and how a system can be reduced by projecting the fine degree of freedom. We are for instance concerned with the question of the controllability of a complex system, namely our ability to act on it to force its behavior towards a desired objective. Dealing with a large number of degrees of freedom makes this question very challenging, both mathematically and numerically. Therefore, there is a great interest to consider the control of a reduced system as a good approximation of the control of the full system. It is worthwhile to note that the problem has already been investigated in the control community, but mainly for the reduction of large scale unstructured linear systems, i.e. described by a large set of differential (or difference) equations. The proposed reduction methods then

B. Chopard et al. (Eds.): ACRI 2022, LNCS 13402, pp. 94–105, 2022.
https://doi.org/10.1007/978-3-031-14926-9_9

rely usually on matrix decomposition algorithms and projections which preserve some system properties such as controllability (see for instance [2] for a textbook on this approach). However these methods do not apply (in general) to nonlinear systems and do not make use of the information on the interaction topology (or *structure*) of the system. In this work we would rather consider reduction methods more specifically adapted to nonlinear complex systems, relying on local dynamics and local interactions topology (agents neighborhood).

The typical problem we have in mind is a stochastic dynamical system on a graph, where each node is an agent that can have a finite number of possible states. Below we will present a version of a voter model that will illustrate our approach. From a general point of view, our goal is act on some agent, impose their state so as to produce a desired global response (e.g. all agents reach the same state). Intuitively, it seems reasonable to assume that the behavior of the system could be obtained by a reduced number of representative agents that aggregate a community of agents that adopt, on average, a similar state.

In what follows, we explore the above question in a simplified topology of agents, namely a periodic one-dimensional system, with only nearest neighbors interactions and two possible states. Such a system corresponds to a probabilistic Cellular Automaton (CA). In short, we want to build "supercells" that aggregate 3 cells of the original system, and see whether we are able to express an evolution rule for a global property of these supercells, for instance the state of the majority of the internal cells.

The process of coarse graining a CA has been addressed by a few authors (see for instance [3–5]). The main difference of the present approach is that we consider probabilistic rules for which any projection of the state of a supercell to $\{0, 1\}$ is possible and will give rise to a new probabilistic rule. In the case of deterministic CA, the challenge is to find whether a projection exists so that the coarse-grained CA is still a deterministic CA. In this work, the questions are rather to decide whether the coarse-grained probabilistic CA is a good approximation of the original (deterministic or probabilistic) one and what *good approximation* means in this context.

The paper is organised as follows. First we develop the formalism for coarse graining a probabilistic CA, and we discuss its applicability in practical cases. Then, we consider the specific case of a CA voter model, its reduction and our capability to design a control strategy on the coarse grained model that would produced the same effect as on the fully resolved CA. We conclude the discussion with open questions and tentative approaches to address them.

2 Problem Formulation

The goal of this section is to provide a general framework to define what we mean by the coarse graining of a CA, or its reduction. We start from a general formulation of a 1D CA model. It is well known that the deterministic, elementary CAs can be specified using the numbering scheme proposed by Wolfram [1].

All possible input configurations are listed and the set of corresponding output is interpreted as a number characterizing the rule of CA. This is sketched below for a two-state, radius 1 rule $11011000_2 = 216_{10}$:

$$\underbrace{111}_{1} \quad \underbrace{110}_{1} \quad \underbrace{101}_{0} \quad \underbrace{100}_{1} \quad \underbrace{011}_{1} \quad \underbrace{010}_{0} \quad \underbrace{001}_{0} \quad \underbrace{000}_{0} \qquad (1)$$

The output $p = 0$ or $p = 1$ can be interpreted as the probability p that the site $s_i(t+1) = 1$ provided the values $s_{i-1}s_is_{i+1}$ at the previous time t. Therefore, using the same approach, we can define a stochastic $k = 2$ states and $r = 1$ radius as

$$\underbrace{111}_{p_7} \quad \underbrace{110}_{p_6} \quad \underbrace{101}_{p_5} \quad \underbrace{100}_{p_4} \quad \underbrace{011}_{p_3} \quad \underbrace{010}_{p_2} \quad \underbrace{001}_{p_1} \quad \underbrace{000}_{p_0} \qquad (2)$$

where p_ℓ is the probability that configuration $\ell = s_{i-1}s_is_{i+1}$ is 1 at the next iteration. Therefore any 1D $r = 1$, $k = 2$ CA, whether stochastic or deterministic can be specified by the vector

$$p = (p_7, p_6, p_5, p_4, p_3, p_2, p_1, p_0)$$

with $p_i \in [0, 1]$.

Note that the number of probability p_i can be reduced if the rule has symmetries or additional properties. For instance, for the so-called totalistic rules, where the outcome depends only on the sum of the state of the neighborhood, $p_6 = p_5 = p_3$, $p_4 = p_2 = p_1$, and only four components are needed to specify the rule, for instance p_7, p_6, p_4 and p_0. The number of components of p is also reduced if the rule is symmetric by permuting the left and right neighbors, or by the transformation $0 \leftrightarrow 1$.

The reason why we are introducing this representation is that the coarse graining procedure that we will present transforms a probability vector p into another one, p', by adding noise. The difference between p and p' indicates how the coarse grained rule differs from the original one. Our formalism allows us to consider both deterministic and stochastic rule within the same framework.

3   Coarse Graining Procedure

Our coarse graining procedure is based on several steps that we illustrate on a $r = 1$ CA whose evolution rule is defined through the transition function (or conditional probability).

$$P(s_i(t+1)|s_{i-1}(t), s_i(t), s_{i+1}(t)) \qquad (3)$$

Generalization to a larger neighborhood or to any kind of interaction graph is left for further investigations.

Figure 1 sketches the process. The cells re grouped in super cells of size 3. A given configuration of 3 such supercells produces one super-cell after 3 iterations of the CA (operation T). This super-cell can then be reduced to $w \in \{0, 1\}$

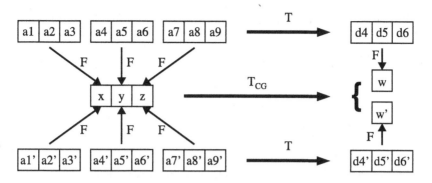

Fig. 1. Schematic illustration of the coarse graining procedure for stochastic CA with radius 1.

according to a projection F. The question is then to determine the rule T_{CG} that would lead to the same result by directly projecting the initial super-cells. As suggested in Fig. 1, there might be different sets of super-cells that have the same projection x, y, z, but a different projected output w. This variability can be considered as a probabilisitic component of the reduced CA.

(1) **Extension of the CA rule** by combining several time steps on the corresponding extended neighborhood. For instance, a $r = 1$, CA, iterated 3 times required the knowledge of the state, $a_1 \ldots a_9$, of 9 consecutive cells and determines the state, $d_4 \ldots d_6$, of 3 cells as illustrated in the following example

$$
\begin{aligned}
t = 0 &: a_1 \; a_2 \; a_3 \; a_4 \; a_5 \; a_6 \; a_7 \; a_8 \; a_9 \\
t = 1 &: \quad\;\; b_2 \; b_3 \; b_4 \; b_5 \; b_6 \; b_7 \; b_8 \\
t = 2 &: \quad\quad\;\; c_3 \; c_4 \; c_5 \; c_6 \; c_7 \\
t = 3 &: \quad\quad\quad\;\; d_4 \; d_5 \; d_6
\end{aligned}
\tag{4}
$$

The lookup table corresponding to this extension amounts to computing the conditional probability

$$
P(d_4, d_5, d_6 | a_1, a_2, a_3, a_4, a_5, a_6, a_7, a_8, a_9)
\tag{5}
$$

Such a quantity can be obtained from the original rule, namely relation (3). First we notice that conditional probability (5) can be expressed as

$$
\begin{aligned}
&P(d_4, d_5, d_6 | a_1, a_2, a_3, a_4, a_5, a_6, a_7, a_8, a_9) \\
&= \sum_{c_3, \ldots, c_7, b_2 \ldots b_8} P(d_4, d_5, d_6 | c_3, c_4, c_5, c_6, c_7) \\
&\quad \times P(c_3, c_4, c_5, c_6, c_7 | b_2, b_3, b_4, b_5, b_6, b_7, b_8) \\
&\quad \times P(b_2, b_3, b_4, b_5, b_6, b_7, b_8 | a_1, a_2, a_3, a_4, a_5, a_6, a_7, a_8, a_9)
\end{aligned}
\tag{6}
$$

Each of these terms can be obtained from the original CA rule as, for instance for $P(b|a)$,

$$
\begin{aligned}
& P(b_2, b_3, b_4, b_5, b_6, b_7, b_8 | a_1, a_2, a_3, a_4, a_5, a_6, a_7, a_8, a_9) \\
& = P(b_2 | a_1, a_2, a_3) \times P(b_3 | a_2, a_3, a_4) \\
& \times P(b_4 | a_3, a_4, a_4) \times P(b_5 | a_4, a_5, a_6) \\
& \times P(b_6 | a_5, a_6, a_7) \times P(b_7 | a_6, a_7, a_8) \\
& P(b_8 | a_7, a_8, a_9)
\end{aligned}
\tag{7}
$$

because, for each cell i, the CA rule is applied independently (new random numbers are drawn for a stochastic rule) and can be computed explicitly with Eq. (3). A similar expression holds for $P(c|b)$. Expression (6) together with (7) is analytically heavy but can easily be computed numerically from the original CA rule (3). In case the original CA is with two states $\{0, 1\}$, one has, using representation (2), that

$$
P(1|xyz) = p_{xyz} \qquad P(0|xyz) = 1 - p_{xyz}
\tag{8}
$$

where the notation xyz means the binary number obtained with bits x, y and z. Note the transformation proposed here is exact and contains no approximation. Using the extended rule $P(d|a)$ simply reduces the number of iterations by 3 compared to the original rule. This transformation is denoted T in Fig. 1.

(2) **Projection of the extended CA rule:** This step of the procedure consists in a projection of the extended CA on a simple one. First one notices that we can group the 9 cells of the extended CA in 3 super-cells. If the original CA has two states, 0 and 1, the super-cells have 3 bits, that is 8 possible states.

We will now define a projection F from these 8 states to $\{0, 1\}$ so that the projected states take the same values 0 and 1 as the original CA (see Fig. 1, left, where it is shown that two different state vectors a and a' for 9 contiguous cells are projected through F on the same state (x, y, z) for the three corresponding super-cells).

A simple choice for F, in the case of super-cells with 3-bit states, is the majority rule

$$
F(x, y, z) = \begin{cases} 1 & \text{if } x + y + z \geq 2 \\ 0 & \text{otherwise} \end{cases}
\tag{9}
$$

This choice will be used in the sequel of the paper, although the proposed reduction method may be applied using any map F with values in $\{0, 1\}$. The reduced, or coarse grained, CA is then defined by the transition probability $P(w|xyz)$ given by

$$
P(w|xyz) = P(F(d_{4:6}) = w) | F(a_{1:3}) = x, F(a_{4:6}) = y, F(a_{7:9}) = z)
\tag{10}
$$

Notation: $\alpha_{p:q} = (\alpha_p, \alpha_{p+1}, \ldots, \alpha_q)$

It is represented as the transition T_{CG} in Fig. 1. This can be written with the joint probability distribution $P(d, a)$ as

$$P(w|xyz) = \frac{P(w, xyz)}{P(xyz)} \tag{11}$$

$$= \left(\sum_{\substack{F(d_4 d_5 d_6) = w \\ F(a_1 a_2 a_3) = x \\ F(a_4 a_5 a_6) = y \\ F(a_7 a_8 a_9) = z}} P(d, a) \right) \left(\sum_{\substack{F(a'_1 a'_2 a'_3) = x \\ F(a'_4 a'_5 a'_6) = y \\ F(a'_7 a'_8 a'_9) = z}} P(a') \right)^{-1} \tag{12}$$

where a is short for $a_1, a_2 \ldots a_9$, a' is short for $a'_1, a'_2, \ldots a'_9$ and d is short for d_4, d_5, d_6.

Expressing the joint probability $P(d, a)$ as $P(d|a)P(a)$ gives

$$P(w|xyz) = \sum_{\substack{F(d_4 d_5 d_6) = w \\ F(a_1 a_2 a_3) = x \\ F(a_4 a_5 a_6) = y \\ F(a_7 a_8 a_9) = z}} \left(P(d|a) \left[\frac{P(a)}{\sum_{\substack{F(a'_1 a'_2 a'_3) = x \\ F(a'_4 a'_5 a'_6) = y \\ F(a'_7 a'_8 a'_9) = z}} P(a')} \right] \right) \tag{13}$$

The term $P(d|a)$ is known from the previous step, but the term

$$\frac{P(a)}{\sum_{\substack{F(a'_1 a'_2 a'_3) = x \\ F(a'_4 a'_5 a'_6) = y \\ F(a'_7 a'_8 a'_9) = z}} P(a')} \tag{14}$$

is unknown as the probability to get the sequence a may depend on the history of the evolution. This probability can be, for instance, estimated by sampling. However, assuming that all configurations are equally likely, (14) can be obtained easily with combinatorial arguments. This is done in the next section for a deterministic CA example which is known to have a uniform configurations distribution. In Sect. 5, a probabilistic voter model will be reduced. In this latter example, on the contrary, it is shown both through numerical (empirical) experiments and from adjacency matrix analysis, that the configurations may not be considered as uniformly distributed. In that case, a corresponding weighted reduction has to be proposed.

4 Example

As an illustration of the previous section, we coarse grain Wolfram CA deterministic rule 30 into a stochastic CA. For this rule, as $P(a)$ is uniform for all configuration $a = a_1 a_2 \ldots a_9$, with the projection F being the majority rule (9), expression (14) equals $1/64$. According to expression (13), to obtain probabilities p_i, we need to compute $P(d|a)$. These values are deduced from (6), (7) and from rule 30. Thus, for this example, by applying the method presented in the previous part, we obtain the following probabilities:

$$p_0 = 0.65625 \quad p_1 = 0.546875 \quad p_2 = 0.671875 \quad p_3 = 0.734375 \quad p_4 = 0.34375$$

$$p_5 = 0.453125 \quad p_6 = 0.328125 \quad p_7 = 0.265625$$

Figure 2 (left) shows the evolution of rule 30, for a periodic CA of length 300, every 3 iterations, and with a projection by F of each supercell of size 3 to a size 1 cell. In the middle we show the evolution of the coarse grained rule 30, which naturally has a time scale and spatial scale reduced by a factor 3. Finally, on the right, we show a fully random rule, with $p_i = 0.5$. Clearly the first two images look very similar and different from the last one. This suggests that the coarse graining preserves some spatio-temporal patterns of rule 30. Of course a quantitative analysis should be performed to measure the quality of the reduction in this case. It is left for further investigations.

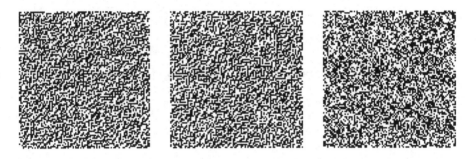

Fig. 2. Wolfram rule 30, projected, reduced and compared to a random rule.

5   Reduced Voter Model

5.1   Description of the Model

We will now apply the projection method to the voter model defined in [6]. This agent-based model is defined on a graph of arbitrary topology, whether directed or not. A binary agent occupies each node of the network. The dynamics is specified by assuming that each agent i looks at every other agent in its neighborhood, and counts the percentage ρ_i of those agents which are in the state $+1$ (in case an agent is linked to itself, it obviously belongs to its own neighborhood). A function f, with $0 \leq f(\rho_i) \leq 1$, gives the probability for an agent i to be in state $+1$ at the next iteration. For instance, if f would be chosen as $f(\rho) = \rho$, an agent for which all neighbors are in state $+1$ will turn into state $+1$ with certainty. The update is performed synchronously over all n agents. Formally, this dynamics for the voter model can be expressed as

$$s_i(t+1) = \begin{cases} 1 & \text{with probability } f(\rho_i(t)) \\ 0 & \text{with probability } 1 - f(\rho_i(t)) \end{cases} \tag{15}$$

where $s_i(t) \in \{0, 1\}$ is the state of agent i at iteration t and where

$$\rho_i(t) = \frac{1}{|N_i|} \sum_{j \in N_i} s_j(t). \tag{16}$$

N_i denotes the set of neighbors of agent i, according to the network topology. The global density of all n agents with opinion 1 is

$$\rho_{all}(t) = \frac{1}{n} \sum_{i=1}^{n} s_i(t) \tag{17}$$

In what follows, we will use the particular function

$$f(\rho) = (1 - 2\epsilon)\rho + \epsilon \tag{18}$$

The quantity $0 \le \epsilon \le 1/2$ is called the noise. It reflects the probability to take a decision different from that of the neighborhood majority.

5.2 Transition Probabilities for a 1D Circular Graph Voter Model

We will consider a 1D voter model where each agent has only left and right neighbors. To avoid boundary effects, we will make use of a 1D circular graph of size n for the network topology. The expression for ρ_i is then

$$\rho_i = \frac{s_{i-1}(t) + s_i(t) + s_{i+1}(t)}{3}, \ i \in \{1, \ldots, n\} \tag{19}$$

where $s_i(t)$ denotes the state of agent i at time t. Following the coarse graining procedure defined in Sect. 3, we make groups of 3 cells defined as "super-agents". The boolean state $S_i(t)$ of the super-agent i is defined by:

$$S_i(t) = \begin{cases} 1 & \text{if } s_{3i+1}(t) + s_{3i+2}(t) + s_{3i+3}(t) \ge 2 \\ 0 & \text{otherwise} \end{cases} \tag{20}$$

Following the notations of Fig. (1), we define the coarse-grained transition probability $P(w|xyz)$ as the probability that $S_i(t+1) = 1$ knowing that the values of $S_{i-1}(t)$, $S_i(t)$ and $S_{i+1}(t)$ are respectively x, y and z. These coarse-grained transition probabilities for super-agents may be computed according to (12) and the resulting probabilistic cellular automaton may be represented using the notation introduced in (2). For instance, with a noise $\epsilon = 0,01$, we obtain

$$p = (p_7, p_6, p_5, p_4, p_3, p_2, p_1, p_0)$$
$$= (0.9512, 0.7898, 0.3836, 0.2108, 0.7838, 0.6111, 0.2116, 0.0501) \qquad (21)$$

5.3   The Transition Function

We compute the values of $P(1|xyz)$, defined by expression (12), through intensive simulations with the original CA, for different noise values ϵ. We look for a transition function, g for the reduced system which is affine as the transition function, f, of the original system (18). However, we observe that when choosing

$$\rho = \frac{S_{i-1}(t) + S_i(t) + S_{i+1}(t)}{3}$$

the function g is not affine. It is therefore useful to consider weights for the values of the block states in the expression of ρ. With the values of $P(1|xyz)$ found by sampling, we compute α and ϵ_1 such that:

$$\begin{cases} g(\rho) = (1 - 2\epsilon_1)\rho + \epsilon_1 \\ \rho = \alpha S_{i-1}(t) + (1 - 2\alpha)S_i(t) + \alpha S_{i+1}(t) \end{cases} \qquad (22)$$

In Fig. 3 (right part), g is computed for several values of ϵ and evaluated for $\rho \in \{0; 0.181; 0.363; 0.637; 0.818\}$. We can see in Fig. 3 (left part) that, for small values of ϵ, ϵ_1 grows linearly with ϵ (the correlation coefficient is 0.99 for values of $\epsilon \in [0; 0.05]$). Using the least squares method, we obtain

$$\epsilon_1 = 3.667\epsilon + 0.0106 \qquad (23)$$

The need to weight state values S_i is due to the fact that the state of a block (or super-agent) at time $t + 3$ is more influenced by its own state at time t, than by the state of its 2 neighboring blocks. The interactions between the agents can be represented by a causality graph. Its adjacency matrix is, in the case of a periodic (circular) topology:

$$A = \begin{pmatrix} 1 & 1 & 0 & \cdots\cdots & 0 & 1 \\ 1 & 1 & 1 & 0 & & 0 \\ 0 & \ddots & \ddots & & & \vdots \\ \vdots & \ddots & \ddots & \ddots & & \vdots \\ \vdots & & \ddots & \ddots & \ddots & \vdots \\ 0 & & & \ddots & \ddots & 1 \\ 1 & 0 & \cdots\cdots & & 0 & 1 & 1 \end{pmatrix}$$

The number of causal paths between 2 agents after 1, 2 or 3 iterations is then given by the coefficients of the matrix $B = A + A^2 + A^3$. We have:

$$B = \begin{pmatrix} C & D & 0_{3,3} & & & 0_{3,3} & D \\ D & C & D & 0_{3,3} & & & 0_{3,3} \\ 0_{3,3} & \ddots & \ddots & & & & \vdots \\ \vdots & \ddots & \ddots & \ddots & & \ddots & 0_{3,3} \\ \vdots & & \ddots & \ddots & \ddots & D & C & D \\ D & 0_{3,3} & \ddots & \ddots & \ddots & D & C \end{pmatrix}$$

with

$$C = \begin{pmatrix} 1 & 4 & 9 \\ 0 & 1 & 4 \\ 0 & 0 & 1 \end{pmatrix}, \; D = \begin{pmatrix} 9 & 11 & 9 \\ 4 & 9 & 11 \\ 1 & 4 & 9 \end{pmatrix}, \; 0_{3,3} = \begin{pmatrix} 0 & 0 & 0 \\ 0 & 0 & 0 \\ 0 & 0 & 0 \end{pmatrix}$$

We may therefore define a parameter b to characterize the influence of the vote of a block of cells at time t on the vote of the same block at time $t + 3$:

$$b = \frac{\sum d_{i,j}}{\sum c_{i,j} + 2 \sum d_{i,j}} = \frac{67}{107} \approx 0.626$$

Similarly, we may define the corresponding influence parameter a for the vote of the two neighbouring blocks at time t on the vote of the central block at time $t + 3$:

$$a = \frac{\sum c_{i,j}}{\sum c_{i,j} + 2 \sum d_{i,j}} = \frac{20}{107} \approx 0.187$$

Note that these weighting parameters are derived directly from the interaction graph and do not require (intensive) sampling to be estimated, contrarily to the estimation of the probabilities in the coarse-grained configuration space by simulations.

For all considered values of ϵ, we obtained for α a mean value of 0.182 and a standard deviation of 0.0028. It may be noticed that these values are very close to the value of a obtained with the matrix B only. Therefore we conjecture that the weights computed from the adjacency matrix B (hence the value of α) give an accurate approximation of the "real" weights which could be computed from the estimation of the coarse-grained configuration probabilities through an intensive simulation effort. For the rest of the simulations in the paper, we will choose $\alpha = 0.182$.

5.4   Simulation of a Controlled Situation

To compare the original system and the reduced one, we look at their behavior while controlling blocks (or supercells). We have done simulations by forcing the vote to 1 of the block agents, and calculate the average opinion ρ_{all} of the population. In the case of the original system we carry out simulations by forcing

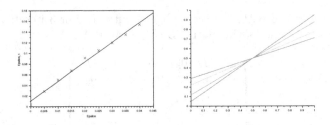

Fig. 3. Left: ϵ_1 as a function of ϵ. Right: $g(\rho)$ with different noises: $\epsilon = 0$(red curve), 0.03 (green curve), 0.07 (yellow curve) and $0, 1$ (purple curve), values calculated for $\rho \in \{0; 0.181; 0.362; 0.638; 0.819\}$. (Color figure online)

the vote to 1 of 3 cells of a block, of 2 blocks and of 4 blocks. We compute the average rate of blocks voting 1 (i.e. 2 or 3 cells of the block vote 1) as a function of t. For the reduced system, we force the values of the coarse-grained cells to 1 for 1, 2 and 4 blocks, and we compute the average fraction of vote 1 over the entire system.

In Fig. 4, we see the results obtained with a ring graph of size $n = 120$. The noise is $\epsilon = 0.01$. We did 10^4 simulations with 600 time steps. The average voting rate is compared for the original and reduced systems. When 1 and 2 blocks are controlled among 40 blocks, we see that the noise induced by the projection generates a slightly lower average rate of blocks voting 1 for the simplified system. On the other hand, when we control 4 blocks, these rates are very close.

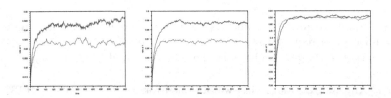

Fig. 4. The fraction of votes 1 for a ring graph of size 120 with controlling blocks of 3 agents during a time period of 600. The blue curves are the fraction of blocks that vote mostly 1 (2 or 3 agents vote 1 among the 3 agents of the block). These curves are obtained with the real system. The red curves are obtained with the simplified system. They give us the rate of blocks that vote 1 in majority. The noise is $\epsilon = 0.01$, and the noise in the reduced model is $\epsilon_1 = 0.047$, as given by Eq. (23). We compute the average of the votes with a sample of 10^4 simulations. The number of controlled blocks of size 3 is 1 (left panel), 2 (middle panel) and 4 (right panel). (Color figure online)

6   Conclusions

Our goal was to explore the possibility to simplify stochastic complex systems on graphs by reducing the number of degrees of freedom, while keeping the essential dynamical features. We believe that the originality of the proposed method is that it can be applied for any projection function and any probabilistic or deterministic CAs. In our theoretical framework an important aspect to correctly build the simplified system is to have hypotheses on the probability distribution of all possible configurations. In the case of the voter model, where we determined the reduced system from a statistical analysis of the real one, we observed that coarse grained agents may have to be defined with a weighted average of the real ones. Anyway, the examples we showed in this study suggest that system reduction is a possible avenue, in particular with the objective of controllability. However, numerous issues need to be investigated: the evaluation of the information loss in the reduction, the comparisons of the stationary probability distributions, etc. Another question is how to best define the blocks or super-agents for the system reduction. When applying the reduction on a dynamical system defined on a graph, a natural way could be to consider the partitions associated with graph communities.

References

1. Wolfram, S.: Statistical mechanics of cellular automata. Rev. Mod. Phys. **55**(3), 601 (1983)
2. Antoulas, A.C.: Approximation of Large-Scale Dynamical Systems. SIAM, Philadelphia (2005)
3. Drasdo, D.: Coarse graining in simulated cell populations. Adv. Complex Syst. **8**(02–03), 319–363 (2005)
4. Israeli, N., Goldenfeld, N.: Coarse-graining of cellular automata, emergence, and the predictability of complex systems. Phys. Rev. E **73**(2), 026203 (2006)
5. Costa, P., De Melo, F.: Coarse graining of partitioned cellular automata. arXiv preprint arXiv:1905.10391 (2019)
6. Toupance, P.A., Lefèvre, L., Chopard, B.: Influence measurement in a complex dynamical model: an information theoretic approach. J. Comput. Sci. **44**, 101115 (2020)

Lyapunov Profiles of Three-State Totalistic Cellular Automata

Milan Vispoel[(✉)][ID], Aisling J. Daly[ID], and Jan M. Baetens[ID]

KERMIT, Department of Data Analysis and Mathematical Modelling,
Faculty of Bioscience Engineering, Ghent University, Coupure Links 653,
9000 Ghent, Belgium
{milan.vispoel,aisling.daly,jan.baetens}@ugent.be

Abstract. Inspired by the theory of continuous dynamical systems, Lyapunov exponents have been previously defined in the framework of cellular automata (CAs) in order to quantify a CA's sensitive dependence on initial conditions, i.e. a CA's sensitivity to a perturbation of an initial configuration. However, the application of these Lyapunov exponents is currently limited to two-state CAs, which limits their usefulness in the framework of CA-based models since these typically involve more than two states. This paper proposes an extension of the existing methodological framework to three-state CAs. Our method is illustrated for some interesting totalistic three-state rules, although it is generally applicable. Our proposed extension to the existing framework reveals some interesting features regarding CAs classified as class IV according to Wolfram's classification.

Keywords: Cellular automata · Lyapunov exponents · Multi-state systems

1 Introduction

In the theory of continuous dynamical systems, Lyapunov exponents are a measure of the exponential divergence rate of two trajectories that are initially infinitesimally close in phase space [9]. As such, they quantify how a dynamical system responds to a perturbation of its initial state. For an N-dimensional dynamical system, this yields a Lyapunov profile consisting of N different Lyapunov exponents, one for each (mutually orthogonal) direction in phase space. As soon as one of the N Lyapunov exponents is non-zero, an initial perturbation will grow exponentially over time - this indicates a sensitive dependence on initial conditions. The details of the Lyapunov profile further specify the kind of dynamics that can occur.

In order to arrive at a comprehensive overview of CAs, many different measures have been proposed [3,11,13]. As a CA is essentially a discrete dynamical system, a measure that captures its sensitivity to the initial configuration and its possible chaotic dynamics is useful to gain insights into the dependence of the dynamical evolution on the initial configuration. However, the extension

B. Chopard et al. (Eds.): ACRI 2022, LNCS 13402, pp. 106–115, 2022.
https://doi.org/10.1007/978-3-031-14926-9_10

of the concept of Lyapunov exponents to CAs is not straightforward. For the case of two-state one-dimensional CAs, two separate viewpoints emerged in the early nineties. The first viewpoint was suggested by Wolfram, who defined the Lyapunov exponents of CA empirically by considering the average propagation velocity to the left and right of the defect pattern [12]. This idea was later formalized for binary one-dimensional CA by Shereshevsky [7] and further refined by other authors [4,8]. This approach yields the left and right Lyapunov exponents $\Lambda^+(x)$ and $\Lambda^-(x)$ respectively for one-dimensional CA. The conditions under which Shereshevsky's definition applies are fairly strict, which prompted Tisseur [8] to define the more generally applicable average Lyapunov exponents that are smaller than or equal to the exponents defined by Shereshevsky.

The second viewpoint, proposed by Bagnoli [2], is more similar to the familiar notion of Lyapunov exponents as the exponential divergence rate of nearby trajectories. This method was later extended by Baetens *et al.* in order to yield the full discrete Lyapunov profile of a CA rule [1].

Both of these approaches are currently only defined for two-state CAs. This significantly reduces their applicability in real-world scenarios, as CA relevant for such applications often require more than two states [5,6]. This paper demonstrates how Bagnoli's [2] approach for obtaining Lyapunov profiles for two-state CAs can be extended to three-state CAs while also distinguishing between the directionality of the defects, i.e. a state change from 1 to 0 is distinct from a change from 0 to 1. In addition to quantifying the exponential divergence rate of initially close trajectories for three-state CAs, this extension also captures the kind of defects that dominate the chaotic dynamics in certain CAs.

2   Lyapunov Profiles of Cellular Automata

2.1   Preliminaries

A CA can be conveniently represented by a sextuple $\mathcal{C} = \langle \mathcal{T}, S, s, s_0, \mathcal{N}, \phi \rangle$. Here, $\mathcal{T}$ denotes a countably infinite tessellation of a one-dimensional Euclidean space, consisting of consecutive intervals $c_i, i \in \mathbb{N}$, referred to as sites, and S constitutes the space of states of the CA. The output function $s : \mathcal{T} \times \mathbb{N} \to S$ yields the state value of site c_i at the t-th discrete time step, i.e. $s(c_i, t)$. The function $s_0 : \mathcal{T} \to S$ assigns to every site c_i an initial state, i.e. $s(c_i, 0) = s_0(c_i)$. $\mathcal{N}(c_i)$ is the neighborhood function with size $|\mathcal{N}|$, i.e. $\mathcal{N}(c_i) = (c_{i-1}, c_i, c_{i+1})$. Finally, the transition function $\phi : S^{|\mathcal{N}|} \to S$, that governs the dynamics of each site c_i, is given by

$$s(c_i, t+1) = \phi(s(c_{i-1}, t), s(c_i, t), s(c_{i+1}, t)).$$

2.2   Two-State CA

Extending the concept of Lyapunov exponents to CAs is not straightforward, as the original definition relies on tools from differential calculus, which are not applicable to CA since the state space $S^{\mathbb{N}}$ is fully discrete. Instead of considering infinitesimally close initial configurations, one can instead consider initial configurations that differ only in a single site. The vector $s(t)$ denotes the defect pattern and indicates how such a perturbation in the initial configuration, referred to as a defect, propagates. For binary one-dimensional CAs, the time evolution of the defect pattern can be written recursively using the Boolean Jacobian matrix $J(s(t), t)$ [2]:

$$\Delta s(t+1) = J(s(t), t) * \Delta s(t), \tag{1}$$

where $*$ denotes the usual matrix multiplication but with the regular summation replaced by summation modulo 2. The matrix $J(s(t), t)$ contains the Boolean partial derivatives of the transition function $\phi : S^{|\mathcal{N}|} \to S$ [10]:

$$\left[J(s(t), t) \right]_{ij} = \frac{\partial s(c_i, t+1)}{\partial s(c_j, t)} \tag{2}$$

$$= \begin{cases} 1, & \text{if } \phi\big(\tilde{s}(\mathcal{N}(c_i), t)\big) = \phi\big(\tilde{s}_j(\mathcal{N}(c_i), t)\big), \\ 0, & \text{otherwise}, \end{cases} \tag{3}$$

where $\tilde{s}_j(\mathcal{N}(c_i), t)$ is the set obtained by replacing $s(c_j, t)$ by its complement in the set $\tilde{s}(\mathcal{N}(c_i), t)$.

These entries simply indicate whether or not flipping the value at site c_j at time t causes a change in the value at site c_i at time $t + 1$. Whether or not a change at site c_j propagates to site c_i depends on the entire neighborhood $\mathcal{N}(c_i)$, which is why $J(s(t), t)$ depends on the configuration $s(t)$. Note that for CA with a neighborhood size of three sites, $J(s(t), t)$ is a tridiagonal matrix since the right hand side of Eq. (3) vanishes when $c_j \notin \mathcal{N}(c_i)$, because perturbations of a certain site c_i can only affect sites in its neighborhood $\mathcal{N}(c_i)$ over the course of a single time step.

Now, we let $H(t)$ denote the sum of all elements of the defect pattern at a certain time step t. This equals the Hamming distance d_h between two configurations evolved from initial configurations differing only in a single site, denoted by $s(t)$ and $s^*(t)$:

$$H(t) = d_h\big(s(t), s^*(t)\big) \tag{4}$$

$$= \sum_i \Delta s(c_i, t), \tag{5}$$

where $\Delta s(c_i, t)$ denotes the ith element of the vector $\Delta s(t)$. Due to the local nature of CAs, $H(t)$ can grow at most linearly with time, so the Hamming distance is not a suitable metric to define exponential divergence in S^N.

Bagnoli resolved this issue for binary one-dimensional CAs by considering the number of ways in which defects can propagate to a certain time step, instead of simply considering the number of defects at a certain time step [2]. The damage vector $n(t)$ is defined as the vector whose i-th entry contains the number of ways in which the initial defect can propagate to site c_i in t time steps (i.e. the number of defect paths). The evolution of $n(t)$ is again written recursively using the Boolean Jacobian matrix:

$$n(t+1) = J(s(t), t), n(t), \tag{6}$$

where regular matrix multiplication takes place. It is clear that the total number of ways in which defects can propagate to time step t is given by the sum of all entries in $n(t)$, further denoted by $\epsilon(t)$. This quantity can grow exponentially with time.

In summary, for one-dimensional binary CAs the defect pattern $s(t)$ and damage vector $n(t)$ are determined by the following recursion relations:

$$\Delta s(t+1) = J(s(t), t) * \Delta s(t), \tag{7}$$

$$n(t+1) = J(s(t), t), n(t), \tag{8}$$

From this, we infer the following upper bounds for $H(t)$ and $\epsilon(t)$ [1]

$$H(t) = \sum_i \Delta s(c_i, t) \le (|\mathcal{N}| - 1)\, t + 1, \tag{9}$$

$$\epsilon(t) = \sum_i n(c_i, t) \le |\mathcal{N}|^t, \tag{10}$$

where $|\mathcal{N}|$ is the size of the neighborhood (e.g. $|\mathcal{N}| = 3$ for elementary CA).

From the above discussion it is clear that considering $\epsilon(t)$ instead of $H(t)$ provides a way to meaningfully define the exponential divergence of trajectories in S^N. This can be used to define Lyapunov exponents in the context of CAs in a way that complies with the definition of Lyapunov exponents for continuous dynamical systems. In particular, Bagnoli defined the total Lyapunov exponent as [2]

$$\Lambda_1 = \lim_{t \to \infty} \frac{1}{t} \log \left(\frac{\epsilon(t)}{\epsilon(0)} \right), \tag{11}$$

where log indicates the natural logarithm. However, this discards the information regarding the distribution of defects in $n(t)$ [1]. A different approach considers a one-dimensional finite CA of size N as an N-dimensional dynamical system, where each site in the lattice corresponds to one of N dimensions, and introduces a finite-time profile of N Lyapunov exponents as follows [1]:

$$\Lambda(T) = \frac{1}{T} \log(n(T)), \tag{12}$$

where the is applied element-wise. The elements of $\Lambda(T)$ may be understood as the time-averaged exponential rates by which the number of defects grows in the sites of the CA. As such, the profile consisting of N Lyapunov exponents is analogous to the spectrum of N Lyapunov exponents associated with an N-dimensional continuous dynamical system.

The above definition relies on the fact that there is only one type of defect (i.e. $1 \to 0$ defects). However, when considering three-state CAs, there are three possible defects (i.e. $1 \to 0$, $1 \to 2$ and $2 \to 0$ defects). Furthermore, when explicitly accounting for the directionality of the defects, there are six possible defects in the case of three-state CAs. This makes the above definition not applicable to CAs with more than two states.

2.3   Three-State CAs

This section discusses how the approach for two-state CAs can be generalized to the three-state directional case. Such a generalization defines six Lyapunov exponents, each one quantifying how one of the six types of defects propagates. Note that in this paper we implement and illustrate our approach for three-state CA, but it is applicable to CA with any number of states. As the number of states k increases, the number of possible types of defects increases as $k(k-1)$, so the required computing power to compute the Lyapunov profiles increases drastically with k.

The extension to three-state CA entails a change in how the entries of the Jacobian $J(s(t), t)$ are defined. Now, $J(s, (t)t)$ contains not only the Boolean partial derivatives of the transition function $\phi : S^{|\mathcal{N}|} \to S$, but also a label that expresses the type of defect that occurs:

$$
\left[J(s(t), t) \right]_{ij} = \begin{cases} \tau_{vw}, & \text{if } \phi\big(\tilde{s}(\mathcal{N}(c_i), t)\big) \neq \phi\big(\tilde{s}_{j,vw}(\mathcal{N}(c_i), t)\big), \\ 0, & \text{if } \phi\big(\tilde{s}(\mathcal{N}(c_i), t)\big) = \phi\big(\tilde{s}_{j,vw}(\mathcal{N}(c_i), t)\big), \end{cases} \tag{13}
$$

where $\tilde{s}_{j,vw}(\mathcal{N}(c_i), t)$ is the set obtained by perturbing $s(c_j, t)$ from state v, to state w in the set $\tilde{s}(\mathcal{N}(c_i), t)$. The values of v and w depend on the kind of defect that arrives at the site c_i.

Now, the evolution of $n(t)$ can be written recursively using the Jacobian matrix:

$$
n(t+1) = J(s(t), t), n(t), \tag{14}
$$

where the regular matrix multiplication takes place. Now, the entries of $n(t)$ contain polynomials in τ_{vw}. Each term in such a polynomial in the ith entry of $n(t)$ represents a certain defect path that arrives at site i in t time steps. The exponent of τ_{vw} in such a term represents the number of times the defect τ_{vw} occurs in this defect path.

We illustrate this approach for the three-state totalistic CA with rule number 420 according to Wolfram's enumeration scheme. We choose this rule because it is the only totalistic rule for which all Boolean derivatives are non-zero, therefore yielding a maximum Lyapunov exponent. For a totalistic rule, the state space is $S = \{0, 1, 2\}$, is endowed with the regular addition, and the updated site value depends only on the sum of the values in its neighborhood at the previous time step: $s(c_i, t+1) = \phi(s(c_{i-1}, t) + s(c_i, t) + s(c_{i+1}, t))$.

Figure 1a shows the defect pattern generated by this rule starting from a random initial configuration of nine sites evolved over three time steps. The damage spreading is shown in Fig. 1b.

In the binary non-directional case, an arrow appears in the damage pattern when the Boolean derivative equals one and no arrow otherwise. In the three-state directional case, the arrows are labelled according to the type of propagating defect. The polynomial at $\left[n(t = 3) \right]_{i=1}$ equals $\tau_{20}\tau_{02}\tau_{12}$. This indicates that there is a single defect path arriving at site $c_i = 1$, which consists of three different defects τ_{20}, τ_{02} and τ_{12}. When moving closer towards the center of the lattice, where the defect was introduced, the number of defect paths

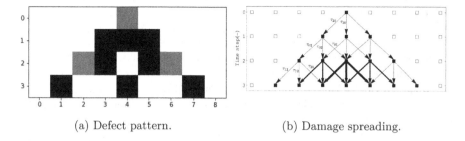

(a) Defect pattern.   (b) Damage spreading.

Fig. 1. The defect pattern generated by totalistic three-state rule 420. For simplicity, only the paths arriving at the two leftmost sites in the defect pattern in Fig. 1b have been labelled.

arriving at a certain site increases. The polynomial at $\left[\boldsymbol{n}(t = 3) \right]_{i=2}$ equals $\tau_{20}\tau_{02}\tau_{12} + \tau_{20}^2\tau_{02} + \tau_{20}^2\tau_{01}$. Now there are three terms in the polynomial, indicating that there are three defect paths arriving at site $c_i = 2$. Note that the sum of the exponents of each term in the polynomial equals the number of time steps.

3   Results and Discussion

3.1   Experimental Setup

Using the definition for directional Lyapunov profiles of three-state CAs, we will illustrate this approach for the case of some exemplary totalistic three-state rules. For each of these rules, the propagation of defects emerging from a single defect was tracked for 15 time steps in a one-dimensional system consisting of 30 sites. We restrict ourselves to random initial configurations and a single initial defect in the center of the lattice, though we should be aware that the Lyapunov profiles might depend on the initial configuration from which they are evolved in the sense that for some rules and initial configuration defects will die out by chance, whereas they will be able to propagate for other initial configurations. In order to yield a more clear visualization of the results, the discrete points which yield the Lyapunov profiles are connected by lines so as to yield continuous profiles.

For each of Wolfram's classes [12], a representative totalistic three-state rule is chosen and its space-time pattern, defect pattern and corresponding Lyapunov profiles are computed. Totalistic rules are chosen for which the steady-state behavior is reached after a single time step, as we want the finite-time Lyapunov profile to reflect the steady-state behavior instead of the transient phenomena. This avoids the need to simulate for long time periods. Computing Lyapunov profiles for rules with long transients is an objective of future work.

3.2 Class I

Class I behaviour is trivial. After a transient, the defect pattern vanishes for all class I rules and the Lyapunov exponents are zero everywhere. This means that any defect introduced in the initial configuration can only propagate over a small finite distance in the lattice, before the system settles on the same equilibrium state. This is true for all class I rules, not just the one-dimensional totalistic rules considered here [2].

3.3 Class II

After a transient, the defect pattern associated with Class II rules becomes non-expanding and periodic. Yet, it often strongly depends on the initial configuration. As the defect pattern is non-expanding, the Lyapunov exponents are non-zero only in certain regions as the defects can only propagate within certain limits. Additionally, the magnitude of the Lyapunov exponents associated with different kinds of defects varies considerably, depending on the type of defects that constitute the periodic section of the defect pattern. This is illustrated in Fig. 2, where the $1 \rightarrow 0$ defects make up an important part of the periodic section of the defect pattern. This is reflected in the corresponding Lyapunov profile. Additionally, it is clear that the Lyapunov profile is non-zero only in those sections of the lattice where the periodic part of the defect pattern persists

3.4 Class III

Class III rules yield defect patterns that are expanding, often at a maximal rate. This in turn yields Lyapunov profiles that are largely overlapping and non-zero everywhere, with their maximal value at the center of the lattice. This is illustrated for rule 420 in Fig. 3. In addition, Lyapunov profiles associated with class III rules are relatively independent of the initial configuration. Class III CA are typically associated with chaotic systems. The resulting space-time patterns are virtually random, with some class III rules finding use as random number generators. As such, class III rules yield defects that are uniformly and randomly distributed over the defect pattern, yielding the largely overlapping profiles. The

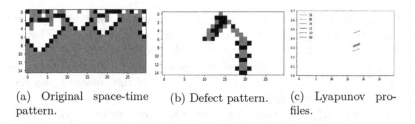

(a) Original space-time pattern.   (b) Defect pattern.   (c) Lyapunov profiles.

Fig. 2. The space-time pattern generated by Class II rule 126 along with the corresponding defect pattern and Lyapunov profiles.

maximum occurs near the center site as the number of paths reaching a certain site decreases when moving away from this center.

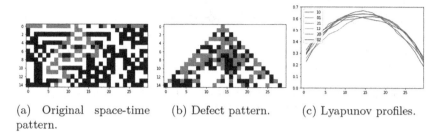

(a) Original space-time pattern.

(b) Defect pattern.

(c) Lyapunov profiles.

Fig. 3. The space-time pattern generated by class III rule 420 along with the corresponding defect pattern and Lyapunov profiles.

3.5   Class IV

Class IV is often seen as lying in the phase transition between Class II and III rules, which is reflected in their defect pattern and Lyapunov profiles: the defect pattern is irregularly expanding and highly dependent on the initial configuration. This yields Lyapunov profiles that are non-zero in an ever increasing part of the lattice, yet there are still zones where a sharp transition to zero occurs. Additionally, whereas the Lyapunov profiles of class III rules have a single maximum that usually occurs near the center of the lattice, class IV rules often lead to Lyapunov profiles exhibiting any number of local extrema, which is illustrated for class IV rule 114 in Fig. 4. This multitude of extrema reflects the irregular nature of the defect pattern that class IV rules tend to generate. In particular, a minimum in the profile can signify the splitting of the defect pattern into two separate clusters.

Figure 5 shows the space-time pattern, defect pattern and Lyapunov profiles for class IV rule 63. It is clear that $2 \rightarrow 0$ defects yield a Lyapunov profile that is significantly higher than those associated with any other type of defect. This highlights the tendency of some class IV rules to yield defect patterns dominated by a single kind of defect. In the large time limit, any given defect path will consist almost entirely of a single type of defect. This is similar to the theory of continuous dynamical systems, where the largest of the N Lyapunov exponents dominates the others and completely determines the type of chaotic behavior. These distinct features exhibited by the class IV profiles are very relevant, as they can be used to distinguish class III from class IV CA, which has been proven to otherwise be exceptionally difficult [11].

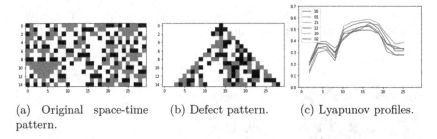

(a) Original space-time pattern.   (b) Defect pattern.   (c) Lyapunov profiles.

Fig. 4. The space-time pattern generated by class IV rule 114 along with the corresponding defect pattern and Lyapunov profiles.

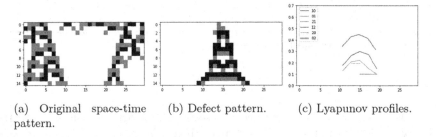

(a) Original space-time pattern.   (b) Defect pattern.   (c) Lyapunov profiles.

Fig. 5. The space-time pattern generated by class IV rule 63 along with the corresponding defect pattern and Lyapunov profiles.

4   Conclusions

In this paper, we have shown how the existing notion of Lyapunov exponents of two-state CA can be extended to three-state CA by specifying the kind of defect that can propagate in each entry of the Jacobian. Aside from permitting similar insights into CA dynamics for the three-state case as for the two-state case, this approach has the additional advantage of distinguishing between the directionality of the defects.

In both theoretical and practical scenarios, the most interesting CA are found in Wolfram's class IV. These CA also provide the most interesting Lyapunov profiles. In particular, they reveal that often a single kind of defect dominates the profile, which indicates that the CA responds to a perturbation in a very particular way, so as to provide a possible characterization of the specific CA. This is useful information to have when a CA is used as a computational model in a practical context. Additionally, the distinctive features the class IV profiles exhibit can be used to address the difficult task of distinguishing class III from class IV CA.

Our approach was illustrated for three-state CA, but is applicable to CA with any number of states, yet the required computing power increases drastically when the number of states increases and hence additional work will be needed to increase the efficiency of the methodology and computation.

References

1. Baetens, J.M., Gravner, J.: Introducing Lyapunov profiles of cellular automata. J. Cell. Autom. **13**, 267–286 (2015)
2. Bagnoli, F., Rechtman, R., Ruffo, S.: Damage spreading and Lyapunov exponents in cellular automata. Phys. Lett. A **172**(1), 34–38 (1992). https://doi.org/10. 1016/0375-9601(92)90185-O, http://www.sciencedirect.com/science/article/pii/ 037596019290185O
3. Bhattacharjee, K., Naskar, N., Roy, S., Das, S.: A survey of cellular automata: types, dynamics, non-uniformity and applications. Nat. Comput. **19**(2), 433–461 (2018). https://doi.org/10.1007/s11047-018-9696-8
4. Courbage, M., Kaminski, B.: Space-time directional Lyapunov exponents for cellular automata. J. Stat. Phys. **124** (2006). https://doi.org/10.1007/s10955-006-9172-1
5. Pfeifer, B., et al.: A cellular automaton framework for infectious disease spread simulation. Open Med. Inform. J. **2**, 70–81 (2008)
6. Reyes, L., Laroze, D.: Cellular automata for excitable media on a complex network: the effect of network disorder in the collective dynamics. Physica A **588**, 126552 (2021). https://doi.org/10.1016/j.physa.2021.126552
7. Shereshevsky, M.A.: Lyapunov exponents for one-dimensional cellular automata. J. Nonlinear Sci. **2**, 1–8 (1992). https://doi.org/10.1007/BF02429850
8. Tisseur, P.: Cellular automata and Lyapunov exponents. Nonlinearity **13**(5), 1547–1560 (2000). https://doi.org/10.1088/0951-7715/13/5/308
9. Vallejo, J., Sanjuán, M.: Predictability of Chaotic Dynamics: A Finite-time Lyapunov Exponents Approach. Springer, Cham (2019). https://doi.org/10.1007/978-3-030-28630-9
10. Vichniac, G.: Boolean derivatives on cellular automata. Physica D **45**(1–3), 63–74 (1990)
11. Vispoel, M., Daly, A.J., Baetens, J.M.: Progress, gaps and obstacles in the classification of cellular automata. Physica D **432**, 133074 (2022). https://doi.org/10. 1016/j.physd.2021.133074
12. Wolfram, S.: Universality and complexity in cellular automata. Physica D **10**, 37 (1984)
13. Wuensche, A.: Classifying cellular automata automatically: finding gliders, filtering, and relating space-time patterns, attractor basins, and the Z parameter. Complexity **4**, 47–66 (1999)

Modelling and Simulation of Physical Systems and Phenomena

Evolving Quantum Circuits to Implement Stochastic and Deterministic Cellular Automata Rules

Shailendra Bhandari[1,2,3](✉) [ID], Sebastian Overskott[1,2,3],
Ioannis Adamopoulos[1,2,3], Pedro G. Lind[1,2,3] [ID], Sergiy Denysov[1,3],
and Stefano Nichele[1,2,3,4,5] [ID]

[1] Department of Computer Science, OsloMet – Oslo Metropolitan University,
P.O. Box 4, St. Olavs Plass, 0130 Oslo, Norway
shailendra.vandari@gmail.com,
{s331402,s350141,pedrolin,sergiyde,stenic}@oslomet.no
[2] AI Lab – OsloMet Artificial Intelligence Lab, Pilestredet 52, 0166 Oslo, Norway
[3] NordSTAR – Nordic Center for Sustainable and Trustworthy AI Research,
Pilestredet 52, 0166 Oslo, Norway
[4] Department of Holistic Systems, Simula Metropolitan Center for Digital
Engineering, Pilestredet 52, 0166 Oslo, Norway
[5] Department of Computer Science and Communication, Østfold University College,
B R A Veien 4, 1757 Halden, Norway

Abstract. The aim of this work is to generate specific rules of deterministic and stochastic cellular automata (CA) using the set of five quantum gates, which is known to generate any quantum circuit. To build such quantum circuits, we use an evolutionary algorithm, based in mutations, which allows the optimization of quantum gate types and their connectivity. The fitness function of the evolutionary algorithm aims at minimizing the difference between the output of the quantum circuit and the CA rule. We also inspect the differences observed when changing the number of gates and the mutation rate. We benchmark our methods with stochastic as well as deterministic CA rules, and briefly discuss the possible extensions their quantum "cousins" may enable.

Keywords: Quantum circuits · Critical behavior · Evolutionary algorithms · Stochastic cellular automata

1 Scope and Motivation

Quantum computing and cellular automata are two important topics in modern computer science, often approached independently from each other. Cellular automata (CA) are classical discrete models for reproducing complex processes of extended systems of coupled elements, based in simple rules which map the present state of each element and its direct neighbors into the next state of each element. Quantum computing (QC) is a field in its infancy aiming at solving

B. Chopard et al. (Eds.): ACRI 2022, LNCS 13402, pp. 119–129, 2022.
https://doi.org/10.1007/978-3-031-14926-9_11

Fig. 1. Example of a quantum circuit [11]

the limitations of classical computation, when dealing with problems which in practice are not computable due to their complexity.

Underlying the difference between classical and quantum algorithms are their respective elementary components, the bit and qubit respectively. While bits can have only two possible states, 0 or 1, qubits can have an infinite number of possible states *if* their state is not measured. If it is, they will "collapse" to the classical pair of possibilities, 0 or 1, and one can know beforehand the probability to observe each one of these final measured states. The gates used to build quantum circuits are also different from the usual classical gates (e.g. NOT, AND, OR), since they can operate on qubits, and only after measurement, retrieve an on- or an off-state with a specific probability. Consequently, they may be good candidates for mimicking so-called stochastic CA, discrete models which define the CA rules with an associated probability. In this paper we introduce a framework to build specific quantum circuits, whose classical counterpart reproduces the behavior of a CA rule. We illustrate the framework for some specific deterministic and stochastic CA rules and argue that it can be, in principle, apply to any other rule.

Moreover, due to its particular features, beyond the common behavior of classic bits and digital gates, there is still no straightforward procedure to build the quantum circuit for one specific computation or algorithm using a minimum number of gates. In this paper we show how evolutionary algorithms can be useful to address this drawback to build optimal quantum circuits. Evolutionary algorithms (EA) are a group of heuristic algorithms that solves problems in a Darwinian way. In short, they start out with a widespread population of possible solution for a problem. The solutions in the population that yielded best results when tested against a target is used to create a new population: the next generation of solution. This process continues until a solution meets the target criteria, based in a so-called fitness function (FF) which plays the role of a cost function. We will focus on a sub-category of EA called genetic algorithms (GA) [1], which built upon the idea of the solution of the algorithm to be chromosomes, compose of genes [2]. In our case the chromosome represents a quantum circuit while a gene represents a quantum gate.

Finally, the framework also enables to explore new contexts of complex behavior. In particular, we focus in critical behavior. We introduce a quantum circuit, which when reduced to a purely classical architecture - with all its components being measured and therefore without superposing their states - retrieves the usual behavior of a critical CA. Having such circuit, and with the sufficiently large number of qubits, one is able to explore the outcome of an evolving critical

CA when "switching-off" the full monitoring of its qubits and leaving their states to superpose in time.

A quantum circuit involves a collection of one or more qubits which are initialized to state $|0\rangle$. Figure 1 shows an example of a quantum circuit involving one qubit. The gate which acts on the qubit is represented by a square and in our case, it is the X gate which flips the state of the qubit from 0 to 1. Each horizontal application of gates for a qubit is called a wire and each wire has a depth which is the number of gates applied on that qubit. In our example we have one wire with depth 1. The measurement symbol at the end is not a gate. It is the component collapsing the state of the qubit into either 0 or 1. The time progress in a quantum circuit goes from the left to the right. [11].

2   The Genetic Algorithm to Evolve Quantum Circuits

Genetic algorithm has been used to evolve quantum circuits with success earlier [3,4,6,8,10,12,14]. Lukac and Perkowski use the unitary matrix representation of the gates and the identity matrix for connections/wires. This way we can use Kronecker products (tensor products) and matrix products to calculate the complete circuit as a matrix. This also makes it possible to represent the FF as a matrix to calculate the error. As we see in [6] and [1] the quantum gates are genes in the algorithm. They never change the properties of the gates themselves, but move, swap, delete gates from the circuit as genetic operators. It is also a possibility to add new gates as a mutation. The gates have been encoded in several ways. Yabuki and Iba [14] encodes the gates with a letter set of four digits 0,1,2,3, and assign each gate a three-letter codon i.e. 231. Here the first letter describes type of gate, and the second and third indicate what qubit will be operated. By using a table we can look up the gate type and placement in the circuit. Here we will focus on one particular set of genes (quantum gates) and compare the results with two different fitness functions. We will use the following set of quantum gates: Hadamard, three Pauli gates (X, Y and Z), Cnot, Toffoli, swap, RZZ, and RXX (Fig. 2).

Initially, a certain number of chromosomes is assigned with the number of quantum gates per circuit, generating the initial number of chromosomes. Then, iteratively, the genetic algorithm evolves the current chromosomes into new ones, identifying in each generation the chromosome with highest fitness, which will be a parent for the next generation. At each evolution step (generation), when a new parent is generated, all chromosomes undergo a mutation process happens either by replacing a gates from the pool of gates in the chromosome with a randomly generated new one, or replacing the chromosome so as to generate four best parents. The mutation process is probabilistic and when the chromosomes get mutated, the four best chromosomes are left unchanged as "elites" the rest of the chromosomes are evolved with a probabilistic selection where each of the current circuit has a probability to become a parent that is proportional to its fitness. This evolution cycle continues throughout a certain prescribed number of generations.

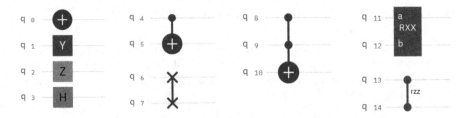

Fig. 2. An overview of quantum gates available to the algorithm: X-gate (q0), Y-gate (q1), Z-gate (q2), Hadamard gate (q3), CNOT (control: q4, target: q5), swap-gate (q6, q7), Toffoli-gate (control: q8 and q9; target: q10), RXX-gate (q11, q12), RZZ-gate (q13, q14).

To assess the performance of the quantum circuits we derive, we measure only the first qubit (q0) and consider two different fitness functions to compare the measured probability $Q(\omega)$ of an initial state ω, computed from the chromosome, and the corresponding desired probability $P(\omega)$. The first one is the sum of the absolute difference between each $P(\omega)$ and corresponding $Q(\omega)$:

$$F = \sum_{\omega \in \Omega} |P(\omega) - Q(\omega)|. \tag{1}$$

This gives a possible fitness value between 0 and 8. The second type of fitness function that is implemented is the Kullback-Leibler (KL) divergence, which measures the difference between two probability distributions and has been used in other works [5,7] as a fitness function as well:

$$D_{KL}(P||Q) = \sum_{\omega \in \Omega} P(\omega) log\Big(\frac{P(\omega)}{Q(\omega)}\Big). \tag{2}$$

In our case those distributions are discrete and each one of them has eight different values which are related to the eight different initial states of the three qubits. If the distributions completely match then both F and D_{KL} fitness functions are zero.

There are some difference between the sum of the absolute differences between the measured and the desired probabilities and the Kullback-Leibler divergence. While the former treats each probability as pure values, the latter considers deviations of higher probability with a stronger weight than low probability values.

In order to address our optimization problem, the performance of the proposed approach has been accessed by running the evolutionary algorithm on a simulator belonging to the IBM Q experience initiative (Qiskit)[1]. For more information about the module and instructions on how to use it, please visit the Github repository https://github.com/Overskott/Quevo. The project was created and done in python version 3.8 with Qiskit version 0.34.1 and scipy.special 1.7.1.

---

[1] https://qiskit.org.

Table 1. The deterministic and stochastic CAs considered in this paper. For the stochastic cases, the values indicate the probability of an update of value 1 for the middle cells in the triad-neighborhood. For the deterministic cases, the values indicate the exact update imposed.

Neighbors	Stoc. CAProb	Rule90	Rule110	Ran. Prob. 1	Ran. Prob. 2	Ran. Prob. 3
[0, 0, 0]	0.394221	0	0	0.6364	0.4778	0.1988
[0, 0, 1]	0.094721	1	1	0.6603	0.5604	0.4701
[0, 1, 0]	0.239492	0	1	0.5261	0.8528	0.9836
[0, 1, 1]	0.408455	1	1	0.1748	0.4818	0.7115
[1, 0, 0]	0	1	0	0.8820	0.3143	0.6616
[1, 0, 1]	0.730203	0	1	0.3371	0.3464	0.1218
[1, 1, 0]	0.915034	1	1	0.0340	0.0678	0.1328
[1, 1, 1]	1	0	0	0.4444	0.9124	0.7306

The code developed for this paper was done in python, and resulted in a python module called quantum_circuit_evolver. The module consists of three classes: `Chromosome`, `Generation` and `Circuit`. The `Chromosome`-class is responsible for handling the series of integers by storing them as a list. The class also handles the creation of random series, the list of angles needed by some of the gates, mutation of the series, and other list related functions. It takes a list of the desired gate types as a parameter on construction, and automatically creates the tables needed for parsing. The `Generation`-class stored a generation of chromosomes, the fitness associated with each, methods for running and retrieving fitness for two different fitness functions, and functions for printing. Last, the `Circuit`-class is handling the parsing from string and generating a Qiskit quantum circuit, the simulations of the circuit, measurements, and visualization of the circuit.

3   Three Different "Flavours" of Quantum Cellular Automata

The quantum CAs we derive will be based in the standard classical one dimensional CA, composed of cells with two possible states, 0 or 1 (Boolean CA), which are updated according to one out of 256 possible rules matching each one of the eight neighborhoods ([0, 0, 0], [0, 0, 1], [0, 1, 0], [0, 1, 1], [1, 0, 0], [1, 0, 1], [1, 1, 0] and [1, 1, 1]) to an update of the middle cell.

We will consider three different types of quantum CA. We will start with a stochastic *critical* CA and then illustrate the robustness of our framework with more general stochastic CA (random updates) and a few deterministic rules, namely rule 90 and 110 [13]. In all cases, the updates are shown in Table 1. We fix a maximum number of chromosomes $N_c = 20$, a maximum number of generations $N_g = 150$, and each simulation is repeated for $N_{ic} = 20$ initial conditions randomly chosen.

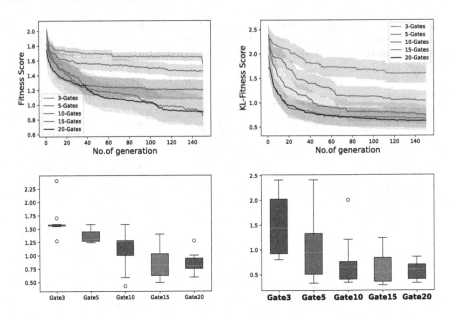

Fig. 3. (Top) The fitness scores as a function of the number of generations, for **different number of gates**. (Bottom) Number of gates vs. the best fitness scores. In each case we show the result for (left) the absolute sum of differences, Eq. (1), and (right) Kullback-Leibler divergence, Eq. (2). The fitness scores of each gates for the box plots are the best fitness scores per run and the fitness scores for the lower two plots are the average fitness scores of 20 runs.

3.1   The Quantum Cousin of a Stochastic Critical Cellular Automata

The authors in [9] have evolved a stochastic CA model in order to reach criticality which is a property of dynamical systems that gives them the possibility to do robust computations. For each triad-pattern a probability has been calculated through genetic algorithm for the central cell to have state 1. These probabilities are shown in Table 1, second column.

We start by considering the number of gates used, evolving quantum CAs with 3, 5, 10, 15 and 20 gates. The mutation probability is fixed to 10%.

Figure 3 shows the result for both fitness functions above. It is clear from the figure that the fitness score improves with increasing the number of gates until 15 gates and the gradual increase is seen for 20 gates. Therefore for experiment 2 and 3, the number of gates used is 15. Notice that the fitness score is optimum for 15 gates in the case of KL fitness function while the fitness score is optimum for 20 gates in the absolute difference of probabilities fitness function. Moreover, while the sum of absolute differences performs better for the cases with lowest number of gates, while KL fitness function is better suited when the number of gates increases.

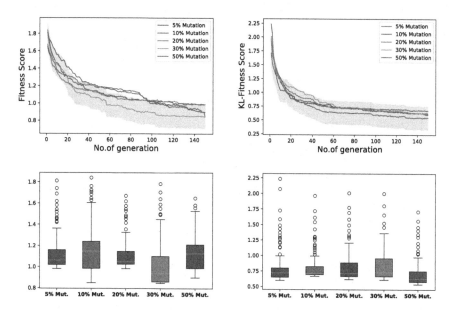

Fig. 4. (Top) The fitness scores as a function of the number of generations, for **different mutation rates**. (Bottom) Mutation rates vs. the best fitness scores. In each case we show the result for (left) the sum of absolute differences (Eq. (1)), and (right) the KL divergence. The fitness scores of each gates are the average fitness scores of 20 runs.

Next we explore how the fitness changes when changing the mutation probability. The goal is to test the impact of mutation over the fitness function at different number of generations. We fix the number of gates to 15 and select mutation probabilities of 5%, 10%, 20%, 30% and 50%.

Figure 4 (left) shows the comparison of the fitness scores with the number of generations at different percentage of mutation rate for the absolute difference of probabilities fitness function, while Fig. 4 (right) shows the comparison of the fitness scores with the number of generations at different percentage of mutation rate for KL-fitness function. In case of KL divergence fitness function we can see the gradual improvement in results with increase in percentage of the mutation rate, however similar conclusion cannot be drawn in other fitness score as the results are random.

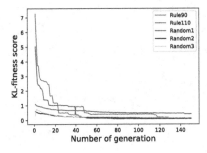 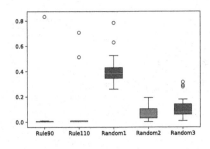

Fig. 5. (Left) Fitness scores for different sets of probabilities against the number of generations for KL-fitness function. (Right) Best fitness scores per runs for KL-fitness function for different sets of probabilities. The fitness scores of each gates are the average fitness scores of 20 runs.

3.2 The Two Other Flavours: Deterministic CA and Stochastic CA but Non-critical

We end our investigation applying the same framework to deterministic rules as well as to stochastic CAs which do not show critical behavior. Here, we fix the parameters with 15 gates and 10% mutation probability. The desired probabilities for Rule 90, and Rule 110 (the deterministic rule, so the probabilities of the 8 neighborhoods will be either 0 or 1), and 8 randomly generated probabilities with three repetitions are used as target probabilities. The target probabilities for each condition are shown in Table 1 and results are shown in Fig. 5. The fitness scores for the deterministic CA (Rule 90 and Rule 110) are very good as shown in figure Fig. 5 (left), therefore it is quite successful to run quantum circuit for deterministic CA. For the stochastic CA with randomly generated probabilities with three repetitions, the results are indeed promising, with best fitness scores 0.14 and 0.27 for Random2 and Random3. While the best fitness score for Random1 is 0.685 which is not bad either but needs further experiments to be able to tune the evolution to reduce the difference even further. Figure 5 (right), shows the fitness scores for the different sets of probabilities against the number of generation for two deterministic CA (Rule 90 and Rule 110) and the stochastic CA with randomly generated probabilities with three repetitions (Random1, Random2, and Random3).

Finally, we illustrate the quantum circuits generated with our algorithms. The circuit in Fig. 6 is the result of a run that scored much better than the average runs for critical stochastic CA. It shows a fitness score of 0.3404, using KL fitness function in Eq. (2).

Similarly, the circuit in Fig. 7, is the result of the deterministic CA Rule 90. It has a best fitness score of 0.000921, with 15 numbers of gates, 10% mutation probability and the KL fitness function.

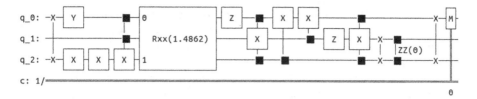

Fig. 6. Visualization of a circuit created by 15 number of gates, 10% mutation probability with KL fitness scores. The circuit is the best produced circuit with fitness score of 0.3404 for critical stochastic CA.

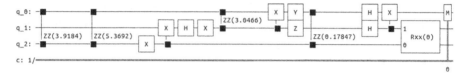

Fig. 7. Visualization of a circuit created by 15 number of gates, 10% mutation probability with KL fitness scores for deterministic CA (Rule 110). The circuit is the best produced circuit with fitness score 0.000921.

4   Discussion and Conclusions

In this paper we showed a simple framework to derive quantum circuits reproducing specific CA rules, using genetic algorithms. We showed that the framework is able to evolve quantum circuits towards several types of CA rules, ranging from deterministic rules to stochastic updates.

An important observation for all the experiments that we did, was that most of the times the fitness functions of the parents that would survive were not the same in the next generations. Their fitness functions in the next generations were sometimes actually worse than those they had in the previous generations. Mutated solutions with better fitness functions would then take their places as parents but still these functions could be worse than those that the first parents had originally. As a result, we did not see a gradually decrease of the value of the best fitness function from generation to generation as we expected or as we wanted but instead, that value had ups and downs. The above phenomenon happened for both types of fitness functions that we used and the reason is the following. Every quantum circuit which corresponds to a chromosome or a solution, is executed multiple times (1000 in our case) with a simulator. The outcome probabilities that are related with the fitness function can not be exactly the same each time we run the same circuit in another generation. If we execute the same circuit another 1000 times for example, we will have slight differences in our results. Even when we increased the number of shots in the simulator (10000 and then 50000) to stabilize the probability value, we did not succeed.

Another thing that we realized, was that for every set of desired probability outcomes, we can reach approximately a common fitness function score for all the mutation rates and for both types of fitness functions (Eqs. (1) and (2)), as it is illustrated in Fig. 4. One possible reason for this could be that the pool of potential solutions is not very big based on the number of gates that we used, although the types of these gates were enough to build almost any quantum circuit.

As far as concerned the two different fitness functions, we can not really say that one performs better than the other. One small observation though is that the diagrams which correspond to the KL fitness function have more gentle fluctuations and they reach their final range of values in the early generations.

Moreover, there are some parameters that could be further tested in future investigations, as well as considering additional genetic operators in evolutionary algorithms, e.g. crossover.

References

1. Giraldi, G.A., Portugal, R., Thess, R.N.: Genetic algorithms and quantum computation. CoRR cs.NE/0403003 (2004)
2. Holland, J.H.: Genetic algorithms. Scholarpedia **7**(12), 1482 (2012). Revision #128222
3. Lahoz-Beltra, R.: Quantum genetic algorithms for computer scientists. Computers **5**, 24 (2016)
4. Li, R., Alvarez-Rodriguez, U., Lamata, L., Solano, E.: Approximate quantum adders with genetic algorithms: an IBM quantum experience. Quantum Measure. Quantum Metrol. **4**, 1–7 (2016)
5. Lucas, S.M., Volz, V.: Tile pattern KL-divergence for analysing and evolving game levels. In: Proceedings of the Genetic and Evolutionary Computation Conference, July 2019
6. Lukac, M., Perkowski, M.: Evolving quantum circuits using genetic algorithm. In: Proceedings of 2002 NASA/DoD Conference on Evolvable Hardware, pp. 177–185 (2002)
7. Martín, F., Moreno, L., Garrido, S., Blanco, D.: Kullback-Leibler divergence-based differential evolution Markov chain filter for global localization of mobile robots. Sensors **15**(9), 23431–23458 (2015)
8. Mukherjee, D., Chakrabarti, A., Bhattacharjee, D., Choudhury, A.: Synthesis of quantum circuits using genetic algorithm. Full Paper Int. J. Recent Trends Eng. **2** (2009)
9. Pontes-Filho, S., et al.: A neuro-inspired general framework for the evolution of stochastic dynamical systems: cellular automata, random Boolean networks and echo state networks towards criticality. Cogn. Neurodyn. **14**(5), 657–674 (2020). https://doi.org/10.1007/s11571-020-09600-x
10. Rubinstein, B.: Evolving quantum circuits using genetic programming. In: Proceedings of the 2001 Congress on Evolutionary Computation, pp. 144–151 (2001)
11. Sutor, R.S.: Dancing with Qubits. Packt Publishing, Birmingham (2019)
12. Williams, C.P., Gray, A.G.: Automated design of quantum circuits. In: Williams, C.P. (ed.) QCQC 1998. LNCS, vol. 1509, pp. 113–125. Springer, Heidelberg (1999). https://doi.org/10.1007/3-540-49208-9_8

13. Wolfram, S.: Cellular automata as models of complexity. Nature (London) **311**(5985), 419–424 (1984)
14. Yabuki, T.Y.: Genetic algorithms for quantum circuit design-evolving a simpler teleportation circuit-. In: In Late Breaking Papers at the 2000 Genetic and Evolutionary Computation Conference, pp. 421–425. Morgan Kauffman Publishers (2000)

Double Population Lattice Boltzmann Model for Magneto-Hydrodynamic Blood Flow in Stenotic Artery

Ikram Cherkaoui🆔, Soufiene Bettaibi$^{(\boxtimes)}$🆔, and Abdelwahed Barkaoui🆔

Laboratoire des Energies Renouvelable et Matériaux Avancés,
Université Internationale de Rabat (UIR), Rocade Rabat-Salé, 11100 Rabat, Morocco
Bettaibisoufiene@gmail.com, soufiene.bettaibi@uir.ac.ma

Abstract. Atherosclerosis, which refers to a reduction in vessels diameter due to fatty deposits, is considered as the main cause of heart attacks, strokes, and peripheral vascular disease. The malfunctioning of cardiovascular system is mainly related to haemodynamics. However, the magnetic properties of blood are of great interest in haemodynamics. In this paper, a double population lattice Boltzmann model is suggested to investigate magnetohydrodynamic blood flow in stenotic artery. Blood is considered as a homogeneous fluid with magnetic properties. The rheological behavior of blood is presented by Carreau-Yasuda model. Blood flow is considered as incompressible and laminar. The vessel walls are assumed to be rigid. The proposed lattice Boltzmann model is found to be accurate, stable and effective. Findings are presented in terms of streamlines, velocity and wall shear stress profiles, based on a variety of parameters, including Reynolds and Hartmann number. The results show that the increase in magnetic intensity causes a considerable decrease in velocity and recirculation zones.

Keywords: Lattice Boltzmann approach · Atherosclerosis · Blood flow · Magneto-hydrodynamic

1 Introduction

The development of blood vessels pathologies such as stenosis, atherosclerosis and spasm disturb blood flow and lead to a malfunctioning of many organs. In order to detect the vessels diseases, a detailed knowledge of blood flow remains a necessity. The study of blood flow is the subject of different numerical methods. However, the traditional conventional computational fluid dynamics method (CFD) are limited and the implementation of boundary conditions still more complicated for complex geometries [1]. In addition, the resolution of mathematical equations used to present the system is complicated. Given the complexity of these equations, the analytical solutions of Navier-stokes equations are generally nonexistent and only an approximated numerical solution is existing. This justifies, the considerable development of the techniques and methods of

© The Author(s), under exclusive license to Springer Nature Switzerland AG 2022
B. Chopard et al. (Eds.): ACRI 2022, LNCS 13402, pp. 130–141, 2022.
https://doi.org/10.1007/978-3-031-14926-9_12

numerical computation in fluid mechanics (CFD) during these last decades. The continuous evolution of numerical methods is related to the computer resources development, what allows the numerical resolution of the equations governing fluid mechanics and heat transfer with great precision and for a wide range of complex geometries. Unlike numerical simulation methods based on the resolution of partial differential equations linking the macroscopic properties of fluids, the lattice gas automata (LGA) method makes it possible to find macroscopic variables such as velocity, pressure or pressure fields and temperature, by simulating the interactions between molecules. Lattice Boltzmann Method (LBM), a numerical method evolving from LGA, has gained popularity in the last few years. It has been used for simulating and modeling different systems including immiscible fluids [2], multiphase flows [3], heat transfer problems [4–7], isotropic turbulence [8] and porous media [9]. It has proven its effectiveness in the field of conventional fluid flows, particularly in complex geometries and porous media. It has attracted the attention of researchers for the simulation of flows in different applications. Higuera and Jimenez [10] proposed an important simplification in LBM by approximating the collision operator in Lattice Boltzmann Equation with a linearized one that assumes that the distribution is close to the equilibrium state. The success of lattice Boltzmann method is related, in large part, to the introduction of the Bhatnagar-Gross-Krook (BGK) collision operator characterized by its simplicity and ease of implementation. Bhatnagar-Gross-Krook (BGK) collision model is a simple linearized collision operator, introduced by Koelman [11] and Chen et al. [12]. The macroscopic Navier-Stokes equations are recovered by the Lattice BGK model through a Chapman-Enskog analysis [13]. The lattice Boltzmann method describes fluids in a mesoscopic scale and provides stable and efficient numerical calculations for the fluids macroscopic behavior [14–16]. The problem of taking into account the initial and boundary conditions was the subject of particular attention by the initiators of the LBM method. Stability and numerical precision are closely related to the nature of the boundary conditions. The lattice Boltzmann approach does not necessitate the resolution of a global system of equations, just information from surrounding nodes is required to describe variables evolution. Because of the nature of the explicit computation with locality, the lattice Boltzmann method is a cost-effective solution to communication between processors and hence excellent for parallel computation.

In this paper, we propose an efficient and accurate lattice Boltzmann model for simulating magnetohydrodynamic blood flow in stenotic arteries. The unique feature of this modelization is that both velocity and magnetic fields are solved using the lattice Boltzmann technique, which allows to investigate the influence of strong magnetic field intensities on blood flow.

2 Mathematical Model

2.1 Problem Description

In this study, blood is considered as a homogeneous magnetic bio-fluid, incompressible and non-Newtonian with density $\rho = 1060\,\text{kg/m}^3$. The Vessel walls are assumed to be rigid and blood flow is considered laminar and steady. The diameter of the artery is D = 6 mm. An idealized geometry of stenosis is considered (Fig. 1) in this study.

Fig. 1. Stenosis geometry

Stenosis refers to a reduction in the vessel section due to a deposition of fatty components on the walls. The geometry of the wall with the presence of stenosis is given by: $y(x) = D - h \sin\left[\frac{\pi(x-d)}{l}\right]$ where D is the diameter of health artery, h the width of the restricted zone, d the length of the inlet region and l the length of the restricted zone. The severity of the reduction zone (degree of stenosis DOS) can be calculated by the following equation: $DOS(\%) = (1 - \frac{A_s}{A}) \times 100$ where A_s is the restricted zone section and A is the section of healthy artery.

2.2 Equations

Taking into consideration the presented hypothesis, the 2-D incompressible, unsteady flow of blood as an electrically conductive fluid is described by Navier–Stokes equations, with an additional term presenting Lorentz force are written as:

$$\frac{\partial u}{\partial t} + (u.\nabla)u = -\frac{\nabla p}{\rho} + \nu \Delta u + \frac{\mathbf{j} \times \mathbf{B}}{\rho} + Q \tag{1}$$

$$\nabla.u = 0 \tag{2}$$

where ν is the fluid kinematic viscosity, ρ is the density, p is the pressure, $u = [u_x, u_y]$ the velocity, $\mathbf{B} = [B_x, B_y]$ the magnetic field, $\mathbf{j} = \nabla \times \mathbf{B}$ and $\mathbf{Q} = [Q_x, Q_y]$ the external body force vectors.

This research investigates the 2-dimensional, laminar and incompressible magnetohydrodynamic blood flow through a restricted vessel. The governing equations, including the impact of viscosity and energy dissipation due to the presence of magnetic field are given by the following equation:

$$\frac{\partial u_x}{\partial x} + \frac{\partial u_y}{\partial y} = 0 \tag{3}$$

$$\rho(u_x\frac{\partial u_x}{\partial x} + u_y\frac{\partial u_x}{\partial y}) = -\frac{\partial p}{\partial x} + \mu(\frac{\partial^2 u_x}{\partial x^2} + \frac{\partial^2 u_x}{\partial y^2}) - \sigma B_0^2 u_x \tag{4}$$

$$\rho(u_x\frac{\partial u_y}{\partial x} + u_y\frac{\partial u_y}{\partial y}) = -\frac{\partial p}{\partial x} + \mu(\frac{\partial^2 u_y}{\partial x^2} + \frac{\partial^2 u_y}{\partial y^2}) \tag{5}$$

The term $\sigma B_0^2 u_x$ in Eq. 4 depicts the magnetic body force ($\mathbf{j} \times \mathbf{B}$) per volume. Where $B = [B_x, B_0]$ and σ is the electrical conductivity of blood.

Carreau-Yasuda Model

Human blood is a composed fluid, containing mainly plasma and blood cells. The plasma acts like a Newtonian fluid, its viscosity depends on the concentration of plasma proteins [17], whereas the whole blood has a non-Newtonian behavior. Many models have been developed in order to predicts the rheological behavior. Carreau-Yasuda model is one of the simplest and accurate models used in blood modeling. The viscosity depends on shear rate and modelled by the Carreau-Yasuda model [18] as following:

$$\mu(\dot\gamma) = \mu_\infty + (\mu_0 - \mu_\infty) + (1 + (\lambda\dot\gamma)^\alpha)^{\frac{n-1}{\alpha}} \tag{6}$$

where μ is the viscosity, $\dot\gamma$ is the shear rate, $\mu_\infty = 0.0035\,Pa.s$ is the viscosity at infinite shear rate, $\mu_0 = 0.16\,Pa.s$ is the viscosity at the absence shear-rate, and $\lambda = 8.2$, $\alpha = 0.64$, and $n = 0.2128$ are material coefficients. The shear rate is given by:

$$\dot\gamma = 2\sqrt{D_{\mathrm{II}}} \tag{7}$$

where D_{II} is the second invariant of the strain rate tensor, given by:

$$D_{\mathrm{II}} = \sum_{\alpha,\beta=1}^{l} S_{\alpha\beta}S_{\alpha\beta} \tag{8}$$

where $l = 2$ for a two-dimensional model.

For incompressible fluids, the stress tensor is written as:

$$\sigma_{\alpha\beta} = -p\delta_{\alpha\beta} + 2\mu S_{\alpha\beta} \tag{9}$$

where $\delta_{\alpha\beta}$ is the Kronecker delta and $S_{\alpha\beta}$ is the strain rate tensor, written as: $S_{\alpha\beta} = \frac{1}{2}(\nabla_\beta u_\alpha + \nabla_\alpha u_\beta)$

3   Numerical Model

3.1   Lattice Boltzmann Method with Single Relaxation Time (LBM-SRT)

Solving two linked lattice Boltzmann equations can be used to solve magnetohydrodynamic equations. The first equation covers fluid dynamics by forecasting the development of the particle distribution function f_i, whereas the second equation incorporates a vector-valued function g_i that represents the evolution of the magnetic field. The two equations are discretized in a D2Q9 space (Fig. 2).

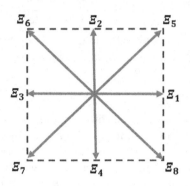

Fig. 2. D_2Q_9 model

The lattice Boltzmann approach (LBM) with single relaxation time, which is based on the Bhatnagar-Gross-Krook (BGK) approximation, is used to forecast the development of both fluid dynamics and magnetic fields. The fluid in the lattice Boltzmann approach is defined by a particle distribution function that develops in discrete space and time. As a result, the lattice Boltzmann equation is stated as:

$$f_i \left(\mathbf{x} + \Xi_i \delta t, t + \delta t \right) - f_i \left(\mathbf{x}, t \right) = C_i \left(f \right) \tag{10}$$

where C_i is the collision operator, presenting the change in particles distribution after collision step. The lattice Bhatnagar-Gross-Krook (BGK) equation can be written as:

$$f_i \left(\mathbf{x} + \Xi_i \delta t, t + \delta t \right) - f_i \left(\mathbf{x}, t \right) = -\frac{1}{\tau} \left[f_i \left(\mathbf{x}, t \right) - f_i^{eq} \left(\mathbf{x}, t \right) \right] \tag{11}$$

where τ is the relaxation parameter, related to viscosity by the following: $\tau = \left(\frac{\nu}{c_s^2} + 0.5 \right)$ with c_s is the lattice speed, given by $c_s = \frac{\delta x}{\sqrt{3}\delta t}$. δx and δt are the lattice width and time step respectively, chosen as $\delta x = \delta t = 1$ and $c = \frac{\delta x}{\delta t}$. f_i^{eq} is the equilibrium distribution function, which depends on the local fluid velocity and density. The equilibrium distribution function is given by:

$$f_i^{eq} = w_i \rho \left[1 + \frac{3 \Xi_i . \mathbf{u}}{c^2} + \frac{9 \left(\Xi_i . \mathbf{u} \right)^2}{2c^4} - \frac{3 \mathbf{u} . \mathbf{u}}{2c^2} \right] \qquad i = 0 \rightarrow 8 \tag{12}$$

In the presence of external magnetic field, the equilibrium distribution function includes an additional term presenting the effect of magnetic field intensity on particles distribution. The equilibrium distribution function becomes:

$$f_i^{eq} = w_i \rho \left[1 + \frac{\mathbf{\Xi_i} . \mathbf{u}}{c_s^2} + \frac{(\mathbf{\Xi_i} . \mathbf{u})^2}{2c_s^4} - \frac{\mathbf{u} . \mathbf{u}}{2c_s^2} \right] + \frac{\lambda_i}{2c_s^4} \left[\frac{1}{2} | \mathbf{\Xi_i} |^2 | \mathbf{b} |^2 - (\mathbf{\Xi_i} . \mathbf{b})^2 \right] \quad (13)$$

where w_i and λ_i are the weighting factors defined in D_2Q_9 as following: $w_i = \lambda_i = \frac{4}{9}$ for $i = 0$, $w_i = \lambda_i = \frac{1}{9}$ for $i = 1, 2, 3, 4$ and $w_i = \lambda_i = \frac{1}{36}$ for $i = 5, 6, 7, 8$.

$$\begin{cases} \mathbf{\Xi_i} = (0,0) & i = 0 \\ \mathbf{\Xi_i} = \left(\cos \left[(i-1) \frac{\pi}{2} \right], \sin \left[(i-1) \frac{\pi}{2} \right] \right) c & i = 1, 2, 3, 4 \\ \mathbf{\Xi_i} = \left(\cos \left[(2i-9) \frac{\pi}{4} \right], \sin \left[(2i-9) \frac{\pi}{4} \right] \right) c\sqrt{2} & i = 5, 6, 7, 8 \end{cases} \quad (14)$$

The magnetic field evolution is described by the following lattice Boltzmann equation:

$$g_i \left(\mathbf{x} + \mathbf{\Xi_i} \delta t, t + \delta t \right) - g_i \left(\mathbf{x}, t \right) = -\frac{1}{\tau_m} \left[g_i \left(\mathbf{x}, t \right) - g_i^{eq} \left(\mathbf{x}, t \right) \right] \quad (15)$$

where τ_m is the magnetic relaxation parameter, related to magnetic resistivity η by: $\tau_m = \left(\frac{\eta}{c_s^2} + 0.5 \right)$. In 2-dimensional space, Eq. 15 is written as following:

$$g_{ix} \left(\mathbf{x} + \mathbf{\Xi_i} \delta t, t + \delta t \right) - g_{ix} \left(\mathbf{x}, t \right) = -\frac{1}{\tau_m} \left[g_{ix} \left(\mathbf{x}, t \right) - g_{ix}^{eq} \left(\mathbf{x}, t \right) \right] \quad (16)$$

$$g_{iy} \left(\mathbf{x} + \mathbf{\Xi_i} \delta t, t + \delta t \right) - g_{iy} \left(\mathbf{x}, t \right) = -\frac{1}{\tau_m} \left[g_{iy} \left(\mathbf{x}, t \right) - g_{iy}^{eq} \left(\mathbf{x}, t \right) \right] \quad (17)$$

The coupling between hydrodynamics and magnetic field takes place in the equilibrium functions:

$$g_{ix}^{eq} = \lambda_i \left[b_x + \frac{\Xi_{iy}}{c_s^2} \left(u_y b_x - u_x b_y \right) \right] \quad (18)$$

$$g_{iy}^{eq} = \lambda_i \left[b_y + \frac{\Xi_{ix}}{c_s^2} \left(u_x b_y - u_y b_x \right) \right] \quad (19)$$

In order to reproduce Navier-Stokes Equations, the following identities must hold:

$$\rho = \sum_{i=0}^{8} f_i \quad (20)$$

$$\rho \mathbf{u} = \sum_{i=0}^{8} f_i \mathbf{\Xi_i} \quad (21)$$

Unlike the other simulation methods that solve Poisson's equation to compute pressure, the pressure p can be directly computed from the equation of state $p = \rho c_s^2$.

The macroscopic magnetic properties are given by:

$$b_x = \sum_{i=0}^{8} g_{ix} \tag{22}$$

$$b_y = \sum_{i=0}^{8} g_{iy} \tag{23}$$

3.2 Boundary Conditions

The problem of taking into account the initial and boundary conditions was the subject of particular attention by the initiators of the lattice Boltzmann method. Stability and numerical precision are closely related to the nature of the boundary conditions. In order to simulate blood flow in stenotic artery in the presence of magnetic field, we implement the Zou-He boundary condition in the inlet and the Bounce back boundary condition in the walls for both velocity and magnetic field (Fig. 3).

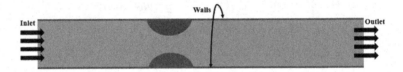

Fig. 3. Boundary conditions

Zou-He Boundary Condition. The Zou-He boundary condition is used to apply certain flux condition in the inlet. The velocity at the inlet is given by the profile of poiseuille:

$$\begin{cases} u_x(y) = 4u_{max} \left(\frac{y}{D} - \frac{y^2}{D^2} \right) \\ \qquad u_y = 0 \end{cases} \tag{24}$$

After streaming, the unknown density and distribution functions f_1, f_5, f_8 at the inlet are given by:

$$\begin{aligned} \rho &= \tfrac{1}{1-u_x} \left[f_0 + f_2 + f_4 + 2(f_3 + f_6 + f_7) \right], \\ f_1 &= f_3 + \tfrac{2}{3}\rho u_x, \\ f_5 &= f_7 - \tfrac{1}{2}(f_2 - f_4) + \tfrac{1}{2}\rho u_y + \tfrac{1}{6}\rho u_x, \\ f_8 &= f_6 + \tfrac{1}{2}(f_2 - f_4) - \tfrac{1}{2}\rho u_y + \tfrac{1}{6}\rho u_x. \end{aligned} \tag{25}$$

3.3   Bounce Back

In the walls, the mid way bounce back boundary condition is applied. This boundary condition is equivalent to no-slip boundary condition, which means that the velocity is zero in the walls. The wall is placed halfway between a wall grid point and a fluid grid point. The bounce back boundary condition assumes that particles hitting the wall disperse back to the fluid following their entering path (Fig. 4).

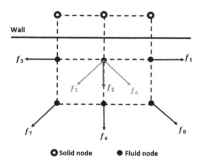

Fig. 4. Mid-way bounce back boundary condition

The unknown distribution functions at the wall are given by:

$$f_5(x, y, t) = f_7(x, y, t)$$
$$f_2(x, y, t) = f_4(x, y, t) \tag{26}$$
$$f_6(x, y, t) = f_8(x, y, t)$$

4   Model Validation

The results given by the suggested lattice Boltzmann model for hemodynamic are compared with in vivo measurements conducted by H. Park et al. [19] in the case of a stenosed aorta with a stenosis degree of 34%. The in vivo measurements were performed by surgically attaching a stenotic clip to a live rat model. The hemodynamic information are obtained by using X-ray PIV method. Figure 5 shows a comparison of velocity field in the stenotic aorta. It is shown that velocity increases considerably in the stenotic section reaching its maximum value of 8 mm/s in both numerical and experimental results. The results found by lattice Boltzmann model are in good agreement with in vivo measurements. It can be concluded that the proposed lattice Boltzmann model is accurate and effective in the treatment of blood flow in stenosed vessels.

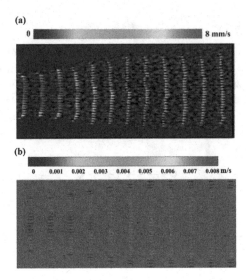

Fig. 5. Comparison of velocity field of in vivo measurement (a) and lattice Boltzmann model (b)

5   Results and Discussion

The aim of this study is to investigate the impact of imposed external magnetic field on blood flow characteristics, mainly velocity and wall shear stress (WSS), in a stenotic artery. The numerical simulations have been carried out for a Reynolds number Re = 360 and various Hartmann numbers Ha = 0, Ha = 5, Ha = 10, Ha = 15 and Ha = 20. The Obtained results of blood flow simulations, indicate that for a fixed stenosis degree (50% in this case), the velocity decreases due to the increasing magnetic field intensity.

Figure 6 and Fig. 7 show the effect of various magnetic field intensities on velocity profiles and recirculation zones in the downstream region of an artery with a 50% stenosis degree. It is apparent that increasing the magnetic field lowers the recirculation zone, resulting in a reduction in hydrodynamic stresses in this area. For Ha = 20, velocity at the stenotic section reduces by approximately 80%, and recirculation zones vanish. This decrease in velocity is produced by RBC aggregation, which increases when blood is exposed to a magnetic field. Our findings are consistent with those reported in the literature by Ilyani et al. [20] who studied the magnetohydrodynamic (MHD) effects on blood flow and discovered that a magnetic field decreases blood flow rate. In their method, a term containing Lorentz force is introduced to Navier-Stokes equations, resulting in a magnetic field with just one conceivable direction. In contrast, in our model, each particle is connected with a vector with nine possible directions, describing the evolution of magnetic field.

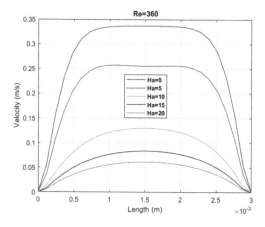

Fig. 6. Velocity profiles at the restricted zone for Re = 360 and Ha = 0, 5, 10, 15 and 20

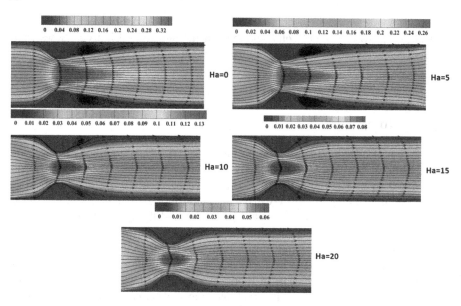

Fig. 7. Velocity streamlines for Re = 360 and Ha = 0, 5, 10, 15 and 20

The WSS is one of the most critical hemodynamic variables in cardiovascular diseases, it has a major impact on stenosis pregression. Figure 8 presents the effect of an external magnetic field on WSS in a stenosed artery for various values of Hartmann number. It is shown that the wall shear stress reaches its maximum at the restricted zone, this is caused by the reduction in diameter in that region. In the stenotic section, the non-Newtonian behavior of blood is more

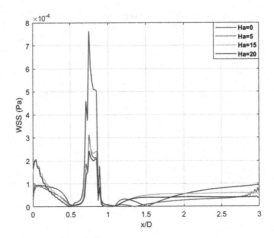

Fig. 8. Wall shear stress (WSS) for Re = 360 and Ha = 0, 5, 15 and 20

noticeable due to red blood cells aggregation in that zone. Figure 8 shows that the WSS in the stenotic region is reduced considerably by applying an external magnetic field. It is found that the WSS decreases by increasing the magnetic field intensity.

6 Conclusion

A simulation of 2-D steady and laminar magnetohydrodynamic blood flow is conducted using a double population lattice Boltzmann model. The blood vessels are assumed to be rigid and blood is considered as non-Newtonian and its rheological behavior is modelled by Carreau-Yasuda model. The effect of magnetic field intensity on blood flow is investigated. The findings show the effectiveness of the proposed Lattice Boltzmann model to study magnetohydrodynamic blood flow problem. In the other hand, it is found that the velocity profiles, recirculation zones and WSS decrease by increasing the magnetic field strength. Which can have interesting application in modulating blood flow rate during medical surgeries and in the treatment of hypertension and other cardiovascular diseases.

References

1. Luo, L.-S., Krafczyk, M., Shyy, W.: Lattice Boltzmann method for computational fluid dynamics. Encycl. Aerosp. Eng. **56**, 651–660 (2010)
2. Gunstensen, A.K., Rothman, D.H.: Lattice Boltzmann model of immiscible fluids. Phys. Rev. A **43**(8), 4320 (1991)
3. Grunau, D., Chen, S., Eggert, K.: A lattice Boltzmann model for multiphase fluid flows. Phys. Fluids A **5**(10), 2557–2562 (1993)
4. Bettaibi, S., Kuznik, F., Sediki, E.: Hybrid lattice Boltzmann finite difference simulation of mixed convection flows in a lid driven square cavity. Phys. Lett. A **378**, 2429–2435 (2014)

5. Bettaibi, S., Sediki, E., Kuznik, F., Succi, S.: Lattice Boltzmann simulation of mixed convection heat transfer in a driven cavity with non-uniform heating of the bottom wall. Commun. Theor. Phys. **63**(1), 91 (2015)
6. Bettaibi, S., Kuznik, F.; Sediki, E.: Hybrid LBM-MRT model coupled with finite difference method for double diffusive mixed convection in rectangular enclosure with insulated moving lid. Phys. A: Stat. Mech. Appl. **444**, 311–326 (2016)
7. Bettaibi, S., Kuznik, F., Sediki, E., Succi, S.: Numerical study of thermal diffusion and diffusion thermo effects in a differentially heated and salted driven cavity using MRT-lattice Boltzmann finite difference model. Int. J. Appl. Mech. **13**(04), 2150049 (2021)
8. Chen, S., et al.: Lattice Boltzmann computational fluid dynamics in three dimensions. J. Stat. Phys. **68**(3), 379–400 (1992)
9. Lallemand, P., Luo, L.-S.: Theory of the lattice Boltzmann method: dispersion, dissipation, isotropy, Galilean invariance, and stability. Phys. Rev. E **61**(6), 6546 (2000)
10. Higuera, F.J., Jiménez, J.: Boltzmann approach to lattice gas simulations. EPL (Europhys. Lett.) **9**(7), 663 (1989)
11. Koelman, J.M.V.A.: A simple lattice Boltzmann scheme for Navier-Stokes fluid flow. EPL (Europhys. Lett.) **15**(6), 603 (1991)
12. Chen, S., et al.: Lattice Boltzmann model for simulation of magnetohydrodynamics. Phys. Rev. Lett. **67**(27), 3776 (1991)
13. Shu, C., Peng, Y., Chew, Y.T.: Simulation of natural convection in a square cavity by Taylor series expansion-and least squares-based lattice Boltzmann method. Int. J. Mod. Phys. C **13**(10), 1399–1414 (2002)
14. Bettaibi, S., Jellouli, O.: Double diffusive mixed convection with thermodiffusion effect in a driven cavity by lattice Boltzmann method. LNTCS **12599**, 209–221 (2021)
15. Cherkaoui, I., Bettaibi, S., Barkaoui, A., Kuznik, F.: Magnetohydrodynamic blood flow study in stenotic coronary artery using lattice Boltzmann method. Comput. Methods Programs Biomed. **221**, 106850 (2022)
16. Mhamdi, B., Bettaibi, S., Jellouli, O., Chafra, M.: MRT-lattice Boltzmann hybrid model for the double diffusive mixed convection with thermodiffusion effect. Nat. Comput. 1–14 (2022). https://doi.org/10.1007/s11047-022-09884-4
17. Alexander, D.E.: Biological materials blur boundaries. Nat. Mach. 99–120 (2017). https://doi.org/10.1016/B978-0-12-804404-9.00004-9
18. Abraham, F., Behr, M., Heinkenschloss, M.: Shape optimisation in steady blood flow: a numerical study of non-Newtonian effects. Comput. Methods Biomech. Biomed. Eng. **8**(2), 127–137 (2005)
19. Park, H., Park, J.H., Lee, S.J.: In vivo measurement of hemodynamic information in stenosed rat blood vessels using X-ray PIV. Sci. Rep. **6**(1), 1–8 (2016)
20. Ilyani, A., Norsarahaida, A., Tasawar, H.: Magnetohydro-dynamic effects on blood flow through an irregular stenosis. Int. J. Numer. Methods Fluids **67**(11), 1624–1636 (2011)

Four State Deterministic Cellular Automaton Rule Emulating Random Diffusion

Henryk Fukś[(✉)] [iD]

Department of Mathematics and Statistics, Brock University,
St. Catharines, ON, Canada
hfuks@brocku.ca

Abstract. We show how to construct a deterministic nearest-neighbour cellular automaton (CA) with four states which emulates diffusion on a one-dimensional lattice. The pseudo-random numbers needed for directing random walkers in the diffusion process are generated with the help of rule 30. This CA produces density profiles which agree very well with solutions of the diffusion equation, and we discuss this agreement for two different boundary and initial conditions. We also show how our construction can be generalized to higher dimensions.

Keywords: Cellular automata · Diffusion · Random walk

1 Introduction

Modeling of diffusion processes with cellular automata (CA) is almost as old as the field of cellular automata itself. Lattice gas automata models [7] can simulate diffusion of real gas [4] very realistically and they were extensively studied in the last several decades, thus abundant literature of the subject exists, including monographs and textbooks [5,11,13,16]. Various models of diffusion using lattice gases were investigated in recent years, for example [1,9,10]

Lattice gas automata are relatively complicated compared to "classical" CA. Even in the simplest HPP model [7] there are up to four particles per lattice site and each particle is characterized by one of the four allowed velocity vectors. Moreover, the update step consists of two substeps, movement of particles in the direction of the velocity vector followed by the collisions step when the directions of velocity vectors of some particles are changed. In more advanced models, such as, for example, reactive lattice gas automata [2,15], there are three substeps, namely interaction, randomization and propagation. In the randomization substep the call to a pseudo-random generator is required for each lattice node.

In contrast to the above, in regular CA there are no velocity vectors attached to particles, and the update is done in a single time step with no need of substeps. The lattice sites change their state simultaneously at each time step according to a specified local rule which is purely deterministic, thus there is no need to call a random number generator.

© The Author(s), under exclusive license to Springer Nature Switzerland AG 2022
B. Chopard et al. (Eds.): ACRI 2022, LNCS 13402, pp. 142–152, 2022.
https://doi.org/10.1007/978-3-031-14926-9_13

We argue that for some applications it would be advantageous to have such a simple deterministic nearest-neighbour cellular automaton mimicking diffusion process, so that it could be used as a building block for various "complexity engineering" tasks. For example, it could be used to constructs solutions of classification problems in which diffusive spreading of agents is required, like in recently proposed "diffusive" solution of density classification problem [6].

What we would like to discuss in this paper, therefore, is a model of diffusion which is not based on lattice gas automata but rather on "classical" cellular automata. It is a model of an assembly of random walkers which perform random walk on a lattice following exclusion principle, that is, one lattice site can be occupied by only one walker at a time.

2   Construction of the Rule

Consider one dimensional lattice with lattice sites being either empty (state 0) or occupied by a single particle (state 1). All particles simultaneously and independently of each other decide whether to move to the left or to the right, with the same probability 0.5 in either direction. We then simultaneously move every particle to the desired position if it is empty, otherwise the particle stays in the same place. If two particles want to move to the same empty spot, only one of them, randomly selected, is allowed to do so. This process, which constitutes a single time step, is then repeated for as many time steps as desired.

In order to describe the process more formally, let us denote by s_i the state of the lattice site i, and let X_i denote binary random variable attached to site i. All variables X_i should be independent and identically distributed such that $Pr(X_i = 0) = Pr(X_i = 1) = 1/2$. We give the following interpretation to values of random variables X_i. If $s_i = 1$, then $X_i = 1$ ($X_i = 0$) means that movement of the particle from site i to the right (left) is allowed. If $s_i = 0$, then $X_i = 1$ ($X_i = 0$) means that arrival from the right (left) of site i is allowed. If movement or arrival is not allowed, the particle does not move. With this notation, the state of the site i at the next time step, denoted by s'_i, can be expressed as follows.

$$s'_i = s_i - \underbrace{s_i X_i (1 - s_{i+1})(1 - X_{i+1})}_{move\ to\ the\ right} - \underbrace{s_i (1 - X_i)(1 - s_{i-1}) X_{i-1}}_{move\ to\ the\ left}$$
$$+ \underbrace{(1 - s_i)(1 - X_i) s_{i-1} X_{i-1}}_{arrive\ from\ the\ left} + \underbrace{(1 - s_i) X_i s_{i+1}(1 - X_{i+1})}_{arrive\ from\ the\ right} \tag{1}$$

The above equation can be simplified,

$$s'_i = s_i + X_i X_{i-1} s_i - X_i X_{i-1} s_{i-1} + X_i X_{i+1} x_i - X_i X_{i+1} s_{i+1}$$
$$- X_i s_i + X_i s_{i+1} - X_{i-1} s_i + X_{i-1} s_{i-1}. \tag{2}$$

It is also easy to verify that for periodic boundary conditions on a lattice of length L,

$$\sum_{i=0}^{L-1} s'_i = \sum_{i=0}^{L-1} s_i,$$

meaning that the number of particles is conserved.

Equation (2) represents a probabilistic cellular automaton, and if we had a way to simulate X_i by some pseudo-random process, we could constructs a purely deterministic CA. This can be done by using elementary rule 30 [12,17],

$$X_i' = f_{30}(X_{i-1}, X_i, X_{i+1}),   \tag{3}$$

where f_{30} denotes local function of rule 30, which can be written as

$$f_{30}(x_0, x_1, x_2) = (x_0 + x_1 + x_2 + x_1 x_2)   \mod 2.   \tag{4}$$

This means that at each site i we have two binary state variables, s_i and X_i, evolving, respectively, according to Eqs. (2) and (3). We can combine them together by introducing another variable,

$$y_i = 2s_i + X_i,$$

so that we obtain CA with four states, $y_i \in \{0, 1, 2, 3\}$. This is a fully deterministic nearest neighbour CA given by

$$y_i' = f(y_{i-1}, y_i, y_{i+1}),$$

where $f : \{0, 1, 2, 3\}^3 \to \{0, 1, 2, 3\}$ is defined in the Table 1. Let us call $\{0, 1\}$ *lower states* and $\{2, 3\}$ *upper states*. Lower states represent empty sites, while upper states sites occupied by particles. Of course this mean that empty cell can be in two states (0 or 1) and a particle can be in two states as well (2 or 3). These "internal" states are used only for generation of random numbers.

Table 1. Rule table for the diffusive rule with four states. The entries represent $(y_{i-1}, y_i, y_{i+1}) \to y_i'$.

$(0,0,0) \to 0$	$(1,0,0) \to 1$	$(2,0,0) \to 0$	$(3,0,0) \to 3$
$(0,0,1) \to 1$	$(1,0,1) \to 0$	$(2,0,1) \to 1$	$(3,0,1) \to 2$
$(0,0,2) \to 0$	$(1,0,2) \to 1$	$(2,0,2) \to 0$	$(3,0,2) \to 3$
$(0,0,3) \to 1$	$(1,0,3) \to 0$	$(2,0,3) \to 1$	$(3,0,3) \to 2$
$(0,1,0) \to 1$	$(1,1,0) \to 0$	$(2,1,0) \to 1$	$(3,1,0) \to 0$
$(0,1,1) \to 1$	$(1,1,1) \to 0$	$(2,1,1) \to 1$	$(3,1,1) \to 0$
$(0,1,2) \to 3$	$(1,1,2) \to 2$	$(2,1,2) \to 3$	$(3,1,2) \to 2$
$(0,1,3) \to 1$	$(1,1,3) \to 0$	$(2,1,3) \to 1$	$(3,1,3) \to 0$
$(0,2,0) \to 2$	$(1,2,0) \to 1$	$(2,2,0) \to 2$	$(3,2,0) \to 3$
$(0,2,1) \to 3$	$(1,2,1) \to 0$	$(2,2,1) \to 3$	$(3,2,1) \to 2$
$(0,2,2) \to 2$	$(1,2,2) \to 1$	$(2,2,2) \to 2$	$(3,2,2) \to 3$
$(0,2,3) \to 3$	$(1,2,3) \to 0$	$(2,2,3) \to 3$	$(3,2,3) \to 2$
$(0,3,0) \to 1$	$(1,3,0) \to 0$	$(2,3,0) \to 1$	$(3,3,0) \to 0$
$(0,3,1) \to 3$	$(1,3,1) \to 2$	$(2,3,1) \to 3$	$(3,3,1) \to 2$
$(0,3,2) \to 3$	$(1,3,2) \to 2$	$(2,3,2) \to 3$	$(3,3,2) \to 2$
$(0,3,3) \to 3$	$(1,3,3) \to 2$	$(2,3,3) \to 3$	$(3,3,3) \to 2$

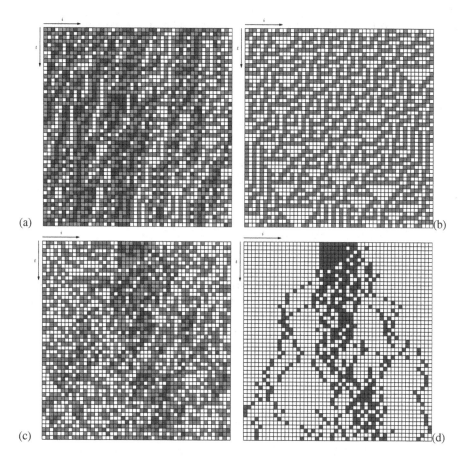

Fig. 1. Spatiotemporal patterns for lattice with periodic boundary conditions and length $L = 50$. (a) Random initial condition. (b) Random initial condition with only 0s and 1s. (c) Initial condition with block of 10 cells in upper states in the middle, lower states elsewhere; every 10th step is shown. (d) Identical pattern as in (c) but with lower states colored white and upper states blue. (Color figure online)

Figure 1 shows examples of spatiotemporal patterns produced by this rule, with upper states shown in blue/green and lower states in grey/white. Random walk performed by individual particles is clearly visible. If we start with a lattice with all sites in lower states, the well known pattern produced by rule 30 can be observed (Fig. 1b).

We will now demonstrate that by taking the appropriate limit, Eq. (2) actually leads to the partial differential equation known as diffusion or heat equation. Let $\rho_i = \langle s_i \rangle$, where the angle bracket denotes the expected value. Taking expected value of both sides of the Eq. (2) we obtain

$$\rho_i' = \rho_i + \frac{1}{4}\rho_i - \frac{1}{4}\rho_{i-1} + \frac{1}{4}\rho_i - \frac{1}{4}\rho_{i+1} - \frac{1}{2}\rho_i + \frac{1}{2}\rho_{i+1} - \frac{1}{2}\rho_i + \frac{1}{2}\rho_{i-1}, \quad (5)$$

where we used the fact that $\langle X_i \rangle = 1/2$ for all i. The above then simplifies to

$$\rho_i' = \frac{1}{2}\rho_i + \frac{1}{4}\rho_{i+1} + \frac{1}{4}\rho_{i-1}. \tag{6}$$

We can write this as

$$\rho_i' - \rho_i = \frac{1}{4}\left(\rho_{i+1} - 2\rho_i + \frac{1}{4}\rho_{i-1}\right). \tag{7}$$

Let us now suppose that the system is updated in discrete time steps, where the time interval between updates is τ. Moreover, let the spacing between lattice sites be ϵ. If we divide both sides of the above equation by τ and multiply its right hand side by $\frac{\epsilon^2}{\epsilon^2}$ we obtain

$$\frac{\rho_i' - \rho_i}{\tau} = \frac{\epsilon^2}{4\tau}\frac{\rho_{i+1} - 2\rho_i + \rho_{i-1}}{\epsilon^2}. \tag{8}$$

It is now clear that the left hand side corresponds to numerical approximation of the first derivative of ρ with respect to time, while the right hand side corresponds to the numerical approximation of the second derivative of ρ with respect to the spatial coordinate. If we take the limit of both sides with $\epsilon \to 0$ and, at the same time, allowing τ tend to zero in such a way that ϵ^2/τ remains constant, we get

$$\frac{\partial \rho}{\partial t} = D\frac{\partial^2 \rho}{\partial x^2}, \tag{9}$$

where $D = \epsilon^2/4\tau$, $x = i\epsilon$ represents spatial coordinate, and $t = k\tau$ represents time with k denoting time step, $k \in \{0, 1, 2, \ldots\}$. This is indeed the diffusion equation. We will now show that orbits of our rule defined in Table 1 approximate solutions of Eq. (9) remarkably well.

3 Experiments

We will consider two numerical experiments highlighting the quality of the rule of Table 1. The first one is usually described in PDE textbooks as a heated finite bar with inhomogeneous boundary conditions [3]. We will consider finite lattice of size L with fixed boundaries where the leftmost site is always occupied by a particle and the rightmost site is always empty. Figure 2 shows the corresponding spatiotemporal patterns. We computed numerical approximations of ρ_i by obtaining average value of s_i after k iterations, where the average is obtained by repeating the simulation 10^4 times. Defining $x = i/L$ we then plotted ρ versus x for various values of k. Results are shown in Fig. 3.

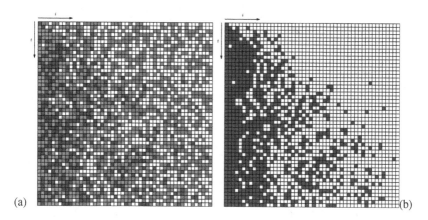

(a)   (b)

Fig. 2. (a) Spatiotemporal patterns for lattice with fixed boundary conditions and length $L = 50$. Left end is the source of particles and the right end is kept empty. (a) Identical pattern as in (a) but with lower states colored white and upper states blue. Only every 10-th step is shown. (Color figure online)

Let us compare the results with solution of Eq. 9 with boundary conditions $\rho(0,t) = 1$, $\rho(1,t) = 0$, given by the following [3] infinite series,

$$\rho(x,t) = 1 - x - \frac{2}{\pi} \sum_{n=1}^{\infty} \frac{1}{n} \exp\left(-n^2\pi^2 Dt\right) \sin\left(n\pi x\right). \tag{10}$$

One can see that as $t \to \infty$, corresponding to our $k \to \infty$, the density profile should tend to a straight line, $\rho(x,\infty) = 1-x$, labelled in Fig. 3 as "steady state" line. For $k = 10^5$ the experimental density profile almost overlaps with $1 - x$, confirming that the approximation of Eq. (9) by rule of Table 1 is indeed very good.

The second experiment we will describe is the case of the initial configuration where all the particles are placed in a solid block in the middle of the lattice, just like in Fig. 1c and 1d. We again computed average densities using 10^4 runs, and the results are shown in Fig. 4a. We used lattice of 300 sites with only 30 sites occupied initially, for $i = 135, 136, \ldots, 165$, the rest being empty. Spatial variable i (upper axis) is rescaled as $x = (i-150)/15$ (lower axis), so that $x = -1$ corresponds to $i = 135$ and $x = 1$ corresponds $i = 165$. The rescaling was done to compare the CA density profiles with solution of Eq. (9) with initial condition

$$\rho(x,0) = \begin{cases} 1 & \text{if } |x| < 1, \\ 0 & \text{otherwise,} \end{cases}$$

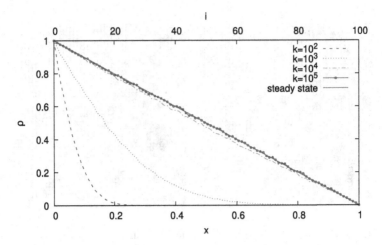

Fig. 3. Density profiles obtained by numerical experiments for finite lattice ($L = 100$) with inhomogeneous boundary conditions. Left end is the source of particles and the Right end is always empty. Vertical axis represents density obtained after k iterations, averaged over 10^4 runs.

which, following [8], is given as

$$\rho(x,t) = \frac{1}{2\sqrt{D\pi t}} \int_{-1}^{1} \exp\left(-\frac{(x-v)^2}{4Dt}\right) dv = \frac{1}{2}\mathrm{erf}\left(\frac{x+1}{2\sqrt{Dt}}\right) - \frac{1}{2}\mathrm{erf}\left(\frac{x-1}{2\sqrt{Dt}}\right).$$
(11)

For $k = 50$, we compared the numerically obtained density profile (shown in Fig. 4a as dotted line) with the corresponding solution of the diffusion equation given by Eq. 11. In Fig. 4b, the density profile obtained by the CA rule for $k = 50$ is shown together with the corresponding graph of the right hand side of Eq. (11). We can again see very good agreement of both, although there are slight discrepancies in the intervals around $x = \pm 1.5$. Given that we are comparing orbits of the discrete process with solution of the continuous PDF, the agreement is still quite remarkable.

4   Two-Dimensional Rule

It is not difficult to construct the deterministic diffusion rule in higher dimensions, following the method outlined in the first section. As an example, we will show two-dimensional version of the rule of Table 1. In this case, two independent pseudo-random variables $X_{i,j}$ and $Y_{i,j}$ are needed, controlling the movement in, respectively, horizontal and vertical direction. These variables can be obtained by using the rule 30 applied in horizontal and vertical direction,

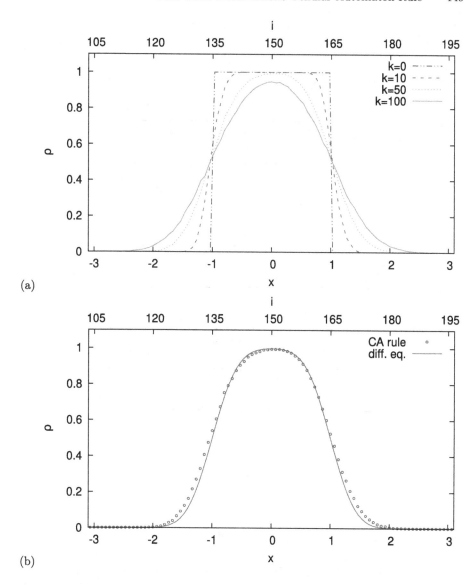

Fig. 4. (a) Development of density profile for lattice of length $L = 300$ with particles initially located only at $i = 135, 136, \ldots 165$. Vertical axis represents density obtained after k iterations, averaged over 10^4 runs. (b) Density profile for CA for $k = 50$ compared with solution of the diffusion equation given by Eq. (11).

$$X'_{i,j} = f_{30}(X_{i-1,j}, X_{i,j}, X_{i+1,j}), \tag{12}$$

$$Y'_{i,j} = f_{30}(Y_{i,j-1}, Y_{i,j}, Y_{i,j+1}). \tag{13}$$

The two-dimensional diffusive rule is then given by

$$s'_{i,j} = s_{i,j} - \underbrace{s_{i,j}X_{i,j}(1 - s_{i+1,j})(1 - X_{i+1,j})Y_{i,j}Y_{i+1,j}}_{move\ to\ the\ right}$$

$$- \underbrace{s_{i,j}(1 - X_{i,j})(1 - s_{i-1,j})X_{i-1,j}Y_{i,j}Y_{i-1,j}}_{move\ to\ the\ left}$$

$$+ \underbrace{(1 - s_{i,j})(1 - X_{i,j})s_{i-1,j}X_{i-1,j}Y_{i,j}Y_{i-1,j}}_{arrive\ from\ the\ left}$$

$$+ \underbrace{(1 - s_{i,j})X_{i,j}s_{i+1,j}(1 - X_{i+1,j})Y_{i,j}Y_{i+1,j}}_{arrive\ from\ the\ right}$$

$$- \underbrace{s_{i,j}X_{i,j}(1 - s_{i,j+1})(1 - X_{i,j+1})(1 - Y_{i,j})(1 - Y_{i,j+1})}_{move\ to\ the\ top}$$

$$- \underbrace{s_{i,j}(1 - X_{i,j})(1 - s_{i,j-1})X_{i,j-1}(1 - Y_{i,j})(1 - Y_{i,j-1})}_{move\ to\ the\ bottom}$$

$$+ \underbrace{(1 - s_{i,j})(1 - X_{i,j})s_{i,j-1}X_{i,j-1}(1 - Y_{i,j})(1 - Y_{i,j-1})}_{arrive\ from\ the\ bottom}$$

$$+ \underbrace{(1 - s_{i,j})X_{i,j}s_{i,j+1}(1 - X_{i,j+1})(1 - Y_{i,j})(1 - Y_{i,j+1})}_{arrive\ from\ the\ top}.$$

We can then introduce variable

$$y_{i,j} = 4s_{i,j} + 2Y_{i,j} + X_{i,j},$$

and with this new variable we will obtain deterministic cellular automaton with 8 states and von Neumann neighbourhood, where lower states $\{0, 1, 2, 3\}$ correspond to empty sites and upper states $\{4, 5, 6, 7\}$ to occupied sites. The rule table of this rule consists of $8^5 = 32768$ entries, thus it cannot be reproduced here. Nevertheless, using compression tool for CA rules included with Golly software [14], this rule table can be reduced to 94 transitions using 31 variables. The .rule file for Golly program is available from the author, allowing to perform interactive experiments with the rule. Results of one of such experiments are shown in Fig. 5, where we used only two colors, white for low states and blue for high states. This is done to emphasize the dynamics of the diffusion process and to "hide" the generation of random variables by two embedded rules 30.

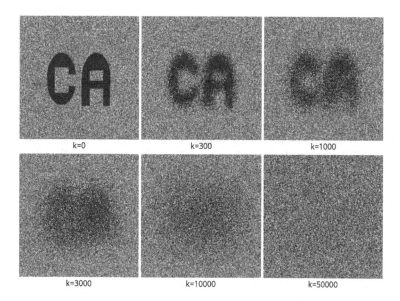

Fig. 5. Patterns produced by two-dimensional diffusive rule starting from the initial image depicting letters "CA" on a lattice 250×250 with periodic boundary conditions. States 0–3 are shown as shades of gray and states 4–7 as shades of blue. (Color figure online)

5   Conclusions

Deterministic nearest-neighbour cellular automaton modelling diffusion process with very high fidelity can easily be constructed providing that sufficient number of states is employed, and in d dimensions 2^{d+1} states are needed. This brings an interesting question and research challenge: could one construct realistic diffusion model with smaller number of states? In particular, in one dimension, can we construct a nearest-neighbour CA rule with only 3 states (instead of our 4), yet emulating diffusion process with similar quality as the rule presented here? The answer is most likely no, yet one would have to formulate the problem in a more rigorous fashion first in order to give the definitive answer. What is certain is that it cannot be done with two states, as none of the elementary CA rules exhibits sufficient diffusion-like properties.

Acknowledgements. The author acknowledges financial support from the Discovery Grant by National Science and Engineering Council of Canada.

References

1. Arita, C., Krapivsky, P.L., Mallick, K.: Bulk diffusion in a kinetically constrained lattice gas. J. Phys. A Math. General **51**(12), 125002 (2018)

2. Boon, J.P., Dab, D., Kapral, R., Lawniczak, A.T.: Lattice gas automata for reactive systems. Phys. Rep. **273**(2), 55–148 (1996)
3. Boyce, W.E., DiPrima, R.C.: Elementary Differential Equations and Boundary Value Problems, pp. 582–583. Wiley, New York (2001)
4. Chopard, B., Droz, M.: Cellular automata model for the diffusion equation. J. Stat. Phys. **64**, 859–892 (1991)
5. Chopard, B., Droz, M.: Cellular Automata Modeling of Physical Systems. Cambridge University Press, Cambridge (1998)
6. Fukś, H.: Solving two-dimensional density classification problem with two probabilistic cellular automata. J. Cell. Autom. **10**(1–2), 149–160 (2015)
7. Hardy, J., Pomeau, Y., de Pazzis, O.: Time evolution of a two-dimensional classical lattice system. Phys. Rev. Lett. **31**, 276–279 (1973)
8. Kreyszig, E.: Advanced Engineering Mathematics, p. 570. Wiley, New York (2011)
9. Medenjak, M., Klobas, K., Prosen, T.: Diffusion in deterministic interacting lattice systems. Phys. Rev. Let. **119**(11), 110603 (2017)
10. Nava-Sedeño, J.M., Hatzikirou, H., Klages, R., Deutsch, A.: Cellular automaton models for time-correlated random walks: derivation and analysis. Sci. Rep. **7**, 16952 (2017)
11. Rothman, D.H., Zaleski, S.: Lattice-Gas Cellular Automata: Simple Models of Complex Hydrodynamics. Cambridge University Press, Cambridge (1997)
12. Shin, S.H., Yoo, K.Y.: Analysis of 2-state, 3-neighborhood cellular automata rules for cryptographic pseudorandom number generation. In: 2009 International Conference on Computational Science and Engineering, vol. 1, pp. 399–404 (2009)
13. Succi, S.: The Lattice Boltzmann Equation: for Fluid Dynamics and Beyond. Clarendon Press, Oxford (2001)
14. Trevorrow, A., Rokicki, T.: Golly (2022). http://golly.sourceforge.net/
15. Voroney, J.P., Lawniczak, A.T.: Construction, mathematical description and coding of reactive lattice-gas cellular automaton. Simul. Pract. Theory **7**, 657–689 (2000)
16. Wolf-Gladrow, D.: Lattice-Gas Cellular Automata and Lattice Boltzmann Models: An Introduction. Springer, Heidelberg (2004). https://doi.org/10.1007/b72010
17. Wolfram, S.: Random sequence generation by cellular automata. Adv. Appl. Math. **7**(2), 123–169 (1986)

The Evolution of Vermicular Structures and Sintering Behavior of Alumina

Francisco Jiménez-Morales[1(✉)] [iD], Pedro Rivero-Antúnez[1,2] [iD],
Manuela González-Sánchez[1] [iD], Laura Garrido-Regife[1],
and Víctor Morales-Flórez[1,2] [iD]

[1] Dept. Física de la Materia Condensada, Universidad de Sevilla,
41012 Sevilla, Spain
`jimenez@us.es`
[2] Instituto de Ciencia de los Materiales ICMS (CSIC-US),
Av. Américo Vespucio, 49, 41092 Sevilla, Spain

Abstract. The evolution of microstructure of the precursor particles during the sintering of ceramic materials has been assessed by a cellular automaton model in which the only physical consideration for the evolution of the system is to minimize the interface energy among the cells and the interface energy alumina-air. The model reproduces qualitatively the vermicular microstructural patterns observed in actual partially-sintered alumina powders for different heat treatments. Moreover, a successful comparison between porosity computed data and experimental data was performed.

Keywords: Cellular automata · Alumina · Vermicular structure · Sinterization · Porosity

1 Introduction

The scientific research of ceramic materials has been an extensive field since centuries due to their outstanding combination of physical, mechanical and chemical properties. Nowadays, many technologies of the every-day life involve ceramics or ceramic matrix composites. In particular, alumina, Al_2O_3, is one of the most researched ceramic materials and it is currently implemented on a wide variety of applications, such as mechanical, high temperature or biomaterials [1–3]. Therefore, there are still major fundamental and technological interests in the fabrication processes of alumina, which involves a high-temperature treatment for the *sintering* (also known as *consolidation* or *densification*) of the precursor compacted powders in order to obtain a fully dense bulk ceramic material.

Despite that the fabrication of ceramics has been known since centuries, the understanding of the sintering behavior and the evolution of the microstructure of the compacted powders are still subjects of research. Hence, a wide variety of procedures have been considered for the fabrication of ceramics, starting from different recipes of the synthesis of the precursor powders, to the employment

B. Chopard et al. (Eds.): ACRI 2022, LNCS 13402, pp. 153–162, 2022.
https://doi.org/10.1007/978-3-031-14926-9_14

of different densification methods, such as pressureless sintering, hot isostatic pressure sintering, spark plasma sintering, or reactive sintering [1,4,5]. Typically, the goal is to obtain the fully dense material and the finest grain size, but saving as much as energy and time as possible.

Sintering is a process that leads to the densification of the material thanks to viscous flow and/or diffusion to reduce porosity [6]. In addition, other processes could be involved such as surface dehydroxylation, crystallization and grain boundary formation, or phase transformations. In brief, the system tends to diminish its energy through the reduction of the interface solid-gas (or solid-vacuum) and grain boundaries. In the case of crystalline materials, the formation of the grains and boundaries are additional mechanisms consuming time and energy during densification, but, again, the driving mechanism is reducing the surface energy, which involves the grain boundaries in addition to the external interface solid-gas. It should be noted that these diffusion processes are energy-activated, being coarsening more relevant at low temperature. For example, viscous sintering is driven by the gained energy through interface surface reduction [6], and the viscosity, η, depends on the temperature through an Arrhenius-like relation with a threshold temperature, T_{th}, namely

$$\eta = \eta_0 e^{[Q/k(T-T_{th})]} \tag{1}$$

In summary, the densification of the powders is a complex phenomenon that involves different concomitant and competing physical processes that govern the morphology of the powders, the crystal and grain sizes, and the disappearance of the porosity. The dependence of each phenomenon with time and temperature, the threshold temperatures of each process, and the influence of the microstructural and chemical composition of the precursor powders have been deeply studied, and they are still under research. In particular, several studies can be found in the literature assessing the sintering behavior, namely, the evolution of the microstructure of the precursor powders, and monitoring the gradual reduction of the porosity among the powders throughout the consolidation process. Moreover, the dependence of the residual porosity is typically analysed by the relative density, that is, the ratio of the actual sample density with regard to the theoretical bulk alumina density of 3.98 g/cm^3. Hence, in all cases, a direct relation between decreasing porosity with time and temperature has been confirmed [1,6,7].

The use of simulation techniques in the field of materials science has a double interest. On the one hand, the improvement of the properties of the material for its industrial use and, secondly, the theoretical interest in the knowledge of the physical processes involved. Traditionally, Monte Carlo simulation methods have been considered but their sequential update of randomly selected points may not be able to capture the simultaneous evolution of grains and the realistic representation of the physical processes also it is very inefficient when applied to large sets of data [8]. On the contrary, in Cellular Automata models, the simultaneous update of every single cell in the lattice of the discretized system appear to reflect more realistically the underlying physical phenomena during

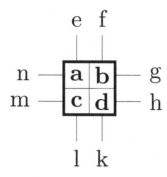

Fig. 1. The neighborhood for the calculus of the surface energy of a given configuration, which is obtained as $E = \sum_{ij} J_{ij}(1 - \delta_{ij})$. If $i = j, \delta_{ij} = 1$ otherwise, if $i \neq j, \delta_{ij} = 0$, and $J_{ij} = 1$ in all cases.

nature process. Recently, numerous studies in the field are using models based on cellular automata [9–12]. Most of these models focus on the study of the dynamic recrystallization [13,14] process and its kinetics [15]. However, there is a lack of studies on the structural patterns that originate during densification, for example, of the boehmite (γ-AlOOH) precursor powders on sapphire substrates, where vermicular structures are formed and studied by electron microscopy [16].

In this work, we present a probabilistic model of cellular automata, in which the evolution of the system is determined exclusively by the minimization of the energy at the interface boundaries. The patterns generated in the simulation qualitatively reproduce the vermicular structures found experimentally [16] for different temperatures. In addition, the decreasing trend of the porosity with the temperature is also well reproduced, allowing the correspondence between simulation and sintering temperatures.

2   The Cellular Automaton Model

We take a two dimensional array of $N = L \times L$ cells with periodic boundary conditions to avoid border effects. The set of possible states is $\sigma = \{0, 1\}$, which correspond to a void lattice cell or cell filled with an elemental portion of alumina, respectively. To conserve the number of filled cells, the Margolus neighborhood is used, the lattice is split in non-overlapping sub-lattices and the updating is done simultaneously on each block of size 2×2. In Fig. 1, one block and its neighborhood are sketched. Note that, in the current model, we have considered only one state for the alumina. But the proposed model is so versatile that different crystallographic orientations can be implemented simply by assigning different states to the alumina cells. This feature will allow the detailed study of crystallographic domains behavior. Nevertheless, different crystallographic orientations are left for elsewhere.

2.1 The Interface Energy

We assume that the energy E of a certain configuration only depends on the interfaces between neighboring cells. Figure 1 shows the elementary block of four cells (a,b,c,d) and the neighbors cells (e,f,g,h,k,l,m,n). The configuration energy is defined as:

$$E = \sum_{ij} J_{ij}(1 - \delta_{ij}) \tag{2}$$

where δ_{ij} is the Kronecker delta, and J_{ij} is the surface energy of one elemental interface, which in this work is considered to be the same for all the alumina-void interfaces ($J = 1$). Thus, the total energy of the system is obtained summing up the energy of all the blocks. In other words, the configuration energy is obtained as the total number of sides of the lattice cells that are found between lattice cells with different states.

2.2 Transition Probabilities

The evolution rule assigns to each configuration at time t a different one at time $t + 1$, depending exclusively on the difference between both energies $\Delta E = E(t + 1) - E(t)$. Table 1 shows the lookup table of the rule. All possible initial states of the elementary blocks, not including rotations, are shown along with all the possible outputs. Each of these possible outputs is assigned a function of Arrhenius type:

$$q_i = A \cdot e^{-\frac{\Delta E_i}{kT}} \tag{3}$$

the prefactor A is taken as 1. And finally the probability is obtained by normalizing between the set of possible corresponding final states.

$$p_i = \frac{q_j}{\sum_i q_j} \tag{4}$$

Therefore, in our probabilistic CA model, all states have a probability of being able to occur, contrary to what happens in other simulation methods in which, for example, transitions with $\Delta E > 0$ are rejected while if $\Delta E \leq 0$ are accepted with probability 1. These different methodologies (namely, the soft one and the hard one, respectively), involve different physical considerations and lead to different final states.

Table 1. Lookup table rule of the cellular automata. All the 5 possible initial states of the blocks at time t and their possible states at instant $t + 1$ are shown. For each transition, the difference between the interface energies of the block is obtained and the Ahrrenius-type coefficient $q_i = e^{-\frac{\Delta E_i}{kT}}$ is calculated. The probability assigned to each of the outputs are normalized $p_i = q_i/(\sum_j q_j)$

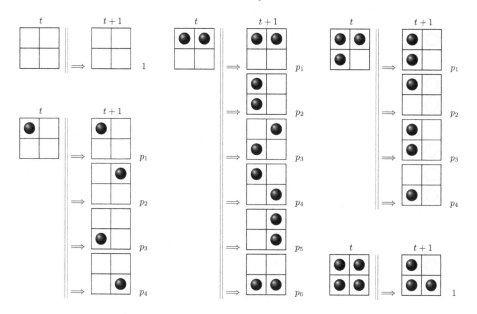

In the hard case, the system reaches the equilibrium state in a few time steps. However, in the final state, the system has a total energy higher than in the soft case. In other words, the system upon the typical hard transition probabilistic methodologies achieves faster some "local" equilibrium, while the soft probabilistic methodology allows a wider exploration of the energy pathway, which leads to a more stable equilibrium state.

3   Results

The simulations are performed on lattices of $N = 500 \times 500$ cells and start from a random initial state with a concentration $\rho = \frac{1}{N}\sum_i^N \sigma_i = 0.6$. The system evolves under the transition rules described above and the different data are recorded after 10^4 time steps. Since $k = 1$ and $J = 1$ the energy and temperature values are in arbitrary units.

3.1   The Total Interface Energy

Figure 2 shows the relative decrease of the total interface energy versus the temperature. It was found that the largest relative decreases of the energy, $\Delta E/E_0$

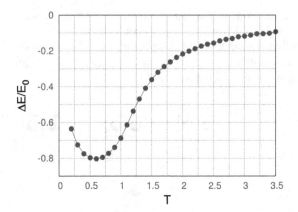

Fig. 2. Simulation results of the CA model. Lattice size 500×500, periodic boundary conditions. Starting from a random initial condition with a density of 0.6. Dependence of the relative decrease of the total energy versus the temperature. The "frozen" system ($T = 0$) would not exhibit any change of the energy, as expected

are observed in the range of lower temperatures, that is, for $0.5 < T < 0.75$. It is below this value of $T = 0.75$ where it makes physical sense that the mechanism to reach equilibrium is the decrease of the total interface energy. On the other hand, when T increases, the thermal energy of the particles is the dominant factor against the minimization of energy.

The analysis of the evolution of the energy can be also made in terms of the distribution of the energy throughout the system. Figure 3 shows the spatial distribution of local energies for two different temperatures. For evaluating this local energy, the Von-Neumman neighborhood of each cell is taken into account. In the case of low temperature, the energy, which is only found in the interface between matter and the vacuum, clearly depicts the contour of the particulate, partially-sintered, system. On the contrary, at higher temperatures, the energy is distributed throughout the network, meaning that, even at the final equilibrium state, there are interfaces throughout the sample. We assume that, during the simulation of the sintering of the sample at high temperature, there are multiple remaining pores (void cells) located within the domains of alumina, due to the soft probabilistic transition methodology, which allows that some kind of thermal agitation of the cells prevails over the minimization of the interface energy. This could also explain the increase of the relative reduction of the energy above $T = 0.75$ observed in Fig. 2.

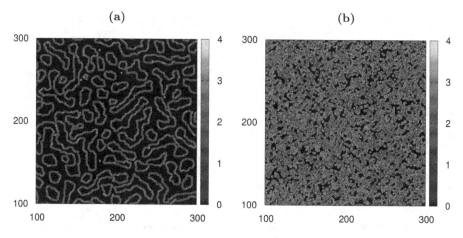

Fig. 3. Contour Plot of the local energy at $t = 10^4$ time steps for two temperatures: (a) $T = 0.5$, (b) $T = 1.5$. The minimum value of the energy are the pixels of black color, while the yellow color represents the maximum values. (Color figure online)

3.2   Vermicular Structures

The spatial arrangements of the matter obtained at the final configurations can be discussed and compared with experimental images in Fig. 4, where the top file shows the patterns generated at various temperatures after 10^4 time steps, in which the equilibrium was reached in all cases. A blue pixel is a lattice with alumina.

In the case of $T = 1.5$, we have plotted the temporal average of σ for 10^4 time steps, so thermal fluctuations at high temperatures are neglected. In the plots, it can be seen how the particles are distributed minimizing the interface energy forming clusters, with vermicular shapes of different sizes that are directly related with the temperature. Surprisingly, this type of patterns has already been observed experimentally in the sintering of alumina on sapphire surfaces, as shown in the bottom file of Figure 4. Therefore, the ability of the proposed CA model for simulating partially sintered structures is clearly supported by the structural similarity of the simulated and experimental systems.

3.3   A Measure of the Porosity

During the preparation of ceramics such as alumina, voids among the precursor particles progressively disappear resulting in the densification of the sample. Nevertheless, partial or imperfect preparations lead to incomplete densifications and then the material exhibits some remaining porosity. In this simple CA model, we can measure the porosity by interpreting the existence of holes in the sample when the time average occupancy of a given cell is less than 0.5. Figure 5 shows the results obtained through the simulation where some experimental data have also been included. The porosity decreases as the temperature increases and

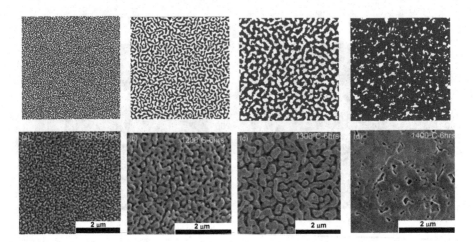

Fig. 4. Top line: Vermicular structures shown by the CA model at different temperatures. a) $T = 0.25$, b) $T = 0.50$, c) $T = 0.80$, d) $T = 1.5$. The initial concentration is 0.6. For d) each pixel is a temporal average of the cell state. A blue pixel if $\langle \sigma \rangle > 0.5$. Bottom line: Scanning electron microscopy images of vermicular structures of partially sintered alumina. Reproduced with permission from [16]. (Color figure online)

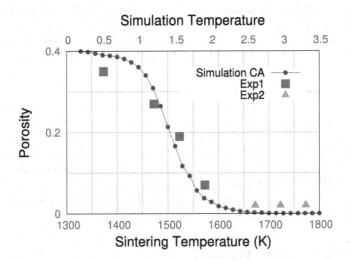

Fig. 5. Evolution of the porosity of the sample vs. temperature. Simulation data (red circles) reproduced reasonably well the decreasing trend exhibited by the experimental data. The temperature of the samples of alumina were maintained during 600 min. (Exp1, green squares) and 300 min (Exp2, cyan triangles). Data from ref. [17]. (Color figure online)

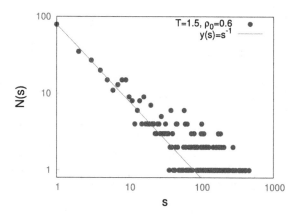

Fig. 6. Log-log plot of the number $N(s)$ of void clusters versus the size s. The initial concentration was $\rho_0 = 0.6$ and the simulation temperature $T = 1.5$. The slope of the straight line drawn is -1.

above a certain critical value it practically reaches a null value, meaning that, above a given T, fully-dense samples are obtained, which makes an absolute realistic sense. Moreover, the correlation between the trends of both sets of results is remarkable. Finally, we have correlated the sintering temperature with the simulation temperature obtaining that $T_{simulated} = 1 \approx T_{real} = 1450\ K$. We have found also that the distribution of the holes within the sample follows a power law $N(s) \approx s^{-1}$ as shown in the Fig. 6.

4 Conclusions

Among the simulation methods used in materials science, CA stand out for their ability to easily capture the complexity of material sintering processes. In this paper we have developed a probabilistic cellular automata in which the transition probability depends on the interface energies as an Arrhenius function. We point out the similarity between the patterns generated by the simulations and the vermicular patterns observed in sol-gel growth of alumina. The model also allows for a measurement of the porosity of the sample as a function of the temperature that qualitatively is in good agreement with experimental data. It is left for a future work the study of the influence of local crystallographic orientations and also the growth kinetics.

Acknowledgements. This research was financed by project PGC2018-094952-B-I00 (INTRACER) from FEDER/Ministerio de Ciencia e Innovación – Agencia Estatal de Investigación, and by project P20_01121 (FRAC) from the Consejería de Transformación Económica, Industria, Conocimiento y Universidades (Junta de Andalucía). Special action I.9 from the VI-PPITUS (Universidad de Sevilla). M. G-S. acknowledges European Social Fund from the Empleo Juvenil European Plan.

References

1. Kingery, W.D.: Introduction to Ceramics. Wiley, New York (1976). ISBN: 978-0-471-47860-7
2. Gocha, A., Liverani, S., De Guire, E.: Ceramics and glass-materials for diverse industries: a 2016 industry profile and manufacturing forecast. Am. Ceram. Soc. Bull. **95**, 10–20 (2016)
3. Gonzalez-Sanchez, M., Rivero-Antunez, P., Cano-Crespo, R., Morales-Florez, V.: Fabrication of porous alumina structures by SPS and carbon sacrificial template for bone regeneration. Materials **15**, 1754 (2022)
4. Orrù, R., Licheri, R., Locci, A.M., Cincotti, A., Cao, G.: Consolidation/synthesis of materials by electric current activated/assisted sintering. Mater. Sci. Eng. R **63**, 127–287 (2009)
5. Rivero-Antúnez, P., Cano-Crespo, R., Sánchez-Bajo, F., Domínguez-Rodríguez, A., Morales-Flórez, V.: Reactive SPS for sol-gel alumina samples: structure, sintering behavior, and mechanical properties. J. Eur. Ceram. Soc. **41**, 5548–5557 (2021)
6. Brinker, C.J., Scherrer, G.W.: The Physics and Chemistry of Sol-Gel Processing. Academic Press, Boston (1990). ISBN: 0-12-134970-5
7. Jagota, S., Raj, R.: Model for the crystallization and sintering of unseeded and seeded boehmite gels. J. Mater. Sci. **27**, 2251–2257 (1992)
8. Maazi, N., Boulechfar, R.: A modified grain growth Monte Carlo algorithm for increase calculation speed in the presence of Zener drag effect. Mater. Sci. Eng. B **242**, 52–62 (2019)
9. He, Y., Ding, H., Liu, L., Shin, K.: Computer simulation of 2D grain growth using a cellular automata model based on the lowest energy principle. Mater. Sci. Eng. **A429**, 236–246 (2006)
10. Wang, D., Bai, Y., Xue, C., Cao, Y., Yan, Z.: Optimization of sintering parameters for fabrication of $Al_2O_3/TiN/TiC$ micro-nano-composite ceramic tool material based on microstructure evolution simulation. Ceram. Int. **47**, 5776–5785 (2021)
11. Li, Z., Wang, J., Huang, H.: Grain boundary curvature based 2D cellular automata simulation of grain coarsening. J. Alloy. Compd. **791**, 411–422 (2019)
12. Raabe, D.: Cellular automata in materials science with particular reference to recrystallization simulation. Annu. Rev. Matter. Res. **32**, 53–76 (2002). https://doi.org/0.1146/annurev.matsci.32.090601.152855
13. Contieri, R.J., Zanotello, M., Caram, R.: Simulation of CP-Ti recrystallization and grain growth by a cellular automata algorithm: simulated versus experimental results. Mater. Res. **20**(3), 688–701 (2017)
14. Ji, X., Shi, Y.: Simulation of the microstructural evolution during dynamic recrystallisation with a modified cellular automaton. Philos. Mag. Lett. **100**(3), 105–115 (2020)
15. Mason, J.K.: Grain boundary energy and curvature in Monte Carlo and cellular automata simulations of grain boundary motion. Acta Mater. **94**, 162–171 (2015)
16. Dutta, S., Kim, T.B., Krentz, T., Vinci, R.P., Chan, H.M.: Sol-gel-derived single-crystal alumina coatings with vermicular structure. J. Am. Ceram Soc. **94**(2), 340–343 (2011). https://doi.org/10.1111/j.1551-2916.2010.04307.x
17. Rivero-Antúnez, P., Morales-Flórez, V., Cumbrera, F.L., Esquivias, L.: Rietveld analysis and mechanical properties of in situ formed La-ß-Al2O3/Al2O3 composites prepared by sol-gel method Ceram. Int. **48**(17), 24462–24470 (2022). https://doi.org/10.1016/j.ceramint.2022.05.058

A Cellular Automaton Model of a Laser with Saturable Absorber Reproducing Laser Passive Q-switching

Francisco Jiménez-Morales[1]([⊠]) [ID], José-Luis Guisado-Lizar[2,3] [ID],
and José Manuel Guerra[4]

[1] Departamento de Física de la Materia Condensada, Universidad de Sevilla,
41012 Sevilla, Spain
jimenez@us.es
[2] Department of Computer Architecture and Technology, Universidad de Sevilla,
Avenida Reina Mercedes s/n, 41012 Sevilla, Spain
[3] Research Institute of Computer Engineering (I3US), Universidad de Sevilla,
Avenida Reina Mercedes s/n, 41012 Sevilla, Spain
[4] Departamento de Optica, Facultad de C.C. Físicas, Universidad Complutense
de Madrid, 28040 Madrid, Spain

Abstract. In this paper, we present a cellular automata model for a two-level laser which includes a saturable absorber. We show that the model reproduces laser passive Q-switching, a behavior in which intense short pulses of laser radiation are produced. Depending on the concentration of the absorbent, the automaton model qualitatively reproduces two operating states of the laser: a stable state and another oscillatory or pulsed state.

Keywords: Laser · Saturable absorber · Q-switching · Cellular automata

1 Introduction

Cellular automata (CA) have proven to be very successful in modeling complex systems in many areas of science and engineering [1,8,12]. One particularly interesting application is to model the dynamics of a laser, which is one of the most paradigmatic examples of a complex system. A CA model to describe laser dynamics was introduced in [3]. It describes the laser system as a collection of simple components: the atoms, electrons or molecules of the active medium of the laser cavity and the radiation laser photons that they produce. Local interactions among these components are described by the CA evolution rules based on the physical processes that occur in a laser system: stimulated emission, absorption, pumping, and noise. It was shown in [3] that different macroscopic laser properties are reproduced by the CA model as emerging properties induced by self-organization: the pumping threshold value, the emission of a laser beam

© The Author(s), under exclusive license to Springer Nature Switzerland AG 2022
B. Chopard et al. (Eds.): ACRI 2022, LNCS 13402, pp. 163–172, 2022.
https://doi.org/10.1007/978-3-031-14926-9_15

above it, the temporal patterns (constant or oscillatory) of the radiation beam, and the dependence of the type of temporal pattern exhibited by a laser on its characteristic parameters.

Since then, it has been possible to model variants of a general laser system by modifying some of the ingredients of the CA model. And for instance in [4] a successful CA model of pulsed-pumped lasers was introduced. Also in [5] another CA model that reproduces antiphase dynamics in lasers was presented. This demonstrates the robustness and usefulness of the CA approach to model laser physics.

The basic idea of modeling laser physics using a microscopic or mesoscopic discrete model has been also developed further by Chusseau et al. to propose related Monte Carlo simulations of laser obtaining very good results for quantum-well and quantum-dot semiconductor lasers [2]. Also recently, Zhang et al. have proposed a CA model of nonlinear optical processes in a phase-change material inspired by this idea (in particular, for a polymorphic gallium film undergoing a light-induced structural phase transition) [13]. They have employed a CA model very similar to our laser model, a three-level system governed by only four transition rules and a sparse set of independent material and process parameters. They have found that their model can phenomenologically describe the complex, non-stationary, spatially inhomogeneous dynamics and resulting nonlinear optical properties of a medium undergoing a light-induced structural phase transition.

In this work, we go a step beyond the original model presented in [3] to introduce a new variant of that model that simulates a laser with a saturable absorber, capable of reproducing the behavior known as laser passive Q-switching. Laser Q-switching is a widely used technique by which a laser can be made to produce an output beam with intense light pulses by modulating the cavity losses, i.e. the Q factor (quality factor) of the cavity, which is the ratio of the stored energy to the energy dissipated per oscillation cycle [6,7,11]. Q factor determines the level of damping of the laser cavity: a laser with a low Q factor has higher losses and is thus more damped than a laser with a higher one. Q-switching is achieved by placing some type of variable attenuator in the laser optical cavity, which provides high attenuation (low Q-factor) for low intensities of laser light circulating through the cavity, and low attenuation (high Q-factor) for higher intensities. In this way, when the laser is switched on, the attenuation is very high, so that the intensity of laser radiation produced by stimulated emission increases only very gradually. Therefore, the pumped energy accumulates in a high population inversion. When the laser radiation intensity exceeds a certain threshold value, the variable attenuator quickly goes from low Q to high Q (the attenuation goes down). This, together with the high population inversion achieved, causes a rapid increase in laser radiation intensity by feedback from stimulated emission. This process consumes the population inversion until it is extinguished and returns to the starting point. The result is a short, intense pulse of laser light, called a giant pulse, which is repeated periodically. In lasers with passive Q-switching, one of the two variants of Q-switching, the variable attenuation is obtained by introducing a saturable absorber inside the laser cavity, a material whose transmission increases when light intensity exceeds some threshold. Some popular saturable absorbers are ion-doped crystals such as $Cr^{4+} : YAG$, $V^{3+} : YAG$, or $Co^{2+} : MgAl_2O_4$, where YAG stands for yttrium aluminum garnet ($Y_3Al_5O_{12}$).

Modeling laser Q-switching using a CA instead of the standard approach based on macroscopic differential equations has different advantages: i) a CA model can be used in cases in which the differential equations are stiff and present convergence problems; ii) it is possible with a CA model to study specific spatial structures of the laser device, for example, structures of the absorbing medium (randomly or regularly distributed); iii) CA models can be implemented very efficiently on parallel computers, due to their intrinsic parallel nature; iV) once a basic CA model has been designed and validated, it is possible and relatively easy to study modifications of the model to deal with different variants of the phenomenon to be studied.

The structure of this paper is as follows. In Sect. 2 the classical description of laser passive Q-switching using rate equations is introduced and the main operation regimes obtained by integrating them are presented. The CA model is introduced in Sect. 3. Results are presented in Sect. 4. Finally, conclusions are drawn in Sect. 5.

2   Laser Rate Equations

The classical balance equations to formulate a two-level laser with a saturable absorber are [11]:

$$\frac{dn}{dt} = K_1 N n - \frac{n}{\tau_n} - K_2 qn \tag{1}$$

$$\frac{dN}{dt} = R_1 - \frac{N}{\tau_N} - K_1 N n \tag{2}$$

$$\frac{dq}{dt} = R_2 - \frac{q}{\tau_q} - K_2 q n \tag{3}$$

where n is the number of photons, N is the population inversion and q is the saturable absorber. K_1 and K_2 are two coupling constants between the radiation and the lasing medium and between the radiation and the absorber. R_1 is the pumping of the laser medium and R_2 is a characteristic property of the absorber.

The laser rate equations allow us a simple interpretation of the different physical processes involved. The intensity of the laser, which is proportional to the number of photons n, increases with the stimulated emission ($K_1 N n$) and decreases due to the effect of the absorber ($-K_2 qn$). The population inversion N, Eq. (2), which is the difference between the electrons that are in the higher and fundamental energy level of the laser active medium, increases due to an external pumping (R_1) and decreases due to stimulated emission. Regarding the absorber, its behavior is similar to that of the population inversion. But in this case, R_2 is a characteristic of the material, although its effect can be understood as if it were an external pump. The absorber q decreases its action as the number of photons increases (K_2qn), this being one of the main characteristics of this type of device: the laser is transparent for high intensity values. Each of the values of the three populations, photons, population inversion, and absorber has a lifetime that represents in each case the decay time of the photon in the resonant cavity $\tau_n = \gamma_n^{-1}$, the decay time of the electron in the upper level of the laser active medium $\tau_N = \gamma_N^{-1}$ and the decay time of the absorber in the active state $\tau_q = \gamma_q^{-1}$.

From the analysis of these laser rate equations, it has been established that for a single mode the main laser regimes are a constant wave (cw) and Q-switching state in which the power shows oscillations [10]. Other unstable laser operations can also be found but are out of the scope of this work [9].

Figure 1 shows the two main operation regimes of the laser which have been obtained by integrating the equations by the fourth order Runge-Kutta method, where we have used the following lifetimes of $\tau_n = 80, \tau_N = 10^3, \tau_q = 2$.

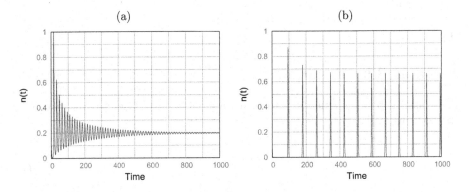

Fig. 1. Time series of the number of photons obtained from the laser rate equations. (a) After a damped transient the laser output is a constant wave. Parameters $R_1 = 0.1$, $R_2 = 0.5$. (b) Pulsed behavior for $R_1 = 0.05, R_2 = 0.9$.

3   A Cellular Automata Model for a Laser with a Saturable Absorber

The CA is defined in a two dimensional lattice of $N = L \times L$ cells with periodic boundary conditions. The state of each cell at a given time, $s_{ij}(t)$, is a vector of 3 values which includes the electronic state of the lasing medium $e \in \{0, 1\}$, the number of photons $f \in \{0, 1, 2, ..., max\}$ and the state of the absorber $q \in \{0, 1\}$.

$$s_{ij}(t) = \{e, f, q\} \tag{4}$$

Table 1. Set of parameters used in the simulations of the CA.

Parameter	Symbol	Value
Photons lifetime	τ_n	80
Population inversion lifetime	τ_N	10^3
Absorber lifetime	τ_q	2
Threshold for stimulated emission	K_1	2
Threshold for absorption	K_2	2
Transient time		50
Number of noise photons		100

The state of every cell changes in parallel according to the following transition rules:

Population Inversion

– Every electron in the ground state $(e = 0)$ can be excited to the state $e = 1$ with a pumping probability R_1. Although in our model we speak of electrons, they are actually the two states of the laser medium. For this reason, we have not included any restrictions on the number of electrons in each level.
– An electron in the state $e = 1$ that is surrounded by a number of photons higher than a given threshold value K goes to $e = 0$. In this process, a new photon is created by stimulated emission. To evaluate this condition the photons in the Moore neighborhood of the cell are considered:

$$\Gamma_{ij} = \sum_{Neig} f_{i,j} \tag{5}$$

– An electron in the state $e = 1$ goes to $e = 0$ after a time τ_N. And this transition is considered to be not radiative.

Photons Evolution

When stimulated emission occurs one new photon is created:

$$f_{i,j}(t+1) = f_{i,j}(t) + 1 \tag{6}$$

Like the electrons, photons vanish after a given time τ_n.

The Absorber $(q \in \{0,1\})$

In our model, the absorber, in the same way as the inversion of the population, has only two possible states: an inactive state $q = 0$ in which it does not interact with radiation and the active state $q = 1$ in which said interaction does occur.

The evolution of the absorber is given by the following rules:

– If $q(t) = 0$ then with a probability R_2, which depends on the physical characteristics of the absorber, $q(t + 1) = 1$.

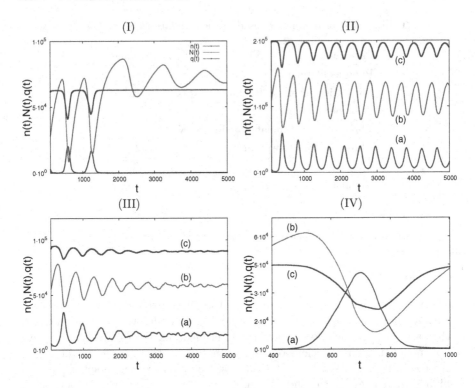

Fig. 2. Time series of **(a)** the number of photons $n(t)$, **(b)** the population inversion $N(t)$ and **(c)** the absorber $q(t)$. For clarity, the last two data sets (b and c) have been shifted slightly along the y-axis in I, II and III. The lattice size is 300×300 cells, the parameters $d_a = 0.5, R_2 = 0.5$. The other parameters used in these simulation are shown in Table 1. The different laser outputs depending on the pumping probability R_1 are: (I) No laser output $R_1 = 0.0035$. (II) Oscilatory behaviour $R_1 = 0.004$. (III) Constant wave $R_1 = 0.007$. (IV) Detail of a pulse corresponding to case (II).

– When the absorber is in the excited state, $q(t) = 1$, it eliminates photons if $\Gamma_{ij} \geq K_2$ and decays to the state $q(t+1) = 0$. This is a deterministic process. In our simulations, we have considered the case in which the absorber eliminates all the photons in the corresponding cell position.
– Also the absorber in the excited state decays to the inactive state after a certain number of time steps τ_q if $\Gamma_{ij} < K_2$.

Another important aspect to take into consideration is that in this lattice model, unlike in the balance equations, it is possible to take into account the spatial distribution of the absorber inside the system. In each and every point of the network we have considered that it can host population inversion and photons. But not so for the case of the absorber where it will be only present in a certain number of cells so that we can introduce a given density of points with absorber d_a.

4   Results

The simulations have been carried out in networks of 300×300 cells with periodic boundary conditions. The values of the different parameters used in most of the simulations are shown in Table 1. Initially the population inversion is null and the random distribution of absorbers is also in the ground state. During a temporary transient we introduce a small amount of noise photons into the system to initiate the action of the laser.

The number of parameters (seven, see Table 1) that define the system are too many to address in this preliminary work an exhaustive study of all the behaviors that can be shown by the CA model. In this way, the simulations that we present below have been carried out by setting the values of the lifetimes and of the constants K_1 and K_2 as indicated in the Table 1. The values of τ_n and τ_N were the typical ones used in previous studies [3]. And as for τ_q we take a value small enough and less than τ_n.

4.1   Dependence with the Pumping Probability R_1

First, we analyze the possible behaviors of the model as we modify the pumping probability of the lasing medium R_1 having fixed $R_2 = 0.5$ and the density of absorber cells $d_a = 0.5$. Figure 2(I) shows the time series of the number of photons $n(t)$, the population inversion $N(t)$ and the absorber in the excited state $q(t)$. For small values of R_1 after a small transient no laser signal is produced. The absorber reaches a fixed value while the population inversion shows damped oscillations until it reaches a fixed value as well.

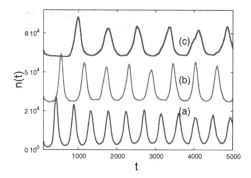

Fig. 3. Dependence of the laser output on the parameter R_2: a) 0.1, b) 0.4, c) 0.8. The pumping is $R_1 = 0.004$ and the density of absorber cells is $d_a = 0.5$.

By increasing the value of R_1 above a certain threshold value (≈ 0.003), the laser shows an oscillatory state that is stable over time as can be seen in Fig. 2(II). A further increase in R_1, Fig. 2(III) results in the disappearance of the oscillatory state after a transient period during which the output intensity dampens and now the laser shows a constant wave output.

The Fig. 2(IV) is an expanded figure of one pulse corresponding to Q-switching. It is interesting to observe that the behavior captured by the CA model reproduces qualitatively the physics of the laser with a saturable absorber. The absorber q reduces its value near the peak in the number of photons due to the bleaching effect.

4.2   Dependence with R_2

We have limited the dependency with the parameter R_2 to the case of the oscillatory state, previously described, being $R_1 = 0.004$ and $d_a = 0.5$. Figure 3 shows the time series of the number of photons for three values of R_2. We have found that as long as R_1 is greater than the threshold value, the oscillatory behavior is maintained as R_2 is modified. But the frequency of pulses decreases as R_2 increases.

4.3   The Effect of the Density of the Absorber

With the discrete model presented here, we can investigate the result of varying the concentration d_a of possible absorbing cells in the lattice. That is an important issue in the preparation of materials with adequate characteristics. Figure 4 is a heat map obtained from the analysis of the time series of $n(t)$ for a fixed value of R_1. Higher values (yellow) are assigned to regular oscillations, and lower values (violet) appear when the signal is constant, down to the null value (black) when there is no output.

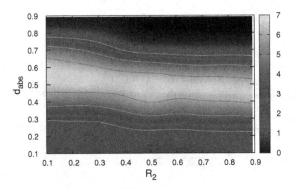

Fig. 4. The different kinds of laser outputs as a function of the density of the absorber and the R_2 parameter. The pumping probability is fixed at $R_1 = 0.004$. a) Black color: there is no laser output for high density of the absorber ($d_a > 0.75$). b) Violet color: constant output of the laser intensity. c) Red color: damped oscillations. d) Yellow color: oscillatory behaviors with an almost constant value of the maximum intensity are observed in the range ($0.45 < d_a < 0.75$) whereas damped oscillations are observed when $d_a < 0.45$. (Color figure online)

Figure 5 shows the time series of the intensity for three values of the density d_a and a fixed value of R_2. We find that in the absence of the absorber (Fig. 5-(a)) the signal has a constant value. As the density increases, the behavior goes from a constant value to an oscillatory behavior; first of all, there are damped oscillations and later they are maintained over time (Fig. 5-(b)). A further increase in the density causes the laser action to stop (Fig. 5-(c)).

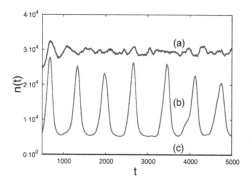

Fig. 5. Time series of the laser intensity for three values of the density d_a of absorber cells in the lattice: a) 0, b) 0.4 and c) 0.8. Other parameter values: $R_1 = 0.004$ and $R_2 = 0.4$. Without the saturable absorber the laser output is a steady state with some noise. The presence of the saturable absorber makes the laser to pulse.

5   Conclusions

In this work we present an extension to a previous CA model used to simulate the laser physics in which a passive saturable absorber is included. Despite its simplicity, the model qualitatively reproduces the main phenomenology of such systems: the inclusion of the absorber can cause the laser to pulse.

Depending on the different parameters that define the system, we have carried out a study modifying the pumping probability R_1 and the parameter R_2 which is a property of the absorber. In this way we obtain that the laser signal can be constant, a damped oscillation, a maintained oscillation (Q-switching) and the absence of laser output.

Finally, this discrete model allows us to analyze the different behaviors that can take place in lasers by modifying the density and location of the points that act as absorbers, something that is not possible with the laser rate equations.

Acknowledgments. This research was financed by projects PGC2018-094952-B-I00 (INTRACER), PID2019-110455GB-I00 (Par-Hot), US-1381077 (CIUCAP-HSF) from FEDER/Ministerio de Ciencia e Innovación – Agencia Estatal de Investigación, and by project P20_01121 (FRAC) from the Consejería de Transformación Económica, Industria, Conocimiento y Universidades (Junta de Andalucía).

References

1. Chopard, B., Droz, M.: Cellular Automata Modeling of Physical Systems. Cambridge University Press, Cambridge (1998)
2. Chusseau, L., Philippe, F., Disanto, F.: Monte Carlo modeling of the dual-mode regime in quantum-well and quantum-dot semiconductor lasers. Opt. Express **22**(5), 5312–5324 (2014)
3. Guisado, J.L., Jiménez-Morales, F., Guerra, J.M.: Cellular automaton model for the simulation of laser dynamics. Phys. Rev. E **67**(6), 66708 (2003)
4. Guisado, J.L., Jiménez-Morales, F., Guerra, J.M.: Simulation of the dynamics of pulsed pumped lasers based on cellular automata. In: Sloot, P.M.A., Chopard, B., Hoekstra, A.G. (eds.) ACRI 2004. LNCS, vol. 3305, pp. 278–285. Springer, Heidelberg (2004). https://doi.org/10.1007/978-3-540-30479-1_29
5. Jiménez-Morales, F., Guisado, J.L., Guerra, J.M.: Simulating laser dynamics with cellular automata. In: Carmona, V., Cuevas-Maraver, J., Fernández-Sánchez, F., García-Medina, E. (eds.) Nonlinear Systems, Vol. 1. UCS, pp. 405–422. Springer, Cham (2018). https://doi.org/10.1007/978-3-319-66766-9_14
6. Keller, U., et al.: Semiconductor saturable absorber mirrors (SESAM's) for femtosecond to nanosecond pulse generation in solid-state lasers. IEEE J. Sel. Top. Quant. Electron. **2**(3), 435–453 (1996)
7. Koechner, W.: Solid-State Laser Engineering, 3rd edn. Springer, Heidelberg (1992). https://doi.org/10.1007/0-387-29338-8
8. Kroc, J., Jiménez-Morales, F., Guisado, J.L., Lemos, M.C., Tkac, J.: Building efficient computational cellular automata models of complex systems: background, applications, results, software, and pathologies. Adv. Complex Syst. **22**(5), 1950013 (2019)
9. Kurtner, F.X., der Au, J.A., Keller, U.: Mode-locking with slow and fast saturable absorbers-what's the difference? IEEE J. Sel. Top. Quant. Electron. **4**(2), 159–168 (1998)
10. Marcuse, D.: Pulsing behavior of a three-level laser with saturable absorber. IEEE J. Quant. Electron. **29**(8), 2390–2396 (1993)
11. Siegman, A.E.: Lasers. Unversity Science Books (1986)
12. Sloot, P.M., Hoekstra, A.G.: Modeling dynamic systems with cellular automata. In: Fishwick, P.A. (ed.) Handbook of Dynamic System Modeling, pp. (21) 1–6. Chapman & Hall/CRC (2007)
13. Zhang, L., Waters, R.F., Macdonald, K.F., Zheludev, N.I.: Cellular automata dynamics of nonlinear optical processes in a phase-change material. Appl. Phys. Rev. **8**, 011404 (2021)

Modeling Phase Change Materials Using Cellular Automata

Yasser Khaddor[1]([✉]) [iD], Abdes-samed Bernoussi[1], Khalid Addi[2][iD],
Mohamed Byari[1][iD], and Mustapha Ouardouz[3]

[1] GAT, Faculty of Sciences and Techniques, Abdelmalek Essaadi University, Tangier,
Morocco
yasserkhaddor@gmail.com

[2] Laboratoire Physique et Ingénierie Mathématique pour l'Energie, l'environnemeNt
et le BâtimenT (PIMENT), University of La Réunion, Saint Pierre, France
khalid.addi@univ-reunion.fr

[3] MMC, Faculty of Sciences and Techniques, Abdelmalek Essaadi University,
Tangier, Morocco

Abstract. This work proposes a recent model for modelling the Phase
Change (PC) phenomenon based on Cellular Automata (CA) of composite and heterogeneous materials with a complex geometry. We aim to
describe the temperature distribution and phases (liquid/solid) evolution
for multi-components materials. The main idea of this paper is to answer
the problem of the high complexity generated when the classical methods for modelling the PC is used in the case of heterogeneous materials
and complex geometry. For this purpose, Each cell was associated with
a set of attributes that characterize each portion of modelled material,
such as thermal conductivity, specific heat capacity, material density, a
specific material phase change temperature, Latent heat, etc.

Keywords: Phase change · Complex system · Multi-components
materials · Heat transfer

1 Introduction

Thermal energy storage represents a solution that will help reduce the gap
between the supply and demand of energy. It also improves the performance
and reliability of energy systems. Phase change materials (PCM) are an effective application for temperature control and consumption reduction. Their ease
of integration makes it a reasonable tool for developing and improving applications in various fields, including building [1,7,12], food transportation [8,19],
medicine [5,9], electronic system cooling [2,11], and clothing [3,10,15]. The use
of PCM is not limited to energy storage, but also provides temperature control
and stabilization. The key to the PCM phenomenon lies in the concept of latent
heat. This was introduced by J. Black [16], who demonstrated by a series of
experiments on water and ice that the process of solid/liquid phase change cannot be studied only in the context of sensible heat. The first study of the phase

© The Author(s), under exclusive license to Springer Nature Switzerland AG 2022
B. Chopard et al. (Eds.): ACRI 2022, LNCS 13402, pp. 173–184, 2022.
https://doi.org/10.1007/978-3-031-14926-9_16

change problem was carried out by Clapeyron and Lamé [16] by considering the secular cooling of the globe. They concluded that the thickness of the solid part that covers our globe increases proportionally to the square root of the time that has elapsed since the beginning of its solidification. The problem of phase change is linked to Jozef Stefan, who introduced the problems of phase change with his work between 1889 and 1891.

The mathematical models found in the literature, to solve the solid-liquid phase change problems, are based on two principal methods: Interface-tracking and no-interface-tracking [20]. Interface tracking methods consist of fixing the interface using a mobile mesh, this leads to the solution of non-linear system equations. The application of interface tracking methods is complex to implement because the time step is fixed and we iterate on the space step so that the phase change interface always coincides with a node of the mesh all the time. The heat transfer equations must be discretized in each phase, and they are linked by the discretization of the energy balance equation at the solid-liquid interface. No-interface-tracking methods simplify the solution of PCM heat transfer without explicitly tracking the solid-liquid interface. In this method class, we can find the two most adopted methods: the enthalpy method [20], and the effective heat capacity method [20]. The enthalpy method uses, for both phases, a single variable (the enthalpy H as an unknown) and therefore reduces the equations system to a single heat transfer equation. In this way, the temperature field is determined without tracking the progression of the solidification front in time. By the enthalpy method, the PC problem becomes easier since the governing equation for the two phases is the same. The effective heat capacity method also reduces the equations system to a single equation. It consists of forming a dependence between latent heat and specific heat capacity.

These models present some limitations, specially when the application in heterogeneous space (media). The heat transfer equations must be discretized in each phase and they are linked by the discretization of the energy balance equation at the solid-liquid interface. It is necessary to establish mathematical models that can correctly link the enthalpy, liquid fraction and temperature [21] plus the different proprieties of different components of the heterogeneous area which are the most difficult to relate since each component got its own proprieties and behaves on its proper way. Thus, heavy numerical instabilities can occur and since in most materials melting or solidification problems can be considered to be multi-dimensional and multi-components problems, which makes them difficult to be solved analytically. Generally, the application of Partial Differential Equations remains difficult to implement to describe the process of phase change with its models in heterogeneous media.

The CA method was applied to many phase change related phenomena, in [6] B. Cortie studied the solidification of a hypothetical liquid using cellular automaton. In [17] the author considered A one-dimensional problem and presented thermodynamic laws applied to CA to take into account phase transition. In [22] a 3D Cellular automata model coupled with finite elements was developed for microstructure evolution. And others mostly focused on material processing

[13,14,18]. Throughout its applications, Cellular Automata showed number of advantages in dealing with this type of problems, especially in proposing solutions dealing with complex geometries and heterogeneous phenomena.

Using cellular automata as an approach will allow us a local description of the evolution of phase change within those types of materials. In this paper we propose a 2D cellular automata model describing the dynamics and behavior of multi-component phase change materials. Conductive heat transfer and solid-liquid phase transition mechanisms are taken into account.

2   Model Description

2.1   Phenomenon Description

Phase change occurs when a substance changes from one state to another. Melting is the transition from solid to liquid, while solidification is the change from solid to liquid. The transition is the result of an energy gain or loss (gain for fusion and loss for solidification). During the phase transition, a zone is created, called a zone phase, characterized by a discontinuity in physical properties. For pure substances, PC occurs with a constant phase change temperature T_{pc} while in the case of impure substances, PC occurs over a temperature range ΔT_{pc}. The PC phenomenon depends on several parameters such as the temperature, thermal conductivity, phase change temperature of each substance, velocity, solid/liquid fraction, etc. The relations between these parameters are non-linear as shown in Eq. 1 that describes the No-interface-tracking model which may be considered the most suitable reference for this problem:

$$\frac{\partial H}{\partial t} + \nabla \cdot (f_s H_s \vec{u}_s + f_l H_l \vec{u}_l) = \vec{\nabla} \cdot (\bar{\lambda} \vec{\nabla} T) \tag{1}$$

f_s is solid fraction, f_l is liquid fraction,
λ is thermal conductivity,
H is enthalpy and its function of temperature and given as:

$$H = f_s \int_{T_0}^{T} \rho_s C_s T d\theta + f_l \int_{T_0}^{T} \rho_l C_l T d\theta + \rho_l f_l L_F \tag{2}$$

ρ_s is solid density, ρ_l is liquid density,
C_s is solid specific heat capacity, C_l is liquid specific heat capacity,
T_0 is the temperature reference point,
L_F is Latent heat of phase change.

2.2   Cellular Automata for Phase Change Phenomenon

For solving the above problem, this paper proposes a new CA model for the phase change phenomenon capable of describing the PC where the material is composite and has complex geometry by an approach more adapted to the computer architecture. The four components of the CA (lattice, neighbourhood, state set and local transition rules) are described in the following.

Lattice and Neighbourhood. The lattice $\mathcal{L}$ is a 2D array that consists of discrete cells c_{ij}. The modelled area is discretized into square or hexagonal elementary cells c_{ij} with centred coordinates (i, j). A cell represents a portion of material in the occupied area. The model works for two cell shapes, square and hexagonal. We consider the Von-Neumann neighbourhood for the square geometric cell and uniform for the hexagonal one.

Attributes. To overcome the problem of modeling a complex phenomenon in the case of a heterogeneous medium (where the cell state depends on several factors and properties that characterize the space). In this way, we consider that the cell can be associated with a set of space attributes. This approach introduced in [4] allows us to separate the state of the phenomenon (the phase of the material in our case) and the space characteristics that impact it. Thus, the attributes are applications linking each cell to a static or dynamic space characteristic, defined by:

$$\sigma: \begin{array}{ccc} \mathcal{L} \times I & \to & F_\sigma \\ (c_{ij}, t_\tau) & \mapsto & \sigma^{t_\tau}(c_{ij}) \end{array}. \tag{3}$$

where $\mathcal{L}$ is the lattice, I is the time interval and F_σ is a bounded set.

States Set. We were interested in the transient of the solid-state towards liquid or vice versa, in that way we distinguished between three main states of matter: solid, transient, and liquid. For more precision, we have considered in transition state an M transient sub-states that can be calculated from the attribute of liquid fraction. So we can present the state of a cell at each iteration t by:

$$\begin{array}{lll} State & S & : \text{Solid state} \\ State & \{T_m\}_{m \leqslant M} & : \text{Transition states} \\ State & L & : \text{Liquid state} \end{array}$$

where m indicates the rate of the liquid part in the material. Each cell is associated with a set of attributes that can be static or dynamic $\mathbb{A}_t = \{T_{pc}, L_{pc}, \phi_t, \lambda_{t_\tau}, Cp_t, \rho, \epsilon\}$. The attributes details are shown in Table 1:

Local Transition Rules. In our model transition rules are based on conductive heat transfer and solid-liquid phase transition principals.

$$f \equiv \boldsymbol{heat\ exchanged} \oplus \boldsymbol{phase\ change}, \tag{4}$$

where the sign $\oplus$ refers to mutual action. The evaluation rules for each process are discussed as follows.

Table 1. Attribute set considered in the model

Phase change temperature	$T_{pc} : \mathcal{L} \mapsto \mathbb{R}^+$	
Latent heat	$L_{pc} : \mathcal{L} \mapsto \mathbb{R}^+$	
Thermal conductivity	$\lambda_t : \mathcal{L} \mapsto \mathbb{R}^+$	$\lambda_t(c_{ij}) = \lambda_l \phi_t(c_{ij}) + \lambda_s(1 - \phi_t(c_{ij}))$
Specific heat capacity	$Cp_t : \mathcal{L} \mapsto \mathbb{R}^+$	$Cp_{t_T}(c_{ij}) = Cp_l \mathbb{K}_{\{\phi_t(c_{ij})=1\}} + Cp_s \mathbb{K}_{\{\phi_t(c_{ij})=1\}}$
Density	$\rho : \mathcal{L} \mapsto \mathbb{R}^+$	$\rho_t(c_{ij}) = \rho_l \mathbb{K}_{\{\phi_t(c_{ij})=1\}} + \rho_s \mathbb{K}_{\{\phi_t(c_{ij})=1\}}$
PC approximation coefficient ϵ :	$\mathcal{L} \mapsto \mathbb{R}^+$	
Liquid fraction	$\phi_t : \mathcal{L} \mapsto [0, 1]$	$\phi_t(c_{ij}) = \frac{T_t(c_{ij}) - T_{pc}(c_{ij}) + \epsilon}{2\epsilon}$

Heat Exchanged. The amount of energy transferred in thermal conduction between two cells can be calculated using the law of heat conduction.

$$Q = -K \Delta T \tag{5}$$

where Q is the local heat flux density (SI unit $[W/m^2]$),
K is equivalent conductivity (SI unit $[W/m^2.°C]$),
ΔT is the temperature difference (SI unit $[°C]$),

By applying Eq. 5 between each cell c_{ij} and its neighbour n, the energy exchanged $\Delta Q_t(c_{ij})$ of each cell is calculated, for example in a case of the hexagonal lattice by

$$Q_t(c_{ij}) = \sum_{n=1}^{6} \Delta Q_t(n) \tag{6}$$

where n indicates the neighbour cell number.

$$\Delta Q_t(n) = K_t(c_{i,j}, n)(T_t(c_{ij}) - T_t(n)) \tag{7}$$

$K_t(c_{i,j}, n)$ is the equivalent thermal conduction coefficient at instant t. Its indicates how heat passes from a cell to another one and equals $\frac{1}{Rth_t(c_{i,j},n)}$, where $Rth_t(c_{i,j}, n)$ is the equivalent thermal resistance between the central cell and its neighbour n. Figure 1 shows a central node and six surrounding nodes and their equivalent thermal resistance. Note that the thermal conductivity $\lambda(n)$ of each cell around the central cell can have a different value. $K_t(c_{i,j}, n)$ is calculated as follow :

$$K_t(c_{i,j}, n) = \frac{1}{Rth_t(c_{i,j}, n)} = \frac{1}{\frac{d/2}{\lambda_t(n)} + \frac{d/2}{\lambda_t(c_{ij})}} \tag{8}$$

$\lambda_t(c_{ij})$: is thermal conductivity of cell c_{ij} at instant t.
$\lambda_t(n)$: is thermal conductivity of cell n at instant t.
d: is the distance between the center of cell c_{ij} and its neighbour cell n. Distance is calculated from the center of the cells.

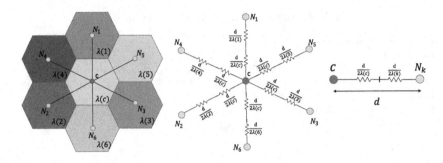

Fig. 1. Equivalent thermal resistance

Phase Change. To take into account the phase change, we use the concept of latent heat. To change its state, a cell requires to gain or lose energy necessary to allow that change. This energy is called latent energy that we introduced as an attribute we first calculate $H_t(c_{ij})$ for each cell, following Eq. 9.

$$
H_t = \begin{cases} \rho_s Cp_s(T_t - T_0) & \text{Solid state } T_t \leq T_1 \\ \rho_s Cp_s(T_1 - T_0) + \rho_l \phi_t L_{pc} & \text{Trans state } T_1 < T_t < T_2 \\ \rho_s Cp_s(T_1 - T_0) + \rho_l L_{pc} + \rho_l Cp_l(T_t - T_2) & \text{Liquid state } T_2 \leq T_t \end{cases}
$$
(9)

$T_0(c_{ij})$ is the temperature reference point. In this paper we choose $T_0(c_{ij})$ the temperature where $H_0(c_{ij}) = 0$
$T_1(c_{ij}) = T_{pc}(c_{ij}) - \epsilon(c_{ij})$
$T_2(c_{ij}) = T_{pc}(c_{ij}) + \epsilon(c_{ij})$
ϵ is used to guarantee phase change.

Adding up the energy exchanged $Q_t(c_{ij})$ to the calculated energy $H_t(c_{ij})$ we obtain $H_{t+1}(c_{ij})$ as shown in Eq. 10.

$$
H_{t+1}(c_{ij}) = H_t(c_{ij}) + Q_t(c_{ij})\Delta t
$$
(10)

The transition from one state to another is illustrated in Fig. 2. We have grouped the transient sub-states $(T_1, \dots, T_N)$ in the middle box. The notation P_{ab} represents the condition that allows a cell to move from a state a to b (solid, transition and liquid states are indicated respectively by 1, 2 and 3). These conditions are represented in Eqs. 12–18.

To determine these conditions, we start from the state of the cell at time t and we base it on the relations between the enthalpy H and the energy necessary to pass from a state to another E. These necessary energies E (E_{rs}, E_{rl}; Eq. 11) depends on the attributes of the cell (type of matter and coefficient of approximation of change of phase ϵ). Moreover, the values of enthalpy H are calculated according to the energy received from the neighborhood (Eq. 10).

$$
E_{rs}(c_{ij}) = c_s(c_{ij})\rho_s(c_{ij})T_1(c_{ij}) \text{ and } E_{rl}(c_{ij}) = c_s(c_{ij})\rho_s(c_{ij})T_1(c_{ij}) + L_{pc}(c_{ij})
$$
(11)

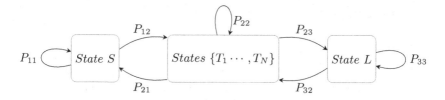

Fig. 2. States transition

P_{11}: if cell is in solid state and did not receive energy necessary to start fusion.

$$P_{11} = \{s_{t+1}(c_{ij}) = 1 \ if \ s_t(c_{ij}) = 1 \ and \ H_{t+1}(c_{ij}) < E_{rs}(c_{ij})\} \qquad (12)$$

P_{12}: if cell is in solid state and receives enough energy to start fusion.

$$P_{12} = \{s_{t+1}(c_{ij}) = 2 \ if \ s_t(c_{ij}) = 1 \ and \ H_{t+1}(c_{ij}) \geq E_{rs}(c_{ij})\} \qquad (13)$$

P_{21}: if cell is changing phase loses enough energy to transform its state to solid.

$$P_{21} = \{s_{t+1}(c_{ij}) = 1 \ if \ s_t(c_{ij}) = 2 \ and \ H_{t+1}(c_{ij}) \leq E_{rs}(c_{ij})\} \qquad (14)$$

P_{22}: if cell is changing phase and did not receive or lose energy necessary to transform its state.

$$P_{22} = \{s_{t+1}(c_{ij}) = 2 \ if \ s_t(c_{ij}) = 2 \ and \ E_{rs}(c_{ij}) < H_{t+1}(c_{ij}) < E_{rl}(c_{ij})\} \quad (15)$$

P_{23}: if cell is changing phase and receives enough energy to transform state to liquid.

$$P_{23} = \{s_{t+1}(c_{ij}) = 3 \ if \ s_t(c_{ij}) = 2 \ and \ H_{t+1}(c_{ij}) \geq E_{rl}(c_{ij})\} \qquad (16)$$

P_{32}: if cell is in liquid state and loses enough energy to start solidification.

$$P_{32} = \{s_{t+1}(c_{ij}) = 2 \ if \ s_t(c_{ij}) = 3 \ and \ H_{t+1}(c_{ij}) < E_{rl}(c_{ij})\} \qquad (17)$$

P_{33}: if cell is in liquid state and did not loose energy necessary to start solidification.

$$P_{33} = \{s_{t+1}(c_{ij}) = 3 \ if \ s_t(c_{ij}) = 3 \ and \ H_{t+1}(c_{ij}) \geq E_{rl}(c_{ij})\} \qquad (18)$$

Remark 1. The time step is integrated into the transition rules in Eq. 10 to calculate the enthalpy in such a way that the information flux between cells depends on the length of the time step. However, we must choose a time step small enough to avoid the direct transaction from the solid to the liquid state, or the reverse.

3   Simulation

3.1   Model Evaluation

To evaluate the model we compared the results with the outputs of the FreeCad software, which was developed in finite elements. The comparison is made only at the temperature level and in the case of a homogeneous material. The comparison of the results for the two types of square (REC) and hexagonal (HEX) cells is through the x-axis. The simulation represents 60 min, we took 4 instants for the comparison 6 min, 15 min, 36 min, and 60 min (Fig. 3).

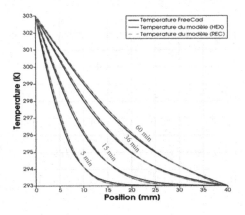

Fig. 3. Temperature distribution along the x-axis, for the 4 instants

3.2   Simulation Results

The simulation represents the heat transfer through a conductive material layer mixed with phase change material (PCM). To apply our approach we consider two types of configurations (circles and fibres) for the Phase Change Material. Figure 4(b) represents the configuration in which the phase change material forms circles of different sizes. Figure 4(c) represents the case of a phase change material in the form of fibres. The initial conditions representing the values of the attributes associated with the phase change materials are shown in Fig. 4(a).

- Layer area: $W = 1 \text{ m}^2$
- Time step used: 10 s
- Mesh size: 100×100 cells
- $T_t(0, j) = 50 \,^\circ\text{C}$.
- Initial temperature: $T_i(\mathcal{L}) = 10 \,^\circ\text{C}$
- Boundary condition: The boundary is considered adiabatic (no heat exchange at the boundaries cells).

Attribute	PCM	Conductive material
λ	$[0.2, 0.22]$	43
ρ	$[640, 660]$	7300
C_s	$[1150, 1258]$	590
L_{pc}	120000	-
T_{pc}	29	1538
ϵ	0.01	-

(a)   (b)   (c)

Fig. 4. Illustration of the simulation conditions. Figure 4(a) initial conditions. Figure 4(b) circles configuration. Figure 4(c) fibres configuration.

Figures 5 and 6 shows the evolution of temperature and liquid fraction over 2000 iterations. We can see that for the same PCM the temperature distribution differs between the circle and the fibre configurations. Liquid fraction figures explains the cold circles and fibres in temperature distribution figures for both configurations, showing the resistance created by the PCM.

The displacement of the heat is almost the same for both configurations, we can see that for the four iterations (100, 500, 1000, 2000) the temperature translation is similar along the horizontal axis. Heat find its way to pass through conductive material.

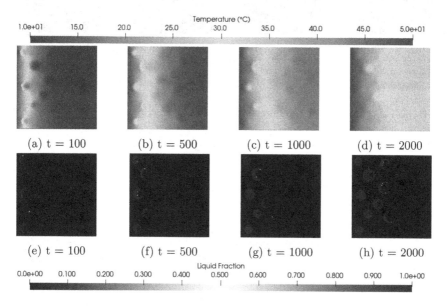

(a) t = 100   (b) t = 500   (c) t = 1000   (d) t = 2000

(e) t = 100   (f) t = 500   (g) t = 1000   (h) t = 2000

Fig. 5. Circle: evolution of temperature and liquid fraction distribution over 2000 iteration

For the same simulation, to observe the temperature evolution of a cell, we have chosen 3 cells at the following positions: (25,25), (50,50) and (75,75). Figures 7(a) and 7(b) shows the variation of temperature for the two configurations (circle and fibre) over 8000 time steps of 3 cells in the following positions: (25,25), (50,50) and (75,75). In the Fig. 7(a) we can see that even if the cell (25,25) was the first one of the 3 to get heated its temperature got dilated because that cell is occupied with PCM and the other two are occupied with conductive material. For the fibre configuration (Fig. 7(b)) the cell at position (75,75) was occupied by the PCM which explain the temperature stabilization between iterations 2000 and 3500.

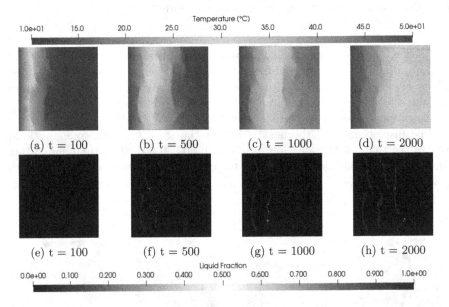

Fig. 6. Fibre: evolution of temperature and liquid fraction distribution over 2000 iteration

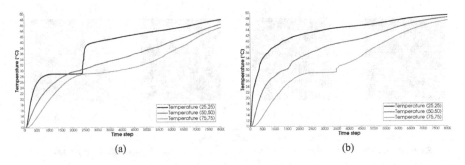

Fig. 7. (a) Circle configuration: plot over 8000 iterations of 3 cells (b) Fibre configuration: plot over 8000 iterations of 3 cells

4   Conclusion and Perspectives

We presented a model based on CA to describe temperature and phases evolution during phase change in complex geometries of multi-components materials. CA have the advantage of being able to consider cases where the space is heterogeneous. Since, we have associated each cell an elementary feature presented by the set of spatial attributes. Consequently, the local description of the phase change phenomenon allows to avoid the computational complexity of the classical methods.

This work allows many perspectives: i) The model can be developed to take into account gas state; ii) The model will be extended to 3D; iii) Optimal control will be introduced in order to design the best configuration and optimize its performance.

Acknowledgement. This work has been supported by MESRSFC and CNRST under the project PPR2-OGI-Env, reference PPR2/2016/79.

References

1. Alawadhi, E.M., Alqallaf, H.J.: Building roof with conical holes containing PCM to reduce the cooling load: numerical study. Energy Convers. Manage. **52**(8–9), 2958–2964 (2011)
2. Bondareva, N.S., Buonomo, B., Manca, O., Sheremet, M.A.: Heat transfer performance of the finned nano-enhanced phase change material system under the inclination influence. Int. J. Heat Mass Transf. **135**, 1063–1072 (2019)
3. Buckley, T.M.: Phase change material thermal capacitor clothing. US Patent 6,855,410, 15 Feb 2005
4. Byari, M., Bernoussi, A.S., Ouardouz, M., Amharref, M.: Control of 3D cellular automata via actuator and space attributes: application to fires forest. In: Gwizdałła, T.M., Manzoni, L., Sirakoulis, G.C., Bandini, S., Podlaski, K. (eds.) Cellular Automata. ACRI 2020. LNCS, vol. 12599. Springer, Cham (2021). https://doi.org/10.1007/978-3-030-69480-7_13
5. Choi, S.-W., Zhang, Y., Xia, Y.: A temperature-sensitive drug release system based on phase-change materials. Angew. Chem. Int. Ed. **49**(43), 7904–7908 (2010)
6. Cortie, M.: Simulation of metal solidification using a cellular automaton. Metall. Trans. B **24**(6), 1045–1053 (1993)
7. Diaconu, B.M., Cruceru, M.: Novel concept of composite phase change material wall system for year-round thermal energy savings. Energy Build. **42**(10), 1759–1772 (2010)
8. Gin, B., Farid, M.M.: The use of PCM panels to improve storage condition of frozen food. J. Food Eng. **100**(2), 372–376 (2010)
9. Hirst, A.R., Escuder, B., Miravet, J.F., Smith, D.K.: High-tech applications of self-assembling supramolecular nanostructured gel-phase materials: from regenerative medicine to electronic devices. Angew. Chem. Int. Ed. **47**(42), 8002–8018 (2008)
10. Hu, Y., Huang, D., Qi, Z., He, S., Yang, H., Zhang, H.: Modeling thermal insulation of firefighting protective clothing embedded with phase change material. Heat Mass Transf. **49**(4), 567–573 (2013)

11. Kandasamy, R., Wang, X.-Q., Mujumdar, A.S.: Application of phase change materials in thermal management of electronics. Appl. Therm. Eng. **27**(17–18), 2822–2832 (2007)
12. Kuznik, F., Virgone, J., Noel, J.: Optimization of a phase change material wallboard for building use. Appl. Therm. Eng. **28**(11–12), 1291–1298 (2008)
13. Łach, Ł, Nowak, J., Svyetlichnyy, D.: The evolution of the microstructure in AISI 304L stainless steel during the flat rolling-modeling by frontal cellular automata and verification. J. Mater. Process. Technol. **255**, 488–499 (2018)
14. Reuther, K., Rettenmayr, M.: Perspectives for cellular automata for the simulation of dendritic solidification-a review. Comput. Mater. Sci. **95**, 213–220 (2014)
15. Salaün, F., Devaux, E., Bourbigot, S., Rumeau, P.: Development of phase change materials in clothing part I: formulation of microencapsulated phase change. Text. Res. J. **80**(3), 195–205 (2010)
16. Šarler, B.: Stefan's work on solid-liquid phase changes. Eng. Anal. Boundary Elem. **16**(2), 83–92 (1995)
17. Selivorstova, T., Selivorstov, V., Guda, A., Ostrovska, K.: Thermodynamic fundamentals of cellular automata model of the process of solidification of metals and alloys considering the phase transition. In: ICTES (2020)
18. Svyetlichnyy, D.S., Nowak, J., Łach, Ł.: Modeling of recrystallization with recovery by frontal cellular automata. In: Sirakoulis, G.C., Bandini, S. (eds.) ACRI 2012. LNCS, vol. 7495, pp. 494–503. Springer, Heidelberg (2012). https://doi.org/10.1007/978-3-642-33350-7_51
19. Tulapurkar, C., Subramaniam, P.R., Thagamani, G., Thiyagarajan, R.: Phase change materials for domestic refrigerators to improve food quality and prolong compressor off time (2010)
20. Voller, V.R., Prakash, C.: A fixed grid numerical modelling methodology for convection-diffusion mushy region phase-change problems. Int. J. Heat Mass Transf. **30**(8), 1709–1719 (1987)
21. Xiaoqing, L., Peng, Y., Renqiang, L., Hui, J., Xiaoyan, L.: A novel model for calculating the melting process of composite phase change materials. J. Energy Storage **30**, 101504 (2020)
22. Zhao, Y., Qin, R., Chen, D.: A three-dimensional cellular automata model coupled with finite element method and thermodynamic database for alloy solidification. J. Cryst. Growth **377**, 72–77 (2013)

Performance Analysis of Regular Clocking Based Quantum-Dot Cellular Automata Logic Circuit: Fault Tolerant Approach

Amit Kumar Pramanik[1,4], Jayanta Pal[2], Biplab K. Sikdar[3],
and Bibhash Sen[4(✉)]

[1] Department of CSE, Dumka Engineering College, Jharkhand, India
[2] Department of Information Technology, Tripura University, Suryamaninagar, India
jayantapal@tripurauniv.ac.in
[3] Department of Computer Science and Technology,
IIEST Shibpur, Howrah, WB, India
biplab@cs.iiests.ac.in
[4] Department of CSE, National Institute of Technology, Durgapur, India
bibhash.sen@cse.nitdgp.ac.in

Abstract. Current CMOS technology suffers from low device density and high power dissipation due to tremendous enhancement of device scaling. Quantum-dot Cellular Automata (QCA) is alternative nanotechnology to overcome these drawbacks. A cell containing four quantum dots and two electrons is a fundamental element for logic circuit realization in QCA. In QCA, clocking plays a vital role in the proper synchronization and flow of information along with the scalability of the QCA circuit. In addition, regular clocking diminishes the fabrication challenges of the nanoscale era. On the other hand, defects remain an issue in nanoscale circuit realization. This work aims to analyze the performance of underlying clocking schemes in terms of fault-tolerant capability. A full adder circuit is realized using different clocking schemes, and the HDLQ and QCADesigner simulators are used for this purpose. According to experimental results, Zig-Zag clocking exhibits better performance under cell deposition defects, whereas RES clocking stands at the top in the case of HDLQ analysis.

Keywords: QCA · Regular clocking · QCA defect · Fault-tolerant · HDLQ · QCADesigner

1 Introduction

As CMOS technology has enhanced tremendously in the last few decades, it encounters serious problems like low device density and high power dissipation. Quantum-dot Cellular Automata (QCA) is one of the emerging technology that can solve these problems [6]. At the same time, a scalable QCA processor was proposed in [3]. It has a strong effect on the development of future fast nano-architecture circuits. In QCA, the fundamental element is the QCA cell. Four quantum dots are present in every cell. Two electrons are positioned in the

© The Author(s), under exclusive license to Springer Nature Switzerland AG 2022
B. Chopard et al. (Eds.): ACRI 2022, LNCS 13402, pp. 185–198, 2022.
https://doi.org/10.1007/978-3-031-14926-9_17

diagonally opposite quantum dots due to the consequence of the columbic inter-action. In contrast with CMOS, the primary gates in QCA are majority voter (MV) and Inverter (INV). Besides these primary gates, other essential elements of QCA circuits are QCA wire and cross-wires. The majority voter is used to realizing traditional AND, OR gate.

In the realization of QCA circuits, clocking plays a vital role. The restoration option of signal with attenuation and loss is a significant advantage of clocking in QCA. Many clocking schemes have been reported till now. Some of the well known clocking schemes are USE [2], RES [5], Optimized 2-D [17], Zig-Zag [11] clocking schemes. Optimized 2-D [17] do not follow a uniform shape; as a result, it is very difficult to fabricate. USE [2] clocking scheme uses a multi-layer clocking scheme, whereas RES [5] uses coplanar wire crossing for QCA circuit realization.

In QCA circuit design, the fundamental idea is to place the QCA cells prop-erly to get desired output. As defect is one of the critical issues in nanoscale, the correctness of any design depends on its fault-tolerant capability. Usually, defects can occur in deposition, fabrication, or both phases. However, the max-imum possibility of defect can occur in the deposition phase. In the fabrication phase, common faults are cell displacement, cell omission, extra cell, and cell misalignment faults. Because of the thermodynamic effect or slight energy vari-ation between excited and ground states, a defect can occur in QCA circuits. A testing mechanism is required to check the fault-tolerant capability as the performance of any QCA circuit depends on its fault-tolerant ability.

In a digital circuit, the adder is a vital circuit. It is used in many logic operations like subtraction, addition, etc. Till now, various methods have been proposed to design adder [8,10,15]. But none of them has investigated which clocking scheme is suitable for this circuit in terms of fault-tolerant capability.

The above factors motivate us to realize 1-bit Full Adder circuit using USE [2], RES [5], Optimized 2-D [17], Zig-Zag [11] clocking schemes. The primary focus of this work is to investigate the fault-tolerant capability of clocking schemes, as mentioned earlier, using a 1-bit full adder. The contributions of the work are as follows:

- A 1-bit Full adder is realized using existing clocking schemes.
- Performance of each clocking-based circuit is investigated in terms of fault-tolerant capability.
- A proper clocking scheme is reported to eradicate the QCA defects.

This article is arranged as follows: Section 2 presents a brief description of the basics of QCA, Regular Clocking, and QCA defects. Section 3 contains an analy-sis about the fault-tolerant capability of different clocking-based 1-bit Full adder (FA). Section 4 presents a detailed discussion about the fault-tolerant capability of underlying clocking schemes. Section 5 concludes the work.

2   Background and Related Work

This section describes the basic concepts of various aspects used in this research work.

2.1 QCA Basic

The basic elements are presented in Fig. 1. Each QCA cell contains four quantum dots, and two electrons are present in diagonally opposite dots, as shown in Fig. 1 (a). Two possible arrangements are formed due to coulombic repulsion, Logic '1' and logic '0' as represented in Fig. 1(b). In quantum dots, electrons switch their places to transmit information from one part to another part. The primary gates are majority voter (Fig. 1(c)) and inverter. Conventional AND, OR gate can be realized from majority voter by fixing any input to 0 or 1. A majority voter has three inputs and one output, as shown in Fig. 1(c), but [14] proposed a five-input majority voter. An inverter is used to flip the input. According to research, many structures of the inverter are available. However, Fig. 1(d) represents one of the structures of the inverter. A QCA wire is formed by arranging cells adjacent to each other. Different wire crossing techniques (multi-layer, rotated cell, and clock zone-based) are available to realize QCA circuits.

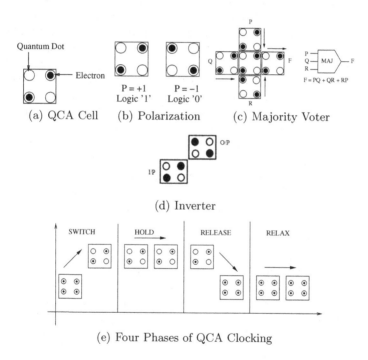

(a) QCA Cell   (b) Polarization   (c) Majority Voter

(d) Inverter

(e) Four Phases of QCA Clocking

Fig. 1. Basic structural components of QCA

QCA clocking is used to synchronize the information flow throughout the circuit. It has four phases, as shown in Fig. 1(e). At the beginning of the switch phase, the QCA cells are un-polarized, and interdot potential barriers are low between them. By the end of this phase, barriers are high, and cell states are fixed. In the hold phase, the barriers remain high, and polarized cells influence the neighbor cell. Cell barriers are lowered and allowed to relax to an unpolarized state in the release phase. Interdot barriers remain lowered in relax phase. According to [2], each array of QCA cells can be divided into sub-array (known as clock zones) to realize multi-phase clocking. A model was developed for calculating the clocking electric field at the device layer in [1].

2.2 Regular Clocking

Clocking plays a vital role in the QCA circuit. Clocking is used to regain the lost signal. [7] has proposed the idea about clocking. Nowadays, many well known clocking schemes are available to realize QCA circuits, like USE Clocking Scheme [2] is a Universal, Scalable, and Efficient clocking scheme (Fig. 2(a)). It can realize the feedback path efficiently. Here information can propagate from Zone 1 to 2, 2 to 3, 3 to 4, 4 to 0, and so on. It also propagates information to the rows and columns. Here information flows in two directions. This clocking scheme uses multi-layer wire crossing to realize QCA circuits, which is challenging to fabricate. RES Clocking Scheme [5] is a Robust, Efficient and Scalable clocking scheme, shown in Fig. 2(b). The advantage of this scheme is that it permits three directional information flow at a particular point, as shown in Fig. 2(b) with the red circle. However, achieving this advantage loses uniformity for the underlying layout for the clock zone 3. As this clocking scheme creates useless wire crossing, it increases the difficulty in fabrication. This scheme utilizes rotated cell-based wire crossing to realize QCA circuits. Optimized 2-D Clocking Scheme [17] is a tile like structure as shown in Fig. 2(c). It has a rectangular structure of clock zone with a 2:1 aspect ratio. It can realize all the functions that other existing clocking schemes can realize. However, it is tough to fabricate due to the movement of clock zones in each row. It allows bi-directional information flow. It solves the problem of underlying wire crossing. Zig-Zag [11] clocking schemes is also known as efficient, scalable, regular clocking scheme. It permits both straight and zig-zag lines (Fig. 2(d)). In this scheme, a bi-directional feedback path is utilized. This clocking permits three directional input and output. This clocking scheme has all the advantages of the clocking schemes mentioned above. In the realization of QCA circuits, [12] has compared RES and USE clocking schemes in terms of the aspects that significantly impact the cost calculation of circuits. Whereas [13] demonstrates the comparison between RES and USE regarding power dissipation. However, the comparison between these four well-established clocking schemes is not reported.

2.3 QCA Defects

Due to various types of cell deposition defects, QCA has high fault rates [16]. In QCA, circuit defects can occur in the deposition phase or fabrication phase [16]. Various types of cell deposition defects are depicted, concerning 3-input majority voter in Fig. 3(a). The defects are **(a) Cell Misalignment:** In this defect cell is misaligned compared to its original alignment. As shown in Fig. 3(b), X is the cell which is wrongly aligned, as compared to the which is fault free (Fig. 3(a)).

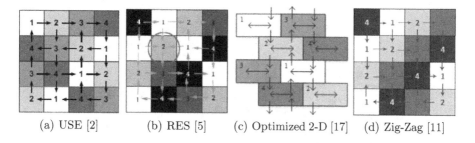

(a) USE [2]   (b) RES [5]   (c) Optimized 2-D [17]   (d) Zig-Zag [11]

Fig. 2. Regular clocking schemes

(b) Cell Displacement: As depicted in Fig. 3(c), X cell is displaced vertically from its actual position. As a result, it may produce an incorrect output. **(c) Extra cell:** In this defect extra cell(s) is doped, termed as 'extra cell' defect. As shown in Fig. 3(d), two extra cells are doped on both sides of the X cell. Due to this defect, the majority gate will provide incorrect output. **(d) Cell Missing:** In this type of defect, any cell may be missing. In Fig. 3(e), input cell X is missing compared to its original structure (Fig. 3(a)) of majority voter. **(e) Rotation Defect:** A cell can be doped as rotated (45°) as compared to its original structure (90°). As shown in Fig. 3(f), input cell X is rotated by $\theta°$ compared to Fig. 3(a). As a result, the output of this defective gate is incorrect.

3   Analysis of Fault Tolerant Capability of Underlying Clocking Schemes

In QCA, some important circuits are Adder, Subtractor, Latch, etc. However, analysis of all QCA circuits is not possible due to page limitations. As many researches [8,15] are targeted towards the full adder (FA) and it is most important circuit, an one bit FA circuit is used to analysis the fault-tolerant capability of different (USE [2], RES [5], Optimized 2-D [17], Zig-Zag [11]) underlying clocking schemes.

The fault-tolerant capability of a circuit is investigated by efficient testing. A defect can occur in the QCA circuit's realization in the synthesis and deposition phases. A serious problem in circuit testing is that logic gates do not have the in-built method for error sensing. Thus, a correct technique is required for circuit testing. Many defects are possible, like cell omission defect, extra cell defect, and cell misalignment defect. In the following sections, cell omission defects of clocking-based full adder circuits are investigated using the HDLQ and QCADesigner simulators. Correct doping of QCA cells is required to provide accurate output on a small scale. As a result, a proper testing technique is necessary to detect faults in boosting the performance of circuits.

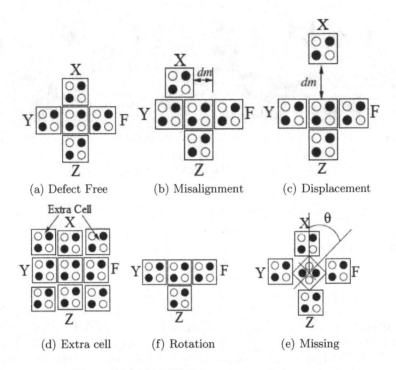

(a) Defect Free   (b) Misalignment   (c) Displacement

(d) Extra cell   (f) Rotation   (e) Missing

Fig. 3. Possible QCA defects in a majority gate

3.1   Analysis Using HDLQ

Different clocking-based Full Adder (FA) circuits are evaluated using the Hardware Description Language (HDL) simulator to find the fault-tolerant clocking scheme [9]. The HDLQ simulator has considered all the feasible faults for a specific cell [4]. In this simulation, HDLQ Verilog library functions are used. This tool is equivalent to Verilog, and it includes Verilog HDL library collections. It contains the library functions for inverter, majority voter, wire crossing, L-shaped, fan-out with the capability to insert defects. The fault tolerance of the QCA is established in literature using HDLQ only. The launder clocking scheme is considered in this case.

The HDLQ diagrams for each clocking based full adder are represented in Fig. 4–7. In this model, "L", "M", "F", "I", "W" represents L-shaped, Majority Voter, Fan-out, Inverter, and Wire Crossing, respectively. Extensive testing for the designed HDLQ diagram is done with the help of the Verilog HDL simulation tool. This diagram or model is tested in the presence of all types of single-cell missing defects. It contains eight input samples for the three inputs and produces 42 different fault samples for the output. The fault samples for different clocking based FA are depicted in Table 1–8. In these tables, ai represents the decimal value for the input combination (i), like a2 represents 10 as 2 is the decimal value for 10. In these tables first, second and last column represents Input

Vector (IV), Expected Vector, and % of fault count (%FT), respectively. %FT indicates the percentage of fault-tolerant outputs out of 42 various fault samples. The fault-tolerant capability of each clocking scheme is investigated below.

USE Clocking Scheme [2]: The 1-bit Full Adder is realized using USE [2] clocking scheme, as shown in Fig. 4(a). It has three inputs (In0, In1, Cin) and two outputs (COUT and SUM). HDLQ diagram or model for Fig. 4(a) is shown in Fig. 4(b). It has 18 L-shaped, 2 Wire Crossings, 6 Fan-outs, 7 Majority Voters, and 2 Inverters. This circuit is tested for 42 different samples, and the results are tabulated in Table 1 and 2. According to these tables, the most fault-tolerant Input Vectors are "a5" and "a6" as it has the highest value for %FT.

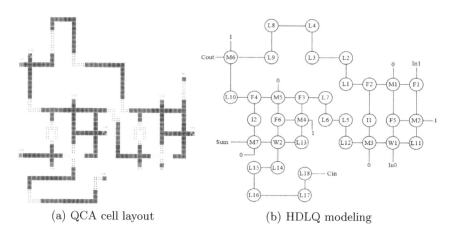

(a) QCA cell layout   (b) HDLQ modeling

Fig. 4. USE clocking based Full Adder

Table 1. Fault pattern (1–22) for USE clocking based FA

IV	EV	1	2	3	4	5	6	7	8	9	10	11	12	13	14	15	16	17	18	19	20	21	22
a0	a0	a2	a0	a2	a0	a0	a0	a0	a1	a0	a0	a0	a0	a0	a0	a0	a1	a0	a0	a0	a0	a1	a1
a1	a2	a1	a2	a2	a0	a2	a2	a2	a3	a2	a2	a2	a2	a2	a2	a1	a1	a2	a2	a2	a2	a3	a3
a2	a2	a0	a0	a0	a0	a1	a1	a2	a2	a0	a0	a2	a2	a0	a0	a2	a2	a2	a2	a2	a2	a3	a3
a3	a1	a2	a2	a1	a3	a3	a2	a1	a1	a2	a2	a1	a1	a1	a1	a1	a1	a0	a0	a3	a3	a1	a1
a4	a2	a2	a0	a0	a0	a2	a1	a1	a1	a2	a2	a2	a2	a0	a0	a2	a2	a2	a2	a2	a2	a3	a3
a5	a1	a1	a2	a1	a3	a1	a2	a3	a3	a1	a1	a1	a1	a1	a1	a1	a1	a0	a0	a3	a3	a1	a1
a6	a1	a1	a3	a3	a1	a2	a1	a1	a1	a1	a1	a3	a3	a1	a1	a1	a1	a1	a1	a1	a1	a0	a0
a7	a3	a3	a1	a3	a1	a1	a3	a3	a3	a3	a3	a1	a1	a3	a3	a1	a1	a3	a3	a3	a3	a2	a2

RES Clocking Scheme [5]: 1-bit Full Adder in RES [5] clocking scheme is represented in Fig. 5(a). It produce 2 output lines (Sum and Carry) from 3 input values (A, B and C). Similar to USE, HDLQ model for Fig. 5(a) is shown in

Table 2. Fault Pattern (23–42) for USE clocking based FA

IV	EV	23	24	25	26	27	28	29	30	31	32	33	34	35	36	37	38	39	40	41	42	%FT
a0	a0	a1	a1	a2	a2	a2	a2	a2	a1	a2	a2	a2	a2	a2	a2	a2	a2	a2	a2	a0	a0	42.86
a1	a2	a3	a3	a1	a1	a1	a3	a3	a3	a1	a1	a0	a0	a0	a0	a0	a0	a1	a0	a2	a0	38.10
a2	a2	a3	a3	a0	a0	a0	a3	a3	a3	a0	a0	a0	a1	a1	a1	a1	a1	a2	a2	a0	a0	28.57
a3	a1	a1	a1	a2	a2	a2	a1	a1	a0	a2	a2	a1	a2	a2	a2	a2	a2	a1	a1	a2	a3	42.86
a4	a2	a3	a3	a0	a0	a0	a3	a3	a3	a0	a0	a0	a1	a1	a1	a1	a1	a0	a2	a0	a0	30.95
a5	a1	a1	a1	a2	a2	a2	a1	a1	a0	a2	a2	a1	a2	a2	a2	a2	a2	a1	a1	a2	a3	45.24
a6	a1	a0	a0	a3	a3	a3	a0	a0	a1	a1	a3	a3	a3	a3	a3	a3	a3	a1	a3	a3	a1	45.24
a7	a3	a2	a2	a1	a1	a1	a2	a2	a3	a3	a1	a1	a1	a1	a1	a1	a1	a3	a1	a1	a1	38.10

Fig. 5(b). It utilizes 10 Fan-outs, 11 L-shaped, 7 Majority Voters, 2 Inverters and 2 Wire Crossings. The results of testing are depicted in Table 3 and 4. "a3" is the most fault tolerant Input Vector.

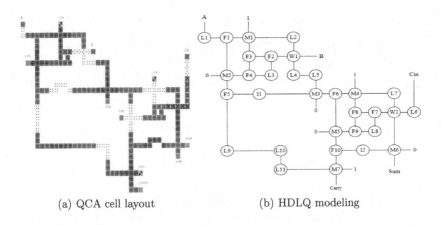

(a) QCA cell layout   (b) HDLQ modeling

Fig. 5. RSE clocking based Full Adder

Table 3. Fault pattern (1–22) for RES clocking based FA

IV	EV	1	2	3	4	5	6	7	8	9	10	11	12	13	14	15	16	17	18	19	20	21	22
a0	a0	a0	a0	a0	a0	a1	a0	a0	a0	a0	a0	a0	a0	a0	a1	a0	a0	a0	a0	a0	a1	a0	a0
a1	a2	a2	a2	a2	a2	a3	a1	a2	a2	a2	a2	a2	a2	a2	a3	a2	a2	a0	a0	a2	a2	a2	a2
a2	a2	a1	a2	a2	a2	a3	a2	a1	a2	a2	a2	a2	a2	a2	a2	a2	a2	a2	a1	a1	a2	a2	
a3	a1	a3	a1	a1	a1	a1	a2	a2	a1	a1	a1	a1	a1	a1	a1	a1	a1	a1	a1	a1	a1	a3	a3
a4	a2	a2	a1	a2	a2	a3	a2	a1	a2	a2	a2	a0	a0	a1	a1	a2	a2	a2	a2	a1	a1	a2	a2
a5	a1	a1	a3	a1	a1	a1	a2	a2	a1	a1	a1	a2	a2	a3	a3	a1	a1	a1	a1	a1	a1	a3	a3
a6	a1	a2	a2	a1	a1	a0	a1	a1	a1	a1	a1	a1	a1	a1	a3	a3	a1	a1	a1	a1	a1	a1	a1
a7	a3	a1	a1	a3	a3	a2	a1	a3	a3	a3	a3	a3	a3	a3	a3	a1	a1	a1	a1	a3	a3	a3	a3

Table 4. Fault Pattern (23-42) for for RES clocking based FA

IV	EV	23	24	25	26	27	28	29	30	31	32	33	34	35	36	37	38	39	40	41	42	%FT
a0	a0	a0	a0	a2	a2	a0	a2	a2	a2	a2	a0	a1	a1	a1	a2	a2	a0	a0	a1	a1	a1	59.52
a1	a2	a2	a2	a1	a1	a2	a1	a1	a0	a0	a2	a3	a3	a3	a1	a0	a2	a2	a1	a3	a3	54.76
a2	a2	a2	a2	a1	a0	a2	a0	a0	a1	a0	a1	a3	a3	a3	a0	a2	a0	a2	a1	a3	a1	47.62
a3	a1	a0	a0	a3	a2	a1	a2	a2	a2	a1	a2	a1	a1	a1	a2	a1	a2	a1	a3	a1	a3	64.29
a4	a2	a2	a2	a0	a0	a1	a0	a0	a1	a0	a1	a3	a3	a3	a2	a2	a0	a2	a1	a0	a1	42.86
a5	a1	a0	a0	a2	a2	a3	a2	a2	a2	a1	a2	a1	a1	a1	a1	a1	a2	a1	a3	a2	a3	47.62
a6	a1	a1	a1	a2	a1	a2	a1	a1	a3	a3	a1	a0	a0	a0	a1	a3	a3	a1	a0	a0	a2	59.52
a7	a3	a3	a3	a1	a3	a1	a3	a3	a1	a1	a3	a2	a2	a2	a3	a1	a1	a3	a0	a2	a1	52.38

Optimized 2-D Clocking Scheme [17]: Fig. 6(a) represents realization of 1-bit FA using Optimized 2-D [17] clocking scheme. It has two outputs (SUMi and C0) and three inputs (Ai, Bi, Ci). Figure 6(b) represents the HDLQ model for Fig. 6(a). This model has 36 L-shaped, 5 Fan-outs, 3 Majority Voters and 3 Inverters. Figure 6(a) is tested for 42 different samples and results are depicted in Table 5 and 6. Result shows that "a3" and "a4" are most fault tolerant Input Vector.

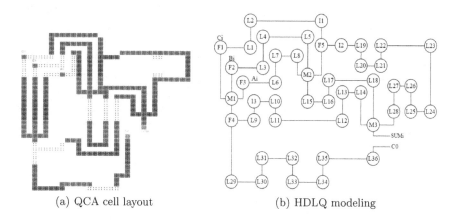

(a) QCA cell layout   (b) HDLQ modeling

Fig. 6. Optimized 2-D clocking based Full Adder

Table 5. Fault Pattern (1–22) for Optimized 2-D clocking based FA

IV	EV	1	2	3	4	5	6	7	8	9	10	11	12	13	14	15	16	17	18	19	20	21	22
a0	a0	a0	a0	a0	a1	a0	a0	a1	a2	a2	a0	a0	a2	a2	a2	a2	a2	a2	a2	a2	a2	a0	a0
a1	a2	a2	a1	a1	a3	a2	a2	a2	a2	a2	a0	a0	a0	a0	a2	a2	a2	a2	a2	a2	a2	a0	a0
a2	a2	a1	a2	a1	a3	a0	a1	a1	a2	a2	a2	a2	a2	a2	a0	a0	a0	a2	a2	a2	a2	a0	a0
a3	a1	a2	a2	a1	a0	a3	a1	a1	a1	a1	a1	a1	a1	a1	a1	a1	a1	a3	a3	a3	a3	a3	a3
a4	a2	a1	a1	a2	a3	a0	a2	a2	a2	a2	a2	a2	a2	a2	a2	a2	a0	a0	a0	a0	a0	a0
a5	a1	a2	a1	a2	a0	a3	a2	a2	a1	a1	a1	a1	a1	a1	a3	a3	a3	a1	a1	a1	a1	a3	a3
a6	a1	a1	a2	a2	a0	a1	a1	a1	a1	a1	a3	a3	a3	a3	a1	a1	a1	a1	a1	a1	a1	a3	a3
a7	a3	a3	a3	a3	a2	a3	a3	a2	a1	a1	a3	a3	a1	a1	a1	a1	a1	a1	a1	a1	a1	a3	a3

Table 6. Fault pattern (23–42) for optimized 2-D clocking based FA

IV	EV	23	24	25	26	27	28	29	30	31	32	33	34	35	36	37	38	39	40	41	42	%FT
a0	a0	a0	a0	a0	a2	a2	a2	a2	a2	a2	a1	a2	a2	a0	a0	a1	a2	a2	a0	a2	a2	35.71
a1	a2	a0	a0	a0	a2	a2	a2	a2	a0	a0	a3	a0	a0	a0	a2	a1	a1	a1	a2	a0	a0	45.24
a2	a2	a0	a0	a0	a0	a0	a0	a0	a2	a2	a3	a2	a2	a0	a1	a1	a1	a1	a0	a2	a2	40.48
a3	a1	a3	a3	a3	a3	a3	a3	a3	a1	a1	a0	a1	a1	a3	a1	a2	a1	a1	a3	a1	a1	50.00
a4	a2	a0	a0	a0	a0	a0	a0	a0	a2	a2	a3	a2	a2	a0	a2	a1	a2	a2	a0	a2	a2	50.00
a5	a1	a3	a3	a3	a3	a3	a3	a3	a1	a1	a0	a1	a1	a3	a2	a2	a2	a2	a3	a1	a1	40.48
a6	a1	a3	a3	a3	a1	a1	a1	a1	a3	a3	a0	a3	a3	a3	a1	a2	a2	a2	a1	a3	a3	45.24
a7	a3	a3	a3	a3	a1	a1	a1	a1	a1	a1	a2	a1	a1	a3	a3	a2	a1	a1	a3	a1	a1	35.72

Zig-Zag Clocking Schemes [11]: The QCA layout for Zig-Zag [11] clocking based 1-bit FA is depicted in Fig. 7(a). The HDLQ model for this layout is shown in Fig. 7(b). This model has 14 L-shaped, 5 Fan-outs, 3 Majority Voters, 2 Inverters, and 3 Wire Crossing. The testing results are tabulated in Tables 7 and 8. Depending on the %FT value, most fault-tolerant input vectors are "a1" and "a6.

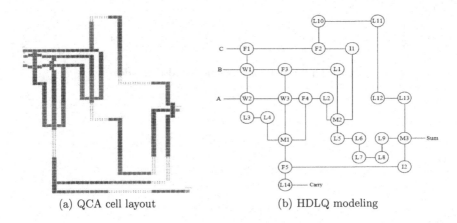

(a) QCA cell layout   (b) HDLQ modeling

Fig. 7. Zig-Zag clocking based Full Adder

3.2   Analysis Using QCADesigner

The Full Adder (FA) circuits are realized using QCADesigner to detect single-cell omission defects. Each clocking-based circuit is tested by deleting one cell at a time (except input, output, and fixed polarized cell). The result of this testing is tabulated in Table 9. In this table, the last column represents (FT %) fault-tolerant capability (%) of that clocking-based FA circuit. It is calculated as (Total cell for which output is not faulty/Total cell except input, output, and fixed polarized cell) * 100.

Table 7. Fault pattern (1–22) for Zig-Zag clocking based FA

IV	EV	1	2	3	4	5	6	7	8	9	10	11	12	13	14	15	16	17	18	19	20	21	22
a0	a0	a0	a2	a0	a0	a1	a0	a1	a0	a0	a0	a0	a2	a2	a0	a0	a2	a2	a2	a2	a2	a2	a2
a1	a2	a2	a0	a1	a1	a3	a2	a2	a2	a2	a2	a2	a2	a2	a2	a2	a2	a2	a2	a2	a2	a0	a0
a2	a2	a1	a2	a2	a1	a3	a1	a1	a2	a2	a0	a0	a0	a2	a1	a1	a0	a0	a0	a0	a0	a2	a2
a3	a1	a2	a1	a2	a1	a0	a1	a1	a3	a3	a3	a3	a1	a3	a2	a2	a3	a3	a3	a3	a3	a1	a1
a4	a2	a1	a2	a1	a2	a3	a2	a2	a0	a0	a0	a0	a2	a0	a1	a1	a0	a0	a0	a0	a0	a2	a2
a5	a1	a2	a1	a1	a2	a0	a2	a2	a1	a1	a3	a3	a3	a1	a2	a2	a3	a3	a3	a3	a3	a1	a1
a6	a1	a1	a3	a2	a2	a0	a1	a1	a1	a1	a1	a1	a1	a1	a1	a1	a1	a1	a1	a1	a1	a3	a3
a7	a3	a3	a1	a3	a3	a2	a3	a2	a3	a3	a3	a3	a1	a1	a3	a3	a1	a1	a1	a1	a1	a1	a1

Table 8. Fault pattern (23–42) for Zig-Zag clocking based FA

IV	EV	23	24	25	26	27	28	29	30	31	32	33	34	35	36	37	38	39	40	41	42	%FT
a0	a0	a2	a2	a1	a2	a0	a2	a0	a2	a0	a0	a0	a0	a1	a0	a0	a1	a1	a1	a3	a1	45.24
a1	a2	a0	a0	a3	a2	a2	a2	a2	a1	a1	a2	a0	a2	a0	a1	a1	a3	a3	a1	a3	a3	52.38
a2	a2	a2	a2	a3	a2	a2	a1	a1	a2	a2	a0	a0	a1	a3	a2	a1	a3	a1	a1	a3	a3	33.33
a3	a1	a1	a1	a0	a2	a2	a1	a1	a1	a1	a3	a3	a1	a1	a2	a3	a2	a2	a2	a3	a3	35.72
a4	a2	a2	a2	a3	a1	a1	a2	a2	a2	a2	a0	a0	a2	a2	a1	a0	a1	a1	a1	a0	a0	35.72
a5	a1	a1	a1	a0	a1	a1	a2	a2	a1	a1	a3	a3	a2	a0	a1	a2	a0	a2	a2	a0	a0	33.33
a6	a1	a3	a3	a0	a1	a1	a1	a1	a2	a2	a1	a3	a1	a3	a2	a2	a0	a0	a2	a0	a0	52.38
a7	a3	a1	a1	a2	a1	a3	a1	a3	a1	a3	a3	a3	a3	a2	a3	a3	a2	a2	a2	a0	a2	42.86

4   Discussion

From Table 1–8, it is clear that the USE [2], Optimized 2-D [17] and Zig-Zag [11] clocking based circuits are most fault-tolerant (FT) for two input vectors (for USE a5 and a6, optimized 2-D a3 and a4, Zig-Zag a1 and a6) whereas RES [5] based circuit is most FT for only one input vector (a3). For HDLQ, the average FT (%) capability for any clocking-based circuit is calculated using %FT values for all the input vectors. It can be called the FT capability of

Table 9. Result of single cell omission defect for FA

Clocking scheme	Total cell	Total input, output and fixed polarized cell	Total cell -output is faulty	Total cell- output is not faulty	Fault-Tolerant (FT%)
USE [2]	286	12	97	177	64.60
RES [5]	206	12	100	94	48.45
Optimized 2-D [17]	300	5	140	155	52.54
Zig-Zag [11]	248	5	69	174	71.60

that clocking-based circuit. Thus, the FT capabilities of the USE, RES, optimized 2-D, and Zig-Zag clocking-based circuits are 38.99, 53.57, 42.86, and 41.37 (in %), respectively. So, by comparing these average % FT values, it is clear that the RES clocking scheme's performance is better than other clocking schemes according to the HDLQ simulator. But Zig-Zag is the most FT clocking scheme, according to QCADesigner, as reported by Table 9. However, these two (HDLQ, QCADesigner) results are combined to find the efficient clocking scheme in terms of fault-tolerant capability as tabulated in Table 10. So the final sequence of fault-tolerant (higher to lower) clocking schemes is Zig-Zag, USE, RES, and Optimized 2-D.

Table 10. Final result of fault tolerant capability for FA

Clocking scheme	Avg. FT (%) for HDLQ	FT (%) for QCADesigner	Average FT (%)
USE [2]	38.99	64.6	51.8
RES [5]	53.57	48.45	51.01
Optimized 2-D [17]	42.86	52.54	47.7
Zig-Zag [11]	41.37	71.6	56.49

5 Conclusion

As the underlying clocking scheme plays a vital role in the realization of QCA circuits, this paper investigates the performance of different (USE, RES, Optimized 2-D, and Zig-Zag) underlying clocking schemes concerning fault-tolerant capability. A Full Adder is one of the vital circuits in digital circuit design. Therefore, a 1-bit Full Adder is used to investigate the performance of the clocking schemes. In this regard, HDLQ and QCADesigner simulators are used. According to the results of the HDLQ simulator, the performance of RES clocking schemes is better than others. But in the case of QCADesigner, Zig-Zag clocking scheme performs better. According to the combined results of these two simulators, Zig-Zag clocking scheme performs better, and the Optimized 2-D performs worse. Therefore, Zig-Zag clocking can be used to realize efficient QCA circuits.

References

1. Blair, E., Lent, C.: Clock topologies for molecular quantum-dot cellular automata. J. Low Power Electr. Appli. **8**(3), 31 (2018)
2. Campos, C.A.T., Marciano, A.L., Neto, O.P.V., Torres, F.S.: Use: A universal, scalable, and efficient clocking scheme for QCA. IEEE Trans. Comput. Aided Des. Integr. Circuits Syst. **35**(3), 513–517 (2015)
3. Fazzion, E., Fonseca, O.L.H.M., Nacif, J.A.M., Vilela Neto, O.P., Fernandes, A.O., Silva, D.S.: A quantum-dot cellular automata processor design. In: 2014 27th Symposium on Integrated Circuits and Systems Design (SBCCI), pp. 1–7 (2014)
4. Fijany, A., Toomarian, B.N.: New design for quantum dots cellular automata to obtain fault tolerant logic gates. J. Nanopart. Res. **3**(1), 27–37 (2001)
5. Goswami, M., Mondal, A., Mahalat, M.H., Sen, B., Sikdar, B.K.: An efficient clocking scheme for quantum-dot cellular automata. Int. J. Electron. Lett. 83–96 (2019)
6. Karim, F., Walus, K.: Efficient simulation of correlated dynamics in quantum-dot cellular automata (QCA). IEEE Trans. Nanotechnol. **13**(2), 294–307 (2014)
7. Lent, C.S., Tougaw, P.D.: A device architecture for computing with quantum dots. Proc. IEEE **85**(4), 541–557 (1997)
8. Mohammadi, M., Mohammadi, M., Gorgin, S.: An efficient design of full adder in quantum-dot cellular automata (QCA) technology. Microelectron. J. **50**, 35–43 (2016)
9. Ottavi, M., Schiano, L., Lombardi, F., Tougaw, D.: Hdlq: a hdl environment for QCA design. J. Emerg. Technol. Comput. Syst. **2**(4), 243–261 (2006)
10. Pal, J., Bhattacharjee, S., Saha, A.K., Dutta, P.: Study on temperature stability and fault tolerance of adder in quantum-dot cellular automata. In: 2019 5th international conference on signal processing, computing and control (ispcc), pp. 69–74. IEEE (2019)
11. Pal, J., Pramanik, A.K., Sharma, J.S., Saha, A.K., Sen, B.: An efficient, scalable, regular clocking scheme based on quantum dot cellular automata. In: IAnalog Integrated Circuits and Signal Processing, pp. 659–670 (2021)
12. Pramanik, A.K., Bhowmik, D., Pal, J., Sen, P., Saha, A.K., Sen, B.: Towards the realization of regular clocking-based QCA circuits using genetic algorithm. Comput. Elect. Eng. **97**, 107640 (2022)
13. Pramanik, A.K., Pal, J., Sen, B.: Impact of genetic algorithm on low power QCA logic circuit with regular clocking. In: Proceedings of First Asian Symposium on Cellular Automata Technology, pp. 191–203. Springer Nature, Singapore (2022), https://doi.org/10.1007/978-981-19-0542-1_14
14. Ravindran, R.S.E., Priyadarshini, K.M., Teja, D.P.M.P., Chakravarthy, P.N., Teja, P.D.: Design of ram using quantum cellular automata (QCA) designer. Int. J. Sci. Technol. Res. **8**, 1385–1390 (2019)
15. Sen, B., Rajoria, A., Sikdar, B.K.: Design of efficient full adder in quantum-dot cellular automata. Sci. World J. **2013** (2013)

16. Tahoori, M., Huang, J., Momenzadeh, M., Lombardi, F.: Testing of quantum cellular automata, Nanotechnology. IEEE Trans. **3**, 432–442 (2005)
17. Wang, L., Xie, G., Zhu, R., Yu, C.: An optimized clocking scheme for nanoscale quantum-dot cellular automata circuit. In: 2019 IEEE 14th International Conference on Nano/Micro Engineered and Molecular Systems (NEMS), pp. 336–341. IEEE (2019)

Idea of Cellular Automata Application in Two-Slit Experiments

Alexander Makarenko[1]([✉]) [ID], Anton Popov[1], and Volodimir Pribega[2]

[1] Institute of Applied System Analysis, National Technical Universities of Ukraine "Igor Sykorski Kiev Polytechnic Institute", Kyiv, Ukraine
makalex51@gmail.com
[2] Physico-Technical Institute, National Technical Universities of Ukraine "Igor Sykorski Kiev Polytechnic Institute", Kyiv, Ukraine

Abstract. One of the most known physical experiments in quantum mechanics and optics is two-slit experiment on transition particles through the screen with two slits. It was important for establishing quantum mechanical description based on probability distribution functions. It is naturally that the mathematical tools of quantum mechanics allow understanding such behavior. However it is interesting to search the analogs of such experiments in other distributed systems. One of such media for investigation is the cellular automata. It is known that the cellular automata are the media constituted from regularly distributed cells with some states and rules for their evolution. In proposed material the description of analogs of two-slit experiment for cellular automata are proposed. The results of computer experiments are given. Some interpretations are proposed including distribution of states frequencies during evolution. Particularly oscillations of quantum trajectory are discussed. Also presumable role of strong anticipation in such experiments is described.

Keywords: Cellular automata · Two-slit experiment · Anticipation · Multivaluednes · Frequency distribution

1 Introduction

Two-slit experiment is so important for the concepts of quantum mechanics that further research attempts that add to the understanding of such phenomena are of interest. In the present paper the results of such an attempt are de-scribed. Namely, a description of the formulation and results of the study based on the model of cellular automata is presented. Let us recall briefly that cellular automata as a model in classical form are represented as follows (see [1–3], etc.). Space is divided into identical cells, which are regularly arranged, cells have a set of certain states (in the simplest case, two), taken at discrete points in time and certain local rules for changing cell states, depending on the cell states in some vicinity of this cell. It is worth noting that the idea of cellular automata has already appeared as one of the means for understanding quantum mechanics (see, e.g., [4–7], etc.) and the number of studies is growing. One is tempted to consider the idea of cellular

© The Author(s), under exclusive license to Springer Nature Switzerland AG 2022
B. Chopard et al. (Eds.): ACRI 2022, LNCS 13402, pp. 199–207, 2022.
https://doi.org/10.1007/978-3-031-14926-9_18

automata applied to the problem of the two-slit experiment. The idea itself has been described, for instance, in [8, 9], and some results of computer experiments with cellular automata are given in [10]. Namely, patterns of cellular automaton activity distribution were investigated, which reveals hidden regularities of the process of passing through an obstacle with holes. In addition, aspects of accounting for anticipating have also been considered. The structure of the paper is the next. In the Subsect. 2 the general idea of two-slit experiments is proposed. Some details of computer experiments are described. Illustration of computer experiment results is described in the Subsect. 3; Sect. 4 is devoted to accounting the strong anticipatory property in proposed experiments. Also presumable interpretations of results are discussed.

2 Description of a Two Dimensional Computer Experiment with Cellular Automata

Let us first describe a scheme of a possible computational experiment in the simplest formulation. There is a partitioning of the binary plane into cells. Each cell has a plurality of states, discrete timing and rules of change of status. In case of strong, anticipating the change of the current state depends on the possible future states (see [1–3]).

2.1 Geometry of the Binary Cellular Automata

The construction of the binary automaton begins with the construction of a lattice, and the area of space in which the behavior of the binary automaton will be investigated. There are two openings in the block (see Fig. 1 below). It allows carrying out computer experiments in a limited time.

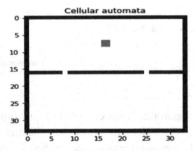

Fig. 1. Geometry and initial conditions of the cellular automaton. The black color shows the walls, the white color shows areas with zero values of the cells, the gray color show areas with value one of the cells. (Color figure online)

A grid size of 34 cells per 34 cells was inverted. The automaton is considered in the restricted area so on the outermost cells on all sides a static value different from the set of states was set. In this implementation the value 2 was set, which will now correspond to wall. The internal wall was constructed as a horizontal line in the middle of the entire domain. The cells, which correspond to the walls have a value of 2.

The wall was implemented in such a way that it is possible to change its width, i.e. to study the behavior of the cellular automaton both on the wall with a width of one cell and larger width. The length and height of the area, the width of the openings and the distance between them and the outside walls are also parameters that can be different in different experiments. It is possible to change both the number of passes and the width of each of the passes. Therefore, the model can be configured differently and its behavior under various conditions can be investigated.

2.2 Dynamic Rules for Cell States

Here (very briefly) we will describe the rules for change of state. The set of states was as in the classic "game life" [1–3, 11], i.e. zero and one. Also, the value two was added, which corresponds to the walls. The value of the over-shoot cells are always static and does not change over time, only cells with value one or zero are changed. Moore's neighborhood (8 subsidiary cells) was used to re-run the cells at the next moment of time. There can be a lot of dynamical rules for the change of state of the cells, starting with the classic ones in the "game life". Initially, a simple rule of state transition was considered in the work: if there is at least one neighboring cell with state 1, then this cell will take on the value 1 at the next moment. Initial conditions can be chosen in the usual way, but in this work it was taken so that to ensure modeling of wave spreading from the initial point. An example of these initial conditions is shown in Fig. 1.

2.3 Frequency Principle of Experimental Processing

Taking into account a possible multivaluedness in systems with strong antici-pation [12, 13], a problem of visualization and processing of results of compu-tational experiments arises. That is why the definition of frequency was added. Frequency in this work is a percentage ratio of the number of time moments when a cell takes value one to the total number of time moments that the cellular automaton passes. This is expressed as a percentage and is described by the following formula for each cell:

$$\left(Frequency_{i,j} = \left(\left(amfc_{i,j} \right) / \text{steps} \right) * 100 \right) \tag{1}$$

where $amfc_{i,j}$ (alive moments for cell) is the number of moments when the cell was in the state "1"; steps is the total number of clock cycles that the cellular automaton operated. It is not very important for this experiment, but will be used in the next section as a very important part of the model.

3 Results of Computational Experiments

We can see that starting from the initial position the cellular automaton develops over time like a circular wave, spreading in all directions. It is possible to draw some parallels with light propagation, where the initial position is the source of light and each moment of time will propagate at the speed of light.

The result of frequency distribution shows (Fig. 2) that the highest frequency of cells with state "1" is in the intervals, which are located at 45° angle to the walls and are

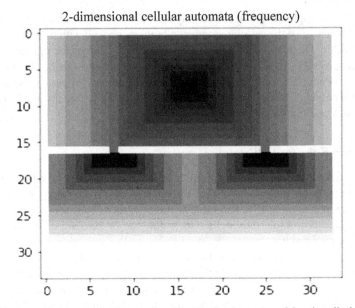

Fig. 2. Frequency for the simple divergence rule at the fixed moment of time in cells domain, The colors from white to black correspond to gradation of frequency from 0 to 1. (Color figure online)

gradually moving away from the openings. The rules for switching states that have been used are similar to the "game life" but slightly modified, if there will be one neighboring cell in state "1" and the central cell in state "1", or if there are two daughter cells in state "1", the central cell will take value one at the next moment on the clock, otherwise it will take the value zero. However, with the addition of the windows, there is the need to expand these rules, because passing through the windows will not be possible. This is taken into account by changing the rules when switching states, so that the cell under the windows goes to state "1".

Rule of thumb reads as follows: "If, for cells interfacing from the bottom of the cells at the beginning of the windows, the number of cells with state "1" in the proximity is equal to one, the cell also accepts state "1", but the rules which apply to all other cells also apply to these cells. As, the initial position was formed by four living cells in the center of the top part of the domain (placed in a gray square, see Fig. 1).

The above described cellular automaton was tested for 10,000 clock cycles. Up to the eighth step, the cellular automaton develops only in the upper part of the domain. Further rules are additionally introduced, which allow the cellular automaton to developments in the lower part of the domain. After the eighth step, the cellular automaton begins to develop in the lower part of the domain. The cellular automaton was investigated for 100,000 times of development. Three different configurations of the automaton at different moments of time were illustrated above: for 10,000, 20,000, 50,000 and 100,000 steps.

For this configuration of the cellular automaton it is very difficult to identify which class the cellular automaton belongs to according to S. Wolfram [1], because the number of cells which change the state is 994. Therefore, the number of possible configurations of this model will be, but there is a likelihood that the cellular automaton will reach a stable state and stop changing or will develop in cycles. However, this work was carried out for 100,000 cycles and none of this behavior was observed. The graphs below show the number of cells with the status of "1" as a percent of all cells (Fig. 3).

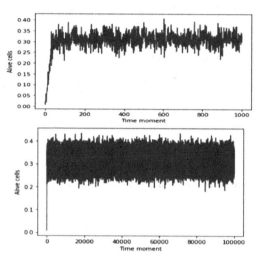

Fig. 3. Upper part: The percent of "1" cells after 1000 steps. Low part: The percent's of living cells with level "1" after 100,000 steps.

We can see from the graphs that with the development of the cellular automaton, the number of cells with a value "1" almost never exceeds 40 percent. We can also say that the development is quite stable. At first we can see growth in the number of such cells, but then the number of cells with level "1" will be in the range of 25% to 40% without significant deviations.

4   Anticipation Based Cellular Automata for Two-Slit Experiments

Already computer-based binary experiments with conventional binary automata show new interesting features in behavior relations. But as shown in [12–14], entirely new features appear in the case of taking into account anticipating. Namely, the possibility of ambiguity of relations appears (D. Dubois calls such behavior in discrete systems hyper-incursion). On the level of cellular automata this phenomenon has been investigated, for instance, in [14]. The next is the investigation of cellular automata with anticipating in two-slit experiments.

4.1   Definition of Anticipation

There are many variants of the description of anticipating. It should be noted that physics itself has long indicated the possibility of manifestation of anticipation in this or that form, starting with R. Feynman. Of the necessity of consideration of non-locality, both in time and space, is indicated by the results of experiments of J. Bell and others. In quantum mechanics there is a transactional interpretation of quantum mechanics by J. Cramers based on micro-processes with delay and anticipation. A significant development and formalization of the foreknowledge concept was introduced by D. Dubois. Dubois described the idea of strong anticipation [12, 13]: "The definition of a discrete system with strong anticipation: it is a system which calculates the current state at time t as a function of past states, ... $t - 3, t - 2, t - 1$, the present state and the state in the future, ... $t + 1$, $t + 2, t + 3,$...

$$x(t + 1) = f(\ldots, x(t - 2), x(t - 1), x(t), x(t + 1), x(t + 2), \ldots), \tag{2}$$

where the x in the future time is computed indirectly from the equation.

4.2 Anticipating in an Cellular Automata Model

In order to add anticipating power to the model, it is necessary to design a function of the next step, which depends on the next (expected) states of the cells. In the simplest, the transition function used in the usual binary cellular automata will be changed to the following function

$$X(t + 1) = a * f(S(t)) + (1 - a) * f(S(t + 1)), \tag{3}$$

where α is a constant that acts as a force and determines which of the rules will have the greatest influence on the value of the cell; $f(*)$a state change function that will describe the value of the cell as at the current time (the same that was used to calculate the value of the cell for the conventional model); $f(S(t + 1))$ is a function that will return the possible values for the next step [14]. The basis of the peculiarity of the solutions is the possible multivaluedness. This phenomenon is called hyperincursion [11, 12].

For cellular automata this also implies the existence of a number of space configurations at a given moment in time. One the method of solution of Eq. (3) is a brute force method, i.e. at the beginning, we put zero in the left part of the equation, then the right part of the equation also must be zero, i.e. both $f(S(t))$ must equal zero and $f(S(t + 1))$ must equal zero, then this case is suitable for the solution. The same calculation is performed for the value of a "1" in the left-hand side of the equation. The function $f(S(t + 1))$ will compute all possible occurrences (configurations) for the evolution of the cellular automaton on the next step.

The difficulty is that these groups of possible configurations become very large and not enough capacity for calculation. For a single variant a maximum 2^3 of possible variants for each cell exists and for a double variant 2^9. Recently in the simplest case of computation $n = 10$ cells and $t = 10$ time steps because of branching we need 1 day for computation.

4.3 Computational Experiments with Cellular Automata with Anticipating

The developed model of a cellular automaton with anticipating was implemented on a smaller grid than the one described in Sect. 3. The grid is de-signed in the size of 13 by 13 cells with two windows, as in the previous model, which is placed in the wall in the middle of the grid (as in Fig. 1). The initial position was used as one central cell at the top of the domain. For experiments with cellular automata anticipating, the Moore neighbor used in the usual experiment in Sect. 2 was changed into the von Neumann neighbor and the transition rules were changed to simplify the calculations.

Let us see how the configuration will change at the next moment, according to Eq. (3). The values are selected for each cell and if they match, the value of the solution is saved. After the calculations, there will be four possible situations for the first step to develop the cellular automaton. However, when the number of possible variants is very large, it is impossible to analyze the obtained results by looking at all sets of configurations. Taking into account the potential for ambiguity, a more appropriate tool for analysis is frequency (1), which takes into account the contribution of all possible configurations. For example, the frequency of different cells after the first step is shown in Fig. 4.

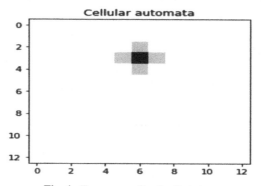

Fig. 4. Frequency after the first step.

For the second step of the calculation, the initial position will be each of the blocks obtained in the first step, i.e. we will consider each of the possible variants by line and calculate the possible variants of development for them. For the following steps, the same rule will be used. Because of the complexity of the calculations (high number of possible links), already on the eighth installment there are more than 4 million possible scenarios, only twenty-five terms were carried out. The following are some of the possible variants of configurations for the twenty-fourth time frame (Fig. 5).

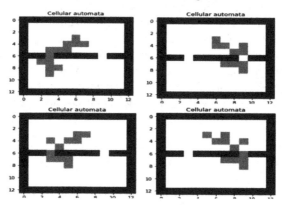

Fig. 5. A few of the many configurations for the development of a 12-step cellular automaton.

It is impossible to make conclusions and analyze the results on so many possible variations of configurations of the cellular automaton, so it is better to investigate the values of frequency at the same moments of time. Therefore, we will consider how the frequency will look only for the lower part of the lattice.

Each of the cells in Table 1 corresponds to the cells of considered cellular automata. The horizontal row corresponds to the row of cells under the obstacles. Upper row is just near the openness. The values into the cell correspond for the total number of 1 accounts of this cell from different branches during the evolution of CA. The symbol 10 m for example corresponds for example to ten millions for example and 47t corresponds to 47 thousand.

Table 1. Frequency for the lower part of the lattice in numerical values

-	-	>20 m	-	-	-	-	-	>20 m	-	-
>2 m	>10 m	>18 m	>10 m	>2 m	340t	>2 m	>10 m	>18 m	>10 m	>2 m
445t	~4 m	>12 m	~4 m	472t	36t	472t	~4 m	>12 m	~4 m	445t
46t	872t	~3 m	872t	47t	1.5t	47t	872t	~3 m	872t	46t
1t	42t	226t	42t	1t	0	1t	42t	226t	42t	1t
0	615	5t	615	0	0	0	615	5t	615	0
0	0	0	0	0	0	0	0	0	0	0

Thus, even with anticipating the given cellular automaton evolves with a *wavelike* behavior, as one can see from the distribution of values in *cell* frequency. From the numbers in Table 1 we can see that the *intermediation* between the leads from different directions has started and similarly we can say that they will reinforce one another and in time will merge into one lead. The main feature revealed in the modeling of such a system with *strong anticipating* is the appearance of a laggard state of such a system. This new behavior allows us to reexamine the classical questions, including unambiguity.

The equations presented in this section are completely new objects and represent a wide field for research. On the other hand, these features are the most promising in terms of interpretation. In the case of strong, anticipating there is a possibility of multivaluedness of states of the individual cell at any moment of time and simultaneous multivaluedness of configurations of the system. This is reminiscent of the structure of classical quantum mechanics, where there is a distribution function, which gives a distribution of probabilities of different states, from which one process of measurement is chosen. Potentially given CA with strong anticipation has another analogy to quantum mechanics.

5 Conclusions

Cellular automata are both fascinating and relatively easy to understand system which has very great potential in modeling both simple and complex real-world processes and phenomena. Local interactions can be modeled by cellular automata; the state of the environment is updated taking into account the states of the neighbors in its periphery. They can calculate functions and solve algorithmic problems.

The space is combined into a grid of neighborhoods, and the behavior of each neighborhood is displayed in varying states, the values of which at any given moment of time are functions dependent on a small circle around the neighborhood. In this work we have built and examined a model of a binary cellular automaton in a circumscribed area. Most of the attention of this work was given to the double-slit experiment, which investigated how the cellular automaton passes and interacts with the wall in which the two windows were placed. In the obtained results one can notice some similarity with the propagation of light in vacuum. The described models can be used as a ground for testing and developing new approaches and ideas in the field of cellular automata and physical systems.

References

1. Wolfram, S.: New Kind of Science. Wolfram Media Inc., USA (2002)
2. Chopard, B., Droz, M.: Cellular Automata Modeling of Physical Systems. Cambridge Univ. Press, Cambridge (1998)
3. Barto, F., Jacopo, T.: Cellular automata. In: Zalta, E.N. (ed.) The Stanford Encyclopedia of Phylosophy (Spring 2022 Edition) (2022). https://plato.stanford.edu/archives/spr2022/entries/cellular_automata/
4. t'Hooft: The Cellular Automation Interpretation of Quantum Mechanics arXiv:[qiant-ph] 1405.1548, v3, 259 p. (2015)
5. Grossing, G., Zellinger, A.: Structures in quantum cellular automata. Physica **B151**, 366–370 (1988)
6. Bisio, A., D'Ariano, G.M., Tosini, A.: Quantum field as a quantum cellular automation: the Dirac free evolution in one dimension. arXiv:12122839v2 [quant-ph] 21 p. (2015).
7. Makarenko A. Presumable applications of cellular automates with strong anticipation in quantum physics. J. Phys.: Conf. Ser. **1251**, 012031 (2019) https://iopscience.iop.org/article/10.1088/1742-6596/1251/1/012031/pdf.
8. Makarenko, A.: Some possible analogues in the behavior of cellular automata with anticipation and quantum-mechanical analogues. Anal. Control Model. Collection of Papers, vol. 3, 5 p.. Kyiv. «Inst. of Appl. Syst. Anal. NTUU KPI» (2018). (in Ukrainian).
9. Makarenko, A.: Two-slit Computer Experiments (2020). http://www.noeticadvancedstudies.us/MakarenkoXII.pdf.
10. Ostrovskiy, Z., Makarenko, A.: Cellular automata in regions with obstacles as the models and tools for analysis and modeling. In: Proceedings of 2019 IEEE 2nd Ukraine Conference on Electrical and Computer Engineering (UKRCON). 2–6 July 2019, 5 p. (2019) https://doi.org/10.1109/UKRCON.2019.887998.
11. Game'Life' (2022). http://en.wikipedia.org/wiki/Conway%27s_Game_of_Life
12. Dubois, D.: Generation of fractals from incursive automata, digital diffusion and wave equation systems. BioSystems **43**, 97–114 (1997)
13. Dubois D.: Incursive and hyperincursive systems, fractal machine and anticipatory ence. In: AIP Conference Proceedings, vol. 573, pp. 437–451. American Institute of Physics (2001).
14. Krushinskiy, D., Makarenko A.: Cellular automata with anticipation. Examples and presumable applications. In: Dubois, D.M. (ed.) AIP Conference Proceedings, USA, vol.1303, pp. 246–254 (2010).

Towards Self–optimizing Sensor Networks: Game–Theoretic Second–Order CA–Based Approach

Franciszek Seredyński[1], Tomasz Kulpa[1(✉)], Rolf Hoffmann[2],
and Dominique Désérable[3]

[1] Department of Mathematics and Natural Sciences,
Cardinal Stefan Wyszyński University, Warsaw, Poland
`{f.seredynski,tomasz.kulpa}@uksw.edu.pl`
[2] Technische Universität Darmstadt, Darmstadt, Germany
`hoffmann@ra.informatik.tu-darmstadt.de`
[3] Institut National des Sciences Appliquées, Rennes, France

Abstract. We propose a second–order Cellular Automata (CA)–based approach to solve a problem of lifetime optimization in Wireless Sensor Networks (WSN). A WSN graph created for a given deployment of WSN in monitored area is considered as a multiagent system, where agents take part in a spatial Prisoner's Dilemma game. We propose a local, agent–player oriented criterion which incorporates issues of area coverage and sensors energy spending. Agents act in such a way to maximize their profits what results in achieving by them a solution corresponding to Nash equilibrium. We show that the system is self–optimizing, i.e. is able to optimize a global criterion not known for players, related to a Nash equilibrium, which provides a balance between requested coverage and spending energy, and results in expanding WSN lifetime. The proposed approach is validated by a number of experimental results.

Keywords: Collective behavior · Network coverage and lifetime · Second–order CA · Spatial Prisoner's Dilemma · Wireless Sensor Networks

1 Introduction

WSN is a system composed of a large number of tiny computer–communication devices called sensors deployed in some area, which sense a local environment. They are one of the key information and communication technologies [9] applied today in the area of Internet of Things and oriented on collecting, sending and processing large amount of data necessary to provide intelligent services termed as Ambient Intelligence. In many applications, such as e.g., monitoring remote and difficult to access areas, sensors are equipped with single use batteries which can not be recharged.

From the point of view of QoS of such WSN, there exist two closely related important issues: an effective monitoring (coverage) some area and an operational lifetime. After a deployment (e.g., by an aircraft) of sensors at random locations they should self–organize: recognize their nearest neighbors to be able to communicate and start taking locally decisions in subsequent moments of time about turning ON or OFF their batteries to monitor events. These decisions will directly influence a degree of area coverage, spending sensors' batteries energy and lifetime of the network. The problem of lifetime maximization is closely related to the coverage problem. A group of sensors monitoring some area is usually redundant, i.e., usually more than one sensor cover monitored targets and forms of redundancy can be different. By solving the coverage problem one can indirectly also solve the problem of maximization of WSN lifetime.

There exists a number of algorithms to solve the problem of coverage/lifetime maximization. They are classified either as centralized and assume availability of entire information and a solution is delivered usually in the form of a schedule of activities of all sensors during the entire lifetime, or distributed, where a solution is found on the basis of only partial information about the network. Because these problems are known as NP–complete [2], WSN centralized algorithms are oriented either on delivery of exact solutions for specific cases (see, e.g. [1]) or applying heuristics or metaheuristics to find approximate solutions (see, e.g. [7,8,11,13]). The main drawback of centralized algorithms is that a schedule of sensors' activities must be found outside the network and delivered to it before starting operation. Therefore, distributed algorithms become more and more popular because they assume reactivity of sensors in real time, and they are scalable in contrast to centralized algorithms.

In this paper we propose a novel approach to the problem of coverage/lifetime optimization based on its multi–agent interpretation, applying game–theoretic interaction between players participating in spatial Prisoner's Dilemma (SPD) game, with the use of a second–order CA as players [6,12]. The paper extends our works and concepts presented in [4] and [5] concerning development of distributed algorithms, where learning automata and classical CA, respectively were applied. The works [10] and [3] are related to our work because they use also game theory and genetic operators for optimization.

The structure of the paper is the following. Section 2 presents the problem of coverage/lifetime optimization in WSN. The next section proposes a multi–agent interpretation of the problem, presents a set of simple heuristics (CA rules) used by agents and shows how their collective behavior influences on solving coverage/lifetime optimization. In Sect. 4, the proposed heuristics are applied in the SPD game, and results related to the collective behavior of them are presented. Section 5 proposes a distributed algorithm based on the SPD game with the use of a second–order CA to solve the coverage/lifetime optimization problem, and the last section contains conclusions.

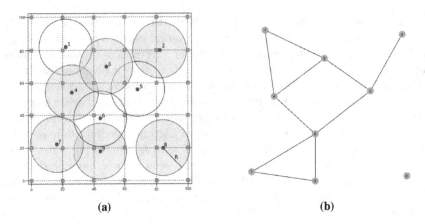

Fig. 1. Example of WSN: 9 sensors cover monitored area containing 36 PoI (a); corresponding WSN graph (b). Sensors currently turned ON monitor their green corresponding areas. (Color figure online)

2   Sensor Networks: Coverage and Lifetime Problems

It is assumed that some area (Fig. 1(a)) contains a number M of "points of interest" (PoI) which should be monitored and covered by N randomly deployed sensors, which can perform monitoring in time. Each sensor has a non–rechargeable battery of capacity *batt_capacity* and can monitor PoI in a sensing range R if its battery is turned ON. An energy capacity of a sensor is decreased on one unit of energy per a single interval of time if a battery is turned ON. Figure 1(a) shows illustrating simplified example with $M = 36$ PoI (in orange), $N = 9$ sensors (in red), and $R = 17$ m; some of sensors are currently turned ON and monitor the corresponding areas (in green).[1]

It is assumed that decisions about turning ON/OFF batteries are taken in discrete moments of time t. It is also assumed that there exists some QoS measure evaluating the performance of WSN. As such a measure, we accept a value of coverage defined as a ratio of a number of PoI covered by active sensors to whole number M of PoI. The coverage q of a target area at j–th time period t_j can be denoted as q_j:

$$q_j = \frac{M_{obs_j}}{M}. \tag{1}$$

Preserving a complete area coverage is a desirable objective, but sometimes it may be more practical to achieve a predefined coverage rate just high enough. So, we assume that at a given moment of time, this ratio should not be lower than some predefined requested value of q_r ($0 < q_r \leq 1$). A lifetime of WSN can be defined as a number of time intervals t_j in the schedule during which the

---

[1] The WSN graph in Fig. 1(b) was obtained under the assumption that the number M of PoI is equal to $21 \times 21 = 441$ as explained in the following section.

coverage of the target area is within δ range of the requested coverage ratio q_r, as follows:

$$lifetime_q = \sum_{j=1}^{T_{max}} t_j \qquad (2)$$

where: $t_j = 1$ if $abs(q_j - q_r) \le \delta$, otherwise $t_j = 0$.

Our objective is to prolong the lifetime of WSN by minimizing the number of redundant sensors during each time interval in order to minimize energy consumption, providing at the same time the requested value of the coverage.

3   Multi–agent System for WSN Coverage and Lifetime Optimization

An important step to interpret WSN Coverage and Lifetime Optimization problem in terms of a multi–agent system is converting a WSN into a corresponding WSN graph. Figure 1(b) shows a WSN graph corresponding to the WSN from Fig. 1(a). The conversion is based on the principle saying that two nodes of a WSN graph are connected, iff they have at least one common PoI within their sensing range R in a corresponding WSN. The number of neighbors of a given node depends on a value of R. The WSN graph was obtained under an assumption that the number M of PoI is equal to $21 \times 21 = 441$ and this value will be used in our experiments. We can see from Fig. 1(b) that the nodes of the WSN graph correspond to the sensors of the WSN. The nodes, except node 8, have a number of neighbors ranging from 1 to 4.

Let us further assume that each node of a WSN graph is controlled by an agent A_i of a multi–agent system consisting of N agents. Each agent has two alternative decisions (actions): $\alpha_i = 0$ (battery is turned OFF) and $\alpha_i = 1$ (battery is turned ON). All agents will make discrete–time decisions regarding the activation of their batteries using certain rules assigned to them (heuristics).

Set of Agents' Rules. We will consider the following set of socially interpreted rules that potentially are useful and inspired by the idea of an underlying game:

- *all–C*: always cooperate (turn ON battery);
- *all–D*: always defect (turn OFF battery);
- *k–D*: cooperate until not more than k neighbors defect, otherwise defect (turn ON battery until not more than k neighbors have batteries turned OFF, otherwise turn OFF the battery);
- *k–C*: cooperate until not more than k neighbors cooperate, otherwise defect (turn ON battery until not more than k neighbors have batteries turned ON, otherwise turn OFF the battery);
- *k–DC*: defect until not more than k neighbors defect, otherwise cooperate (turn OFF battery until not more than k neighbors have batteries turned OFF, otherwise turn ON the battery).

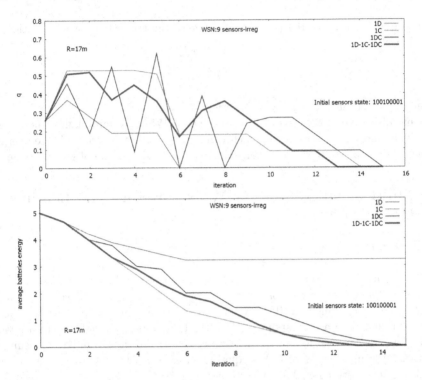

Fig. 2. Example of running a multi–agent system with classical CA–based agents: changes of coverage q (upper), corresponding changes of sensors' batteries energy volume (lower).

One can see that the presented model corresponds to classical non–uniform CA–based models, with a graph structure. We may ask further how the CA rules of the considered multi–agent system will collectively influence on QoS parameters of WSN, such as q and $lifetime_q$.

Motivating Example. Figure 2 shows some results of experiments with the use of the WSN presented in Fig. 1 under the assumption that the initial battery volume of each sensor is $batt\_capacity = 5$, and the initial setting of sensors battery states ON/OFF is equal likely. Figure 2 (upper) shows how the coverage q changes during a run of the multi–agent system when all agents use the same rule, either: 1–D (in green), 1–C (in blue), or 1–DC (in violet), or these rules are randomly assigned to agents with the same probability and work collectively (in red). Figure 2 (lower) shows how these rule assignments change the average batteries energy volume. One can notice that in each case when rules are used separately or working collectively we have to do it with a specific influence on the coverage and batteries energy change. We cannot identify the best rule for this single and small example, but we see that the actual applied rule(s) make a big difference in performance. The main problem with this model is that classical CA–based agents do not have any feedback from the WSN environment saying how their actions influence on QoS of the network. Therefore we will replace these agents by a *second–order CA* (time-variant rules influenced by neighbors) to establish such a feedback that shall depend on the outcome of SPD game. In short, our scheme of the *method* to solve the problem is the following:

- Model the area to be monitored as a 2D grid of PoI. Locate the sensors with a given sensor range R. Compute the WSN graph.
- Consider the sensors as agents that have neighboring agents as given by the WSN graph. Each agent switches ON or OFF according to a local rule taking into account the neighbors' states.
- The local rule is taken from a given *set of rules* that are useful in the context of playing a game, and which potentially can be applied to our problem.
- SPD game explained in Sect. 4 is used as an underlying heuristic to evaluate in a decentralized way a global objective.
- Our problem is mapped to the SPD game (Sect. 5) by designing a payoff function related to the considered problem and used by the players in the game.
- The agents' rules are changed dynamically (second–order CA) taking into account the neighbors rules, states, and game payoffs, in order to find an optimal solution; driving forces of a process of searching a solution are mechanisms of competition and mutation.

4   Collective Behavior of Second–Order CA–Based Players in Spatial Prisoner's Dilemma Game

The purpose of this section is to show that second-order CA operating in a SPD game environment are able to self-optimize. Note that we don't address the whole problem here, and the cells (not the sensors) take the role of agents. In order to solve our optimization problem we further need to express the global criteria as a local criterion (next Sect. 5).

To recognize the applicability of second–order CA to solve the problem of WSN coverage and lifetime optimization, we extend the SPD game model [6,12] by including the set of rules presented in Sect. 3. We consider a 2D spatial array of size $m \times n$. We assume that a cell (i, j) will be considered as an agent–player participating in the SPD game with neighbors. At a given discrete moment, each cell can be in one of two states: either C or D. The state of a given cell will be considered as an action C (cooperate) or D (defect) of the corresponding player against an opponent from its neighborhood. The payoff function of the game is given in Table 1. Each player playing a game with an opponent in a single round (iteration) receives a payoff equal to R, T, S or P, where $T > R > P > S$. We assume that $R = 1$, $T = b$, $S = c$, and $P = a$. We assume that players are rational and act in such a way to maximize their payoff defined by the payoff function. To evaluate a level of collective behavior of the system, we will use an external criterion (not known for players) and ask whether it is possible to expect from players selecting such actions s_{ij} which will maximize the average total

Table 1. Payoff function of a player in the SPD game.

Player's action	Opponent's action	
	Cooperate (C)	Defect (D)
Cooperate (C)	$R = 1$	$S = c$
Defect (D)	$T = b$	$P = a$

payoff (ATP) $\bar{u}()$ (what corresponds to the maximization of the total number of cooperating agents) of the whole set of players:

$$\bar{u}(s_{11}, s_{12}, ..., s_{mn}) = \frac{1}{mn}\sum_{j=1}^{m}\sum_{i-1}^{n}\sum_{k=1}^{n_{ij}} u_{ij}(s_{ij}, s_{i_k j_k})/n_{ij} \qquad (3)$$

where n_{ij} is the number of opponents in the neighborhood.

Game theory predicts that the behavior of players is oriented towards achieving a Nash equilibrium (NE). We call the price of a NE a value of ATP at this point. The game can have many NE points with different ATP. The maximal ATP equal to $R = 1$ corresponds to selecting action C by all players. We will call this ATP the *maximal price point*, however, a solution corresponding to this point is not always a Nash point. To solve this problem we introduce an income sharing mechanism [12] to the game, if necessary.

Cells (i, j) of a 2D array are considered as CA–based players. States D or C are used by the player as actions in games with opponent players. For each cell, a local neighborhood is defined. We apply a cyclic boundary condition. We will assume the Moore neighborhood with eight immediate neighbors. That means that each player has eight ($n_{ij} = 8$) opponents in the game. At discrete moments, CA–based players will use their current states as actions to play games with opponents, they will receive payoffs, and next they will change their states applying *rules* (also called *strategies*) assigned to them.

To convert classical CA into a second–order CA we use the mechanism of *competition*, based on the principle "adapt to the best neighbor". It assumes that each player participating in games with neighbors collects some total score. If the competition mechanism is turned ON, each agent compares its cumulated payoff with the total payoffs of its neighbors. If a more successful player exists in the neighborhood, this player with his rule is replaced by the most successful one. This mechanism converts a classical CA into a *second–order* CA, which can adapt in time.

Figure 3 presents experimental results (with $b = 1.2, c = 0$) showing how a fraction of cooperating agents depends on subsets of rules presented in Sect. 3. First, let us notice that a high level of global collective behavior can be achieved for the value of the parameter of the payoff function $a < 0.3$. The highest level of cooperation is observed when all players used the k–D rule. While using separately rules *all–C* and *all–D* does not make sense, using them together provides also very good results. The performance of rules k–C and k–DC is

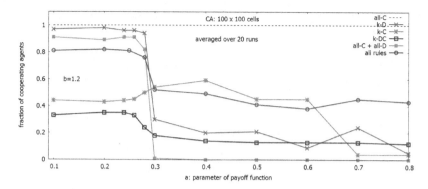

Fig. 3. Fraction of cooperating agents for different subsets of rules.

low when they are used separately, but it can be good if they work collectively together with the remaining rules.

A general conclusion from the conducted experiments is such that a second–order CA operating in SPD game environment are able to *self–optimize*, i.e. maximize a global criterion in the form of Eq. (3) without an explicit knowledge of agents about this criterion. To be able to apply this approach to solve the coverage and lifetime optimization problem, we need to express both the global criteria Eqs. (1) and (2) representing the issues of coverage and batteries energy spending in the form of a local agent criterion as discussed in the next section.

5 Coverage and Lifetime Optimization: Spatial PD Game with the Use of a Second–Order CA

Mapping of the Problem onto the SPD Game. We will assume that the i–th agent (sensor) of the multi–agent system presented in Sect. 3 will take part in a variant of the SPD game related to a WSN coverage and lifetime optimization problem. It will be assumed that each agent knows the value of a global parameter q_r and this value can be considered as a local value, i.e. $q_r^i = q_r$. An agent will receive for his actions in the game some payoffs which depend on whether his current q_{curr}^i is below or above the requested q_r^i. The payoff function of a player is given in Table 2. The payoff function assigns values to the i–th player in the following way:

(a) if he "turns OFF battery" then he calculates his local value of coverage q_{curr}^i; if this value $q_{curr}^i \geq q_r^i$ then he receives reward b, otherwise some punishment equal to a;

(b) if he "turns ON battery" then he calculates what would be his value of q_{curr}^i (denoted as q_{curr}^{i-off}) if in fact he would have "turned OFF" his battery; if $q_{curr}^{i-off} < q_r^i$ then he receives the reward equal to 1, otherwise a penalty equal to c. It is assumed that values of rewards and penalties should fulfill the inequality: $b > 1$ and $b > c > a$. In our experiments we will use $b = 1.2, c = 0.5, a = 0$.

Table 2. SPD approach to solve WSN coverage and lifetime optimization problem: payoff function

i–th agent's action	Fulfilment of q_r^i	
Turn ON batttery (C)	$q_{curr}^{i-off} \geq q_r^i$	
	No	Yes
	$rev_i^{on+} = 1$	$rev_i^{on-} = c$
Turn OFF batttery (D)	$q_{curr}^i \geq q_r^i$	
	No	Yes
	$rev_i^{off-} = a$	$rev_i^{off+} = b$

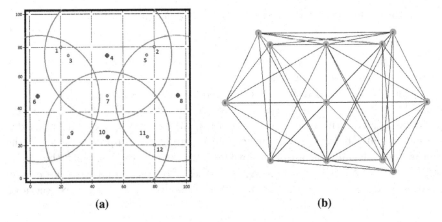

(a)   (b)

Fig. 4. Instance of the problem: WSN with 12 sensors, and R=35 (a), corresponding WSN graph (b).

Experiments and Results. Figure 4 presents a WSN which will be used in our experiments. It consists of 12 sensors with a sensing range $R = 35$ m located in a monitored area (100 m × 100 m) as shown in Fig. 4a. The corresponding WSN graph of the multi-agent system is shown in Fig. 4b. Let us assume that, e.g. $q_r = 0.8$. In the space of 2^{12} possible solutions (combinations of states ON/OFF of sensors' batteries) there exist 3 feasible solutions consisting of 4 sensors turned ON, which provide a cover $q \geq q_r$, and one of such solutions is shown in Fig. 4a (in green). Generally, under a constant value of R and a given value of q_r there can exist some number of feasible solutions.

We assume generally that the multi–agent system for a coverage and lifetime optimization performs a number of rounds, each consisting of 3 steps: (a) find a unique solution (b) full exploitation of the solution found, and (c) deleting sensors with dead batteries from the WSN graph, resulting in changes in the graph. If we assume, e.g. *batt_capacity* $= 5$, it means that in the case of our example each solution will be exploited 5 units of time, and *lifetime* $= 15$.

The purpose of our experiments was to see how the proposed second–order CA will act in different situations related to different values of q_r. We will focus

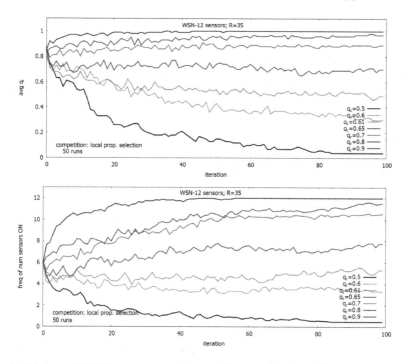

Fig. 5. Solving of WSN coverage problem with second–order CA. Evolving in time steps of: a final coverage (upper) and corresponding number of active sensors (lower). (Color figure online)

on the most important, the first step of each round: *searching of a single solution*. The used rules from the whole set are: *all–C* and *all–D*. These rules and also the sensors states will initially be assigned to agents with equal probability. Agents will change their rules participating in a competition. Our initial experiments had shown that competition based on the principle "adapt to the best neighbor" is not effective for irregular graph structures. We found out that the mechanism based on "a local proportional selection" (similar to one used in genetic algorithms) performs well and this mechanism is used in the competition. Each run of the multi–agent system lasted 100 iterations. As we have to do it with a probabilistic CA, we will present statistical results averaged over 50 runs.

Figure 5 presents some preliminary results of our experimental study and shows (upper) how a value of the coverage q evolves for different values of q_r, and (lower) how a number of active sensors evolves corresponding to the found coverage. Let us analyze these results from the perspective of a difference $\triangle q = \bar{q} - q_r$ which can be calculated from Fig. 5 (upper). For the subsequent values of $q_r = 0.9, 0.8, 0.7, 0.65, 0.61, 0.6, 0.5$ we have the corresponding values of $\triangle q = 0.1, 0.17, 0.19, 0.05, -0.12, -0.3, -0.44$. It can be seen that there exist two regions of behavior of the multi–agent system with respect to the values of $\triangle q$. In the first region ($0.65 \leq q_r \leq 0.9$) the algorithm finds solutions that satisfy the requirement defined by a value of q_r, and in the second region ($q_r < 0.65$) the solutions found do not meet the requirements.

When $q_r = 0.9$ the algorithm finds on average a coverage equal to 1 (Fig. 5 (upper—in violet)), exceeding the required coverage by 0.1, and for this purpose it requires to turn ON all 12 sensors on average (Fig. 5 (lower—in violet)). A similar behavior can be observed for $q_r = 0.8$ and $q_r = 0.7$ with even higher values of $\triangle q$. For $q = 0.65$ we can observe (Fig. 5 (upper—in red)) a behavior of the algorithm with the lowest difference equal to 0.05 between requested and found values of q with the use of around 7.5 sensors on average to be turned ON. This solution seems to be an optimum for the given instance of the problem and the values of the payoff function.

The presented method and simulation algorithm is complex but preliminary results are promising. For a detailed analysis and performance evaluation, it is necessary to conduct an extensive experimental study with use of different WSN instances and different settings of the payoff function.

6   Conclusions

In this paper we have proposed a second–order CA–based approach to solve the problem of lifetime optimization in Wireless Sensor Networks. A WSN represented by a graph was considered as a multi–agent system with agents participating in the Spatial Prisoner's Dilemma "SPD" game and where players could use different rules (heuristics) to maximize their profits.

We considered two models, where we used either classical CA or second–order CA. For the second–order CA model, we have proposed an agent–player payoff function which incorporates issues of area coverage and sensors energy spending, and it is used by agents to maximize their profits, what results in achieving a solution corresponding to Nash equilibrium. We have shown experimentally that the system is able to optimize in a fully distributed way a global criterion not known for players, which provides a balance between the requested coverage and the energy spending, and results in a prolongation of WSN lifetime. Our future work will be oriented towards a more detailed study of the proposed approach and the influence of specific model parameters on the performance.

References

1. Berman, P., Calinescu, G., Shah, C., Zelikovsky, A.: Power efficient monitoring management in sensor networks. In: 2004 IEEE Wireless Communications and Networking Conference (IEEE Cat. No.04TH8733), pp. 2329–2334 (2004)
2. Cardei, M., Du, D.-Z.: Improving Wireless Sensor Network Lifetime through Power Aware Organization. Wireless Netw. **11**(3), 333–340 (2005)
3. Cerruti, U., Dutto, S., Murru, N.: A symbiosis between cellular automata and genetic algorithms. Chaos, Solitons Fractals **134**, 109719 (2020)
4. Gąsior, J., Seredyński, F., Hoffmann, R.: Towards self-organizing sensor networks: game-theoretic ε-learning automata-based approach. In: Cellular Automata, ACRI 2018, pp. 125–136 (2018)

5. Hoffmann, R., Désérable, D., Seredyński, F.: Cellular Automata Rules Solving the Wireless Sensor Network Coverage Problem. Nat. Comput. (to appear)
6. Katsumata, Y., Ishida, Y.: On a Membrane Formation in a Spatio-temporally generalized prisoner's dilemma. In: Umeo, H., Morishita, S., Nishinari, K., Komatsuzaki, T., Bandini, S. (eds.) Cellular Automata, ACRI 2008, pp. 60–66 (2008)
7. Manju, Chand, S., Kumar, B.: Genetic algorithm-based meta-heuristic for target coverage problem. IET Wireless Sen. Syst. 8(4), 170–175 (2018)
8. Musilek, P., Krömer, P., Bartoň, T.: Review of nature-inspired methods for wake-up scheduling in wireless sensor networks. Swarm Evol. Comput. 25, 100–118 (2015)
9. Östberg, P., Byrne, J., et al.: Reliable capacity provisioning for distributed cloud/edge/fog computing applications. In: European Conference on Networks and Communications (EuCNC 2017), pp. 1–6 (2017)
10. Pereira, R.L., et al.: Game theory and social interaction for selection and crossover pressure control in genetic algorithms: an empirical analysis to real real-valued constrained optimization. IEEE Access 8, 144839–144865 (2020)
11. Rathee, M., Kumar, S., Gandomi, A.H., Dilip, K., Balusamy, B., Patan, R.: Ant colony optimization based quality of service aware energy balancing secure routing algorithm for wireless sensor networks. IEEE Trans. Eng. Management 68(1), 170–182 (2021)
12. Seredyński, F., Gąsior, J., Hoffmann, R.: The second order CA-based multiagent systems with income sharing. In: Cellular Automata ACRI 2020, pp. 134–145
13. Zhong, J., Huang, Z., Feng, L., Du, W., Li, Y.: A hyper-heuristic framework for lifetime maximization in wireless sensor networks with a mobile sink. IEEE/CAA J. Automatica Sinica 7(1), 223–236 (2020)

Cellular Automata and Spreading Dynamics

Spreadability and Vulnerability via Attributes for Systems Described by Cellular Automata: Application to Wildfire

Mohamed Byari[1]([⊠]) ⓘ, Abdes-samed Bernoussi[1], Hamidou Kassogué[1,2] ⓘ,
and Mina Amharref[1]

[1] GAT, Faculty of Sciences and Techniques of Tangier, University Abdelmalek
Essaadi, Tétouan, Morocco
mohamedbyari@gmail.com
[2] High Institute of Applied Technologies (TechnoLAB-ISTA),
Bamako, BP E3123, Mali

Abstract. In this paper, we investigate two concepts of system theory in the framework of cellular automata: spreadability and vulnerability. We have proposed adapting the definitions of these concepts for CA associated with a set of information characterizing the modeled space. The spreadability concept describes the expansion of property in space-time, and vulnerability describes the possibility for a region to be affected by this spreadability. The redefinition of these concepts will be based on the impact of the space structure translated into attributes notion. The interest is to study the spatial configuration effect as an environment favors or resists the property. This way, we can study vulnerability through an internal vision rather than only through external effects. Illustrations of our approach will be discussed in a 3D wildfire modeling application.

Keywords: 3D-CA · Attributes · Spreadability · Vulnerability · Wildfire

1 Introduction

Forest growth, the spread of an epidemic, or the way a colony of bees is formed are large networks of interacting entities that can be grouped and studied under the name of "complex dynamical systems", which refers to a branch of mathematics that studies the properties of a dynamic system. Today, they constitute a major scientific challenge that goes far beyond the specificities of the fields in which they are encountered and require a particular research effort. Historically, the system theory was initially introduced via the stability concept which formalizes the properties that bring a system to an equilibrium state [1]. Other concepts have been developed subsequently, notably the controllability that refers to the system's behavior study under the actions that bring it to the desired states

© The Author(s), under exclusive license to Springer Nature Switzerland AG 2022
B. Chopard et al. (Eds.): ACRI 2022, LNCS 13402, pp. 223–234, 2022.
https://doi.org/10.1007/978-3-031-14926-9_20

[2]. Observability is a controllability concept dual that consists in studying the system solution by measuring the output [3]. The concept of spreadability was introduced by El Jai [4,5] in 1994 which describes the spatiotemporal expansion of a given property, while the vulnerability concept [6] was introduced to study the areas susceptible to be affected by the spreadability of a property. El Yacoubi and El Jai couple the spreadability and controllability by a spreadable control [7]. It is a control that makes a system spreadable. Also, Bernoussi introduced the concept of control protector [8] that consists in modifying the spreadability of a property to protect an area where the system is vulnerable.

In the last decades, systems theory has contributed to the development of CA as a particular discrete system [9]. Indeed, the local vision of the CA allows describing a complex phenomenon by focusing exclusively on the interactions of a cell and its neighborhood. We produce a model that takes into account the space's heterogeneity since the cells have specific information about the space they occupy. CA represents an ideal framework to study dynamic system complexity. Moreover, it constitute a remarkable model for its formal simplicity and capable of producing very rich and often difficult to predict behaviors. However, the study of systems theory concepts through CA is considerably younger compared to the continuous approach. Therefore, CA is poor compared to the richness offered by continuous systems such as PDE. In the case of CA, in the early 2000 s,s, El Yacoubi and El Jai enlarged the controllability concept by discussing additive and boolean case of CA [10]. An application of the closed-loop controllability concept was considered in [11] for industrial maintenance processes modeled by CA. Spreadability and vulnerability concepts have been extended to CA by Jellouli [12] considering only the inclusion sense. An application on forest fire problem have been presented. Moreover, Kassogué [13] improved these two concepts by considering the spreadability in the area sense and extended the vulnerability indexes. He considered two CA models [14] for water flow problems (flooding and erosion) as applications for which he adapted the vulnerability indexes in order to take into account the cells structures. The use of cells parameters values in transition rules is introduced rather than just cells states. Then, Byari developed recently in [15,16] the formalism of attributes-based CA (state as a summary of cell attributes values and transition rules as a mutual action of processes on cells attributes). From this formalism he addressed the concept of controlability with actuator and protector control via cells attributes for 3D CA. As applications he considered wildfire problem.

In this paper, we focus on the two concepts: spreadability and vulnerability. We redefine them basing on cells attributes in order to take into account the impact of the space structure locally. Indeed, spreadability and vulnerability are seen in two aspects: an external aspect represented by the intensity of the property that drives the cells to be infected as discussed in [13]; and an internal aspect (attributes resistance) that represents the cells reaction to the external excitation that we discuss here. In this case, the values taken by the attributes are decisive to know if the cell will be infected or not. Our contribution will then concern the study of the effect of a zone attributes on the spreadability of a given property and this zone vulnerability to this spreadability. We propose a readaptation of the vulnerability indexes according to these attributes. To illustrate our approach, we have developed a CA model based on 3D geometry cells for the wildfire phenomenon. The model was developed by taking into account several vegetation attributes as well as climatic constraints. The input data for the regions considered for use in this project were acquired by a terrestrial LiDAR scanner and processed in a GIS environment. Simulation results were performed in a decision support software we have developed in Java programming language. Details on this software are given in [17].

The paper is organized as follow. In Sect. 2, we first recall the formalism of attributes-based CA from [15,16] and the original spreadability and vulnerability concepts from [12,13]. We pursue then with our contribution on spreadability and vulnerability via cells attributes while discussing adapted vulnerability indexes. Section 3 will deal with an application on wildfire phenomenon. We describe first the considered 3D model and we discuss then simulation results on the wildfire spreadability and vulnerability. Finally we conclude our work by giving some perspectives in Sect. 4.

2   CA, Spreadability and Vulnerability

2.1   Attributes-Based CA

CA's originality is manifested not only in the evolution of the system through a local view but also in its ability to solve the problem of space heterogeneity, based on the attributes that characterize each space portion. A CA is the quadruplet

$$\mathcal{A} = (\mathcal{L}, \mathcal{N}, \mathcal{S}, f), \tag{1}$$

where $\mathcal{L} = \{c_i;\ i \in \mathbb{Z}^d\}$ is the d-dimensional lattice; $\mathcal{N} : c \mapsto (c_1, \ldots, c_m)$ is the neighbourhoods that a cell c interacts with; $\mathcal{S} = \{s_1, \ldots, s_n\}$ is the set of states, that is denoted for a cell c as $s_t(c) \in \mathcal{S}$ at time t with $t \in I$ the time horizon indices; and $f : s_t \mapsto s_{t+1}$ is the local transition function. For attributes-based CA, each cell is associated with a set of attributes $\mathbb{A}_t(c) = \{\sigma_t^1(c), \cdots, \sigma_t^l(c)\}$ that can be static or dynamic depending on the modelled phenomenon. During the evolution, state and attributes have a mutual influence on the cell represented by $\Phi(\mathbb{A}_t) = s_t$. Then transition function in this case reads $f : \Phi(\mathbb{A}_t) \mapsto \Phi(\mathbb{A}_{t+1})$. More details are in [15,16].

2.2   Original Spreadability and Vulnerability

Let $\mathcal{A} = (\mathcal{L}, \mathcal{N}, \mathcal{S}, f)$ be a CA modelled a spatio-temporal evolving system. We consider a given property $\mathcal{P}$ and let $\omega_t = \{c \in \mathcal{L};\ \mathcal{P}s_t(c)\}$ be the set of cells satisfying the property $\mathcal{P}$. We say that the property $\mathcal{P}$ is spreadable in the inclusion sense if:

$$\omega_t \subset \omega_{t+1}, \ \forall t \in I. \tag{2}$$

We say that the property $\mathcal{P}$ is spreadable in the area sense if :

$$\mu(\omega_t) \leqslant \mu(\omega_{t+1}), \; \forall t \in I, \tag{3}$$

where $\mu(\omega) := \sum_{c \in \omega} \mu(c)$ is the measure of ω in the sense that $\mu(c)$ is the area of c. Not that if $\mathcal{L}$ is regular, Definition in (3) reduces to $card(\omega_t) \leqslant card(\omega_{t+1})$, $\forall t \in I$.

Now, let $\mathcal{A}$ be a CA on which we have the spreadability of a property $\mathcal{P}$ during a time horizon I. $\mathcal{A}$ is vulnerable over the area $\mathcal{Z} \subset \mathcal{L}$ to the spreadability of property $\mathcal{P}$ or ($\mathcal{P}$-vulnerable) during I if:

$$\exists t \in I; \; \mathcal{Z} \cap \omega_t \neq \emptyset. \tag{4}$$

See [13, pp. 513–515] where some results have been discussed for vulnerability index in the external point of view. In the following sections, we contribute on the internal point of view of these concepts.

2.3   Spreadability via Attributes

The spreadability concept can be seen in two aspects, external: represented by the neighborhood impact, and internal by the values of the attributes (reaction of the cell on the external excitation). In this way, a cell will be infected by a property $\mathcal{P}$ if it is located near another infected one and its attributes values favour the spreadability of the property $\mathcal{P}$. See illustration in Fig. 1. To couple these two criteria (distance and attributes values) in a property spreadability, we define a cell sensitivity radius at time t as the distance between this cell infected at time $t + 1$ and another nearest infected cell at time t:

$$r_t(c) = \min\{d(c, c'); \; c' \in \omega_t \; and \; c \in \omega_{t+1}\}, \tag{5}$$

where $d(c, c')$ is a distance between two cells.

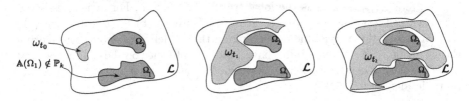

Fig. 1. An illustration of attributes impact on the evolution of $\omega_t \subset \mathcal{L}$ where the attributes values of the areas Ω_1 and Ω_2 do not allow them to be infected by the property $\mathcal{P}$.

Remark 1. We use either the Euclidean distance or the distance defined by:

$$d(c, c') = \min\{k \in \mathbb{N}; \; c' \in \mathcal{N}^k(c)\}, \tag{6}$$

where

$$\mathcal{N}^0(c) = \{c\} \quad \text{and} \quad \mathcal{N}^k(c) = \mathcal{N}(\mathcal{N}^{k-1}(c)), \tag{7}$$

denote successive neighbourhoods for a cell c.

Proposition 1. *Some results are consequences of the definition in (5):*

- $r_t(c) = +\infty \Rightarrow c \notin \omega_{t+1}$ or $\omega_t = \emptyset$.
- $\sum_{c \in \mathcal{L}} r_t(c) = 0 \Rightarrow \omega_{t+1} \subseteq \omega_t$ then $\mathcal{A}$ is not $\mathcal{P}$ – spreadable.

Next, we also define the set $\mathbb{P}_k$ of attributes values taken by the cells that allow satisfying the property $\mathcal{P}$ if they are close by a sensitivity radius equal to k:

$$\mathbb{P}_k = \bigcup_{c \in \mathcal{L}} \{\mathbb{A}_t(c);\ r_t(c) = k\}. \tag{8}$$

Remark 2. – $\mathbb{P}_0$ represents the attributes values allowing the cells, which satisfies the property $\mathcal{P}$ at the time t, to stay at the time $t+1$

$$\mathbb{P}_0 = \bigcup_{c \in \mathcal{L}} \{\mathbb{A}_t(c);\ c \in \omega_t \cap \omega_{t+1}\}.$$

– $\mathbb{P}_1$ represents the attributes values that can allow the cells to satisfy the property $\mathcal{P}$ if one of its neighbors satisfies it at time t

$$\mathbb{P}_1 = \bigcup_{c \in \mathcal{L}} \{\mathbb{A}_t(c);\ \mathcal{N}(c) \cap \omega_t \neq \emptyset \text{ and } c \in \omega_{t+1}\}.$$

– $\mathbb{P}_k$ for $k > 1$, represents the values of the attributes that allow the cells to satisfy $\mathcal{P}$ without needing a neighbourhood that satisfies it.

According to the definition in (8), the attributes of a cell c are said to support the spreadability of the property $\mathcal{P}$ at time t if:

$$\exists k > 0\ ;\ \mathbb{A}_t(c) \in \mathbb{P}_k. \tag{9}$$

2.4   Vulnerability via Attributes

Let $\mathcal{A}$ be a CA on which we have spreadability of a property $\mathcal{P}$ and ω_t be the set of cells satisfying $\mathcal{P}$ at time t.

Definition 1. *We define the sensitivity radius $r_t(\mathcal{Z})$ of a zone $\mathcal{Z}$ as the minimal distance between $\mathcal{Z}$ and the infected zones ω at time t which impacts a part of $\mathcal{Z}$ at the next time:*

$$r_t(\mathcal{Z}) = \begin{cases} d_1(\mathcal{Z}, \omega_t) & \text{if } \mathcal{Z} \cap \omega_{t+1} \neq \emptyset \\ +\infty & \text{else} \end{cases}, \tag{10}$$

where $d_1(\mathcal{Z}, \omega_t) = \min\{k \in \mathbb{N} : \mathcal{N}^k(\mathcal{Z}) \cap \omega_t \neq \emptyset\}$, with $\mathcal{N}^k(\mathcal{Z}) = \bigcup_{c \in \mathcal{Z}} \mathcal{N}^k(c)$ and $\mathcal{N}^k(c)$ defined in (7).

Proposition 2. *Let $\mathcal{A}$ be a CA, $\mathcal{P}$ a property and $\mathcal{Z}$ a zone in $\mathcal{L}$.*

- $\forall c \in \mathcal{Z}$; $r_t(\mathcal{Z}) \leqslant r_t(c)$.
- *if $\exists t \in I$; $r_t(\mathcal{Z}) = 0$ then the CA is $\mathcal{P}$-vulnerable in $\mathcal{Z}$ at the time t.*
- *if $\exists t \in I$; $r_t(\mathcal{Z}) \in \mathbb{R}_*^+$ then the CA will $\mathcal{P}$-vulnerable in $\mathcal{Z}$ at the time $t+1$.*
- *if $\forall t \in I$; $r_t(\mathcal{Z}) = +\infty$ then the CA is not $\mathcal{P}$-vulnerable in $\mathcal{Z}$.*

Definition 2 (Internal Resistance).
A cell's internal resistance to the vulnerability of a property $\mathcal{P}$ is the set of attributes values that does not allow the cell to be affected by $\mathcal{P}$:

$$\overline{\mathbb{P}}(c) = \bigcap_{t \in I} \{\mathbb{A}_t(c); \ r_t(c) = +\infty\}. \tag{11}$$

Proposition 3. *Let $\mathcal{Z} \subset \mathcal{L}$ a non-empty zone of the lattice. The CA $\mathcal{A}$ is vulnerable on $\mathcal{Z}$ if at a given time t the distance between $\mathcal{Z}$ and the zone affected ω_t is less than the sensitivity radius of $\mathcal{Z}$, that is*

$$d_1(\mathcal{Z}, \omega_t) < \min\{k \in \mathbb{N}; \ \mathbb{A}_t(\mathcal{Z}) \cap \mathbb{P}_k \neq \emptyset\}, \tag{12}$$

with $\mathbb{A}_t(\mathcal{Z}) = \bigcup_{c \in \mathcal{Z}} \mathbb{A}_t(c)$.

2.5   Vulnerability Indexes via Attributes

Different zones may react differently to the effect of a property $\mathcal{P}$. Zones may be partially or totally affected. This can also relate to the speed at which areas are affected or the mode of spreadability. The attributes govern the reaction of a zone to the external effect. Thus, to determine which zone is more vulnerable among several zones, the attributes values of each zone must be compared. And this, using vulnerability indexes: the iterative one is used to compare zones vulnerability at each instant; the average one is used to compare zones vulnerability between two instants; and the global one is used to compare zones vulnerability during whole time horizon. Fist defined in [13, pp. 513–514] in the external point of view, we adapt them via attributes in order to take into account the internal effect of cells in the spreadability of $\mathcal{P}$.

Iterative Vulnerability Index

- We call the vulnerability index at a time t, the rate of cells that have favorable attribute values to satisfy the property $\mathcal{P}$:

$$Iv_t(\mathcal{Z}) = \frac{\mu(\mathcal{Z}_{\mathbb{P}_{k>0},t})}{\mu(\mathcal{Z})}, \tag{13}$$

where $\mathcal{Z}_{\mathbb{P}_{k>0},t} = \{c \in \mathcal{Z}; \mathbb{A}_t(c) \in \mathbb{P}_{k>0}\}$ and $\mu(\mathcal{Z})$ the area of $\mathcal{Z}$.
- We call the rate of cells with attributes favoring the property $\mathcal{P}$ and which are located near to the infected area, the quantity.

$$Iv_{d_t}(\mathcal{Z}) = \frac{\mu\{c \in \mathcal{Z}; \ d(c, \omega_t) < r_t(c)\}}{\mu(\mathcal{Z})}. \tag{14}$$

Average and Global Vulnerability Index

- Between two iterations t_0 and t_f, the average vulnerability index is defined by:

$$Iv(\mathcal{Z}) = \sum_{t=t_0}^{t_f} \frac{I_t(\mathcal{Z})}{(t_f - t_0)}. \tag{15}$$

- During a time horizon I, the global vulnerability index takes into account the satisfaction rate of the property $\mathcal{P}$, the contact time of the zones and the crossing speed of $\mathcal{P}$ through the zones. That is:

$$\mathrm{Iv}_g(\sigma) = \frac{\mu(\mathcal{Z}_{\mathbb{P}_{k>0}})}{t_r \, (t_{\ell r} - t_r) \, \mu(\mathcal{Z})}, \quad t_{\ell r} > t_r > 0, \tag{16}$$

where

$$\mathcal{Z}_{\mathbb{P}_{k>0}} = \bigcup_{t \in I} \{ c \in \mathcal{Z}; \; \mathbb{A}_t(c) \in \mathbb{P}_{k>0} \},$$

is the global rate of cells in $\mathcal{Z}$ having attributes values favoring the spreadability of $\mathcal{P}$ during time horizon I. t_r and $t_{\ell r}$ are respectively the first iteration where the area is affected and the first iteration where most part of the area is affected.

3   Case Study: Forest Fire Modelling

3.1   Model Description

As an illustration of the proposed approach, we apply it to an example of 3D wildfires modeling that we have developed [15–17]. The lattice consists of 3D hexagonal cells c_{ijk} whose centered coordinates i, j, k represent a part of the soil, vegetation, or air (Fig. 2a). For the neighbourhood, we consider the D_3Q_{21} model. At an instant t, the cell state is given by the absence or existence of fire in the cell. The set of states S considered is: state 0 for the non-flammable cell such as the cell represents air, ground or smoke, state 1 for the vegetation without fire and state 2 for the vegetation on fire. Each cell is associated with a set of attributes defined in Table 1.

The evolution of the CA is identified as the mutual action between two mechanisms:

$$f \equiv \text{Heat transfer} \oplus \text{Catalyst transfer} \tag{17}$$

The transition rules are defined from two mechanisms: the first is defined from heat transfer which depends on three processes (conductivity, convection, and radiation). The cell temperature is calculated at each iteration where a cell will ignite if its temperature is higher than the auto-ignition temperature. The second mechanism determines the cell dryness by calculating the fuel and air humidity where a cell will ignite if it receives a fire catalyst and its humidity is low. That is:

$$A_t(c) = \begin{cases} 1 & if \; [T_t(c) > T_{auto}] \; or \; [\varrho_t(c) > 1 \; and \; \mathcal{H}_t^{in}(c) < \beta] \\ 0 & else \end{cases} \tag{18}$$

Table 1. Attributes considered for wildfire model.

Cell classification	$\delta : \mathcal{L} \mapsto \{0,1,2\}$	{air, fuel, soil}
Temperature	$T_t : \mathcal{L} \mapsto \mathbb{R}$	
Temperature	$T_{auto} : \mathcal{L} \mapsto \mathbb{R}$	
Packing ratio of the plant species	$\beta_t : \mathcal{L} \mapsto [0,1]$	
Air and vegetation humidity	$\mathcal{H}_t : \mathcal{L} \mapsto [0,1]$	
Thermal conductivity	$\lambda_t : \mathcal{L} \mapsto [0,1]$	
Inflammation rate	$\Gamma_t : \mathcal{L} \mapsto [0,1]$	
Ignition catalyst	$\varrho_t : \mathcal{L} \mapsto \{0,1\}$	{without catalyst, with catalyst}
Porosity	$\phi_t : \mathcal{L} \mapsto [0,1]$	$\phi_t(c) = 1 - \beta_t(c)$
Slope factor	$P_t : \mathcal{L} \mapsto \mathbb{R}^n$	$P_t^{[i]}(c) = 5.275\beta_t(c)^{-3}\tan^2(\theta_i(c))$
Radiative conductivity	$b_t : \mathcal{L} \mapsto \mathbb{R}^+$	$\sigma_n \varepsilon_{r,t} \varphi$
Wind vector	$W_t : \mathcal{L} \mapsto \mathbb{R}^n$	$W_t(c) = (w^{[1]}(c), \cdots, w^{[n]}(c))_t$

More details on lattice and cells geometry, neighborhood, attributes, states, transition rules and simulation aided software are available in [17]. We pursue in the following sections with the simulation results.

3.2 Wildfire Spreadability

Figure 2 presents some snapshots of fire propagation with the developed wildfire model from iteration 200 to iteration 1000. The lecturer can found a simulation example video at (this link).

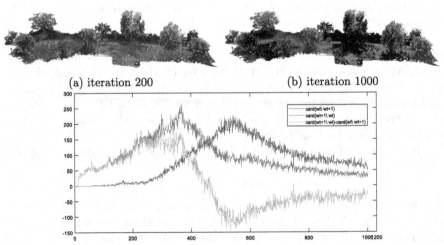

(a) iteration 200   (b) iteration 1000

(c) Evolution of cell numbers in the zones ω_t and ω_{t+1} between t_{200} and t_{1000}.

Fig. 2. Fire propagation from initail conditions to iteration 1000 and spreadability evolution of $\mathcal{P}$.

From this simulation, we can observe that the property $\mathcal{P}s_t(c) \Leftrightarrow s_t(c) = 2$ that describes the cells on fire at an instant t is spreading. In order to check the spreadability mode, we draw in Fig. 2c the number of old cells on fire $card\{\omega_t \backslash \omega_{t+1}\}$, the number of new cells burned $card\{\omega_{t+1} \backslash \omega_t\}$ and the difference between the two values $card\{\omega_{t+1} \backslash \omega_t\} - card\{\omega_t \backslash \omega_{t+1}\}$ where ω_t represents the set of cells satisfying the property $\mathcal{P}$, and this between t_200 and t_{1000}.

According to the graph in Fig. 2c the property $\mathcal{P}$ is spreadable in area sense from the initial time until iteration 450. Then, after iteration 450, the number of new burned cells is lower than the number of extinguished cells. So $\mathcal{P}$ is not spreadable in area sense even if the fire is still spreading.

To capture the values of the attributes with the distance between a given cell and the nearest burning cell, we made a series of simulations by modifying at each one the burned areas at the initial state. We record for each burned cell three values at time $t + 1$: the distance between the cell and the nearest burning cell, the temperature of the cell, and the dryness of the cell at a time t. We present these values in Figs. 3a, 3b and 3c by averaging the values associated with the vertically arranged cells to create a 2D map of the modeled space. Figure 3a shows the vertical average of the sensitivity radius r_t using the distance d defined in (6). It is seen that the sensitivity radius of the areas containing trees is the largest due to convection as the warm air closest to the thermal source decreases in density and tends to rise. Figure 3b shows the vertical average of dryness R_t degree of the cells defined by :

$$R_t(c) = \beta_t \min\{\mathcal{H}_t(c) + \mathcal{H}_t^{int}(c), 1\} + 1_{\{0,2\}}(\delta(c)), \qquad (19)$$

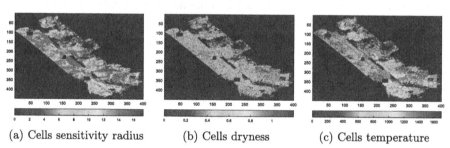

(a) Cells sensitivity radius   (b) Cells dryness   (c) Cells temperature

Fig. 3. Vertical average values of sensitivity radius, dryness and temperature of each cells at the moment before ignition.

where β_t, $\mathcal{H}_t(c)$, $\mathcal{H}_t^{int}(c)$ and $\delta(c)$ represent respectively packing Ratio, air humidity, vegetation humidity, and cell type. Figure 3c represents the cells temperature at the moment before ignition. To capture the cell ignition conditions and the sufficient ratio associated with the attribute values, several simulations were performed by recording the three values presented above in order to identify a map of attributes values that enable cells ignition. Figure 4 shows the function $\mathcal{E}$ defined by :

$$\mathcal{E}(R, T) = \max_{c \in \mathcal{L}, t \in I} \{r_t(c); \ R_t(c) = R \ et \ T_t(c) = T\},$$

from the values of $\mathcal{E}$, we can determine the cells that favour the spreadability of $\mathcal{P}$ at the initial time (Fig. 4b) by dividing the lattice into cells that favour fire spread and others whose attributes resist.

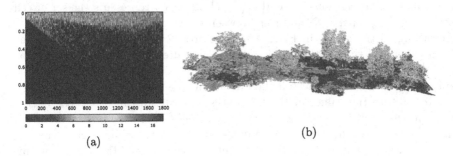

(a)   (b)

Fig. 4. Determination of attributes values that favour the spreadability of $\mathcal{P}$ in order to determine which cells have these values at the initial time. Figure 4a represent the maximum sensitivity radius depending on dryness and temperature and Fig. 4b represent cells classification that favour or not the spreadability of $\mathcal{P}$ at time t_0.

3.3   Wildfire Vulnerability

To compare zones vulnerability based on the attributes we consider two zones $\mathcal{Z}_1$ and $\mathcal{Z}_2$ for a time interval $[t_0, t_{4500}]$ as simulation illustrated in Fig. 5 for iterations 250, 500, 1000 and 4000. Based on the values of the attributes favouring the spreadability of $\mathcal{P}$ as classified in 4b, we calculate at each iteration for the two zones considered the vulnerability indices, the cells on fire number, and the burned cells number (Fig. 6a). We can observe that the zone 2 is more vulnerable than the zone 1 at most time. Figure 6a presents details on vulnerability index for these two zones for classification need. It shows an oscillation of most vulnerable zone. From Fig. 6a observation and the use of iterative and average vulnerability indexes, we give the most vulnerable zone classification into Table 6b according to time intervals.

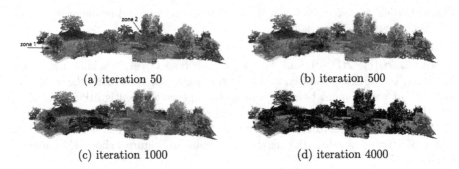

(a) iteration 50   (b) iteration 500

(c) iteration 1000   (d) iteration 4000

Fig. 5. Simulation results of fire spreadability and system vulnerability on two zones

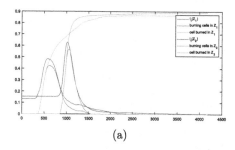

Time interval	Most vulnerable zone
$[t_0, t_{400}[$	zone 2
$[t_{400}, t_{900}[$	zone 1
$[t_{900}, t_{1450}[$	zone 2
$[t_{1450}, t_{2000}[$	zone 1
$[t_{2000}, t_{4000}[$	zone 2

(a)   (b)

Fig. 6. Figure 6a represent the vulnerability index, cells on fire and cells burned number. Figure 6b represent classification of most vulnerable zone.

4   Conclusion and Perspectives

In this paper, we have considered two concepts of systems theory via the cellular automata approach: spreadability and vulnerability. Our contribution concerns the redefinition of spreadability and vulnerability based on spatial attributes in order to take into account the cells internal reaction. This redefinition allows the development of new vulnerability indexes. As a practical application, we have considered a 3D-CA model for the wildfire phenomenon, a recent model we have proposed to simulate and represent wildfires dynamics. We have described an innovative mechanism that allows taking into account the environment heterogeneity as well as the possibility to follow the evolution while keeping a simplified point of view on the wildfire propagation.

As a future study, we will work on the question of optimal control and protector control of vulnerable areas. To address this objective, we will focus on a new type of control based on Reinforcement Learning (RL) to solve problems such as: i) the choice of zones and attributes in which the action will operate; ii) the possibility and feasibility of doing the action; iii) the action cost and intensity; iv) the cost of the system damage over time. The RL can learn how to control this system over time through systematic trial and error, guided by a vast variety of algorithms

Acknowledgements. This work was supported by ministry of National Education Professional training, Higher Education and Scientific Research (MENFPESRS) and the Digital Development Agency (DDA) of Morocco. Project Al Khawarizmi: Outil de Gestion Intelligente des Eaux d'irrigation et du patrimoine forestier.

References

1. Salle, J.P.: The stability of dynamical systems, In: CBMS-NSF Regional Conference Series in Applied Mathematics, vol. 25 (1976)
2. Lions, J.-L.: Controlabilité exacte des systèmes distribués: remarques sur la théorie générale et les applications. In: Analysis and optimization of systems, pp. 3–14. Springer (1986). https://doi.org/10.1007/BFb0004029

3. El Jai, A., Zerrik, E., Simon, M.C., Amouroux, M.: Regional observability of a thermal process. IEEE Trans. Autom. Control **40**(3), 518–521 (1995)
4. El Jai, A., Kassara, K.: Spreadable distributed systems. Math. Comput. Model. **20**(1), 47–64 (1994)
5. Bernoussi, A., El Jai, A.: New approach of spreadability. Math. Comput. Model. **31**(13), 93–109 (2000)
6. Bernoussi, A.: Spreadability and vulnerability of distributed parameter systems. Int. J. Syst. Sci. **38**(4), 305–317 (2007)
7. El Yacoubi, S., El Jai, A.: Cellular automata modelling and spreadability. Math. Comput. Model. **36**(9–10), 1059–1074 (2002)
8. Bernoussi, A.: Spreadability, vulnerability and protector control. Math. Modell. Nat. Phenom. **5**(7), 145–150 (2010)
9. Toffoli, T.: Cellular automata as an alternative to (rather than an approximation of) differential equations in modeling physics. Physica D **10**(1–2), 117–127 (1984)
10. El Yacoubi, S., El Jai, A., Ammor, N.: Regional controllability with cellular automata models. In: Bandini, S., Chopard, B., Tomassini, M. (eds.) ACRI 2002. LNCS, vol. 2493, pp. 357–367. Springer, Heidelberg (2002). https://doi.org/10.1007/3-540-45830-1_34
11. Ouardouz, M., Bernoussi, A., Kassogué, H., Amharref, M.: Maintenance process control: cellular automata approach. In: Vinh, P.C., Barolli, L. (eds.) ICTCC 2016. LNICST, vol. 168, pp. 287–296. Springer, Cham (2016). https://doi.org/10.1007/978-3-319-46909-6_26
12. Jellouli, O., Bernoussi, A., Amharref, M., El Yacoubi, S.: Vulnerability and protector control: cellular automata approach. In: Wąs, J., Sirakoulis, G.C., Bandini, S. (eds.) ACRI 2014. LNCS, vol. 8751, pp. 218–227. Springer, Cham (2014). https://doi.org/10.1007/978-3-319-11520-7_23
13. Kassogué, H., Bernoussi, A.: Vulnerability for systems described by cellular automata: application to flood phenomena. Appl. Math. Model. **50**, 509–523 (2017)
14. Kassogué, H., Bernoussi, A., Maâtouk, M., Amharref, M.: A two scale cellular automaton for flow dynamics modeling (2cafdym). Appl. Math. Model. **43**, 61–77 (2017)
15. Byari, M., Bernoussi, A.S., Ouardouz, M., Amharref, M.: Control of 3D cellular automata via actuator and space attributes: Application to fires forest. In: Gwizdałła, T.M., Manzoni, L., Sirakoulis, G.C., Bandini, S., Podlaski, K., (eds.) Cellular Automata, pp. 123–133. Springer International Publishing, Cham (2021), https://doi.org/10.1007/978-3-030-69480-7_13
16. Byari, M., Bernoussi, A.-S., Ouardouz, M., Amharref, M.: Protector control of 3D cellular automata via space attributes: Application to wildland fire. J. Cell. Automata (2022)
17. Byari, M., Bernoussi, A.-S., Jellouli, O., Ouardouz, M., Amharref, M.: Multi-scale 3d cellular automata modeling: Application to wildland fire spread. Chaos, Solitons Fractals (2022). https://doi.org/10.2139/ssrn.4046576

Automatic Evolutionary Adjustment of Cellular Automata Model for Forest Fire Propagation

Maria Eugênia A. Ferreira[1]([envelope])[iD], André L. M. P. Quinta[1][iD],
Danielli A. Lima[2][iD], Luiz G. A. Martins[1][iD], and Gina M. B. Oliveira[1][iD]

[1] Federal University of Uberlândia (UFU), Uberlândia, MG, Brazil
{maria.eugenia,andre.morais,lgmartins,gina}@ufu.br
[2] Federal Institute of Triângulo Mineiro (IFTM), Patrocínio, MG, Brazil
danielli@iftm.edu.br

Abstract. Forest fires have faced a huge increase due to climate change threatening different biomes. Fire propagation modeling is a critical issue to prevent and control the damage of this phenomenon. Cellular automata shown to be efficient in the construction of such models. However, tuning the various parameters involved in these models is a difficult task. This work proposes a method of parameters adjustment of fire propagation models based on genetic algorithms. Different experiments in various scenarios showed that was possible to use evolutionary computation that automatically adjusts the parameters of a fire spread model.

Keywords: Cellular automata · Fire spread · Forest burning · Computational modelling · Genetic algorithms · Bio-inspired simulation

1 Introduction

Forest fires are notably harmful to the ecosystem, resulting in environmental, economic and social impacts. Recently in Brazil, a considerable increase in forest fires has been observed, mainly in the biomes known as Amazon, Pantanal and Cerrado. To prevent and fight fires, it is necessary to understand how fire spreads in environments and how factors related to vegetation, topography, climate and wind impact the propagation. Furthermore, it is important to choose an adequate modeling approach, capable of reproducing the phenomenon satisfactorily, allowing a model parameters adjustment by simple implementations.

Cellular automata (CA) have been studied as a tool for modeling natural phenomena, and fire propagation is one of the main investigations of such simulation models [2]. Regardless of the modeling used, a wildfire simulation must consider different environmental characteristics, such as soil type, climate, vegetation, wind and terrain topography [9], which leads to a considerable number of parameters in the resulting model. Therefore, setting the parameters of a fire

© The Author(s), under exclusive license to Springer Nature Switzerland AG 2022
B. Chopard et al. (Eds.): ACRI 2022, LNCS 13402, pp. 235–245, 2022.
https://doi.org/10.1007/978-3-031-14926-9_21

propagation model is a critical task. Furthermore, even if a model has been previously tuned for a particular area, its applicability to others may depend on a parameters adjustment that takes into account the differences between areas.

The objective of this work is to investigate an approach based on a genetic algorithm (GA), which allows an automatic adjustment in the parameters of the fire spread models based on CA, from historical data of fires occurred in a target area. In the experiments reported, it was possible to verify that the evolutionary approach was able to find a good fit of parameters for different scenarios.

2   Related Work

CA models have been applied in different areas, such as cryptography [15], task scheduling [1], path planning [10], swarm robotics [8], among others. It is noteworthy that one of the main applications of CA has been in the modeling of natural phenomena that produces a complex behavior from local interactions, such as the epidemiological models [14], urban traffic and fire spread [2], which is also investigated in the present work. Several fire propagation models CA based have been proposed in the literature. Most of these models use probabilistic transition rules applied in two-dimensional grids of cells, which represent the environments where the fire is propagated. The model proposed in [2] consists of a probabilistic CA with three states and it uses the Moore's neighborhood, which was the basis for several rule-based models of CA that emerged later. The study described in [3] considered data from a forest fire in USA. The model has random neighborhoods, wind direction and magnitude, as well as air temperature and relative humidity. The model described in [7] uses scenarios with homogeneous and non-homogeneous forests, considering climatic conditions and the topography of the area.

The model proposed by Louzada & Ferreira Jr. (2008) [11], uses a 2D-CA with Moore's neighborhood and two parameters: LQ (number of firing stages) and LR (forest age). The fire spread model proposed in Lima & Lima (2014) [9] is represented by a 2D-CA with Moore's neighborhood and there are 3 possible states: tree alive, burning and ashe. The burning state can assume 4 different values burning = {1, 2, 3, 4}, depending on the fire intensity. A preference matrix $W_{m \times m}$ representing wind speed and direction was used in their model. A new model for fire simulation based on CA update rules is proposed here. It has the parameters LQ and LR, used in [11], with the preference matrix $W_{3 \times 3}$, which represents the wind, similar to that proposed in [9].

Genetic algorithms consist of a search and optimization technique based on the mechanisms of natural selection and genetics. GA usage allied to CA has already been described in the literature, whether in the adjustment of model parameters as discussed here, or even in the specification of rules [12,13]. The evolutionary search approach has been applied in CA-based models for simulating natural and biological phenomena, such as modeling debris and lava flow [4] and vegetarian recovery [6]. A GA was used in [5] to adjust the parameters of the CA-based model based of proliferation of insect vectors of Chagas disease, which is also used herein.

3   Proposed Model for Forest Fire Simulation

The model proposed herein uses a 2D-CA with Moore's neighborhood (η_{ij}^v), where $v = (2r + 1)^2 - 1 = 8$, $r = 1$ (radius), L (lattice) in $t = 0$ and L' (lattice) for $t \geq 1$. The cell's state x_{ij} is expressed by the pair (Type, Stage), with Type $\in$ {fire, tree} and Stage $\in [1 \cdots$ LQ], if Type = fire (represents tree burning time) or Stage $\in [1 \cdots$ LR], if Type = tree (represents tree recovery time).

A cell of type fire will go through different LQ stages while burning. When changing to fire type, it starts with Stage = 1 and at each subsequent time step (t), the Stage is incremented up to the maximum value equal to LQ. After reaching Stage = LQ, a cell of type fire is changed to type tree with Stage =1, which represents a tree that has just been burned and will start its regeneration. A cell of type tree will go through up to LR different stages of recovery. This represents the dry organic matter amount presented in $x_{ij} \in L'$ that can be fuel for burning. At each subsequent t in which it remains in the tree state, it is incremented (+1) up to the maximum value (LR). The simulation starts defining all cells being of type tree with Stage = LR. Matrix $W_{3 \times 3}$ represents the wind speed as a probability of a neighbor fire cell ignite a tree in the center. Each position $w_{ij} \in W_{3 \times 3}$ assumes a value between [0, 1], modelling the wind direction and intensity $\boldsymbol{w}$. Figure 1 shows examples of $W_{3 \times 3}$. It indicates the probability

0.85	1.00	0.85
0.50	0.00	0.50
0.14	0.00	0.14

(a) Sc$_1$, Sc$_5$

0.14	0.50	0.85
0.00	0.00	1.00
0.14	0.50	0.85

(b) Sc$_2$, Sc$_6$

0.85	0.50	0.14
1.00	0.00	0.00
0.85	0.50	0.14

(c) Sc$_3$, Sc$_7$

0.00	0.14	0.50
0.14	0.00	0.85
0.50	0.85	1.00

(d) Sc$_4$, Sc$_8$

0.85	1.00	0.95
0.46	0.00	0.81
0.74	0.16	0.01

(e) Sc$_1$

0.19	0.75	0.91
0.00	0.00	1.00
0.16	0.59	0.96

(f) Sc$_2$

0.71	0.98	0.00
0.94	0.00	0.15
0.91	0.77	0.06

(g) Sc$_3$

0.00	0.00	0.57
0.31	0.00	0.84
0.34	0.97	1.00

(h) Sc$_4$

0.84	0.99	0.89
0.51	0.00	0.51
0.10	0.01	0.00

(i) Sc$_5$

0.09	0.50	0.82
0.00	0.00	1.00
0.08	0.51	0.81

(j) Sc$_6$

0.82	0.41	0.35
1.00	0.00	0.00
0.85	0.53	0.14

(k) Sc$_7$

0.00	0.12	0.49
0.15	0.00	0.86
0.49	0.91	1.00

(l) Sc$_8$

0.12	0.19	0.72
0.00	0.00	1.00
0.03	0.65	0.70

(m) Sc$_9$

0.08	0.60	0.85
0.00	0.00	1.00
0.00	0.41	0.65

(n) Sc$_{10}$

Fig. 1. Probabilities matrices $W_{3 \times 3}$ representing the wind ($\boldsymbol{w}$) vector forces, where (■) represents the references and (■) represents GA matrix.

for a flame propagate to the center cell x_{ij} from each one of the 8-outer cells $x_{mn} \in \eta_{ij}^8$, that represents wind direction $\boldsymbol{w} = (\boldsymbol{w}_N, \boldsymbol{w}_S, \boldsymbol{w}_E, \boldsymbol{w}_W, \boldsymbol{w}_{NE}, \boldsymbol{w}_{NW}, \boldsymbol{w}_{SE}, \boldsymbol{w}_{SW})$. At each iteration, a tree cell x_{ij} has a probability $P(x_{ij})$ becoming fire: $P(x_{ij}) = \frac{Stage_{ij}}{LR} \times \frac{\Delta}{LQ}$, where $\Delta = \sum_{ab}^{\eta} Stage_{ab} \times w_{ab}$, which $\forall x_{ab} \in \eta_{ij}^8$ neighbor cells of the center x_{ij} that are in the fire state. The Δ is saturated in 1.

4   Evolutionary Approach to Adjust the Model Parameters

Our proposal is to use an evolutionary search, more specifically a GA, to specify the main parameters involved in the fire propagation model described in the previous section, in order to obtain a simulation very close to the one observed in the propagation of flames from a forest fire in a given area.

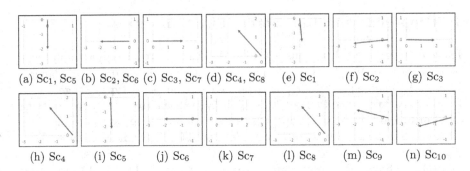

(a) Sc$_1$, Sc$_5$ (b) Sc$_2$, Sc$_6$ (c) Sc$_3$, Sc$_7$ (d) Sc$_4$, Sc$_8$ (e) Sc$_1$ (f) Sc$_2$ (g) Sc$_3$

(h) Sc$_4$ (i) Sc$_5$ (j) Sc$_6$ (k) Sc$_7$ (l) Sc$_8$ (m) Sc$_9$ (n) Sc$_{10}$

Fig. 2. Vector forces ($\boldsymbol{w}$) from $W_{3\times3}$ representing the wind direction and intensity, where (■) represents the references and (■) represents GA matrix.

In this stage of the work, we used artificial databases generated by fire simulations, using a model with different parameter settings related to fire scenarios. In this way, it is possible to evaluate the ability of the GA to specify an adequate set of parameters, from temporal sequences of L', which represent the images captured of the area during the evolution of a fire. For each scenario evaluated, the model was configured with a set of different parameters that were simulated to generate a base with 50 lattices L' of size $10^2 \times 10^2$ that represent the temporal evolution of the fire, simulating a base of images taken at 50 time intervals. Each time interval corresponds to 200 evolution steps of the CA. We will call each set of 50 registered lattices (representative simulation of each fire scenario), the reference lattice base, or simply, the reference base. The parameters extracted from the fire propagation model and which must be specified by the GA are: LQ (maximum burning time), LR (maximum recovery time) and the 8 values of probabilities that make up the matrix $W_{3\times3}$, representing the wind direction $\boldsymbol{w}$. In a preliminary stage, different GA specifications were evaluated until reaching an efficient configuration for the parameter adjustment. The individual (chromosome) is a length-10 vector composed by genes, 8 real values and 2 integer (LQ, LR) values. The real value fields are relative to the eight positions of the $W_{3\times3}$ and each field stores a float value in the range $[0, 1]$. GA initial population is composed of 100 solutions generated at random. The selection of parents for each generation is done through a simple tournament (Tour = 3). A two-point crossover (rate of 90%) is used. A mutation rate of 20% is applied, adding or subtracting a random value to the genes. At each generation end, the best 25% individuals are kept. GA evolves for 10^2 generations. To calculate the fitness $F(k), 0 \le k \le 100$, the simulation of the model using the parameters of the individual k is compared, image by image, with the referential set of 50 lattices ($L'_{100\times100}$) generated for the chosen scenario.

The series of lattices (L') associated with the individual is then paired with the reference data set and the individual is evaluated by the difference in the number of **fire** cells for each pair of lattices (individual, reference), that means $F(k) = \sum_{k=0}^{|L|} |(x_{ij}^{Ref}) - (x_{ij}^{GA})|$, where $x_{ij}^{Ref} \in L'_{Ref}$ and $x_{ij}^{GA} \in L'_{GA}$.

In an initial stage of our experiments, an evaluation was given by the simple sum of the differences in the number of `fire` cells calculated in the 50 capture instants. However, two requirements proved to be important for a good evaluation of the individuals: considering the spatial distribution of the differences in the `fire` cells and seeking to attenuate the stochastic characteristic of the simulation. To meet the first requirement, in an analogy to the compass rose (CR), the lattice is divided into 9 parts and the difference in the number of `fire` cells is calculated for each part, considering each pair of (L'_{Ref}, L'_{GA}), and them the sum is calculated. The assessment of the individual for each simulation is given by the simple average of the sum of the calculated differences.

Finally, to meet the second requirement, two actions were taken. For each scenario, the baseline stores the value of each cell at each time step for a complete simulation. In addition, 10^2 executions were performed for each scenario and the average amounts of `fire` cells in each of the 9 lattice parts were recorded. Furthermore, in the evaluation of each individual, 5 different simulations are performed using the values of parameters specified in their chromosome and at each simulation the average of the sums of the 9 lattice parts is obtained. In calculating the differences between each simulation and the reference, the difference between the average value obtained in the 10^2 runs and the value obtained in each individual simulation is considered. At the end, the evaluation of the individual is calculated by the simple average, considering the 5 simulations, of the average sum per lattice part obtained in each simulation.

5   Experiments

Experiments were carried out considering different scenarios. To analyze the results, the following aspects were taken into account: (i) the values of the parameters LQ, LR and $W_{3\times3}$, which are compared with the values used in the bases of reference; (ii) the vector obtained by the resultant force of the $W_{3\times3}$ and representing the direction and intensity of the wind; (iii) the temporal evolution in which the best individual obtained by the GA was used to define the parameters of the CA model and visually compared with the referential CA temporal evolution at the time instants $t = \{5, 20, 30, 50\}$. Each result will be given by a 3-uple $(\bar{x}, s, w_{CR}^{GA})$, being $\bar{x}$ the fitness average, s the observed standard deviation and w_{CR}^{GA} the length of the resulting vector that points in one of the directions of the CR. For all 8 experiments the value $w_{CR}^{Ref} = 2.0$, for the reference model (Ref).

In the first experiments, 4 scenarios were evaluated using a **single fire spot** in which, although we applied different $W_{3\times3}$, the fire was started from the same point. In those scenarios (LQ, LR) were fixed at $(3, 30)$. The referential matrices $W_{3\times3}$ are shown in Fig. 1 (a to d). The best individual evolved for each of the 4 scenarios also has (LQ, LR) equal to $(3, 30)$, but differences were observed in the matrices. The scenario Sc_1 applies a reference $W_{3\times3}$ with larger values at the top (Fig. 1(a)), resulting in $(2.63, 0.008, 1.60)$, where $\bar{x} = 2.63$, $s = 0.008$ and $w_S^{AG} = 1.60$. The evolved $W_{3\times3}$ (Fig. 1(e)) is similar to the reference with the wind direction to the south (w_S). The intensity of the evolved vector (Fig. 2(d)) is

$w = 1.60$, lesser than $w_S^{Ref} = 2.0$ (Fig. 2(a)). A slight inclination is noticed. Despite the differences between matrices, the behavior observed in Fig. 3 by applying the individual (e to h) is similar to that of the reference (a to d): the fire propagates to the south and the edges are reached between $t = 20$ and $t = 35$.

Considering scenario Sc_2, the result is $(3.60, 0.12, 2.07)$. Although the evolved (Fig. 1f) and the reference (Fig. 1(b)) matrices have differences, they have similar balances: the highest values are on the right. As a consequence, the wind direction is the same. When analyzing the vector that represents the resultant wind force, it can be seen that the GA vector (Fig. 2(e)) presents an angle a little larger than the reference (Fig. 2(b)). Moreover, the intensity of the evolved vector w_W^{GA} is slight bigger than w_W^{Ref}: $2.07 > 2.0$.

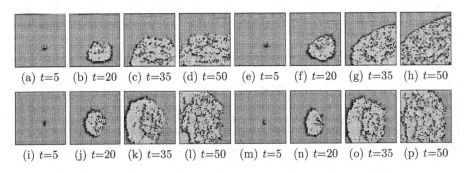

(a) $t=5$ (b) $t=20$ (c) $t=35$ (d) $t=50$ (e) $t=5$ (f) $t=20$ (g) $t=35$ (h) $t=50$

(i) $t=5$ (j) $t=20$ (k) $t=35$ (l) $t=50$ (m) $t=5$ (n) $t=20$ (o) $t=35$ (p) $t=50$

Fig. 3. Sc_1 (1st line): w_S, reference matrix (a, b, c, d) and GA individual (e, f, g, h). Sc_2 (2nd line): w_W, reference matrix (i, j, k, l) and GA individual (m, n, o, p).

The fire spreads to the west of the lattice in both simulations. Figure 3 (i to l) shows the reference data, while Fig. 3 (m to p) shows the simulation using the evolved parameters obtained.

Scenario Sc_3 considered a $W_{3 \times 3}$ with the opposite propagation in the east direction. Figure 1(g) shows the obtained $W_{3 \times 3}$ with greater intensity in the fields on the left, as well as the reference, Fig. 1(c), resulting in $(2.06, 0.03, 1.89)$. In the vector comparison, as shown in Fig. 2(f), it was obtained a vector similar to the reference (Fig. 2c), but there is an angle and $w_E^{AG} < w_E^{Ref}$, where $1.89 < 2.0$. The resultant behaviors can be seen in the first line of Fig. 4. In both cases, $t \in [20, 25]$, the fire spread has already reached the right edges of the lattice.

Finally, a scenario Sc_4 we have the following result $(2.92, 0.16, 2.06)$. The scenario was generated with the largest diagonal fields, according to the $W_{3 \times 3}$ shown in Fig. 1(d). The GA $W_{3 \times 3}$, Fig. 1(h), also obtained values with equilibrium of diagonal fields. In relation to vector comparison, the angles and direction were similar. The GA wind intensity (Fig. 2(g)) $2.06 > 2.0$ (reference) (Fig. 2(d)). The second line of Fig. 4 compares the reference (i to l) and the best individual evolved by GA (m to p), they have a similar behavior. This spread initially took place towards the w_{NW}. In both cases, the initial position of the fire favored

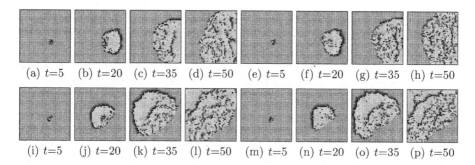

Fig. 4. Sc_3 (1st line): $\boldsymbol{w}_E$, reference matrix (a, b, c, d) and GA individual (e, f, g, h). Sc_4 (2nd line): $\boldsymbol{w}_{NW}$, reference matrix (i, j, k, l) and GA individual (m, n, o, p).

automatic adjustment: the edges took a long time to be reached. GA was successful in the adjustment of the 3-parameters (LQ, LR, $W_{3\times3}$).

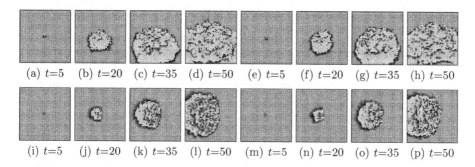

Fig. 5. Sc_5 (1st line): $\boldsymbol{w}_S$, reference matrix (a, b, c, d) and GA individual (e, f, g, h). Sc_6 (2nd line): $\boldsymbol{w}_W$, reference matrix (i, j, k, l) and GA individual (m, n, o, p).

In this step, we simulated the CA **different fire spots** initialization. We sought to know the impact of the initial focus position on the GA performance. Each individual was evolved 5 times, starting the fire from a different spot. The first fire spot evaluated was the central point of L. Also, L was divided into 4 parts and a fire spot was placed in the center of each part, resulting in more 4 fire starts. The Sc_5 experiment uses the same scenario of Sc_1, because we sought to understand the behavior of the worst case of the initial experiments. However, the GA evaluation is based on 5 runs, each one starting from a different fire spot. The reference $W_{3\times3}$ had propagation to the south $\boldsymbol{w}_S$, as shown in Fig. 5 (a to d). The $W_{3\times3}$ is the one obtained by the GA (Fig. 1(i)), resulting in $(2.99, 0.08, 2.12)$. Compared to the reference, Fig. 1(a), it can be seen that the fields have intensities distributed in the same proportion, and $\boldsymbol{w}_S^{GA}$ (Fig. 2(i), is slight greater than $\boldsymbol{w}_S^{Ref}$ (Fig. 2(a)). However, this result is better than the one obtained in the previous experiment Sc_1 (Fig. 2(d)), in which just one simulation was used. As a consequence the simulation obtained using GA solution (Fig. 5 (e to h)) is better than the previous one observed in scenario Sc_1 (Fig. 3 (e to h)). We only show here the simulation starting from central spot.

We sought to evaluate the impact of **changing the parameters LQ and LR** in the last experiments. The GA evaluation based in 5 simulations was also used here. In scenario Sc_6, the pair (LQ, LR) are $(6, 30)$, respectively, and final result is $(3.20, 0.15, 1.84)$. Despite the different values in matrices (Fig. 1(b) and Fig. 1(j)), it shown to be balanced. The vector has the same intensity, albeit a greater angle. Figure 5 (i to p) shows the simulation starting from the central spot: the fire reaches the L' edges in $t \in [35 - 50]$. It is also possible to perceive the influence of LQ. With a higher value (6), the cells burn longer, therefore, there are more fire cells. In scenario Sc_7, the pair (LQ, LR) are $(3, 90)$ and uses the $W_{3 \times 3}$, Fig. 1(c), resulting in $(2.2, 0.13, 2.07)$. Figure 1(k) shows the values of the evolved $W_{3 \times 3}$. The intensity 2.07 of the GA (Fig. 2(j)) slightly larger than the reference. Figure 6 (a to h) shows the CA evolution. A higher value for LR causes cells to take a while to get back on fire. The last experiment (Sc_8) uses (LQ, LR): $(4, 40)$ and the $W_{3 \times 3}$ in Fig. 1(d), where the highest values are on the lower diagonal. The GA search resulted in $(3.27, 0.16, 2.06)$, has the $W_{3 \times 3}$ shown in Fig. 1(l). The wind vector (Fig. 2(l)) has a smaller angle to the reference (Fig. 2(d)), but with similar intensity. The wind direction is equal to the reference: it spreads to the NW. The influence of (LQ, LR) is noted in Fig. 6: cells spend more time burning, take a little longer to become organic matter, which may (or not) catch fire again. The best starting is the central spot with a larger spreading. To analyze the sensitivity of the model, we checked whether the initial settings of the CA affect the behavior of the GA to mimic the fire. This was done by changing the position of the fire spots, but still using the database generated for the Sc_6 scenario shown above. In the Sc_9, in the GA configuration, the five initial fire spots were moved two spaces to the left and two spaces down, resulting in $(3.89, 0.048, 3.81)$, where $\bar{x} = 3.81$, $s = 0.048$ and $w_S^{AG} = 1.93$. The $W_{3 \times 3}$ obtained by AG is shown in Fig. 1(m). The wind vector (Fig. 2(m)) has a smaller angle to the

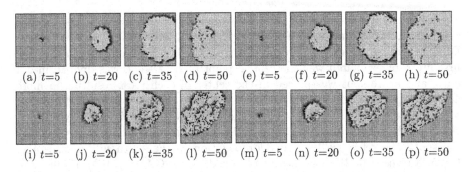

(a) $t=5$ (b) $t=20$ (c) $t=35$ (d) $t=50$ (e) $t=5$ (f) $t=20$ (g) $t=35$ (h) $t=50$

(i) $t=5$ (j) $t=20$ (k) $t=35$ (l) $t=50$ (m) $t=5$ (n) $t=20$ (o) $t=35$ (p) $t=50$

Fig. 6. Sc_7 (1st line): $\boldsymbol{w}_E$, reference matrix (a, b, c, d) and GA individual (e, f, g, h). Sc_8 (2nd line): $\boldsymbol{w}_{NW}$, reference matrix (i, j, k, l) and GA individual (m, n, o, p).

reference (Fig. 2(b)) and the intensity is also lower (1.93). The temporal evolution of the CA with the obtained parameters had a behavior similar to the reference. In Sc_{10}, the fire spots were shifted two spaces to the right and two spaces up. The result was $(4.15, 0.080, 4.00)$, where $\bar{x} = 4.00$, $s = 0.080$ and $w_S^{AG} = 2.01$. The wind vector (Fig. 2(n)) has a bigger angle to the reference (Fig. 2(b)) and the intensity is similar (2.03). The $W_{3\times 3}$ obtained by AG is shown in Fig. 1(n). In the temporal evolution of the model, the behavior is also similar to the reference. Despite the initial fire positions being different from the reference database, the result of scenarios is quite satisfactory.

Finally, we verified if an individual with delay or fire propagation anticipation would have a large error. We choose the values from the Sc_2 reference and run the CA. In our model each time interval corresponding to 200 evolution steps of the CA, Fig. 7 displays the fitness values of the execution with lead and lag. Fitness has a considerable increase in cases with delay. When the fire starts with anticipation, the L' is occupied faster, which causes a smaller increase in fitness, since it is not so easy to capture the fire spread behavior.

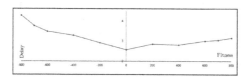

Fig. 7. Fitness variation where there is a delay and an anticipation in fire propagation.

6   Final Considerations

The GA shown to be efficient to adjust the parameters involved in the fire spread model. Regarding LQ and LR, the GA found solutions with the same values used in the referential simulations in all tested scenarios. Regarding the matrices, although the GA did not evolve exactly the same parameters used in the reference data, it was possible to observe that the solutions configured $W_{3\times 3}$ with effects on fire dynamics similar to those observed in the different scenarios. The initial scenarios that shown more difficult to adjust were those that started from fire spots in unfavorable positions to observe their dynamics. Thus, the strategy of GA evaluating from 5 simulations started at different points of the lattice, made the tuning approach more robust in relation to the initial point chosen to start the simulation. From a practical point of view, when using real fire images to evolve the model parameters, we can emphasize the importance of capturing sequences of images from different perspectives of the area. As future work, we intend to evaluate the proposed approach in more complex scenarios, with more than one type of vegetation, in addition to other landscape elements such as water body and buildings. Moreover, we intend to apply this approach to more complex fire models that involve a greater number of parameters, such as topography, humidity and spontaneous combustion. We aim to optimize the fitness function so that it is able to consider the behavior of the model with delay. We also aim to use real data, especially from the Brazilian Cerrado, for model adjustments. In this sense, we intend to create a generic GA adaptable to other models of CA. Finally, we intend to develop a GA that is able to learn the transition rule of the CA model.

Acknowledgements. Authors thank for FAPEMIG, CNPq and CAPES support and scholarships.

References

1. Carvalho, T.I., Carneiro, M.G., Oliveira, G.M.B.: A comparison of a proposed dynamical direct verification of lattice's configuration and a forecast behavior parameter on a cellular automata model to task scheduling. In: El Yacoubi, S., Was, J., Bandini, S. (eds.) ACRI 2016. LNCS, vol. 9863, pp. 258–268. Springer, Cham (2016). https://doi.org/10.1007/978-3-319-44365-2_26
2. Chopard, B., Droz, M.: Cellular automata modeling of physical systems (1998)
3. Clarke, K.C., Brass, J.A., Riggan, P.J.: A cellular automaton model of wildfire propagation and extinction. PE&RS **60**, 1355–1367 (1994)
4. D'Ambrosio, D., Spataro, W.: Parallel evolutionary modelling of geological processes. Parallel Comput. **33**, 186–212 (2007)
5. Fraga, L.M., Oliveira, G.M.B., Martins, L.G.A.: Multistage evolutionary strategies for adjusting a cellular automata-based epidemiological model. In: IEEE CEC (2021)
6. García-Duro, J., et al.: Hidden costs of modelling post-fire plant community assembly using cellular automata. In: Mauri, G., El Yacoubi, S., Dennunzio, A., Nishinari, K., Manzoni, L. (eds.) ACRI 2018. LNCS, vol. 11115, pp. 68–79. Springer, Cham (2018). https://doi.org/10.1007/978-3-319-99813-8_6
7. Karafyllidis, I., Thanailakis, A.: A model for predicting forest fire spreading using cellular automata. Ecol. Model. **99**, 87–97 (1997)
8. Lima, D.A., Tinoco, C.R., Oliveira, G.M.B.: A cellular automata model with repulsive pheromone for swarm robotics in surveillance. In: El Yacoubi, S., Was, J., Bandini, S. (eds.) ACRI 2016. LNCS, vol. 9863, pp. 312–322. Springer, Cham (2016). https://doi.org/10.1007/978-3-319-44365-2_31
9. Lima, H.A., Lima, D.A.: Autômatos celulares estocásticos bidimensionais aplicados a simulação de propagação de incêndios em florestas homogêneas. In: Workshop of Applied Computing for the Management of the Environment and Natural Resources (2014)
10. Lopes, H.J., Lima, D.A.: Cellular automata in path planning navigation control applied in surveillance task using the e-Puck architecture. In: IEEE SMC (2020)
11. Louzada, V.H.P., Ferreira Junior, W.: Incêndios florestais em autômatos celulares, simples e grandes queimadas. Biomatemática-Unicamp (2008)
12. Mitchell, M., Crutchfield, J.P., Hraber, P.T.: Evolving cellular automata to perform computations: mechanisms and impediments. Physica D **75**, 361–391 (1994)
13. Oliveira, G.M.B., De Oliveira, P., Omar, N.: Improving genetic search for one-dimensional cellular automata, using heuristics related to their dynamic behavior forecast. In: IEEE CEC (2001)

14. Slimi, R., El Yacoubi, S., Dumonteil, E., Gourbiere, S.: A cellular automata model for Chagas disease. Appl. Mathe. Model. **33**, 1072–1085 (2009)
15. Wolfram, S.: Cryptography with cellular automata. In: Williams, H.C. (ed.) CRYPTO 1985. LNCS, vol. 218, pp. 429–432. Springer, Heidelberg (1986). https://doi.org/10.1007/3-540-39799-X_32

Wildfire Simulation Model Based on Cellular Automata and Stochastic Rules

Claudiney R. Tinoco$^{(\boxtimes)}$ ⓘ, Heitor F. Ferreira ⓘ, Luiz G. A. Martins ⓘ, and Gina M. B. Oliveira ⓘ

School of Computer Science, Federal University of Uberlândia, Uberlândia, Brazil
{claudineyrt,lgamartins,gina}@ufu.br, heitor.ff@hotmail.com

Abstract. A significant increase in the occurrence of large wildfires has been observed in the last decades. Several works seek ways to attenuate the side effects of these events. In this work, it is proposed a simulation model for wildfires propagation based on stochastic cellular automata. Its main objective is to understand the dynamics of these wildfires in order to speed the decision-making on the main actions to be taken by firefighter forces. The model presents different states, fire intensities and wind currents that redirect the flames. In addition, a non-linear vegetation recovery function is proposed, which brings the model closer to the real characteristics of natural systems. According to the results obtained, it was possible to conclude that the model achieves the expected objectives, satisfactorily simulating the analysed phenomenon.

Keywords: Cellular automata · Stochastic rules · Wildfire simulation · Complex phenomena · Firefighting efficiency

1 Introduction

Spontaneous wildfires occur in nature and are part of the natural cycle necessary for the conservation of some biomes [13]. However, the occurrence of these events has increased throughout the planet in the last decades due to the impacts of climate changes, indiscriminate exploitation and extraction [9]. Since this increase is not part of its natural cycle, in most cases these environments end up collapsing. In addition to the loss of the fauna and the flora, which are irreparable, these wildfires can advance to areas of human occupation [11], especially those of marginalised populations (e.g., indigenous tribes, *quilombolas*, riverside dwellers and *favelas*) where there is no ideal physical infrastructure.

In order to mitigate negative effects, many works propose wildfire simulation models [12], seeking to understand the behaviour of the flames as a means to recommend countermeasures, strengthening the capacity to prevent and suppress wildfires while protecting human lives, nature itself and property.

Cellular Automata (CA) [4] stand out as a simulation technique due to their simplicity of implementation and high correspondence with natural behaviour.

B. Chopard et al. (Eds.): ACRI 2022, LNCS 13402, pp. 246–256, 2022.
https://doi.org/10.1007/978-3-031-14926-9_22

Among the several dynamic models that use CA, we can highlight models for urban growth [1], pedestrian evacuation [3], coordination of swarm of robots [16], epidemiology [14], and disease vector spreading [6]. Considering that a wildfire can be categorised as a complex natural phenomenon, the application of CA facilitates its simulation, since they are discretised both in time and in space [5]. On the other hand, the implementation of continuous systems for the spread of fire would demand a greater computational processing. Furthermore, since the cells evolve independently, it is easily adaptable for multiprocessing, allowing the exploration of high-performance simulations.

Therefore, considering the points raised, this work proposes a computational model to simulate wildfires as a way to speed the decision-making process and, thereby, enabling a greater efficiency for management and firefighting forces. The model is based in CA with stochastic rules for fire propagation. Applied in areas of vegetation, the model does not only take into account the burning time, but other important characteristics during a wildfire, such as the fire intensity, the presence of wind currents and obstacles. Furthermore, this work also contributes from an experimental perspective, since it performs a set of experiments in order to analyse how different parameters influence the evolution of wildfires.

2   Related Works

This section describes a brief literature review including some works related to the application of cellular automata in wildfires simulation. At the end of this review, a table (Table 1) is presented in order to compare key characteristics of the models described by these works with our proposed model.

One of the seminal works proposing CA models to simulate fire spreading is [5]. The model employs three states and stochastic transition rules to recover burnt cells and provide spontaneous combustion. In order to enhance simulations with wildfires, the application CA with hexagonal tessellation spaces was proposed in [20]. Experiments with artificial and real data allowed to conclude that the model can be useful in managing wildfires with heterogeneous characteristics. In [19], it was proposed the integration of CA and Geographic Information Systems for the simulation of forest fires. Focusing on modelling the environment, the system presents different options for terrain, vegetation and weather. According to the authors, the results showed that the proposed model can be adapted to other spatiotemporal modelling applications based on CA. Bringing the models closer to reality, a case study related to a forest fire (Spetses Island, 1990) was carried out in [2]. The authors proposed a simulation model using a non-linear optimisation approach to approximate its behaviour to that of the analysed event. The simulation results were promising in terms of the predictive capacity of the model. More recent works still present CA as an important tool for fire simulation models. In [8] is proposed a model for the simulation of forest fires based on CA that applies a numerical optimisation approach to find values that correlate the model parameters. Simulations showed promising results, bringing the proposal closer to the classical methods. In [18], the authors evaluated a set of factors that influence the spread of flames in forest fires. Among the analysed factors, the authors highlight combustible materials, wind, temperature, and terrain. Implemented through CA rules, the model demonstrates to be able to satisfactorily simulate the flame spread trends under different conditions. Finally, a model for simulating forest fires was proposed by combining different techniques, including CA, in [15]. The main objective of the authors was to improve the accuracy of the model in relation to the spread speed of the flames. According to the results, the model was able to simulate and predict the spread of forest fires, ensuring accuracy in the simulations.

Table 1. Detailed comparison between CA-based wildfire simulation models

Authors	Year	CA States				Prblty.	Wind	Topog.	Veg. recover
		Veg.	Fire	Obst.	Total				
Chopard et al. [5]	1998	1	2	0	3	Yes	No	2D	Linear
Yongzhong et al. [20]	2004	1	2	0	3	No	Yes	3D	No
Yassemi et al. [19]	2008	1	[0.0...1.0]	0	~	Yes	Yes	3D	No
Alexandridis et al. [2]	2008	1	2	1	4	Yes	Yes	3D	No
Ghisu et al. [8]	2015	1	2	0	3	No	Yes	3D	No
Xuehuaet al. [18]	2016	1	2	1	4	No	Yes	3D	No
Sun et al. [15]	2021	1	4	0	5	No	Yes	3D	No
Our Model	**2022**	1	4	1	6	**Yes**	**Yes**	2D	**Non-linear**

3   Model Description

Inspired by the works presented in Sect. 2, we propose a wildfire simulation model based on CA. Applying a stochastic evolution, the model is characterised by the composition of a combustion matrix with wind currents. Furthermore, in order to maintain the environment cycle realistic, it is also proposed a non-linear recovery function based on an exponential probability for burnt cells.

Figure 1 shows the possible states for each CA cell. The state "vegetation" (in green) represents the cells that have fuel material. It is a state that does not influence others, but can be influenced by the fire states. States "initial-fire", "stable-fire" and "ember" (orange, red and dark-red, respectively) represent the fire states, where each one has a different local fire intensity (defined later). When a fire is over, the cells change to the state "ash" (grey). In this state, there is no likelihood of spreading fire to other cells or catching fire again, unless fuel material in this position recovers. Finally, the state "water" (blue), is a state defined at the beginning of the simulation, and does not interact with any other state, but it can serve as a barrier if a fire takes its direction.

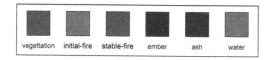

Fig. 1. Possible states for the cells of the CA described by different colours. (Color figure online)

Cells change state according to transition rules, which here we call fire propagation rules. These rules use a combustion probability matrix that defines the probability of the central cell to ignite through the propagation of fire from its closest cells (Moore's Neighbourhood), whether they are already in some state of fire. The proposed combustion probability matrix can be seen in Fig. 2a. The figure shows a central cell in the state "vegetation", i.e., capable of igniting. Each cell in the neighbourhood of the central one has a probability of propagating the fire. For example, the cell to the right of the central cell has a probability of 25% of propagation. Furthermore, the total burning time of a cell lasts a few time steps and the central cell is influenced by all the cells in its neighbourhood, increasing the probability of ignition when accumulated.

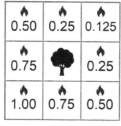

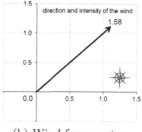

(a) Combustion matrix   (b) Wind force vector

Fig. 2. Combustion probability considering a northeast wind: (a) combustion matrix and (b) force vector with the direction and intensity of the wind.

It is known that certain factors can influence how the flames spread in a wildfire [18]. In our work, the wind was defined as an influencing factor. In the combustion matrix (Fig. 2a), one can see that the lower-left cell has a higher probability of propagation (100%) in comparison to the upper-right cell (12.5%). This difference in the probability is due to the composition of the combustion matrix and wind currents. In order to facilitate the visualisation, Fig. 2b presents the wind influence as a force vector. This vector constitutes the influence composition of all cells that are in the neighbourhood of the central cell. As a result, we have the wind direction and its intensity.

The model has two coefficients to adjust the fire behaviour: the calorie (λ) and the wind factor (δ). The calorie λ is used to produce different scales of wildfires, i.e., it represents the global fire intensity. For its implementation, the coefficient is applied to each cell of the combustion matrix (Fig. 2a). In turn, the wind factor δ represents a cardinal/collateral value that indicates the direction of the wind. For instance, considering Fig. 2b, the value of δ would be "northeast". From this coefficient, it is possible to rearrange the combustion matrix (done by means of rotations) in such a way that its values represent the specified direction. Since the combustion matrix represents a predefined proportionality of fire propagation, both coefficients, λ and δ, modifies these values maintaining the same proportion. Furthermore, from these coefficients, the model derives all parameters used in the simulation, including the CA rules.

In addition to the fire propagation rules, our model also implements a transition rule for the recovery of burnt vegetation. That is, unlike the other models of the literature presented in Sect. 2, in our model, a cell that is burnt, i.e., in the state "ash", can return to be a cell in the state "vegetation". Vegetation recovery is an important process to consider, as some biomes are highly resilient to wildfires and have a rapid recovery capacity. Described by the Generating Function (GF) in Eq. 1, it defines the probability of recovering P_r of a cell x_{ij} of the 2D lattice. If a time of idleness is defined, i.e., a period after the burn where no recovery occurs, then the probability is zero. Otherwise, the probability is equal to the square of the counting of time steps since the cell x_{ij} turn to ash (ts_r) over a power of 10. Defined by the variable a, this exponential represents the longitudinal extent of the probability distribution.

$$P_r(x_{ij}) = \begin{cases} 0.0, & \text{if } idle \\ (ts_r)^2/10^a, & \text{otherwise, such that } ts_r \geq 1 \ and \ a \geq 1 \end{cases} \tag{1}$$

In order to take the model closer to reality, the GF is defined as an exponential, in which the applied probability is proportional to the number of time steps, i.e., cells that have been burnt for a long time are more likely to change state. Other types of functions would not print the desired behaviour. On the one hand, a constant probability function would not have a temporal effect on the recovery of the flora, i.e., it would not imply that the longer a cell is burnt, the more likely it is to be reborn. On the other hand, using a linear probability function, although the temporal characteristic is present, would imply an accentuated probability of recovery for cells that have just been burnt.

Figure 3 illustrates examples of Probability Density Functions (PDF) (Fig. 3a) and Cumulative Distribution Functions (CDF) (Fig. 3b), obtained through the GF (Eq. 1). The PDF and CDF curves were computed using a process derived from the Monte Carlo method [10] (each curve with a sample size of 100m). The variable a affects the height of the PDF curve, i.e., it increases the distribution of data over more time steps. According to the data obtained, the value of a equal to six ($a = 6$) presented the best behaviour intended. In this case, the PDF shows that the highest probability of a cell being reborn is reached around the time step 160. In turn, in CDF, from the time step 300, the probability of a burnt cell being reborn is almost 100%, considering that the $\lim_{x \to \infty} CDF = 1.0$.

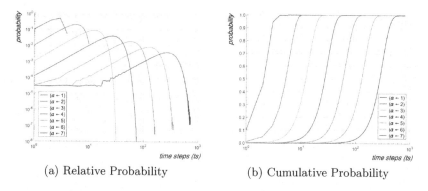

(a) Relative Probability   (b) Cumulative Probability

Fig. 3. Probability distribution for the recover of cells after a complete burning.

CA Rules: Taking into account the characteristics and parameters of the model presented, the fire propagation rules can be described as follows:

- If the central cell is in the state *"vegetation"* and there are no cells in a fire state in the neighbourhood: maintain the same state;
- If the central cell is the in state *"vegetation"* and a cell *cl* in the neighbourhood is in a fire state: there is a probability to change to the state *"initial_fire"*; $\{P(\text{"initial\_fire"}) = combustion\text{-}matrix(cl) \times local\text{-}fire\text{-}intensity \times (\lambda)\}$
- If the central cell is in the state *"initial_fire"*: it is not influenced by other cells, maintains this state for 3 time-steps and switches to the state *"stable_fire"*;
- If the central cell is in the state *"stable_fire"*: it is not influenced by other cells, maintains this state for 3 time-steps and switches to the state *"ember"*;
- If the central cell is in the state *"ember"*: it is not influenced by other cells, maintains this state for 10 time-steps and switches to the state *"ash"*;
- If the central cell is in the state *"ash"*: it is not influenced by other cells. It can change to the state *"vegetation"* according to the recovery function (Eq. 1);
- If the central cell is in the state *"water"*: there is no interaction with others states.

Model Parameters (Values Obtained by Preliminary Experiments): calorie ($\lambda = \{0.08, 0.16, 0.24\}$); wind factor ($\delta = \{\{cardinal\} \cup \{collateral\}\}$); local fire intensity (*"initial_fire"* = 0.6; *"stable_fire"* = 1.0; *"ember"* = 0.2); dwell time of states with active fire (*"initial_fire"* = $3ts$; *"stable_fire"* = $3ts$; *"ember"* = $10ts$); recovery time step ($ts_r = \{1..\} \parallel ts_r \in \mathbb{N}^*$); and, the exponent ($a = 6$).

4   Simulations and Analyses

This section describes the simulations and analyses performed with the proposed model. It was implemented in the GameMaker [7] engine and in the C programming language, where the former was used for visualisation and the latter for mass processing. All simulations have run for 300 time steps, while the mass experiments consist of 100 executions per simulation, using different seeds to avoid outliers. Screenshots are composed of a CA lattice (1024 × 1024) in the same time step intervals $ts = \{20, 50, 100, 200, 300\}$.

Figure 4 presents three scenarios (S1, S2 and S3) of wildfires using our proposed model. Each scenario implements a different caloric coefficient: $\lambda_1 = 8\%$ (Fig. 4); $\lambda_2 = 16\%$ (Fig. 4b); and $\lambda_3 = 24\%$ (Fig. 4c), respectively. The evaluation of different calories is very important, since some biome and climate characteristics (e.g., type of vegetation, seasonality, humidity, temperature) can influence

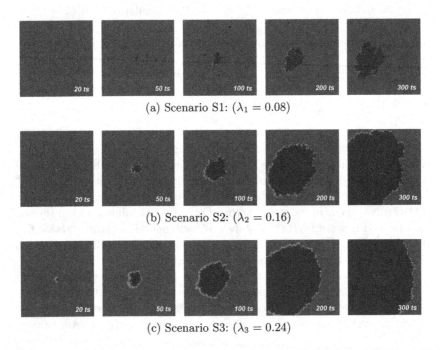

(a) Scenario S1: ($\lambda_1 = 0.08$)

(b) Scenario S2: ($\lambda_2 = 0.16$)

(c) Scenario S3: ($\lambda_3 = 0.24$)

Fig. 4. Evolution of the model in three different scenarios, in which there is the presence of wind currents from east to west and different calorie coefficients.

how the flames behave whether a wildfire occurs. Thus, the main objective of these simulations is to, empirically, observe the evolution of the flames in relation to the caloric coefficient, so that it would be possible to calibrate the model and bring its behaviour closer to the characteristics of real wildfires.

In the beginning, all cells are in the state *"vegetation"*. Intentionally, a spark is placed in the centre of the lattice to start the fire. In the scenario S1, one can observe that the propagation of the fire is slower compared to the other two scenarios. In S2 and S3, all cells within the wildfire radius went into combustion, differently from scenario S1. This is due to the fact that the coefficient calorie was weakened in S1. Observing Fig. 4a ($ts = 300$), there are several intact green areas within the burnt area, not resulting from the recovery of the vegetation (depending on environmental conditions, a part of the vegetation may not be affected in real wildfires). In the scenarios S2 and S3, in which the coefficient calorie is stronger, all cells ignited within the radius of the wildfire. In S3, in addition to the burning of all cells, the speed of fire propagation was faster. For instance, in S3 with 200 time steps, the burn radius is close to that of S2 with 300 time steps. Finally, it is worthy to highlight the recovery of cells in the state "ash", from the centre (older burnt cells) to the edges (recently burnt cells), which characterises the proposed recovery function (see Eq. 1).

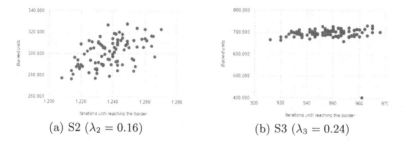

(a) S2 ($\lambda_2 = 0.16$)   (b) S3 ($\lambda_3 = 0.24$)

Fig. 5. Simulations performance in the scenarios S2 and S3.

This analysis is even more evident by observing the charts of Fig. 5, which show the total number of burnt cells and time steps required for the fire to reach one of the lattice edges in all simulations, considering scenarios S2 and S3 (Figs. 5a and 5b, respectively). As it can be noticed, the increase of 50% in the combustion coefficient resulted in an increase upper than 100% in the number of burnt cells (300,000 vs. 700,000) and a reduction of approximately 33% in the time steps needed to reach the lattice edge (950 vs. 1,240).

In a second experiment, an obstacle was built in the direction of the fire (southwest). Figure 6 presents a scenario (using $\lambda = 0.16$ and $a = 6$) where the fire goes towards a lake (cells in blue representing state "water" [5]). From 100 time steps, it is possible to notice that the flames reach the lake and, in that direction, the fire propagation is interrupted. However, the flames manage to go around the lake and reach the opposite shore. Despite being an initial experiment, this is an important variable to be considered in wildfires, to understand which factors would influence the blocking of the flames. For instance, although water flows are obstacles, in some real wildfires, flames are able to cross rivers, depending on their width, through the dispersion of sparks by the wind.

In order to better visualise the influence of wind currents, Fig. 7 shows two scenarios where the wind force (δ) is opposite. In the first one (Fig. 7a) the wind current is cardinal *east* ↔ *west*, whereas in the second one (Fig. 7b) it is collateral *northwest* ↔ *southeast*, both using ($\lambda = 0.16$) and ($a = 6$). Besides, the figures were divided into Cartesian quadrants, making it possible to compare and quantify burnt cells (state "ash"). Figure 7a, in which the wind current is from *east* → *west*, has a total of 6435 burnt cells, where 76.93% (4951 cells) are

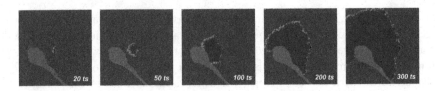

Fig. 6. Propagation of the wildfire towards a lake as an obstacle.

in quadrants II and III, and 23.06% (1484 cells) in quadrants I and IV. On the other hand, when the wind current from *west* → *east*, the fire spreads in the opposite direction. From 5743 burnt cells, 92.72% (5325 cells) are in quadrants I and IV, while 7.27% (418 cells) are in quadrants II and III. The same behaviour is observed in Fig. 7b. Applying a wind current from *southeast* → *northwest*, from 5581 burnt cells, 47.84% (2670 cells) are just in quadrant II, while 52.15% are distributed over the others. When the wind current is from *northwest* → *southeast*, from 6457 burnt cells, 62.36% (4027 cells) are in quadrant IV, while 37.63% are distributed. These results are consistent with the expected influence of wind currents, since the fires have started exactly at the centre of the lattice.

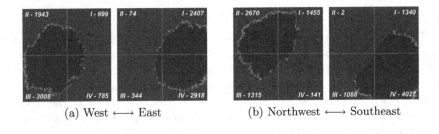

(a) West ⟷ East   (b) Northwest ⟷ Southeast

Fig. 7. Assessment of the influence of wind currents through Cartesian planes.

5   Conclusion and Future Work

This work proposed a model for wildfire simulation through the application of cellular automata. Among its main characteristics, one can highlight (i) the presence of different states for the fire, which makes it possible to simulate different intensities of flames; (ii) the presence of wind currents that influence the fire direction; and, (iii) a non-linear recover function for the burnt vegetation.

According to the preliminary analyses, it was possible to conclude that our model achieves the expected behaviour. It was able to satisfactorily simulate, considering the characteristics presented, the fire behaviour in the event of a wildfire. The spreading of the flames presented clear characteristics of a stochastic model, and the wind currents were able to direct these flames. Moreover, the proposition of a recovery function allowed to print more realistic characteristics, mainly, compared to a random function, which, in turn, gave a high probability to the vegetation to grow in the time step subsequent to its burning.

Regarding future works, we intend (i) to add more states to the vegetation, bringing it closer to the characteristics of the Cerrado, a biome in our location that frequently suffers from wildfires; (ii) to compare our model with other wildfire simulation models present in the literature; (iii) to evaluate the construction of a three-dimensional model, which would allow the implementation of fire propagation by roots and wind; (iv) to make a deep study of the sensitivity of the model's parameters; and (v) to apply evolutionary computation in the optimisation this parameters [17], taking into account real data.

Acknowledgements. Authors are grateful to FAPEMIG, CNPq and CAPES support and scholarships.

References

1. Aburas, M.M., et al.: The simulation and prediction of spatio-temporal urban growth trends using cellular automata models: a review. Int. J. Appl. Earth Observ. Geoinf. **52**, 380–389 (2016). https://doi.org/10.1016/j.jag.2016.07.007
2. Alexandridis, A., et al.: A cellular automata model for forest fire spread prediction: the case of the wildfire that swept through spetses island in 1990. Appl. Math. Comput. **204**(1), 191–201 (2008). https://doi.org/10.1016/j.amc.2008.06.046
3. Bandini, S., Crociani, L., Vizzari, G.: An approach for managing heterogeneous speed profiles in cellular automata pedestrian models. J. Cell. Autom. **12**(5) (2017). https://doi.org/10.17815/CD.2020.85
4. Bhattacharjee, K., Naskar, N., Roy, S., Das, S.: A survey of cellular automata: types, dynamics, non-uniformity and applications. Nat. Comput. **19**(2), 433–461 (2018). https://doi.org/10.1007/s11047-018-9696-8
5. Chopard, B., Droz, M.: Cellular automata modeling of physical systems. J. Stat. Phys. **97**(5/6), 1031–1032 (1998). https://doi.org/10.1142/S0219525902000602
6. Fraga, L.M., de Oliveira, G.M.B., Martins, L.G.A.: Multistage evolutionary strategies for adjusting a cellular automata-based epidemiological model. In: IEEE Congress on Evolutionary Computation, pp. 466–473 (2021). https://doi.org/10.1109/CEC45853.2021.9504738
7. YoYo Games: Gamemaker: Studio (2014). https://www.yoyogames.com/gamemaker
8. Ghisu, T., et al.: An improved cellular automata for wildfire spread. Procedia Comput. Sci. **51**, 2287–2296 (2015). https://doi.org/10.1016/j.procs.2015.05.388
9. Keenan, R.J.: Climate change impacts and adaptation in forest management: a review. Ann. For. Sci. **72**(2), 145–167 (2015). https://doi.org/10.1007/s13595-014-0446-5
10. Kroese, D.P., et al.: Why the Monte Carlo method is so important today. Wiley Rev. Comput. Stat. **6**(6), 386–392 (2014). https://doi.org/10.1002/wics.1314
11. Lozano, O.M., et al.: Assessing climate change impacts on wildfire exposure in mediterranean areas. Risk Anal. **37**(10), 1898–1916 (2017). https://doi.org/10.1111/risa.12739

12. Sakellariou, S., Tampekis, S., Samara, F., Sfougaris, A., Christopoulou, O.: Review of state-of-the-art decision support systems (DSSs) for prevention and suppression of forest fires. J. For. Res. **28**(6), 1107–1117 (2017). https://doi.org/10.1007/s11676-017-0452-1

13. Schmidt, I.B., Eloy, L.: Fire regime in the Brazilian Savanna: recent changes, policy and management. Flora **268**, 1–5 (2020). https://doi.org/10.1016/j.flora.2020.151613

14. Slimi, R., Yacoubi, S.E.: Spreadable probabilistic cellular automata models: an application in epidemiology. In: Conference on Cellular Automata, pp. 330–336 (2006). https://doi.org/10.1007/11861201_39

15. Sun, L., et al.: Adaptive forest fire spread simulation algorithm based on cellular automata. Forests **12**, 1431 (2021). https://doi.org/10.3390/f12111431

16. Tinoco, C.R., Lima, D.A., Oliveira, G.M.B.: An improved model for swarm robotics in surveillance based on cellular automata and repulsive pheromone with discrete diffusion. Int. J. Parallel Emergent Distrib. Syst. **34**, 53–77 (2017). https://doi.org/10.1080/17445760.2017.1334886

17. Tinoco, C.R., Vizzari, G., Oliveira, G.M.B.: Parameter adjustment of a bio-inspired coordination model for swarm robotics using evolutionary optimisation. In: Gwizdalla, T.M., Manzoni, L., Sirakoulis, G.C., Bandini, S., Podlaski, K. (eds.) Cellular Automata. ACRI 2020. LNCS, vol. 12599, pp. 146–155. Springer, Cham (2020). https://doi.org/10.1007/978-3-030-69480-7_15

18. Xuehua, W., et al.: A cellular automata model for forest fire spreading simulation. In: IEEE Symposium Series on Computational Intelligence, pp. 1–6 (2016). https://doi.org/10.1109/SSCI.2016.7849971

19. Yassemi, S., Dragićević, S., Schmidt, M.: Design and implementation of an integrated GIS-based cellular automata model to characterize forest fire behaviour. Ecol. Model. **210**(1–2), 71–84 (2008). https://doi.org/10.1016/j.ecolmodel.2007.07.020

20. Yongzhong, Z., et al.: Simulating wildfire spreading processes in a spatially heterogeneous landscapes using an improved cellular automaton model. In: IEEE International Geoscience and Remote Sensing Symposium, vol. 5, pp. 3371–3374 (2004). https://doi.org/10.1109/IGARSS.2004.1370427

Crowds, Pedestrian, and Traffic Dynamics

Integrating the Implications of Distance-Based Affective States in Cellular Automata Pedestrian Simulation

Stefania Bandini[1,2], Daniela Briola[1], Alberto Dennunzio[1], Francesca Gasparini[1], Marta Giltri[1(✉)], and Giuseppe Vizzari[1]

[1] Department of Informatics, Systems and Communication, Università degli Studi di Milano-Bicocca, Viale Sarca 336, 20126 Milan, MI, Italy
{stefania.bandini,daniela.briola,alberto.dennunzio,francesca.gasparini, marta.giltri,giuseppe.vizzari}@unimib.it
[2] RCAST - Research Center for Advanced Science and Technology, The University of Tokyo, Komaba Campus, 4-6-1 Meguro-ku, Tokyo 153-8904, Japan

Abstract. Cellular Automata have successfully been applied to the modeling and simulation of pedestrian dynamics. These simulations have often been focused on the evaluation of situations of medium-high density, in which the motivation of pedestrians overcomes natural proxemic tendencies. The COVID-19 outbreak has shown that in certain situations it is instead crucial to focus on situations in which proxemic is amplified by the particular affective state of the individuals involved in the studied scenario. We present the first steps in a research effort aimed at integrating results of quantitative analyses concerning effects of affective states on the perception of mutual distances by pedestrians of different type and the modeling of movement choices in a cellular automata framework.

Keywords: Cellular automata · Pedestrian simulation · Affective state modeling

1 Introduction

The perception and evaluation of distances, especially mutual distances among people, is a topic of relevance to different disciplines and decision making activities, ranging from psychology to architectural design. In general, having a model of this phenomenon is relevant whenever one needs to understand how pedestrians move throughout an environment in situations where their comfort zones may be threatened.

The concept of proxemic distances introduced by Hall [8] describes how people perceive space differently when interacting with others, with their behaviour heavily influenced by internal (e.g., age, gender, emotions) and external factors (e.g., the environment, culture, existing relationships with the other person or people involved).

© The Author(s), under exclusive license to Springer Nature Switzerland AG 2022
B. Chopard et al. (Eds.): ACRI 2022, LNCS 13402, pp. 259–270, 2022.
https://doi.org/10.1007/978-3-031-14926-9_23

The global pandemic brought by the COVID-19 virus also contributed to change even more how people approach others, modifying the way distances are perceived not only according to the different regulations that every country implemented to deal with the outbreak, but also according to the fear of being infected. This topic has become even more relevant for scientific investigation, although unfortunately pedestrian models are usually more focused on situations in which medium-high densities are easily reached, and also easily accepted by pedestrians since their motivations (e.g., the need to employ a public transport facility) are preponderant over the natural tendencies they adopt in normal situations.

Pedestrian dynamics have always been of interest for multiple disciplines, and have always been investigated from different points of view. Including the Cellular Automata (CA) modelling approach, in which the spreading of emotions and proxemics have also been investigated. Works concerning the introduction of emotions [10,12,13] and proxemics [1,14] in cellular automata models are already present in the literature, but they tend to mainly involve emotional models [3,5,11], proxemic theories [8] and well-grounded cellular automata concepts [2] with changes in the pedestrians' behaviour only dictated by ad-hoc formulas. What is missing, in these cases, is the utilization of information about actual measurements regarding distances and their perception, acquired through systematic experiments carried out more recently than the pioneering work of Hall. Considerations that can be obtained from these times of global pandemic are also important to be brought on board, since they would have been impossible to even conceive only a few years ago.

This is why, in this work, we focus our efforts on investigating the influence of affective states, intended as states containing a measure indicating how a person feels when faced with a particular situation, influenced both by internal factors related to the person himself/herself and external ones tied to the environment in which the person is. In particular, this preliminary investigation involves pedestrian proxemic tendencies, basing the modeling of these states on data collected from an experiment performed with human subjects rather than relying only on theories presented in the literature.

Our aim is to investigate pedestrian dynamics with a focus on the proxemic behaviours of people influenced by different affective states, investigation carried on through the modeling of a 1-dimensional and a 2-dimensional cellular automata. In order to do this, data acquired from an online experiment involving the perception of proxemic distances in the COVID-19 era [6] are analysed to gain knowledge about how pedestrians with different affective characteristics handle distances from others. Moreover, the work here presented concerns itself with low density simulations, to effectively see how pedestrians modify their behaviour given different affective factors without having crowding mechanics overpower their natural proxemic tendencies as they move inside the environment.

The outline of the paper is the following: Sect. 2 briefly explains the online experiment through which we gathered the data we used; in Sects. 3 and 4 the formal models of the 1D and 2D CA respectively are presented, together with some preliminary results obtained with a virtual simulation carried on with the NetLogo tool; lastly, conclusions regarding the presented work are drawn in Sect. 5.

2   Affective State Design: Data from Experiments

In order to parametrize affective states inside the CA models according to real data, we started working on data coming from a previously executed online experiment, carried out with the aim of studying how distances perceived as comfortable varied in COVID-19 times in different circumstances.

The experiment was made public in the period between 27/12/2020 and 18/01/2021[1], and it involved 80 Italian subjects whose only requirement for the study was not to have previously contracted COVID-19. The population age varied between 16 and 92 years old and, regarding demographics, 44 of them were women and 25 of them were elderly (i.e., aged 65 and older).

The designed procedure was composed of two main phases: the first one focused on questionnaires to gather information about the participant, while the second one proposed the active part of the experimentation in which the subjects were involved in a *figure-stop activity* inspired by previous studies [4].

In the figure-stop activity, subjects were presented an avatar, chosen in respect of their indicated gender and age group, positioned on the left side of an environment. They were then asked to move their character along a line and towards another figure, of the opposite gender and age group, positioned at the other side of the environment. Their objective was to move closer to the other figure and stop the second they sensed that shortening the distance even more could make them uncomfortable (Fig. 1).

Fig. 1. One of the figure-stop activities performed by the participants.

---

[1] We think it is relevant to mention the precise period since the perception of COVID-related risk changed significantly according to trend in the number of infections.

This activity was proposed for a total of eight time during the experiment, with changes regarding the environment the participants had to move their avatar into (an indoor one, a restaurant, and an outdoor one, a park) and the presence or absence of masks on both the moving figure and the still one, which led to the creation of four different configurations where: (1) the subject's avatar and the other avatar both had a mask on, (2) only the subject's avatar had a mask on, (3) only the other avatar had a mask on and (4) no avatar had a mask on.

The experiment allowed us to gather demographic data together with information about the proxemic distances adopted by the participants in the figure-stop activity. Through the collected questionnaires, we then managed to gather gender, age, mask condition, sociality levels and fear of contagion data, which all proved to influence in some way the distances the subjects chose as they performed the tasks.

Thus, from the data analysis of this experiment results it is possible to correlate the distance perceived as safe with the other factors, and to relate the distances, chosen varying the environmental conditions, to the 4 distances of the Hall's space. The information then extracted from the experiment to be included in the models were then gender, age group, mask information, sociality levels, fear index and Hall's proxemic spaces derived from the recorded distances.

3   1D CA Model

We are firstly going to describe the simplest CA that can be used to model the experimental scenario described in Sect. 2 in the most natural way possible. In order to keep the model as simple as possible, the affectivity has been embedded into their local rules. As a matter of fact, introducing it inside the CA state set would have produced a too complex design with respect to the considered scenario.

This approach leads us to have a family of different cellular automata since the local rule depends on the value m, which is the minimum distance the moving person can have from the non-moving person in the environment. This happens because the m value is derived from the affective states of the two people involved in the situation described by the CA. In particular, the moving person's information derived from the experiment and the other person's mask condition are used to select a Hall's space with a certain probability, which gives the upper and lower bound for the m value to be randomly selected between them. The scale of discretization is of course important: traditionally, CA based pedestrian models employ 40 cm sided cells [2] and we also considered this as a baseline value for the model.

The involved one-dimensional CA are then triples (S, r, f) where the set of states $S = \{0, 1, 2\}$, the radius $r \in \mathbb{N}$ and the local rule $f : S^{2r+1} \to S$ are defined as follows.

As far as any cell of the one-dimensional lattice is concerned, states $0, 1, 2$ correspond to an empty cell, a cell containing a moving person and a cell containing a resting person, respectively.

The radius r of the CA assumes the value of the ceiling of m, the minimum distance we described before, and this could lead us to two different CA classes.

When m is an integer, the CA radius is $r = m$ and the local rule f is defined for any $(a_{-r}, ..., a_0, ..., a_r) \in S^{2r+1}$ as follows:

- if $a_0 = 2$,

$$f(a_{-r}, ..., a_0, ..., a_r) = a_0,$$

- if $a_0 = 1$,

$$f(a_{-r}, ..., a_r) = \begin{cases} 0 & \text{if } a_1 = ... = a_r = 0 \\ 0 & \text{if } \exists\, 0 < i < r \text{ s.t. } (a_i = 1 \vee a_i = 2) \wedge a_{-1} = 0 \\ a_0 & \text{if } (a_r = 1 \vee a_r = 2) \wedge a_1 = ... = a_{r-1} = 0 \\ a_0 & \text{if } \exists\, 0 < i < r \text{ s.t. } (a_i = 1 \vee a_i = 2) \wedge (a_{-1} = 1 \vee a_{-1} = 2) \end{cases},$$

- if $a_0 = 0$,

$$f(a_{-r}, ..., a_r) = \begin{cases} a_0 & \text{if } a_{-1} = a_1 = 0 \\ a_0 & \text{if } a_1 = 1 \wedge a_2 = ... = a_r = 0 \\ a_0 & \text{if } a_{-1} = 1 \wedge \text{ if } \exists\, 0 < i < r \text{ s.t. } (a_i = 1 \vee a_i = 2) \\ 1 & \text{if } a_{-1} = 1 \wedge a_1 = ... = a_{r-1} = 0 \\ 1 & \text{if } \exists\, 1 < i < r \text{ s.t. } (a_i = 1 \vee a_i = 2) \wedge a_1 = 1 \end{cases}.$$

When m is not an integer, on the other hand, the CA radius is $r = \lceil m \rceil$. The local rule f is defined for any $(a_{-r}, ..., a_0, ..., a_r) \in S^{2r+1}$ as specified before, except for the following case:

- if $a_0 = 1$,

$$f(a_{-r}, ..., a_0, ..., a_r) = 0 \quad \text{if } (a_r = 1 \vee a_r = 2) \wedge a_1 = ... = a_{r-1} = 0.$$

As usual, the lattice is a one-dimensional array of cells where every cell is associated with a certain state from S. Moreover, the state of each cell is updated at every discreet time step by the local rule f on the basis of its own state and the ones of both its r-neighbouring cells on the left and on the right.

The second CA class we described causes an oscillatory movement in the CA dynamics, since the moving person finds himself/herself switching from a position where it is still far enough from the other to a position where it is already too close to the other, which is absent when the CA with $r = m$ are considered.

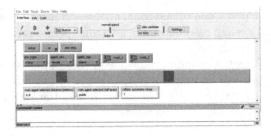

Fig. 2. The user interface of the NetLogo model used for the 1D CA simulation.

3.1   Implementation and Results

After the formalization of the cellular automaton was concluded, we then proceeded to try and simulate the automaton transition function through the NetLogo platform [15] (Fig. 2).

The simulation allows the user to choose different options for the setting, such as the environment of the experiment, the gender and age of the main moving pedestrian and the mask configuration for both the moving and the resting person, basically following the specification highlighted in the online experiment to obtain the same condition in the in-vitro simulation involving the automaton.

Since every parameter is easily set and visible throughout the entire execution of the simulation, the different colours are used to differentiate the two types of pedestrians presented in the simulation: the one highlighted in *red* on the left is the moving person, while the one coloured in *blue* is the resting person. Just like it happened in the online experiment, the moving person is always setup to be on the left of the resting person, and the only modification regards the place in which it gets set up: the positions of both pedestrians are, in fact, randomly selected before the simulation can be started, with each of them being in one specific half of the environment.

Given how the simulation is built in order to feed on the data and the information gathered from the experiment, reproducing the same situations proposed during the online trials performed by human participants, the CA behaviour mirrors the one already observed. The conditions on the moving and on the resting pedestrians are the same that were implemented in the experiment, so that we could see if the transition function of the CA worked to correctly show what we were expecting after analysing those results.

The only notable difference from the online experiment lies in how the moving person behaves in the case $r = \lceil m \rceil$, regarding the oscillatory behaviour described in the formalization. This behaviour was not shown in the experiment, given how space was treated differently, but it is well described by the transition function defined for the CA.

4 2D CA Model

The two-dimensional CA we are going to introduce is based on a rectangular lattice $L = \{0, ..., M - 1\} \times \{0, ..., N - 1\}$ representing the discretization of the real space, where M and N are the horizontal and vertical sizes respectively. Periodic boundary conditions are applied to L so that it can be viewed as a two-dimensional discrete torus.

For any cell $x \in L$ and any h, the h-radius Moore neighborhood of x is defined as:

$$N_h(x) = \{y \in L : ||x - y||_\infty \leq h\}$$

where $|| \cdot ||_\infty$ is the usual infinity (or maximum) norm.

The set of states of the CA is $S = DIR \times AS \times G \times AG \times M \cup \{\oslash\}$, where $\oslash$ is the state assigned to empty cells (i.e., in which there is no person) while a tuple from the cartesian product is the state assigned to cells containing a person. The sets involved in the cartesian product are defined as follows:

- $DIR = \{0, 1, ..., 8\}$ is the set of the possible moving directions for a person. Namely, numbers from DIR refer to the following direction vectors: $v_0 = (0, 0), v_1 = (1, 0), v_2 = (1, 1), v_3 = (0, 1), v_4 = (-1, 1), v_5 = (-1, 0), v_6 = (-1, -1), v_7 = (0, -1), v_8 = (1, -1)$. In this way, 0 concerns a resting person, while every other value $j \in DIR$ with $j \neq 0$ refers to a person at a certain position $x \in L$ with a moving direction v_j;
- $AS = \{relaxed, worried, scared\}$ is the set of the so-called affective states of a person. Each value from AS is obtained by combining data about sociality and fear previously obtained through the experiment and structured in three different levels;
- $G = \{male, female\}$ is the set of the genders of a person. Given the data that were collected, we only involved the $male$ and $female$ options without including more genders;
- $AG = \{y, ya, a, e\}$ is the set of age groups a person could belong to ($y =$ young, $ya =$ young-adult, $a =$ adult, $e =$ elderly);
- $M = \{on, off\}$ is the set of the possible settings for a person as far as a mask is concerned, i.e., the values specifying if the person wears a mask or not.

We point out that, unlike the case of the 1D CA model, the affectivity details are now included inside the set of states of the CA, since we want to model more complex situations contemplating people with different characteristics moving together inside a two-dimensional environment. With an abuse of notation, for any state $s \in S$ and any $i \in \{1, ..., 5\}$, s_i will denote the i-th component of s whenever $s \neq \oslash$.

This way, the CA configuration is a map $c : L \to S$ associating every cell $x \in L$ with a state $c(x) \in S$. Thereafter, regarding the dynamical evolution of the CA, for every $t \in \mathbb{N}$, any $x \in L$ and every $i \in \{1, ..., 5\}$, c^t, $c^t(x)$ and $c_i^t(x)$ will denote the CA configuration at time t, the state of the cell x inside c^t, and the $(c^t(x))_i$, i.e., the i-th component of $c^t(x)$, respectively. The radius of the CA, on the other hand, is the value $r \in \mathbb{N}$ defining the largest set $N_r(x)$ of positions that a person located in any cell $x \in L$ is able to detect and observe around himself/herself.

Regarding its evolution, the considered CA is non deterministic. Because of this, in order to describe its dynamical evolution $\{c^t\}_{t \in \mathbb{N}}$ starting from any initial configuration $c^0 \in S^L$, we will illustrate how the configuration c^t at time t is transformed by the CA into the configuration c^{t+1} at time $t + 1$.

Before proceeding we point out that, in our model, one time step corresponds to 0.33 s which, in addition to also considering 40 cm sided cells, leads to a walking speed of about 1.2 m/s, which is in line with typically observed values [7]. Moreover, each time step consists of three different stages.

During the first one, for any time $t \in \mathbb{N}$ the configuration c^t is transformed into the intermediate configuration d^t in such a way that $\forall x \in L$, $\forall i \neq 1$, $d_i^t(x) = c_i^t(x)$. In other words, only the direction of every cell x containing a person may change during this stage.

For any cell $x \in L$ with $c^t(x) \neq \oslash$, the value $d_1^t(x)$is computed as follows. Firstly, the cells $y \in N_r(x)$ s.t. $c^t(y) \neq \oslash$, i.e., containing a moving or resting person, are identified. Then, according to the values $c_i^t(y)$ with $i \in \{2, ..., 5\}$ (i.e., the components of the state of the neighboring people previously detected), the minimum possible distances between the person at cell x and each of them is determined through an appropriate function. Such distances are computed taking into account the affective information of the person in cell x and the mask condition for the person in cell y. These information are used to designate a probabilistic distribution weighting the selection of a certain Hall's space, then proceeding to randomly select an m distance between the upper and lower bound of the drafted space as we previously described for the 1D CA.

This process results in a subset $D(x) \subseteq \{1, ..., 8\}$ of possible directions the person at x could adopt for their next movement. Namely, $j \in D(x)$ if and only if the person, moving alongside the direction v_j, is not going to get nearer to the other people in cells $y \in N_r(x)$ that are already at a smaller distance than or on the edge of the distance m computed between them and the person at x. Once $D(x)$ has been computed, we have two different cases; in the first one, when $D(x) = \emptyset$, it holds that $d_1^t(x) = 0$, corresponding to the person at cell x not move; in the second one, when $D(x) \neq \emptyset$, $d_1^t(x)$ gets randomly chosen from $D(x)$, corresponding to the person standing at x moving in the selected direction. In this way, $d^t(x)$ has been defined.

Then, the second stage manages possible conflicts. In fact, it may happen that, referring to the configuration d^t, for a certain empty cell x there exist at least two non-empty cells y^1 and y^2 belonging to its neighborhood $N_1(x)$ where there are non-null $d_1^t(y^1) = k^1$ and $d_1^t(y^2) = k^2$ with $k^1, k^2 \in DIR$ such that $x = y^1 + v_{k^1} = y^2 + v_{k^2}$. In other words, there are two people in two distinct cells whose directions $d_1^t(y^1)$ and $d_1^t(y^2)$ would move them into the same empty cell x. The configuration d^t is then transformed into another intermediate configuration e^t. When a conflict is found, every person involved in it, with the exception of a randomly chosen one, has their direction set to 0, blocking their movement.

Finally, the third stage allows getting c^{t+1} from e^t. Namely, this step describes the movement of each moving person from a cell x towards the adjacent one identified by the moving direction of the person in $e_1^t(x)$. This behaviour is formally expressed as:

– if $e^t(x) = \oslash$,

$$c^{t+1}(x) = \begin{cases} e^t(y) & \text{if } \exists\ y \in N_1(x) \text{ s.t. } x = y + v_k \text{ with } k = e_1^t(y) \\ e^t(x) & \text{otherwise} \end{cases},$$

– if $e^t(x) \neq \oslash$,

$$c^{t+1}(x) = \begin{cases} \oslash & \text{if } e_1^t(x) \neq 0 \\ e^t(x) & \text{otherwise} \end{cases}.$$

4.1 Implementation

The model allows the user to set the preferred environment to observe during the simulation (indoor or outdoor, as presented in the online experiment) and to set the initial density for both the moving people and the non-moving ones. The maximum density that can be set for both type of people is 10%, so that the total population density in the environment will never exceed 20%. This is aligned with our intention of utilizing low densities for these trials.

The moving pedestrians inside the simulation have been modeled to roam inside the environment by *random walk*, using a built-in NetLogo function to randomly select one of their allowed directions to plan their next step. Also, given that the data acquired through the experiment pointed how the distances selected by the participants were not only influenced by their personal parameters but also by the mask condition of the other person they had to get close to, every pedestrian computes two different preferred distances: one to be maintained from masked people, and the other to be maintained from non-masked people.

Monitors allow the user to have under control the quantities of the pedestrians on screen together with the indication of the current automaton range considered and of how many times a moving person found himself/herself unable to move around due to it being surrounded too closely by others. For an easier visualization, the moving people are represented by *circles* and the non-moving ones by *squares*. With the same purpose, masked pedestrians are identified by the color *white* while the non-masked pedestrians are shown with the color *red* (Fig. 3).

Regarding possible conflicts and collisions, a clarification needs to be made: in our specific case, as this is only a preliminary simulation of the model, it is not contemplated that two moving pedestrians could find themselves walking to and standing on the same patch. This is given by the fact that, as it was mentioned before, we intended to work with low crowd density inside the environment and, moreover, because the behavioural rules we implemented actively

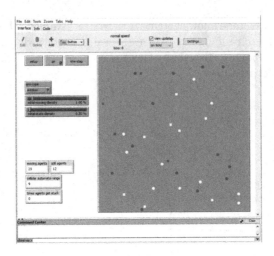

Fig. 3. The user interface of the NetLogo model used for the 2D CA simulation. (Color figure online)

keep the pedestrians far from each other. They move around, but always keeping into consideration that they have to avoid others in order to remain comfortable. The combination of these two factors lead the pedestrians to remain at a distance from others and never actually occupying the same space out of necessity, for example. A generalization of the model here proposed, without the clear limitations introduced regarding density and pedestrians' behaviour, should then be able to properly address conflicts for space and avoid collisions. There are already some approaches, in the literature, that could be adopted in order to deal with this issue, like the one presented in [9] regarding friction.

4.2   Preliminary Results

Table 1. Table showing the percentage of pedestrian remaining stuck for each timestep in simulation performed with different initial densities.

Density (%)	Moving	Still	Stuck Events (on 100 ts)	Pedestrian stuck per ts (mean)
1%	11	16	4	0.04 (0.36%)
5%	56	68	2770	27.70 (49.46%)
10%	123	127	8551	85.51 (69.52%)
15%	177	188	15358	153.58 (86.77%)
20%	277	329	27269	272.69 (98.44%)

Table 1 shows some preliminary results obtained by making the 2D simulation run for 100 timesteps at a time, each time with different pedestrian densities as initial configurations. We previously showed how the densities of moving people and non-moving people can be set separately, in order to set them differently for different trials, but in this case we kept them equal so that, summed up, they could reach the densities that are reported into the table. The different numbers of people are derived from the way the environment is set up, since every empty patch randomly chooses a number than, if smaller than the density set through the slider, allows them to spawn a turtle representing a person.

As we can see from the data, as the pedestrian density inside the environment grows, the number of events recording how a moving person find himself/herself stuck grows rather quickly, and that is clearly visible looking at the percentage indicating the mean of moving people recorded as still per timestep. The percentage reached even with a density of only 20%, which is not considered a high density in terms of crowding, indicates how, despite the environment not being too crowded for people to move around into, the distances set by the affective state of every person are held in high regard and prevent the pedestrians from moving around when others are perceived too close to allow movement. Despite being gathered from a preliminary trial based on data coming from an experiment in a 1D environment, the results reported here are already quite promising in terms of how affective states modify pedestrian behaviour. The affective state we modeled in the CA effectively influences the pedestrians' choices, driving them to get farther from people too close to them and making them stop the moment every choice regarding direction they could take would only make them uncomfortable.

5   Conclusion

In the work hereby presented, we aimed at tackling the problem of introducing affective states inside cellular automata modeling by starting from realistic data rather than on theoretical frameworks already studied in the literature. We then proceeded to show the 1D and 2D models we designed in order to address the matter, illustrating how data coming from a previously executed online experiment was used in order to insert the concept of affective inside the models. Simulations showing both of the models through NetLogo were then presented, together with some preliminary results highlighting the effects of affective states influencing proxemic distances on pedestrians' behaviour.

Future work in this direction includes the investigation of more experiments, in order to see if it is possible to also use other types of data to model the affective states to be introduced in the models, together with a transition towards agent modeling: with the 2D CA model, in fact, as other works in this same research area, we focused on the behavioural rule for the single cell rather than on the local rule used for the 1D model, which is a method near to agent modeling. Shifting towards that approach would also help us manage more easily the heterogeneity intrinsically present in the simulation.

Acknowledgments. This research is partially supported by Fondazione Cariplo, for the project LONGEVICITY - Social Inclusion for the Elderly through Walkability (Ref. 2017-0938).

References

1. Bandini, S., Crociani, L., Gorrini, A., Nishinari, K., Vizzari, G.: Unveiling the hidden dimension of pedestrian crowds: introducing personal space and crowding into simulations. Fund. Inform. **171**(1–4), 19–38 (2020)
2. Burstedde, C., Klauck, K., Schadschneider, A., Zittartz, J.: Simulation of pedestrian dynamics using a two-dimensional cellular automaton. Physica A **295**(3–4), 507–525 (2001)
3. De Raad, B.: The Big Five Personality Factors: The Psycholexical Approach to Personality. Hogrefe & Huber Publishers, Kirkland (2000)
4. Dosey, M.A., Meisels, M.: Personal space and self-protection. J. Pers. Soc. Psychol. **11**(2), 93 (1969)
5. Ekman, P.: An argument for basic emotions. Cogn. Emot. **6**(3–4), 169–200 (1992)
6. Gasparini, F., Giltri, M., Briola, D., Dennunzio, A., Bandini, S.: Affectivity and proxemic distances: an experimental agent-based modeling approach. In: Proceedings of the Italian Workshop on Artificial Intelligence for an Ageing Society 2021, vol. 3108, pp. 81–92. AIxIA, CEUR Workshop Proceedings (2021)
7. Gorrini, A., Vizzari, G., Bandini, S.: Age and group-driven pedestrian behaviour: from observations to simulations. Collective Dyn. **1**, 1–16 (2016)
8. Hall, E.T.: The Hidden Dimension, vol. 609. Doubleday, Garden City (1966)
9. Kirchner, A., Nishinari, K., Schadschneider, A.: Friction effects and clogging in a cellular automaton model for pedestrian dynamics. Phys. Rev. E **67**, 056122 (2003)
10. Li, X., Guo, F., Kuang, H., Zhou, H.: Effect of psychological tension on pedestrian counter flow via an extended cost potential field cellular automaton model. Physica A **487**, 47–57 (2017)
11. Ortony, A., Clore, G.L., Collins, A.: The Cognitive Structure of Emotions. Cambridge University Press, Cambridge (1990)
12. Saifi, L., Boubetra, A., Nouioua, F.: An approach for emotions and behavior modeling in a crowd in the presence of rare events. Adapt. Behav. **24**(6), 428–445 (2016)
13. Wang, G.N., Chen, T., Chen, J.W., Deng, K., Wang, R.D.: Simulation study of crowd dynamics in pedestrian evacuation concerning panic contagion: a cellular automaton approach. Chinese Phys. B (2022)
14. Wąs, J., Gudowski, B., Matuszyk, P.J.: Social distances model of pedestrian dynamics. In: El Yacoubi, S., Chopard, B., Bandini, S. (eds.) ACRI 2006. LNCS, vol. 4173, pp. 492–501. Springer, Heidelberg (2006). https://doi.org/10.1007/11861201_57
15. Wilensky, U.: NetLogo. Center for Connected Learning and Computer-Based Modeling, Northwestern University, Evanston, IL (1999). http://ccl.northwestern.edu/netlogo/

Density Estimates in Cellular Automata Models of Pedestrian Dynamics

Marek Bukáček$^{(\boxtimes)}$ (ORCID) and Jana Vacková (ORCID)

Faculty of Nuclear Sciences, Czech Technical University in Prague,
Trojanova 13, 12000 Prague, Czech Republic
{marek.bukacek,jani.vackova}@fjfi.cvut.cz

Abstract. Presented contribution deals with general concept of pedestrian density estimate appropriate even for cellular models of pedestrian dynamics. Using kernel approach, authors are able to cover multiple density estimate methods (e.g. point approximation, Voronoi approach) and to control required features by "blur" parameter. With respect to specific setting, final density can be smooth enough even for discreet lattice and still keep other requirements.

Keywords: Pedestrian dynamics · Density estimate · Cellular model

1 Introduction

Models simulating pedestrian movement may differ with purpose, level of complexity, dynamic definition or e.g. the way how space and time is handled. These differences affect the outputs, some models brings just macroscopic estimates of total occupancy, average flows or total evacuation time. Multiple model classes, including cellular automata, go deeper providing essential pedestrian quantities as actual density in given area or actual velocity of agents representing single pedestrians.

Even flow, velocity and density are considered to be fundamental quantities in the both traffic flow [1] and pedestrian dynamics [2,3] the optimal estimate of pedestrian density is still the contemporary topic in question. The proper estimate in cellular models is much more complex as both the space and time are roughly discretized.

In this contribution, we will recall complex density estimate approach using kernels [4] and illustrates its features. Presented concept was developed for an arbitrary data source and it is fully compatible with CA model data structure, as will be shown further.

Applying the same or at least similar approach for model and real world data is crucial for proper calibration and any further analysis and applications. The purpose of this article is to spread developed methodology among the pedestrian modelers community and, in general, discuss all possibilities how to evaluate pedestrian density.

© The Author(s), under exclusive license to Springer Nature Switzerland AG 2022
B. Chopard et al. (Eds.): ACRI 2022, LNCS 13402, pp. 271–280, 2022.
https://doi.org/10.1007/978-3-031-14926-9_24

1.1 Quantities

The standard approach using physical definitions counting the number of pedestrians (N) passing through a cross-section within the interval ΔT or standing in the area (A) enriched by the hydrodynamic approximation

$$J = \frac{N}{\Delta T} \; [\text{ped} \cdot \text{s}^{-1}], \qquad \rho = \frac{N}{|A|} \; [\text{ped} \cdot \text{m}^{-2}], \qquad J = \rho \cdot v \qquad (1)$$

were widely studied [5,6].

Such approach can be used for discrete CA data, just the sampling frequency ΔT or detector area A should be defined with respect to the discretization applied in the model. Unfortunately results generated by this method are highly scattered and they could be hardy compared with real data on microscopic level [7].

The need of more sophisticated analysis based on statistics methods, including kernel estimates [3,8–12] or even the methods expressing the density based on time to collision or minimal distance were derived from Eq. 1. More general methods interpreting the comfort or crowdeness as independent variables related to density became popular as they may be more relevant for several use cases.

Authors considered several parametrized kernels types (Gaussian, conic, cylindrical, cubic) together with Voronoi diagram approach to estimate the density distribution in the observed area. Voronoi method was studied further and stabilized by averaging over time in [13].

But, according to us, it is critical to keep comparing used methods and to identify common aspects as well as differences. From our perspective, *individual density distribution* based on kernel approach may be interpreted as general concept where many other methods could be introduced as special cases. Moreover, with appropriate scaling, kernel approach can be used as good proxy for multiple above mentioned approaches.

Here should be noted that any outputs of model may be smoothed during post processing phase. Such approach is completely acceptable as far as the smoothing techniques conserves the mean (ergodicity requirements) as discussed further. In cellular automata universe, it make sense to transform pedestrian trajectory from points to smooth curve using some smart interpolation similarly to [14] and then resample it with higher frequency. Such approach would enable to use measurements for continuous space without any limits. Moreover, alternations of cellular automata avoiding discretization issues has been studied in [15].

1.2 Data-Driven Study

The following parametric study is based on the egress experiment organized in the study hall of FNSPE, CTU in Prague in 2014, see [16–18] for details. Pedestrians (undergraduate students wearing recognition caps) randomly entered the room by one of three entrances, walked to the opposite wall and left the room by one exit. By controlling input flow, different conditions from free flow to congestion in the exit area were achieved. In total, our sample is made up of 2000 paths through 10 experimental runs captured using 48 frames per seconds.

Cellular model generating the data represent a variant of floor filed model enhanced by pedestrian heterogeneity, adaptive time span and conflict solution using bonds [19,20].

In order to examine the kernel shape and size, the parametric study is based on a rectangular static detector 2 m width and 1 m long placed symmetrically in front of the exit.

To compare experimental runs with different length, the normalized time t_{norm} in the meaning that the start is represented by $t_{norm} = 0$ and the end by $t_{norm} = 1$ will be used.

Cone, cylinder, cubic and Gaussian kernels are evaluated for wide range of parameter $R \in \{0.1, 0.2, \ldots, 3\}$ while Voronoi distribution, point approximation were evaluated only once (there is no parameter). First, we will verify the possibility to mimic all mentioned density evaluation methods by conic kernel and then, quantitative comparison will be provided.

2   Concept and Definitions

Let us rewrite the definition of *density* in an area A using distribution inspired by kernel distribution theory [21–23]

$$\rho = \frac{N}{|A|} = \frac{\int_A p(\boldsymbol{x})\, \mathrm{d}\boldsymbol{x}}{|A|} = \frac{\int_A \sum_{\alpha=1}^N p_\alpha(\boldsymbol{x})\, \mathrm{d}\boldsymbol{x}}{|A|} = \sum_{\alpha=1}^N \frac{\int_A p_\alpha(\boldsymbol{x})\, \mathrm{d}\boldsymbol{x}}{|A|}, \qquad (2)$$

where N represents the number of pedestrians, $|A|$ the size of considered area A, $p_\alpha(\boldsymbol{x})$ the individual density distribution generated by each pedestrian $\alpha \in \{1, 2, \ldots, N\}$ and $p(\boldsymbol{x}) = \sum_{\alpha=1}^N p_\alpha(\boldsymbol{x})$ the *density distribution* in the area A.

In a case that area A fills the whole examined area, the individual density distribution holds normalization condition $\int_A p_\alpha(\boldsymbol{x})\, \mathrm{d}\boldsymbol{x} = 1$, therefore the relation $\int_A p(\boldsymbol{x})\, \mathrm{d}\boldsymbol{x} = N$ is fulfilled and the density ρ_A is called *global*.

Most of applied kernels used in relation (2) can be parametrized, thus the density distribution should be written as $p_\alpha(\boldsymbol{x}, R)$. No matter the kernel type is, R expresses the smoothing factor, i.e. we refer it as *blur*.

Blur manipulates the size of area affected by one pedestrian. Let us label this area as pedestrian *support* A_α fulfilling

$$A_\alpha = \{\boldsymbol{x} \in A \,|\, p_\alpha \boldsymbol{x} > 0\} \qquad (3)$$

i.e. A_α is the smallest possible subset of A fulfilling $\int_{A_\alpha} p_\alpha(\boldsymbol{x})\, \mathrm{d}\boldsymbol{x} = 1$.

When an area $B \subset A$ covers only the part of the possible area A, the pedestrian α contributes to the density ρ_B only partially in case $A_\alpha \not\subset B$, i.e. $\int_B p_\alpha(\boldsymbol{x})\, \mathrm{d}\boldsymbol{x} < 1$.

If the kernels intersect the walls or obstacles, they are normalized to keep pedestrian volume in the eligible area, i.e. their support A_α is trimmed and the kernel is re-scaled – therefore the peak of the individual density distribution will be higher than usual.

2.1 Type of Kernels

If the surroundings is set to the whole considered area and Dirac function is used as the individual density distribution, the standard approach (1) is obtained. However there is more different choices of kernels as the individual density distribution. Denoting $\boldsymbol{x}_\alpha := \boldsymbol{x}_\alpha(t)$ as the (head) position of pedestrian α at fixed time $t \in \mathbf{R}_0^+$, let us mention a few of them which will be used in further analysis.

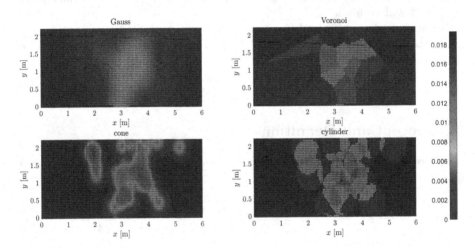

Fig. 1. Density map produced by four different kernels with $R = 0.5$ m. Selected frames from experimental data [18].

Point Approximation with Dirac delta function

$$p_\alpha(\boldsymbol{x}) = \delta_{\boldsymbol{x},\boldsymbol{x}_\alpha}$$

Stepwise Function levels density on whole support

$$p_\alpha(\boldsymbol{x}, R) = \Theta\left(\boldsymbol{x} \in A_\alpha(R)\right) \frac{1}{|A_\alpha(R)|}$$

with **Cylindrical kernel** $A_\alpha(R) = \left\{\boldsymbol{x} \in \mathbf{R}^2 : \|\boldsymbol{x} - \boldsymbol{x}_\alpha\| \le R\right\}$
or **Cubic kernel** $A_\alpha(R) = \left\{\boldsymbol{x} \in \mathbf{R}^2 : |\boldsymbol{x} - \boldsymbol{x}_\alpha| \le R\right\}$.
Voronoi kernel represent a step-wise approach with fluid kernel shape influenced by agents around.

Each spatial point $\boldsymbol{x} \in \mathbf{R}^2$ is assigned to the nearest pedestrian α at position $\boldsymbol{x}_\alpha$. The set of these points is called Voronoi cell and it is denoted as A_α for pedestrian α [8].

A_α does not depend on any blur parameter R, only occasionally Voronoi cell is limited by some maximal size. This can be analytically covered overlapping of Voronoi and cylindrical support.

For CA models, Voronoi approach is reduced to the question how to assign/split cells that aren't occupied. The simplest method would be to assign the whole cell to nearest neighbor or to split it. As the cell is a unit, it is much easier than the task to find edges of cells in continuous environment even such approach may be used as well, assuming pedestrian sits in the middle of the cell.

Conic Kernel

$$p_\alpha(\boldsymbol{x}, R) = \frac{3}{\pi R^3} \mathbb{1}_{A_\alpha(R)}(\boldsymbol{x}) \ (R - \|\boldsymbol{x} - \boldsymbol{x}_\alpha\|),$$

where

$$\mathbb{1}_{A_\alpha(R)}(\boldsymbol{x}) = \Theta\left(R - \|\boldsymbol{x} - \boldsymbol{x}_\alpha\|\right).$$

It has several desired features for representing pedestrians compared to the stepwise kernels, e.g. decreasing trend with increasing distance, limited support and the independence of one pedestrian to the others.

Gaussian Kernel in a symmetric version, i.e. with diagonal covariance matrix,

$$p_\alpha(\boldsymbol{x}, R) = \frac{1}{2\pi R^2} \exp\left\{ -\frac{\|\boldsymbol{x} - \boldsymbol{x}_\alpha\|^2}{2 R^2} \right\}.$$

This is the only representative with a limitless area of influence (i.e. with unbounded support) in this study.

Blur Parameter. R represents the kernel bandwidth in our study, thus it is comparable through all used kernel shapes. The example of density distribution with blur equal to 0.5 m for different kernels can be seen in Fig. 1.

We work with all mentioned kernels in their symmetric version here, but in general, the pedestrian support A_α it could be modified, e.g. elliptical shape with axis dynamically reacting to pedestrian velocity might be introduced. Furthermore the kernel size can be definitely enhanced by varying in time in accordance with the conditions in pedestrian surroundings. We will not cover that in presented study, it is the main point of the following research.

2.2   Smoothing Techniques

The smoothing of density could be realized either by providing measurements that are less scatter or by filtering of final time series. Both approaches can trivially replace density jumps caused by entering a new pedestrian into the detector. As visualized in Fig. 2, weighted moving averages (time smoothing) may be completely equivalent to kernel estimates (space smoothing) with respect to the assumption to pedestrian velocity or border conditions.

To be more specific the two options are

- **space smoothing** that replace jump-like pedestrian contribution (delta function) by a space representation of a person. One can imagine kernels, distance-weighted contributions or cell approach. In highly discrete environment, space smoothing may by degradated.
- **time smoothing** that balanced ups and downs. Typically weighted moving averages, possibly any filtration method conserving mean value

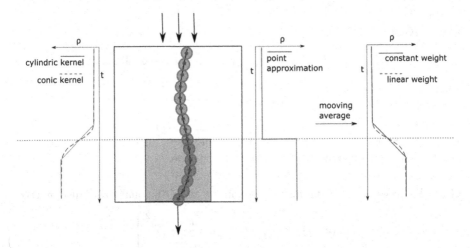

Fig. 2. Equivalence of kernel approach (left) and point approximation processed by moving average (right).

3   Illustrations and Analysis

As mentioned earlier, the kernel approach may be applied even in situations when the space is roughly discretized, see illustration in Fig. 3. Two pictures visualize two consecutive steps of any CA model with square lattice (cell edge 0.5 m). The number of agents in the detector (red rectangle) differs thus the standard density would jump by 0.5 ped/m^2. In case of kernel approach, this jump would be significantly reduced due to the presence of more agents in front of the detector. Assuming the average flow through the detector would be equal to 1.5 ped/TU, the kernel method returning density fluctuating around 1.25 ped/m^2 would be more satisfying then saw-like pattern alternating 1 ped/m^2 and 1.5 ped/m^2.

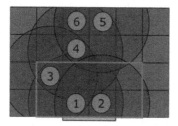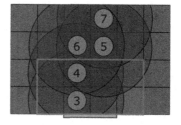

Fig. 3. Comparison of point approximation and kernel approach ($R = 0.9$ m) for discrete environment, one time step visualized. (Color figure online)

3.1   Similarity to Point Approximation

As we already mentioned that cylinder has similar properties as point approximation for some values of R, let us research this similarity. We prepared for this examination Fig. 4, where we compare pedestrian count obtained by the point approximation versus pedestrian count (obtained as median for fixed value of pedestrian count of point approximation) for an examined kernel - Gauss, Voronoi, cone and cylinder. It is evident that the closer the axis of the first quadrant, the closer the Dirac count.

It is seen that the count for blur $R = 0.1$ m is very similar to the Dirac count for every kernel. Interesting fact is that the deviation is greater for greater pedestrian count (and greater values of blur) - the highest the blur, the slope of the line is lower for every kernel.

3.2   Alternatives of Voronoi Diagram

Time development of pedestrian count (left) and pedestrian count distribution for different kernels versus Voronoi distribution (right) are denoted in Fig. 5. We can say that Voronoi diagram has its alternatives among other kernels, specifically for $R \in (0.7, 1.5)$ m. However there is greater range for Voronoi than for other kernels and also slight differences for low densities in Fig. 5 (left). This undervaluation of Voronoi pedestrian count is evident in Fig. 5 (right). The greater range could be caused due to the property that Voronoi can resemble Dirac distribution under specific condition (dense crowd).

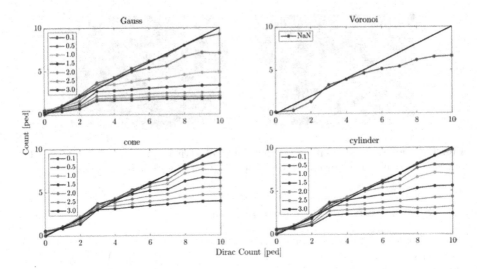

Fig. 4. Similarity to Point Approximation. Median value of kernel pedestrian count estimates is plotted against corresponding point approximation value. Data taken from experiment [18].

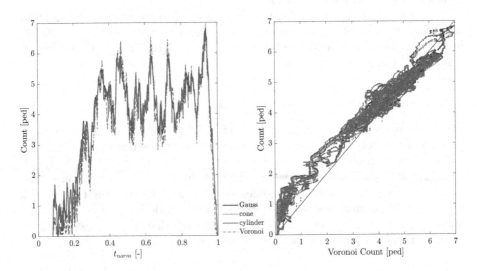

Fig. 5. Similarity to Point Approximation. Time development of Voronoi and kernel methods (left) and value of kernel pedestrian count estimates is plotted against corresponding voronoi value (right). Data of experimental round 6 taken from [18] used.

4 Conclusions

No matter the level of discretization is, it worth trying to evaluate the density in analyzed area using smooth approach conserving desired features of standard point approximation. Proposed kernel approach represents valid and general approach covering generally used methods, enabling to control "smoothness" through blur parameter. To get really smooth values even for model with low actualization frequency, it would be beneficial to combine presented approach with trajectory oversampling techniques, but even without that simple application of kernel density estimate brings satisfying results.

We would like to note that the calibration and detail parametric study introduced in [4] were used for cellular automata case without any modification. Though more detail metrics analyzing discrete systems are a subject of further research.

Acknowledgements. This work was supported by the grant TAČR ZETA Effective spatiotemporal predictions using machine learning methods and grant SGS21/165/OHK4/3T/14.

References

1. Treiber, M., Kesting, A.: Traffic Flow Dynamics: Data, Models and Simulation. Springer, Heidelberg (2013). https://doi.org/10.1007/978-3-642-32460-4
2. Daamen, W., Hoogendoorn, S.: Flow-density relations for pedestrian traffic. In: Schadschneider, A., Pöschel, T., Kühne, R., Schreckenberg, M., Wolf, D.E. (eds.) Traffic and Granular Flow 2005, pp. 315–322. Springer, Heidelberg (2007). https://doi.org/10.1007/978-3-540-47641-2_27
3. Schadschneider, A., Chraibi, M., Seyfried, A., Tordeux, A., Zhang, J.: Pedestrian dynamics: from empirical results to modeling. In: Gibelli, L., Bellomo, N. (eds.) Crowd Dynamics, Volume 1. MSSET, pp. 63–102. Springer, Cham (2018). https://doi.org/10.1007/978-3-030-05129-7_4
4. Vacková, J., Bukáček, M.: Kernel estimates as general concept of pedestrian density estimates. Transportmetrica A (submitted). https://arxiv.org/abs/2205.10145
5. Seyfried, A., Steffen, B., Klingsch, W., Boltes, M.: The fundamental diagram of pedestrian movement revisited. J. Stat. Mech. 10002 (2005)
6. Georgoudas, I.G., Koltsidas, G., Sirakoulis, G.C., Andreadis, I.T.: A cellular automaton model for crowd evacuation and its auto-defined obstacle avoidance attribute. In: Bandini, S., Manzoni, S., Umeo, H., Vizzari, G. (eds.) ACRI 2010. LNCS, vol. 6350, pp. 455–464. Springer, Heidelberg (2010). https://doi.org/10.1007/978-3-642-15979-4_48
7. Craesmeyer, M., Schadschneider, A.: Simulation of merging pedestrian streams at T-junctions. Transp. Res. Procedia **2**, 406–411 (2014)
8. Steffen, B., Seyfried, A.: Methods for measuring pedestrian density, flow, speed and direction with minimal scatter. Physica A **389**(9), 1902–1910 (2010)
9. Helbing, D., Johansson, A.: Analytical approach to continuous and intermittent bottleneck flows. Phys. Rev. Lett. **97**(16), 168001 (2006)
10. Johansson, A., Helbing, D.: From crowd dynamics to crowd safety: a video-based analysis. Adv. Complex Syst. **11**(4), 497–527 (2008)

11. Duives, D., Daamen, W.: Quantification of the level of crowdedness for pedestrian movements. Physica A **427**, 162–180 (2015)

12. Hillebrand, A., Hoogeveen, H.: Comparing different metrics quantifying pedestrian safety. Collective Dyn. **5**, 158–166 (2020)

13. Liddle, J., Seyfried, A.: Microscopic insights into pedestrian motion through a bottleneck, resolving spatial and temporal variations. arXiv preprint arXiv:1105.1532 (2011)

14. Plaue, M., Chen, M., Bärwolff, G., Schwandt, H.: Trajectory extraction and density analysis of intersecting pedestrian flows from video recordings. In: Stilla, U., Rottensteiner, F., Mayer, H., Jutzi, B., Butenuth, M. (eds.) PIA 2011. LNCS, vol. 6952, pp. 285–296. Springer, Heidelberg (2011). https://doi.org/10.1007/978-3-642-24393-6_24

15. Yamamoto, K., Kokubo. S.: Simulation for pedestrian dynamics by real-coded cellular automata (RCA). Physica A **379**(2), 654–660 (2007)

16. Bukáček, M., Hrabák, P., Krbálek, M.: Experimental analysis of two-dimensional pedestrian flow in front of the bottleneck. In: Chraibi, M., Boltes, M., Schadschneider, A., Seyfried, A. (eds.) Traffic and Granular Flow 2013, pp. 93–101. Springer, Cham (2015). https://doi.org/10.1007/978-3-319-10629-8_11

17. Bukáček, M., Hrabák, P., Krbálek, M.: Individual microscopic results of bottleneck experiments. In: Knoop, V.L., Daamen, W. (eds.) Traffic and Granular Flow 2015, pp. 105–112. Springer, Cham (2016). https://doi.org/10.1007/978-3-319-33482-0_14

18. Bukáček, M., Hrabák, P.: Microscopic travel-time analysis of bottleneck experiments. Transportmetrica A **14**(5–6), 375–391 (2018)

19. Hrabák, P., Bukáček, M.: Influence of agents heterogeneity in cellular model of evacuation. J. Comput. Sci. **2017**(21), 486–493 (2017)

20. Bukáček, M., Hrabák, P., Krbálek, M.: Cellular model of pedestrian dynamics with adaptive time span. In: Wyrzykowski, R., Dongarra, J., Karczewski, K., Waśniewski, J. (eds.) PPAM 2013. LNCS, vol. 8385, pp. 669–678. Springer, Heidelberg (2014). https://doi.org/10.1007/978-3-642-55195-6_63

21. Baszczyńska, A.: Kernel estimation of cumulative distribution function of a random variable with bounded support. Stat. Trans. **17**(3), 541–556 (2016)

22. Wand, M., Jones, M.: Kernel Smoothing. Chapman and Hall/CRC, New York (1994)

23. Chacón, J., Duong, T.: Multivariate Kernel Smoothing and Its Applications. Chapman and Hall/CRC, New York (2018)

Maximum Traffic Flow Patterns in Interacting Autonomous Vehicles

Nathan Cohen, Bastien Chopard[ID], and Pierre Leone[(⊠)][ID]

Computer Science Department, University of Geneva, Geneva, Switzerland
Nathan.Cohen@etu.unige.ch, {Bastien.Chopard,Pierre.Leone}@unige.ch

Abstract. We consider the auto-organization of a set of autonomous vehicles following each other on either an infinite or circular road. The behavior of each car is specified by its "speed regulator", a device that decides to increase or decrease the speed of the car as a function of the head-tail distance to its predecessor and the speed of both cars. A collective behavior emerges that corresponds to previously proposed cellular automata traffic models. We further analyze the traffic patterns of the system in the long term, as governed by the speed regulator and we study under which conditions traffic patterns of maximum flow can or cannot be reach. We show the existence of suboptimal flow conditions that require external coordination mechanisms (that we don not consider in this paper) in order to reach the optimal flow achievable with the given density.

1 Introduction

The collective behavior of interacting autonomous vehicles is an interesting question in view of its impact on traffic conditions, such as security or reduced congestion. Our goal is to investigate the capability of autonomous cars, following each other, to reach a state of global maximum flow, by only interacting deterministically with the preceding car.

Our approach follows the work initiated in [14] of modeling traffic using cellular automaton. The road is seen as a collection of cells and cars are moving from one cell to another following some rules that we refer to as the *speed regulator*. Among the questions of interest is the determination of the maximum flow as a function of the number N of cars. This is described as the fundamental diagram, a relation between the traffic flow and the car density $\rho = N/L$ [cars per unit of length], where L is the length of the road section. This fundamental diagram usually shows two distinct dynamics, a first where increasing the density increases the flow and a second one where, due to high density, the cars interact and traffic jams occur.

Classical analysis of traffic models amount to classify the different dynamics and identify the conditions for transition, for instance the existence of on/off-ramp [4,6,7], traffic lights [2], lane changing [15], mixed-traffic [13], and combinations [5].

B. Chopard et al. (Eds.): ACRI 2022, LNCS 13402, pp. 281–291, 2022.
https://doi.org/10.1007/978-3-031-14926-9_25

Real Traffic have been subject to empirical studies where sensors located on the road provide measurements of various parameters like speeds and head-tail distances between cars. These works lead to an understanding of the various dynamics depending on the traffic conditions. In particular to the three-phase traffic theory [8,10,11]. Roughly, this theory distinguishes the free-flow phase where cars update their speeds independently, the synchronized flow where speeds and head-tail distances decrease and tend to synchronize and, lastly the jammed flow where we observe cars with null speed.

The large amount of data collected from real traffic conditions and the accurate analysis, foster speed regulator designers to devise models that reproduce the observed dynamics [9,12,17,19,20]. These models introduce new parameters, such as probabilities, that are wisely tuned to reproduced the observed dynamics.

This paper follows a different approach. We consider a simple collision-free, deterministic speed regulator, that mimics the behaviour of an autonomous car. This speed regulator the behaviour of each car. Collectively, it leads to various possible flow patterns that we want to compute rigorously and check whether the resulting traffic flow is maximum. We do not intend to reproduce real traffic patterns like those mentioned in the literature. Rather, our long-term goal is the search for an efficient speed regulator to equip autonomous car whose performance are better that human drivers.

We start here to consider the simplest speed regulator, which could be used by autonomous cars, ensuring that: (i) no collision occurs and, (ii) speed is maximized. We analyze the dynamic of a pool of cars obeying the speed regulator.

In particular, we find a bound for the maximum flow as a function of the density that leads to the fundamental diagram. We identify the traffic patterns of maximum flow - reaching the bound. We show as well that in some non optimal traffic patterns the cars involved cannot increase their speed due to the no-collision constraint. In this situation, some external mechanism, that we do not consider in this paper, is required to allow the cars to switch to a more efficient traffic pattern.

In Sect. 2 we define the speed regulator. It maximizes the speed v_a of a car a according to the head-tail distance d with a leading car b, ensuring that no-collision occurs. We call viable a configuration where no-collision occurs and shows that for viable configurations the property $d < v_a$ is transient, see Proposition 1. Hence, the long-term traffic patterns show $d \geq v_a$, see Proposition 2. This leads in Sect. 3 to bound the maximum flow, see Proposition 4. The fundamental diagram and related maximum flow traffic patterns are presented in Sect. 4.

Interestingly, the condition $d \geq v_a$ plays a similar role as the synchronization distance in the KKW-model [9,20].

The evaluation of the speed regulator performance requires to understand the traffic patterns generated. We show traffic patterns where the car's speeds are locked to non-optimal values, and the general form of flow-optimal traffic patterns in Proposition 2. We have also found other traffic patterns that are metastable in the sense of [16] not included due to the lack of space.

Unsurprisingly, our speed regulator is similar to several CA traffic models proposed in the literature. For instance in [12] where it is complemented with parameters that are tuned to reproduce some traffic patterns and human behavior. Our use of the regulator is different.

2 The Speed Regulator

A (one-lane) road section consists in L cells that can be occupied by only one car at a time. Cars are moving from cell to cell. Time is discrete $t \in \mathbb{N}$. We use letters $a, b, \ldots$ to denote cars, $v_a, v_b, \ldots$ to denote the speeds of the cars and $x_a, x_b, \ldots$ to denote the positions of the cars along the section of the road. If the speed of a, is v_a at time t the position update of the car a is $x_a + v_a$ at time $t+1$, we do not write the factor $\Delta_t = 1$, i.e. $x_a + v_a \Delta_t$. Usually, the distance of a cell is 7.5 meters and speeds belong to $\{0, \ldots, v_{max}\}$. For our numerical experiments we use $v_{max} = 5$. Similarly, acceleration is bounded and belongs to $\{-1, 0, 1\}$. Once the position is updated, the velocity is adjusted as explained below. The updated quantities are indicated with a tilde on top (e.g. $\tilde{v}_a$ and $\tilde{d}$). Distances, positions and speeds are all natural numbers.

Because the speed is bounded we use the following definition for the bounded operators (adding a dot on top of the plus and minus signs).

Definition 1. *The bounded addition and subtraction are defined by:*

$$v \dotplus 1 = \min(v + 1, v_{max}),$$
$$v \dotminus 1 = \max(0, v - 1).$$

To denote that the speed regulator updates the speed of a we use the notation $\tilde{v}_a$ and similarly for the updated head-tail distance $\tilde{d}$. This shorten the notation $v_a = v_a(t)$ and $v_a(t + 1) = \tilde{v}_a$. Distances, positions and speeds are all natural numbers.

We first focus on the dynamics of two cars a following b and the state of the dynamical system is (v_a, v_b, d), where d is the head-tail distance of cars a and b (i.e. the number of empty cells).

In one step $(t \mapsto t+1)$ two operations are done: (1.) move the cars according to their speed, i.e. $\tilde{x}_a = x_a + v_a$, $\tilde{x}_b = x_b + v_b$ hence $\hat{d} = d - v_a + v_b$ and, (2.) cars revise their speed following the speed regulator. We consider the succession of configurations of the form

$$(v_a, v_b, d) \underset{\text{1. position updates}}{\Longrightarrow} (v_a, v_b, \hat{d} = d - v_a + v_b) \underset{\text{2. speed updates}}{\Longrightarrow} (\tilde{v}_a, \tilde{v}_b, \tilde{d}) \quad (1)$$

For the simulation where many cars are present the updates are done synchronously.

Definition 2. *We define the function* $df : \mathbb{N} \to \mathbb{N}$ *as* $df(v) = v \dotplus (v-1) \dotplus \ldots \dotplus 1 = \frac{v(v+1)}{2}, \quad v \geq 0.$

The function df gives the braking distance for a car moving at speed v and decelerating constantly such that $\Delta v = 1$ each time step. The speed regulator shown in Algorithm 1 sets the speed $\tilde{v}_a$ in such a way that no-collision occurs even if the leading car b brakes constantly to 0.

Algorithm 1 Basic speed regulator.

1: **if** $\tilde{d} + df(v_b \dot{-} 1) >= df(v_a + 1)$ **then**
2:     $\tilde{v}_a = v_a \dot{+} 1$
3: **else if** $\tilde{d} + df(v_b \dot{-} 1)) >= df(v_a)$ **then**
4:     $\tilde{v}_a = v_a$
5: **else**
6:     $\tilde{v}_a = v_a \dot{-} 1$
7: **end if**

For a configuration (v_a, v_b, d) we define the viability condition ensuring that the traffic dynamic avoids collisions.

Definition 3. *We say that a configuration (v_a, v_b, d) is viable if*

$$d \geq df(v_a) - df(v_b),$$

or equivalently $\tilde{d} \geq df(v_a \dot{-} 1) - df(v_b \dot{-} 1)$.

It can be shown that the regulator preserves the viability condition hence, the no-collision condition. In the next sections it is implicit that the viability property holds for the initial states and hence at any time. **This ensures that the speed regulator can at any time sets the maximum speed that avoids collision.**

Next, we show that the configurations with $d < v_a$ are transient and the speed regulator eventually leads to $d \geq v_a$.

Proposition 1. *If (v_a, v_b, d) is viable and $d < v_a$ then $v_b \geq v_a$. Moreover, such configuration is transient in the sense that eventually $d \geq v_a$ holds.*

Proof. $v_a + df(v_b) > d + df(v_b) \geq df(v_a)$ results from viability and $d < v_a$. Hence, $df(v_b) > df(v_a) - v_a = df(v_a \dot{-} 1)$, which implies $v_b \geq v_a$. For the second statement, the argument rests on $v_b > v_a$ except when b is decelerating. Each time $v_b > v_a$ the head-tail distance increases and when b decelerates $\tilde{v}_a$ decreases. The first case leads to $d \geq v_a$ because v_a is bounded and the second as well because v_a decreases to 0.

To exemplify Proposition 1 consider a configuration $(3, 3, 2)$, the two cars move at speed 3 and distance 2. This condition is viable (no-collision occurs in the future). Indeed, after updating the position, the trailing car reduces its speed to 2 and then, $d \geq 2 \geq v_a$. In the long term the configuration $(3, 3, 2)$ cannot be observed since it is transient and the property $d \geq v_a$ is preserved by the speed regulator as shown in Proposition 2. Such a configuration could only be observed because of the initial condition.

Proposition 2. $d \geq v_a \Longrightarrow \tilde{d} \geq \tilde{v}_a$.

Proof. If $d \geq v_a$ then $\tilde{d} = d - v_a + v_b \geq v_b$ and the result is true if $v_b \geq \tilde{v}_a$. Let us assume that $v_b < \tilde{v}_a$.
Case 1. We assume that $\tilde{v}_a = v_a + 1$ which occurs if $\tilde{d} \geq df(v_a + 1) - df(v_b \dot{-} 1)$ from which we deduce $\tilde{d} \geq \tilde{v}_a$.
Case 2. We assume that $\tilde{v}_a = v_a$ which occurs if $\tilde{d} \geq df(v_a) - df(v_b \dot{-} 1)$ from which we deduce $\tilde{d} \geq \tilde{v}_a$.
Case 3. We assume that $\tilde{v}_a = v_a - 1$ which occurs if $\tilde{d} \geq df(v_a - 1) - df(v_b \dot{-} 1)$ from which we deduce $\tilde{d} \geq \tilde{v}_a$.

The next proposition shows a set of configurations where the car copies the behavior of the leader car. This behavior is referred to lag synchronization in the literature [1]. Interestingly, such configurations are flow optimal, see Proposition 4.

Proposition 3. *If* $\mid v_a - v_b \mid \leq 1$ *and* $d = v_a$ *then* $\tilde{v}_a = v_b$ *and* $\tilde{d} = \tilde{v}_a$, *in particular* $\mid \tilde{v}_a - \tilde{v}_b \mid \leq 1$.

Proof. $\tilde{d} = d - v_a + v_b$, hence $d = v_a \Longrightarrow \tilde{d} = v_b$, it remains to see that $\tilde{v}_a = v_b$.
$\mid v_a - v_b \mid \leq 1 \Longrightarrow v_a = v_b - 1$ or $v_a = v_b$ or $v_a = v_b + 1$.
If $v_a = v_b - 1$: (in particular $v_b \neq 0$) $\tilde{d} + df(v_b - 1) = df(v_b) = df(v_a + 1)$. The speed regulator follows line 1 $\tilde{v}_a = v_a + 1 = v_b$.
If $v_a = v_b$: $\tilde{d} + df(v_b \dot{-} 1) = df(v_b) = df(v_a)$). The speed regulator follows line 3 and $\tilde{v}_a = v_a = v_b$ (condition $\tilde{d} + df(v_b \dot{-} 1) \geq df(v_a + 1)$ is not fulfilled).
If $v_a = v_b + 1$: $\tilde{d} + df(v_b \dot{-} 1) = df(v_b) = df(v_a - 1)$, the regulator follows line 6 and $\tilde{v}_a = v_a - 1 = vb$ (conditions $\tilde{d} + df(v_b \dot{-} 1) \geq df(v_a + 1)$ and $\tilde{d} + df(v_b \dot{-} 1) \geq df(v_a)$ are not fulfilled).

3   Analysis of the Flow

In the previous sections we analyzed the speed regulator by considering configurations of the form (v_a, v_b, d). Here, we consider a flow of cars. Recall that if N cars are on a road section of length L, we define the density $\rho = N/L$ [cars per length units] and the flow $j(N, L) = \rho \bar{v}$ [cars per time unit] where $\bar{v}$ is the average speed of the N cars.

Propositions 1 and 2 show that in the long term configurations satisfy $d \geq v_a$. This leads to the next proposition.

Proposition 4. *In the long term, for N cars are on a road of length L the maximum flow $j(N, L)$ is bounded by*

$$j(N, L) \leq 1 - \frac{N}{L}.$$

In particular, the flow is maximal if all the cars configurations (v_a, v_b, d) belong to the invariant set defined by Proposition 3.

Proof. Because in the long term configurations satisfy $d \geq v$ by Propositions 1 and 2 we have $N + \sum_{i=1}^{N} v_i \leq N + \sum_{i=1}^{N} d_i = L$, from which we get $j(N, L) = \frac{\sum v_i}{L} \leq 1 - \frac{N}{L}$. Proposition 3 defines a flow-optimal invariant set since the condition $v = d$ ($v_a = d$ in the notation of the proposition) is fulfilled.

It is common to express the flow as a function of the density $\rho = N/L$, i.e. $j(N, L) = j(\rho)$.

We represent flows with a typewriter style using . to denote an empty cell of the road and a number to indicate that the cell is occupied by a car and the speed of the car. For instance a configuration ($v_a = 3, v_b = 4, d = 3$) is represented as $\underbrace{3}_{v_a} \underbrace{\ldots}_{d} \underbrace{4}_{v_b}$.

We start with a counterexample of Proposition 4. The traffic pattern `3..3..3..` etc. is viable (does not lead to collision), of density $\frac{1}{3}$ and of flow $\rho = 1$, hence it seems to contradict the statement of Proposition 4. However, this traffic pattern is transient (notice $d < v_a$) because at the next step cars decrease their speed to 2 and we get the traffic pattern `2..2..2..etc.` which satisfies the bound of Proposition 4 and $d \geq v_a$. In general, our analysis of the flow is in the long term and transient traffic patterns are ignored. It is not stated systematically that only long term traffic patterns are considered although everywhere assumed in the following.

A (long term) traffic pattern of maximal flow is

$$\ldots\ldots5\ldots\ldots5\ldots\ldots5\ldots\ldots5\ldots\ldots5\ldots\ldots5\ldots\ldots \text{ etc.} \tag{2}$$

This flow is maximal because the head-tail distance d equals the speed as proved in Proposition 4. Notice, that the flow is regular if measured on a road section of length L with $L = 6N$ where N is the number of cars, i.e. the configuration maximizes the function $j(N, L) = j(N, 6N)$. Hence for density $\rho = 0.16\bar{6}$. The reader can imagine the same pattern repeating infinitely often.

Another example of maximal flow is

$$\ldots3\ldots3\ldots3\ldots3\ldots3\ldots3\ldots3\ldots3\ldots \text{ etc.} \tag{3}$$

which is maximal for $L = 4N$ hence for density $\rho = 0.25$.

Maximal flow can be obtained by other regular patterns for different values of N and L. For instance, the flow of `.1.2..3...2..1 etc.` is maximal for $N = 5k$ and $L = 14k$ for any $k > 1$, hence for density $\rho = 5/14 = 0.36$.

In general, for traffic patterns with $v = d$ and N_i cars at speed i satisfy

$$\sum_{i=0}^{v_{max}} i N_i = L, \text{ and } \sum_{i=0}^{v_{max}} N_i = N. \tag{4}$$

Equations (4) are useful to generate flow-equivalent traffic patterns. For instance, if we assume that there exists a configuration with $N_2, N_3, N_4 > 0$ we can find a traffic pattern with one less car in N_2 and N_4 and two more in N_3. Consider a car $a \in N_4$ at speed 4, it can be turned to speed 3. To ensure flow-optimality

($v_a = d$) the next cars are moved one cell back until the speed of the car moved back is 2. The speed of this last car is turned to 3. We obtain a new configuration still satisfying (4). Actually this process can be repeated until N_2 or N_4 is empty. For instance, .1.2..3...2..1. etc. can be turned to .1.2..2..2..2.. etc. without modifying the flow-optimality of the traffic pattern.

The following traffic patterns are not optimal and of same density than (3):

.....4.....4.....4.....4..... etc. and

.....3.....3.....3.....3..... etc..

Indeed, in both configurations the density is $\rho = 0.16\bar{6}$ and no car changes his speed due to the regulator speed in Algorithm 1. Indeed, for the traffic pattern 4.....4..... to increase the speed to 5 the condition $df(5) \leq d + df(3)$ (the trailing car pays attention to the fact that the leading car can break) must be satisfied which is not the case, i.e. $25 \nleq 5 + 6$. The same argument holds for the second traffic pattern, i.e. $10 \nleq 5 + 3$.

Another non flow-optimal traffic pattern is given by

$$3....4.....5......4.....3....4.....5...... \text{ etc.} \tag{5}$$

This configuration is not optimal since the following one with same density has a higher flow 5.....5.....5.....5.....5..... etc.. Indeed, both configuration have density $\rho = 1/6$ but the flows are 16/24 and 20/24 respectively.

In summary, all these examples show that some traffic patterns are permanent but not optimal. This means that the flow of cars can be trapped in a sub-optimal state. Escaping such a state requires coordination. For instance, all the cars must agree to accelerate at the same time. Otherwise, an accelerating car would violate the viability condition.

Jam Formation. A classical traffic pattern is the appearance of a jam without bottleneck, see [18] for real traffic experiment and [3] for a recent review. For instance, cars are following a traffic pattern of the form of 3...3...3...etc.. For a reason a car slow down to speed 2 then 1 at some time and for a given period. The trailing cars are following the speed changes and the cars are platooning at speed 1. When the braking car restarts following the speed regulator we observe that the flow increases. **The relevant observation is that no trailing car is slowing below speed 1.** Notice that the constant speed pattern seems hard to restore and we observe a regular pattern of the form of (5).

The point is that, this is not what may be observed in real traffic conditions where some cars are going to stop (at speed zero) [18]. Such an observation is then not compatible with the respect of the viability condition.

4   Fundamental Diagrams

In this section we evaluate the average speed of cars $\bar{v}$ and the corresponding flow j for a traffic pattern where at most one car does not satisfy $v = d$. Consider N cars separated by a distance d on a circular road of length L, $d = \max\{x \mid n(x + 1) \leq L\}$ except for one car where the distance between it and the next

can be greater than d. Therefore, we can set the speed $v = min(d, v_{max})$ of the cars without having a risk of collision and the flow is maximal by proposition 4.
Case d $\geq$ v$_{max}$. In this part, the density of the road is low enough so that the cars can be at $v = v_{max}$ and the flow $\mathbf{j} = \mathbf{v_{max}}\rho$.

As the number of cars increases, we reach a critical density ρ_{crit} where their distance $d = v_{max}$. We denote the critical number of cars $N_{crit} = \frac{L}{(v_{max}+1)}$. If this value is an integer, we can reach the maximal flow $j_{max} = \frac{v_{max}}{(v_{max}+1)}$.
Case d < v$_{max}$, i.e. $N > N_{crit}$. It is still possible that some cars reach the maximum speed but overall the cars will have their speed $v = d = \lfloor \frac{L}{N} \rfloor - 1$. Let $M + d$ be the remaining distance between the last car and the first car. This distance can be written as: $M = L - N(d+1) \geq 0$.
Subcase M = 0. Every car have exactly a head-tail of d, no more, no less. The cars are in a synchronized state as their speed will never change i.e. $v = \bar{v} = d$ and the flow $\mathbf{j} = \mathbf{1} - \boldsymbol{\rho}$. This is the maximal achievable flow (see Proposition 4). Using $\rho_{crit} = \frac{N_{crit}}{L}$ we can substitute into the equation to get the maximal flow:

$$j_{max} = 1 - \rho_{crit} = 1 - \frac{N_{crit}}{L} = 1 - \frac{L}{L(v_{max}+1)} = 1 - \frac{1}{v_{max}} = \frac{v_{max}}{v_{max}+1}$$

This is the value where the two flow functions intersect (see Fig. 1). Below shows such a configuration.

$$4....4....4....4....4....4....4....4....4....$$

Subcase 0 < M < d + 1. The last car cannot increase its speed, therefore all cars are driving at the same speed $v = \bar{v} = d$. But the last car has some extra space which it will never catch up. The flow is given by $\mathbf{j} = (\lfloor \frac{1}{\rho} \rfloor - 1)\boldsymbol{\rho}$. Below shows a configuration where all cars have a head-tail of 4 except the last one who has 7 but cannot increase its speed.

$$4....4....4....4....4....4....4....4.......$$

Subcase M $\geq$ d + 1. The last car l has more head-tail and will increase its speed to $v = d + 1$. This happens only when $M \geq d + 1$, see the speed regulator. Such speed updates are going on for all trailing car successively. Eventually l reaches a head-tail of $2d$ to the next car and reduces its speed to $v = d$. The global flow follows the dynamic of Proposition 3. In the example below, most of the cars are at speed 3 except the ones that take advantage of $M \geq d + 1$ to accelerate. In this case, we have $\bar{v} = \frac{L-d}{N} - 1$, since one car has head-tail $2d$ and cannot accelerate, and the corresponding flow is $\mathbf{j} = \mathbf{1} - \frac{\mathbf{d}}{\mathbf{L}} - \boldsymbol{\rho}$. Notice that $d < v_{max}$.

$$3...3....4....4....4....4...3...3...3...3......$$

In Fig. 2a, we see the results of our simulation in dark blue dots. The plain lines are the theoretical solutions of $j = 1 - \frac{d}{L} - \rho$. The dashed vertical line

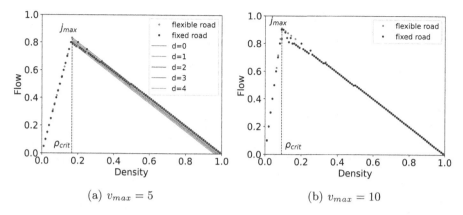

(a) $v_{max} = 5$ (b) $v_{max} = 10$

Fig. 1. Fundamental diagrams of our simulation with $L = 100$ and going through all the possible densities ($\rho = [0.01, 1]$). Starting initial position as described in the text.

shows the value of the maximal flow j_{max}. As stated, this value is not reachable since $N_{crit} = 16.6\overline{7}$ is not an integer. For a density N/L the car reaches a traffic pattern where $d \in \{0, 1, 2, 3, 4\}$.

In cyan we simulated a flexible road which changes its length $L_f = \lfloor \frac{L}{N} \rfloor \cdot N$ in order to always satisfy the condition $M = 0$. This implies that the flow is always maximal and that we can reach the maximum flow. In Fig. 2b, we see the same diagram with a higher speed. We observe the same pattern but with a j_{max} bigger and pushed to the left. The what seems to be random points after j_{max} are density who follows the flow $j = (\lfloor \frac{1}{\rho} \rfloor - 1)\rho$. From these observations, we can conclude that there are configurations where the flow is optimal. This happens only when the cars use all the space available, i.e. $M = 0 \implies v_i = d_i$ for all cars i. A configuration not optimal cannot go to an optimal one with our regulator conditions. It would require one car to violate the condition $\tilde{d} + df(v_b \dot{-} 1) >= df(v_a + 1)$ thereby risking a collision. Finally, the state depends on the initial conditions. If we start the cars at $v = d = 0$, like at a traffic light, they will reach the maximum flow since our regulator assure $v_i = d_i$. Nevertheless it only happens if the last car reaches the first car before it starts closing the gap M to zero. Otherwise, $M > 0$ and the flow will not be optimal.

To conclude the presentation of these experiments, we show the fundamental diagram obtained with random starting initial conditions, the positions of the cars are random and the speed is 0. We observe various flow value that are due to more general traffic patterns. These traffic patterns are not optimal and can be explained with an extended version of Proposition 3. In particular, it is always the case that $\tilde{v}_a = v_b$ meaning that the trailing cars copy the speed of their leading car, this correspond to lag synchronization.

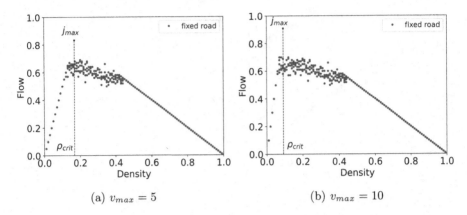

(a) $v_{max} = 5$ (b) $v_{max} = 10$

Fig. 2. Fundamental diagrams of our simulation with $L = 100$ and going through all the possible densities ($\rho = [0.01, 1]$). Starting with random initial positions.

5   Conclusions

In this paper we analyzed theoretically and numerically the traffic patterns that are accessible for autonomous vehicles equipped with a simple, local and deterministic speed regulator. We consider a simple traffic situations (cars following each other) and identified the potential strength and weakness of an automatic driving system, such as stop and go waves or non-optimal flow conditions. Of course, more complex situations need to be investigated, such as junctions, merging or lane changing to better understand the emergent collective behavior of autonomous cars.

References

1. Brown, R., Kocarev, L.: A unifying definition of synchronization for dynamical systems. Chaos Interdisc. J. Nonlinear Sci. **10**(2), 344–349 (2000)
2. Chacoma, A., Abramson, G., Kuperman, M.N.: A phase transition induced by traffic lights on a single lane road. Phys. A **568**, 125763 (2021)
3. Chou, F.-C., Bagabaldo, A.R., Bayen, A.M.: The lord of the ring road: a review and evaluation of autonomous control policies for traffic in a ring road. ACM Trans. Cyber-Phys. Syst. (TCPS) **6**(1), 1–25 (2022)
4. Gupta, A.K., Katiyar, V.K.: Phase transition of traffic states with on-ramp. Phys. A **371**(2), 674–682 (2006)
5. Hanumappa, D., Ramachandran, P.: Cellular automata model for mixed traffic flow with lane changing behavior. Model. Simul. Eng. **2021** (2021)
6. Jiang, R., Qing-Song, W.: Phase transition at an on-ramp in the Nagel-Schreckenberg traffic flow model. Phys. A **366**, 523–529 (2006)
7. Karakhi, A., Laarej, A., Khallouk, A., Lakouari, N., Ez-Zahraouy, H.: Car accident in synchronized traffic flow: a stochastic cellular automaton model. Int. J. Mod. Phys. C **32**(01), 2150011 (2021)
8. Kerner, B.S.: The physics of traffic. Phys. World **12**(8), 25 (1999)

9. Kerner, B.S., Klenov, S.L., Wolf, D.E.: Cellular automata approach to three-phase traffic theory. J. Phys. A Math. Gen. **35**(47), 9971 (2002)

10. Kerner, B.S.: The Physics of Traffic: Empirical Freeway Pattern Features, Engineering Applications, and Theory. Understanding Complex Systems, Springer, Heidelberg (2004). https://doi.org/10.1007/978-3-540-40986-1

11. Kerner, B.S.: Understanding Real Traffic: Paradigm Shift in Transportation Science. Understanding Complex Systems, Springer, Cham (2021). https://doi.org/10.1007/978-3-030-79602-0

12. Lee, H.K., Barlovic, R., Schreckenberg, M., Kim, D.: Mechanical restriction versus human overreaction triggering congested traffic states. Phys. Rev. Lett. **92**(23), 238702 (2004)

13. Meng, J., Dai, S., Dong, L., Zhang, J.: Cellular automaton model for mixed traffic flow with motorcycles. Phys. A **380**, 470–480 (2007)

14. Nagel, K., Schreckenberg, M.: A cellular automaton model for freeway traffic. J. Phys. I **2**(12), 2221–2229 (1992)

15. Naito, Y., Nagatani, T.: Effect of headway and velocity on safety-collision transition induced by lane changing in traffic flow. Phys. A **391**(4), 1626–1635 (2012)

16. Nishinari, K., Fukui, M., Schadschneider, A.: A stochastic cellular automaton model for traffic flow with multiple metastable states. J. Phys. A Math. Gen. **37**(9), 3101 (2004)

17. Qian, Y.-S., Feng, X., Zeng, J.-W.: A cellular automata traffic flow model for three-phase theory. Phys. A **479**, 509–526 (2017)

18. Sugiyama, Y., et al.: Traffic jams without bottlenecks-experimental evidence for the physical mechanism of the formation of a jam. New J. Phys. **10**(3), 033001 (2008)

19. Tian, J., Jia, B., Li, X., Jiang, R., Zhao, X., Gao, Z.: Synchronized traffic flow simulating with cellular automata model. Phys. A **388**(23), 4827–4837 (2009)

20. Tian, J., Zhu, C., Jiang, R., Treiber, M.: Review of the cellular automata models for reproducing synchronized traffic flow. Transportmetrica A Transp. Sci. **17**(4), 766–800 (2021)

Stimulus-Induced Swarming in Soldier Crabs
A Behavioral Model by Cellular Automata

Claudio Feliciani[1]($\boxtimes$)(iD), Hisashi Murakami[2], Takenori Tomaru[2],
and Yuta Nishiyama[3]

[1] Research Center for Advanced Science and Technology, The University of Tokyo,
Tokyo 153-8904, Japan
feliciani@g.ecc.u-tokyo.ac.jp
[2] Faculty of Information and Human Science, Kyoto Institute of Technology,
Kyoto 606-8585, Japan
[3] Information and Management Systems Engineering,
Nagaoka University of Technology, Niigata 940-2188, Japan

Abstract. Collective self-organization is a widely studied topic in animal behavior, but it also attracts the attention of researchers studying crowds of people. The creation and dynamics of self-organized structures in animals have been often studied by means of numerical simulation, also considering how they would change in relation to the surrounding environment (e.g. a predator approaching a flock of birds). However, little has been done to research possible means to influence swarm behavior as a whole. In this work, we study how soldier crabs react to a moving light and how their individual reaction is amplified by swarm size. A numerical model is created to reproduce experimental data and used to assess more in detail swarm dynamics. Results show that crabs can self-organize better in the presence of an external stimulus and their capacity to show a collective behavior also depends on swarm size. In particular, the moving light results particularly efficient in inducing swarming for medium-sized swarms, while becoming potentially detrimental at high densities. Results are expected to increase the knowledge on self-organized structures in animals, but also help in the assessment of efficacy in the frame of information-provision in human crowds.

Keywords: Swarming · Soldier crab · Crowd steering · Light-stimuli

1 Introduction

A large number of animal species are known for their striking capability to form swarms resulting in a collective motion where the whole group moves as a single entity, apparently following rules of motion unrelated to the behavior of the single individuals. What is most impressive in such structures is the fact that they lack a centralized command and the collective motion is merely the result of a large number of individual-level interactions [16]. Flocks of birds are probably the most

B. Chopard et al. (Eds.): ACRI 2022, LNCS 13402, pp. 292–302, 2022.
https://doi.org/10.1007/978-3-031-14926-9_26

impressive, most known and most studied collective structure in animals [1,14], but also school of fishes [12,15] are often studied for their capability to create self-organized structures. Although some studies considered how swarms would react to a change in the surrounding environment [2,9] or tried to influence them by introducing robotic lures [10], only few attempted to artificially steer swarms by modifying environmental conditions.

Humans create collective structures too; what is generally known as crowds. However, although animal behavior can be mostly studied from a cognitive perspective, to understand phenomena related to crowd behavior, psychology also needs to be accounted for, thus making human crowds more difficult to study. Nonetheless, a number of theories have been developed to explain the formation of a shared identity in groups of people and numerical models allow us to reproduce phenomena typically formed in crowds [7]. Still, influencing crowds is not an easy task and typically crowd control is performed in an invasive manner through policing or physical means [7]. Alternative methods relying on the so-called "nudging" approach and aiming to drive people into a particular behavior by intervening on the environment are also emerging, for example through light stimuli [4] or music [17]. Such studies are still pioneering and they mostly aim at pinpointing methods which could stimulate behavioral changes in crowds.

In this work, we will try to move one step forward and examine under which conditions non-invasive crowd steering is likely to be effective and to which extent individual compliance could affect overall behavior. On this purpose, a particular species of crab, *Mictyris guinotae*, known under the name of soldier crab [5], is employed. Although the cognitive capacities of this small crab are clearly much lower than humans, they show a collective organization underlying spontaneous formation in swarms. This hints to the possibility that they share the fundamental principle of collective self-organization with human crowds. They therefore represent a good testbed to investigate how a stimulus effective on a single individual could be reinforced by the interactions within the swarm/crowd. Clearly, we are not trying to state that behavior observed in swarms of crabs can be directly compared to human crowds, but learnings gained through the investigation of collective motion in animals may help lay the fundamentals to study methods to change crowd's behavior.

Specifically, we will study how a moving light can affect swarming behavior in soldier crabs and under which conditions it is particularly effective in stimulating the creation of self-organized structures. Since the cognitive mechanisms leading to the behavior of soldier crabs on the individual level can be only hypothesized, a Cellular Automata model will be used to test whether the hypotheses are at least likely to be correct[1].

2   Experiment and Outcomes

In this section, a brief introduction will be given for the specific experiment considered here. But before discussing the experiment, a few words would be

---

[1] If a model can reproduce experimental results, it does not necessarily mean that assumptions are correct. It is simply a first step toward a longer validation process.

needed to describe the species involved: the soldier crab. This small crab (adults have a carapace width of about 15–20 mm) can be found in sandy beaches with "soft" fine gravel in the southern parts of Japan. Activity of the soldier crab is governed by tidal periods. At low tide, individuals emerge from below the sand and start wandering in large colonies, forming self-organized structures resembling a "moving army". When sea level rises, soldier crabs dig again under the sand until the next tidal period. Another remarkable characteristic of soldier crabs is that they walk forwards, rather than sideways as most crab species.

Interestingly, soldier crabs are likely to approach a flashlight on the tidal flat at night, so-called phototaxis. This characteristic was found first by a research group (including some of the authors) when studying collective behaviors of soldier crabs both in nature and in laboratory. Those initial investigations showed that crabs could be guided by the moving light even in laboratory experiments [8]. Here, to test the influence of a moving light on swarms of soldier crabs, the animals were collected from their habitat and taken to an experimental facility (Iriomote Station, Tropical Biosphere Research Center, The University of Ryukyus, Japan). Care was taken to not harm them and all individuals were released into their natural habitat after the experiments. Experimental setup consisted of a ring-shaped path 50 mm wide and having a centerline length of 1 m. The course was delimited with high transparent walls, preventing crabs from moving out of it. To allow the recognition of crabs, markers painted using a UV-reflecting material were used.

(a) Normal condition   (b) External stimulus

Fig. 1. Experimental conditions considered in this work. Left: The course is fully lighted and crabs are clearly recognizable. Right: A rotating light illuminates only a small part of the course (roughly 30°), while the rest is left in darkness. UV-light allows locating crabs also in darkness.

As shown in Fig. 1 two different conditions were tested. In one condition the course was fully lighted and crabs could be easily recognized from the green floor. In the other condition all external light sources were covered, leaving the course in darkness. A rotating light mounted at a height of around 30 cm created a beam shining from azimuthal direction above the course, which was used to try influencing the motion of soldier crabs. The rotating light illuminated a section of the course with an arc length of 30° and moved at a speed of 7.3 rpm (a speed from 4.7 rpm to 13.4 rpm was found adequate to stimulate crabs according to [8]). Direction was randomly changed during each trial, which lasted around 5 minutes for both conditions. Tested swarm size consisted of 3, 10 and 30 individuals and each crab was used only once in each trial. In addition, isolated single individuals were also studied to grasp features of the fundamental behavior when stimulated through the moving light.

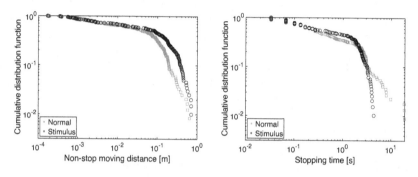

Fig. 2. Experimentally obtained CDFs for individual crabs moving along the course in the normal (fully lighted) and stimulated condition (rotating light). Stopping time distribution is approximated as a power law using the tail, with the exponents being 2.50 and 7.15 in the normal condition and with external stimulus, respectively. The exponent for the non-stop moving distance was taken as 3.25 for both conditions.

Experiments on individual crabs revealed that crab's kinematic behavior can be divided into two activities: moving and stopping. Both moving distance and stopping time can be generally described using a power law as shown in Fig. 2. In addition, observations of individuals showed that the moving light has a stronger effect on the stopping time, drastically reducing long stops. Since the scope of this work is to focus on self-organization in swarms, rules used for individual motion in simulation were taken for granted. Thus, we assumed that each crab will move a given distance and stop for a given time according to a power law distribution gained from the data of Fig. 2. In addition, we observed that, regardless of the condition, crabs typically moved at a speed of 4.5 cm/s and, when alone, inverted their moving direction every 30 s on average.

Experimental results for swarms of crabs will be presented while comparing numerical simulation results, but here we want to provide a list of outcomes from the experiments, which will be used in developing the simulation model.

– Especially for large swarms, clusters would occur with many crabs concentrated in a small area and trying to move in different directions. A dominant direction would eventually result from the conflict, with most crabs adopting that direction.

- Preliminary experimental results showed that crabs tended to be particularly receptive when light is approaching. Consequently they would resume moving if resting and increase their speed if already moving. This could be explained considering that food is typically found in areas close to the water, which appears brighter in their natural habitat.

- Observations showed that crabs were not particularly able to assess the moving direction of light, but, in general they were more likely to start moving in the same direction of light rather than the opposite one when the beam approached.

- Although observations are difficult in the condition with light stimulus (right under the light is too bright to clearly recognize crabs and in the dark area only markers are visible), some cues indicate that crabs were more likely to imitate peers' behavior when in darkness. An hypothesis would be that uncertainty caused by the darkness and the resulting low visibility prompted crabs to sense the environment through vibrations, resulting in a coping behavior which could explain the stronger collective motion.

3   Numerical Simulation

Swarm dynamics of soldier crabs has been already studied using numerical simulation and the discrete approach has been successfully applied to describe different mechanisms [11,13]. Also considering the almost unidimensional nature of the experiment considered here, a Cellular Automata (CA) model was employed to numerically model swarm behavior under the influence of light. The course was discretized into a lattice composed of 50 cells, each having a size of 2 cm. At the start of each simulation, crabs were randomly positioned over the lattice with random orientation. In the experiments, about two crabs could move on different "lanes" along the course, but sometimes they would partially overlap moving on top of each other's. Based on this observation a limit of 3 crabs per cell was set in simulation. Time step was set at 0.44 s based on crabs' moving speed of 4.5 cm/s.

Update procedure is performed by parallel-update, i.e. each crab reserve the target cell before actually moving. Whenever a number of crabs exceeding the maximum limit reserve the same cell, only 3 of them are chosen randomly (three being the limit here) with the remaining ones reassigned to their original positions. When all conflicts are resolved positions are updated at once. Additional details on motion rules are given as follows.

3.1   Universal Behavior

Fundamental Motion. In accordance with the results obtained from individual observations, crabs are modeled as moving for a power-law distributed distance and stopping for a time also distributed according to a power law. In addition, we assumed that only the distribution for the stopping time changes due to darkness and moving distance will remain unchanged. In the model, moving direction randomly changes every 30 s on average, regardless of the interaction with other crabs.

Group Interaction. To reproduce the mechanisms related to the change in direction seen in the experiments, each crab is assumed to interact over 3 cells in both directions, as shown in Fig. 3.

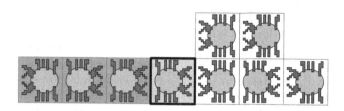

Fig. 3. Schematic representation of a cluster potentially resulting in a direction inversion for the crab highlighted in the middle. Note that the model is unidimensional and crabs added over the lattice are intended to show the number of individuals in each cell (a maximum of 3 is possible). For the sake of clarity, we should point out that perception on the overall condition in the cluster is assumed to be based on the pressure exerted on the body and transmitted through the legs and not through visual assessment.

A change in direction will occur proportionally to the force balance within the 7-cells cluster, with this size based on evidence gained by observing videos of the experiment (but not measured explicitly). For a specific crab, if the difference between the crabs pushing in the opposite direction and the ones moving in the same direction is large, then a direction change will occur with a probability proportional to this difference. From the example of Fig. 3 we obtain that 3 crabs are moving in the same direction and 5 in the opposite one. In this condition, the crab in the middle is likely to invert its direction with a probability given by:

$$p_{invert} = k_{change} \cdot \frac{|n_{same} - n_{opposite}|}{n_{max} \cdot \Delta x_{cluster}} = 5.0 \cdot \frac{2}{3 \cdot 7} = 0.476 \qquad (1)$$

where n_{same} and $n_{opposite}$ are the number of crabs moving the in same and opposite direction, respectively, n_{max} the maximum number of crabs per cell, $\Delta x_{cluster}$ the cluster size (including the central crab) and k_{change} a model parameter. This mechanism of direction inversion is considered both in the normal condition and when stimulus was added since we assume that crabs perceive the force acting on them regardless of visibility[2].

---

[2] An hypothesis is that the fairly omnidirectional distribution of crab's legs allows them to estimate the pressure from each direction and thus feel which one is dominant when inside a cluster.

3.2   Behavior in the Presence of External Stimulus (Moving Light)

Alignment to Light Direction. In accordance with experimental observations, we assume that when light is approaching (starting from 30° before the beam) each crab may align its direction with the one of the light with a probability of 0.05. Each crab can align with the light only once per turn, meaning that the assessment is not repeated at every time step during the approach of the light, but only once[3].

Imitation in the Dark Section. As discussed earlier, a sort of coping mechanism was observed in the dark areas and could be explained by the capability of crabs to sense vibrations on the ground. To reproduce this imitating behavior, similar to the following behavior observed for humans in lanes, a "pheromone trace" was used[4]. A virtual trace is left when each crab moves, reporting its direction. This trace may decay (i.e. decrease by a random value over one time step) or diffuse to a random neighbor cell (i.e. the trace is reduced by a random value in the "central" cell considered and increased by the same amount in a randomly selected neighbor cell) with a probability of 0.10 and 0.05, respectively (for details on this method see [3,6]). Each crab takes into account traces from both directions and will align to the dominant direction with a probability given by:

$$p_{align} = 1 - \exp(-k_{coping} \cdot f_i) \qquad (2)$$

where f_i is the (total) trace value at cell i and k_{coping} is a model parameter (set at 0.1).

Interaction in Darkness. Finally, to take into account the difficulty while interacting with other crabs in darkness, hopping rate was reduced from 1 (certain motion to a neighbor cell) under normal conditions to lower values when under complete darkness (not directly under the light nor beam approaching). In this step, the number of crabs in the 7-cells cluster considered earlier is computed (n_{crabs}) and hopping rate is set according to:

$$p_{hop} = \left(1 - \frac{n_{crabs}}{n_{max} \cdot \Delta x_{cluster}}\right)^{k_{density}} \qquad (3)$$

where $k_{density}$ is a model parameter (set at 1.5).

---

[3] An assessment at each time step would be also reasonable, but the "once per turn" approach was chosen because it is closer to the quantity measured experimentally.

[4] Note that this is not to be intended in its strict biological meaning; crabs are not known for releasing pheromone while moving.

3.3   Results

Simulations were performed for a duration of 5 min (same as the experiments) by varying swarm size from 1 to 45. A total of 750 repetitions were performed for each swarm size. Model parameters were manually adjusted by trial-and-error to match experimental results reported as follows, paying particular attention in having a similar qualitative trend. The rather inefficient manual approach was preferred to an algorithm due to the limited availability of experimental data and because the aim of this work is not to reach a perfect fit, but rather to understand the model while considering its dynamics. On top of that, we ensured that parameters having a specific meaning would remain within acceptable limits.

Two quantities were selected to evaluate the results and compare them with experimental data: absolute and collective flow. The absolute flow represents the total number of crabs transiting to any given cross section along the course over 1 min and it roughly represents crabs' activity. The collective flow uses the same approach but takes into account the balance between crabs transiting in one direction and the ones transiting in the opposite one. It can be said to represent the capability of the swarm to self-organize. Both quantities are normalized by the swarm size to allow a systematic analysis on the effect of this variable.

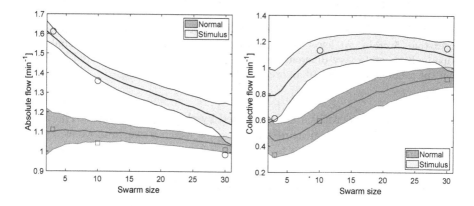

Fig. 4. Absolute and collective flow in relation to swarm size and comparison with experimental results (shown by circles and squares). Shaded areas represent the variance among simulation repetitions. Note that swarm size is shown from 2 to 31 to restrict the graphs to experimentally investigated conditions.

Absolute and collective flow from simulations is compared with experimental data in Fig. 4. In general a good agreement is found, especially for the collective flow, which accounts for more subtle interactions. From an ethological perspective it can be observed that the light has an influence in inducing swarming in soldier crabs, but its effect is related with swarm size. At low (swarm) densities the stimulus affects individuals and thus the increase in collective flow is limited. At medium densities interactions within the swarm amplify the effect of the stimulus. However, at high densities self-organization is already obtained without external stimuli, thus minimizing the swarming effect brought by the moving light.

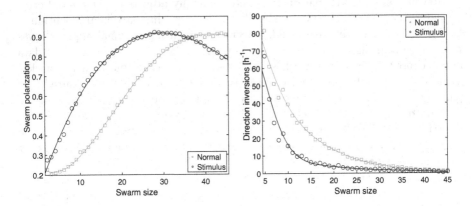

Fig. 5. Swarm polarization and frequency of (collective) direction inversion. Both results presented here are relative only to the simulation as such quantities could not be measured experimentally. Markers are relative to each numerical result for the given swarm size and a fitting curve is employed to better show the trend (a general smoothing function is used). In the right graph results are visualized only for swarm sizes larger than 5 crabs. At lower sizes, swarms composed of odd and even numbers of individuals generate very different results due to (a)symmetry. The initial transition from the random alignment to an organized state is not counted.

The above considerations are confirmed by the graphs of Fig. 5. The polarization (index) is used to measure the degree to which a swarm move as a single entity and is defined according to:

$$PI = \frac{|n_{clockwise} - n_{counterclockwise}|}{n_{swarm}} \tag{4}$$

where $n_{clockwise}$ and $n_{counterclockwise}$ is the number of crabs moving in the clockwise and counterclockwise direction, respectively, and n_{swarm} the swarm size. Thus, polarization will be 0 for completely unorganized swarms (random motion) and 1 for a perfectly organized one. Differences between the normal and stimulated conditions disappear for swarms larger than 35 individuals and, above it, the stimulus of light is detrimental and swarms get less organized. The right graph of Fig. 5 shows the number of changes in direction (per hour) of the whole swarm. To avoid counting fluctuations around 0, a swarm is considered as moving in a given direction when polarization exceeds 0.5 (excluding the initial transition). In this representation, it is confirmed that light has an influence in conforming the behavior among crabs, although the effect is negligible for large swarms and, as we saw earlier, it may even undermine self-organization.

4   Conclusions

The possibility to influence self-organization in animal swarms has been studied using soldier crabs, a particular species of crab walking forwards and known to produce large swarms in nature. A narrow ring-shaped path was created thus influencing the formation of an almost-unidimensional swarm structure, moving in a specific direction (clockwise or counterclockwise) if fully self-organized. The normal condition, fairly close to the natural habitat, was compared with a condition in which a light beam was rotated along the course in a specific direction, potentially influencing the collective behavior. To help confirm some hypothesis on crabs' behavior and allow a better investigation of related mechanisms, a CA model was developed, reproducing with sufficient accuracy experimental data.

Results reveal that the rotating light has indeed an effect on self-organization, specifically helping crabs to align toward a common direction. In addition, we found that the stimulus provided by the light is amplified by the interactions between crabs and this mechanism is particularly effective at medium swarm densities, where distance between crabs is sufficiently small to let interactions happen but without hindering motion. At high densities, a common behavior emerges to limit the number of conflicts, but motion is also more difficult, especially in darkness, thus minimizing the stimulating effect of the moving light.

Although care is needed in generalizing the results to other types of social animals, some outcomes may help in the management of human crowds, in particular when the stimulus provided by the moving light in crabs is associated with information provision to crowds of people. Because crabs possess very simple cognitive mechanisms, a simple stimulus such as a moving light is already sufficient to induce changes on the collective level. However, similar effects may be obtained in human crowds through information provision, for example through information display or by smartphone notifications. In this context, it is possible that, like for animal swarms, also in crowds, efficacy of information provision could be limited to low-to-medium densities, thus stressing on the importance of a crowd control strategy starting from low densities.

In the future, we plan to study whether the conclusions obtained for crabs applies indeed to human crowds while also investigating more in detail collective behavior of soldier crabs, for example by changing the rotating speed of light or testing other swarm sizes to further validate the simulation model.

Acknowledgements. This work was partially supported by JST-Mirai Program Grant Number JPMJMI20D1 and by JSPS KAKENHI Grant Number 20K14992 and 20K20143. In addition, the authors are grateful to Yasuko Makino, Xiaolu Jia and Sakurako Tanida for their help in the experiments and video analysis. Finally, a special thanks to Lorenzo Vanoni (Attratech Sagl) who helped in the construction of the experimental equipment.

References

1. Ballerini, M., et al.: Interaction ruling animal collective behavior depends on topological rather than metric distance: evidence from a field study. Proc. Natl. Acad. Sci. **105**(4), 1232–1237 (2008). https://doi.org/10.1073/pnas.0711437105

2. Berdahl, A., Torney, C.J., Ioannou, C.C., Faria, J.J., Couzin, I.D.: Emergent sensing of complex environments by mobile animal groups. Science **339**(6119), 574–576 (2013). https://doi.org/10.1126/science.1225883

3. Burstedde, C., Klauck, K., Schadschneider, A., Zittartz, J.: Simulation of pedestrian dynamics using a two-dimensional cellular automaton. Phys. A **295**(3–4), 507–525 (2001). https://doi.org/10.1016/S0378-4371(01)00141-8

4. Corbetta, A., et al.: A large-scale real-life crowd steering experiment via arrow-like stimuli. Collective Dyn. **5**, 61–68 (2020). https://doi.org/10.17815/CD.2020.34

5. Davie, P.J., Shih, H.T., Chan, B.K.: A new species of Mictyris (Decapoda, Brachyura, Mictyridae) from the Ryukyu Islands, Japan. In: Studies on Brachyura: a Homage to Danièle Guinot, pp. 83–106. Brill (2010). https://doi.org/10.1163/ej.9789004170865.i-366.61

6. Feliciani, C., Nishinari, K.: An improved cellular automata model to simulate the behavior of high density crowd and validation by experimental data. Phys. A **451**, 135–148 (2016). https://doi.org/10.1016/j.physa.2016.01.057

7. Feliciani, C., Shimura, K., Nishinari, K.: Introduction to Crowd Management. Springer, Cham (2022). https://doi.org/10.1007/978-3-030-90012-0

8. Kawai, H., Nishiyama, Y., Moriyama, T., Nomura, S.: An intervention of phototaxis on swarming behavior of a soldier crab, Mictyris Guinotae - an experimental study. In: Joint Meeting of the 22nd International Congress of Zoology (ICZ) and the 87th Meeting of the ZSJ (2016)

9. Lima, S.L., Dill, L.M.: Behavioral decisions made under the risk of predation: a review and prospectus. Can. J. Zool. **68**(4), 619–640 (1990). https://doi.org/10.1139/z90-092

10. Mondada, F., et al.: A general methodology for the control of mixed natural-artificial societies, Technical report. Pan Stanford Publishing (2013)

11. Murakami, H., Niizato, T., Gunji, Y.P.: Emergence of a coherent and cohesive swarm based on mutual anticipation. Sci. Rep. **7**(1), 1–9 (2017). https://doi.org/10.1038/srep46447

12. Murakami, H., Niizato, T., Tomaru, T., Nishiyama, Y., Gunji, Y.P.: Inherent noise appears as a lévy walk in fish schools. Sci. Rep. **5**(1), 1–11 (2015). https://doi.org/10.1038/srep10605

13. Murakami, H., Tomaru, T., Nishiyama, Y., Moriyama, T., Niizato, T., Gunji, Y.P.: Emergent runaway into an avoidance area in a swarm of soldier crabs. PLoS ONE **9**(5), e97870 (2014). https://doi.org/10.1371/journal.pone.0097870

14. Nagy, M., Ákos, Z., Biro, D., Vicsek, T.: Hierarchical group dynamics in pigeon flocks. Nature **464**(7290), 890–893 (2010). https://doi.org/10.1038/nature08891

15. Pitcher, T.J.: Heuristic definitions of fish shoaling behaviour. Anim. Behav. (1983). https://doi.org/10.1016/S0003-3472(83)80087-6

16. Vicsek, T., Zafeiris, A.: Collective motion. Phys. Rep. **517**(3–4), 71–140 (2012). https://doi.org/10.1016/j.physrep.2012.03.004

17. Zeng, G., Schadschneider, A., Zhang, J., Wei, S., Song, W., Ba, R.: Experimental study on the effect of background music on pedestrian movement at high density. Phys. Lett. A **383**(10), 1011–1018 (2019). https://doi.org/10.1016/j.physleta.2018.12.019

Analysis of Congestion Caused by a Bottleneck in a Crowded Aquarium with a Fixed One-Way Route

Riho Kawaguchi[1]([✉]), Claudio Feliciani[2], Daichi Yanagisawa[1,2,3],
Shigeto Nozaki[4], Yukari Abe[5], Makiko Mita[5], and Katsuhiro Nishinari[1,2,3]

[1] Department of Aeronautics and Astronautics, School of Engineering,
The University of Tokyo, 7-3-1, Hongo, Bunkyo-ku, Tokyo 113-8656, Japan
riho-k@g.ecc.u-tokyo.ac.jp
[2] Research Center for Advanced Science and Technology, The University of Tokyo,
4-6-1, Komaba, Meguro-ku, Tokyo 153-8904, Japan
[3] Mobility Innovation Collaborative Research Organization, The University of Tokyo,
5-1-5, Kashiwanoha, Kashiwa-shi, Chiba 277-8574, Japan
[4] Kaiyukan, 1-1-10 Kaigandori, Minato-ku, Osaka 552-0022, Japan
[5] GOODFELLOWS CO., LTD., 1-15-5 Nakacho, Musashino-shi,
Tokyo 180-0006, Japan

Abstract. In this research, we introduce a modified TASEP model with a bottleneck in order to model visitors' behavior in a crowded aquarium, Kaiyukan in Japan, and to propose a congestion reduction method. It is distinct in that visitors walk through a fixed one-way aisle, as opposed to a typical museum or aquarium where visitors can move freely in an open space. Using theoretical analysis and numerical simulation, we investigated the basic congestion features caused by the bottleneck and developed new indicators to estimate congestion.

Keywords: ASEP · Pedestrian behaviour · Crowd control · Aquariums

1 Introduction

The quantitative analysis of visitors' behavior at museums or exhibitions has recently increased because of the advancements in tracking systems and the development of IT infrastructure knowledge [1,2]. Statistics of visitors' behavior enables us to create a model of real-life visitors' motions at museums. Thus, the applications of a mathematical model or a digital twin for visitors' behaviors in museums have been extensively studied [3,4]. Yoshimura et al. [5] simulated visitors' sequential movements in a global network of the museum by a random

This research work was in part supported by JST-Mirai Program Grant Number JPMJMI20D1 and JSPS KAKENHI Grant Numbers 20K14992, JP21H01570 and JP21H01352.

B. Chopard et al. (Eds.): ACRI 2022, LNCS 13402, pp. 303–313, 2022.
https://doi.org/10.1007/978-3-031-14926-9_27

walk and compared the results to data collected at the Louvre Museum. Centorrino et al. [6] acquired real-life data to create stochastic digital-twins of the visitor dynamics at the Galleria Borghese museum in Italy, by acquiring real-life data and they also optimized ticketing and entrance/exit management.

Although many mathematical tools are available, for hyper-congestion [7] situations that impact visitors' choices, current data collection and quantitative analysis are insufficient and literature is mostly lacking. As a result, we simplify the situation to a one-way route museum model that addresses this problem and focuses on heavily crowded situations. Our case study is Kaiyukan in Osaka, Japan, which is one of the largest aquariums in the world. Kaiyukan is unique in that visitors walk through a fixed one-way aisle, as opposed to a typical museum or aquarium where visitors can move freely in an open space, which is consistent with our aim. We construct a model using the totally asymmetric simple exclusion process (TASEP), which has been intensively investigated for many years to reproduce a transportation system. It has been extensively studied to describe non-equilibrium systems such as production flow [8], vehicular traffic [9], biological transport [10] and exclusive-queuing processes [11]. In TASEP, each site can only accommodate one particle at a time. However, in our model, each site can hold multiple particles up to a maximum accommodation limit. Sites represent the exhibition area in front of the aquarium's water tanks, while particles represent visitors. Additionally, we consider a bottleneck in the system, which represents a significantly packed area compared to other exhibitions. In the case of Kaiyukan, it is in front of the whale shark tank which is displayed halfway through the route.

Usually levels of congestion are estimated based on flow or density for TASEP models. Congestion level for specifically pedestrian crowds has been discussed [12, 13]. However, it is questionable whether those indicators are effective in estimating the congestion level in areas where visitors want to take their time gazing around the exhibitions with preference, such as museums and aquariums, where moving fast unimportant. As a result, we are introducing a new congestion level that can be used for museums and aquariums. We also propose a control method that involves establishing a new bottleneck and testing it to see if it reduces congestion.

The rest of this paper is structured as follows. Section 2 defines and compares our modified TASEP to the original TASEP. Section 3 introduces new indices for estimating. Section 4 presents the results of theoretical analysis and steady state simulation results. Section 5 includes simulations to test the reduction of congestion in an unsteady state. Finally, Sect. 6 brings the paper to a conclusion.

2   Model Description

2.1   Original TASEP

The original TASEP with open-boundary is defined on a one-dimensional discrete lattice of L sites, whose sites are labeled as $i = 1, 2, \ldots, L$, respectively (see Fig. 1 (a)). Here, we adopt discrete time and parallel updating scheme.

Particles hop into the system from the leftmost site 1 with probability α, go through the bulk, and after reaching the rightmost site L, they leave the lattice with probability β. Each site is either empty or occupied by the particles. When the ith site at time t is occupied by a particle, its state is represented as $n_i(t) = 1$; otherwise, its state is $n_i(t) = 0$. At each time step, a particle at site i can hop to the next site $i + 1$ with a certain hopping probability p if the site $i + 1$ is empty; otherwise it remains at its present site.

2.2 Modified TASEP

Our modified TASEP differs from the original TASEP in several ways (see Fig. 1 (b)). In our model, each site ($i \geq 2$) can hold multiple particles to a maximum accommodation limit, i.e. $1 \leq n_i(t) \leq n_{\max}$. For $n_{\max} = 1$, the system corresponds to TASEP, therefore, our TASEP can be interpreted as an modified TASEP with a maximum occupation number of particles. Note that we adopt discrete time and parallel updating scheme for particles and that multiple particles can move at the same time step. There is no limit for the first site store, thus $n_{\max} = \infty$, as an exception in order to avoid a call loss at the first site. This is because the entrance of the aquarium can hold no matter how many visitors come. Next, we introduce a hopping probability p_i allocated to the sites determined by the expected staying time on the site, in the case of an aquarium, the tank. At each time step, a particle at site i can hop to the next site $i + 1$ with a hopping probability p_i if the number of particles at site $i + 1$ is less than $n_{\max}$; otherwise they remain at their present site. Note that if multiple particles try to hop to the same site $i + 1$, $\{n_{\max} - n_{i+1}(t)\}$ particles can hop; however other particles cannot hop to the next site. More specifically, if multiple particles try to hop to the same site $i + 1$ at time step $t + 1$, particles hop to site $i + 1$ from the first particle to the $n_{\max} - n_{i+1}(t)$ th one that hopped on site i at time step t. Particles at the right boundary, leave the lattice with $\beta = p_L$. Note that particle can overtake each other in the system.

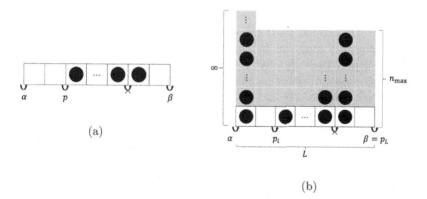

(a)

(b)

Fig. 1. (a) Schematic of the original TASEP with open-boundary conditions. (b) Schematic of the modified TASEP with open-boundary conditions.

3   Definition of New Indexes to Estimate Congestion

3.1   Traditional Indicators to Estimate Congestion

Many studies modeling transportation systems with TASEP, especially vehicular traffic, usually investigate velocity, flow and density to estimate the level of congestion of the system. When considering a vehicular traffic system, average velocity can be used to understand how smoothly the particles can move. Similarly, flow has been used to evaluate the amount of motion or movement of the particles. Furthermore, density and flow are connected through the fundamental diagram, which is one of the most important principles that can be used to predict capability of a system [14,15].

However, it is questionable whether velocity and flow are sufficient indicators to estimate the congestion level of the system where visitors take their time looking around the exhibitions, such as museums and aquariums. Since how fast the visitors can move is not the objective in museums and aquariums, maximizing the velocity and flow does not make sense. Low velocity does not necessarily mean that the system is congested, but visitors would rather walk slowly of their own free will regardless of the congestion.

Level of Service (LOS), an approach to classify congestion in pedestrian crowds, was proposed by Fruin [16]. Different types of facilities are ranked on a scale from A to F based on qualitative remarks using LOS. However, implementing the LOS in real-time crowd would be difficult since the density differs with time and space. From the perspective of previous studies on museums where visitors walk around the systems enjoying the exhibitions, the number of visitors or density and length of stay at each room or throughout the whole-building is investigated to estimate the congestion level. Centorrino et al. [6] identified keeping the number of visitors in each room below a certain room-dependent safety limit as one of the objectives and optimized ticketing and entrance/exit management in the Galleria Borghese museum in Rome. In this research, they also consider the length of stay at the museum as one of the basic illustrative statistics. However, they constructed a model only for a mild congestion level situation where the length of stay can be assumed to be independent from the congestion. They suspect that, in a hyper-congestion [7] which has impact on visitors choices, congestion can either increase or decrease the length of stay, depending on the perceived importance and fame of the room content. Yoshimura et al. [17] investigated the relationship between length of stay and density and figured out that crowd density around exhibitions largely affects a visitor's length of stay either positively or negatively, and that the effect can differ depending on the exhibition.

Although there is no doubt about the importance of density and length of stay in museums, connecting them with congestion directly can be difficult and may not be appropriate. There are few previous research that has challenged to quantitatively define hyper-congestion with density [6]. High density or long length of stay do not necessarily mean that the visitors are stuck in a congestion and the relationship between density and length of stay is vague.

3.2   Mean Experienced Density for Particle

Considering the argumentation above, we present two new indicators, "Mean experienced density for particles" and "Number of waiting particles" that can be used to estimate congestion level. Total experienced density for particle j presented in this work is defined with the time particle j entered Subsystem 2, $t = t_j^{in}$, the time particle j exited Subsystem 3, $t = t_j^{out}$ and the density on the site where particle j is at time t, $\rho_j(t)$ as:

$$u_j = \sum_{t=t_j^{in}}^{t_j^{out}} \rho_j(t). \tag{1}$$

Mean experienced density which particle j experienced can be also calculated as:

$$\bar{u}_j = \frac{u_j}{t_j^{out} - t_j^{in}}. \tag{2}$$

Density is usually calculated as the density at a room or the whole building and the time-variation or difference between rooms are investigated. However, note that, in our research, u_j focuses on the density that the visitor experiences.

Number of waiting particles, $W(t)$ is defined as the number of particles that could not move to another site because the next site reached the capacity n_{max} at the time step t. Thus, if $W(t)$ is a large value, it indicates that a lot of visitors cannot move forward because other visitors are in their way.

Mean experienced density for particles and number of waiting particles can be used as indicators of congestion at steady state and unsteady state respectively. In the case of our research which focuses on museums and aquariums, the system does not necessarily reach steady state because of operating hours. Therefore, considering unsteady state is important as well.

4   Theoretical Analysis and Simulation Results of Steady State

4.1   Theoretical Analysis

In this section, we theoretically analyze the steady state of our modified TASEP in the presence of a bottleneck, i.e. a defect site with reduced hopping probability $p_k = q < p_i$ $(k \neq i)$, in order to model the influence of a bottleneck at a aquarium. In the case of Kaiyukan, the whale shark tank attracts the visitors' attention the most and creates a heavily crowded area infront of it, which can be considered as the bottleneck of the whole aquarium. We calculate the steady-state in the limit $L \to \infty$ so that we can obtain theoretical results. In order to simplify the calculation and elucidate the influence of the bottleneck, we set $p_1 = p_i = \ldots = p_L = p = $ const. $(i \neq k)$.

When α is small, we refer to it as low density (LD) phase. The flow approximates to $J = \alpha$ because the capacity of each site is large enough to neglect failure of hopping due to the exclusion in LD, even though the exact steady state flow can be calculated as $\alpha\frac{p-\alpha}{p-\alpha^2}$ for TASEP with open boundary and parallel updating [20,21].

When α is larger than a certain value, particles pile up behind the bottleneck. We call this phase as high-density with bottleneck (HDB) after the HD phase with TASEP with open boundary. As shown in Fig. 2 (a), the system can be virtually divided into three subsystems, Subsystem 1, 2 and 3. Thus, in HDB Subsystem 1 and 2 are congested. Note that Subsystem 2 accommodates $n_{max}(k-1)$ particles at most. On the other hand, particles in Subsystem 3, which is after the bottleneck are relatively scarce. For Subsystem 3, the input probability can be written as qn_k as shown in Fig. 2 (a). Therefore, the steady state flow for the whole system is given by:

$$J = qn_k(t \to \infty),\qquad(3)$$

since in steady state the flow of Subsystem 1, 2 and 3 should be equal due to the rule of current conservation in [18].

We calculate the occupation number of particles at site $i = k$, i.e. $n_k(t \to \infty)$ approximately. At time $t-1$ the time evolution of the number of particles at site $i = k$ can described as,

$n_k(t) =$ Occupation number of particles at site k at time $t-1$

$+$ Inflow term to site k at time t

$-$ Outflow term from site k at time t.

When we assume that there are enough particles at site $k-1$ and can fill in the holes at site k, the inflow term to site k at time t can be written as $n_{max}-n_k(t-1)$. Therefore,

$$n_k(t) = n_k(t-1) + \{n_{max} - n_k(t-1)\} - qn_k(t-1).\qquad(4)$$

When $t \to \infty$, $n_k(t) \approx n_k(t-1)$. Thus,

$$n_k(t \to \infty) = \frac{n_{max}}{q+1}.\qquad(5)$$

Therefore, the steady state flow of the system can be calculated by Eq. (3) and Eq. (5) as:

$$J = \frac{qn_{max}}{q+1}.\qquad(6)$$

Theoretical results can be summarized as:

$$J = \begin{cases} \alpha & \text{for LD phase} \quad (\alpha \leq \frac{qn_{max}}{q+1}) \\ \frac{qn_{max}}{q+1} & \text{for HDB phase} \quad (\alpha > \frac{qn_{max}}{q+1}) \end{cases}\qquad(7)$$

We discuss the density at the systems and the average staying time in order to calculate the mean experienced density for particles and the number of waiting particles. Here we focus on Subsystem 2 and 3. In this paper, we exclude

Subsystem 1 because waiting area at Subsystem 1 represents the entrance area of the aquarium which can hold ever so many visitors and we want to focus on Subsystem 2, we assume that the average number of particles at sites $i = 2, \ldots, k-1$ equals to that of site k, thus the average density is $\overline{\rho}_2 = \frac{1}{q+1}$. The average staying time is $\overline{T}_2 = \frac{\overline{\rho}_2 n_{\max} L_2}{J} = L_2/q$. For Subsystem 3, average density $\overline{\rho}_3$ can be calculated as $\overline{\rho}_3 = \frac{J}{pn_{\max}} = \frac{q}{p(q+1)}$. The average staying time is $\overline{T}_3 = L_3/p$. The mean experienced density for particles can be described as:

$$\overline{u} = \overline{\rho}_2 \overline{T}_2 + \overline{\rho}_3 \overline{T}_3 = \frac{1}{q+1}\left(\frac{L_2}{q} + \frac{qL_3}{p^2}\right). \tag{8}$$

The mean of the number of waiting particles can be written as:

$$\overline{W} = L_2(p\overline{\rho}_2 - (1 - \overline{\rho}_2)) = \frac{(p-q)L_2}{q+1}. \tag{9}$$

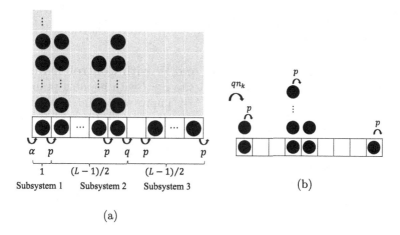

(a)

(b)

Fig. 2. (a) Schematic of an modified TASEP with one bottleneck and (b) Subsystem 3 with open boundaries.

4.2   Simulation Results

Basic Analysis. In this section, we perform numerical simulations to validate the theoretical results in the preceding section. In all the simulations below, we set the system size, $L = 101$, $k = \frac{L+1}{2}$, $n_{\max} = 5$, over 10 trials and run for 5×10^3 steps for each calculation.

First, we investigate the flow when there is a bottleneck, i.e. q is sufficiently smaller than α and p. Figure 3 (a) compares the simulation and theoretical results of steady state flow, J for $p = 1$ and various $q \in \{0.05, 0.1, 0.15\}$ and shows good agreement with our theoretical analyses.

Next, we explore the mean experienced density for particle, $\overline{u}_j$ and number of waiting particles, $\overline{W}$. Figure 3 (b) and Fig. 3 (c) compares the simulation and theoretical results of $\overline{u}_j$ and $\overline{W}$, respectively, $\overline{u}_j$ for $\alpha = 1$, as functions of p and various $q \in \{0.05, 0.1, 0.15\}$ and show good agreements with our theoretical analyses. As shown in Fig. 3 (b), $\overline{u}_j$ of $q = 0.05$ is considerably large compared to that of $q = 0.1$ and $q = 0.15$.

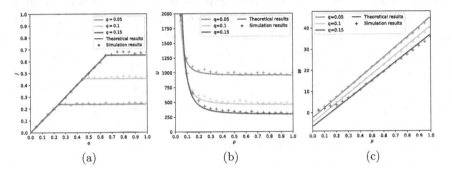

(a)   (b)   (c)

Fig. 3. Simulation and theoretical results of (a) J as functions of α, (b) $\overline{u}_j$ as functions of p and (c) $\overline{W}$ as functions of p for various $q \in \{0.05, 0.1, 0.15\}$.

Investigation of Improvement of $\overline{u}_j$ and $\overline{W}$ with Control. In this section, we verify if putting a new bottleneck at site $i = l$ with hopping probability q_1 before the existing bottleneck at site $i = k$ improves $\overline{u}_j$ and $\overline{W}$. We examine how $\overline{u}_j$ and $\overline{W}$ changes between $0 < q_1 < 1$. Here, we set the position of a new bottleneck at site $i = l = 25$, which is the middle of subsystem 2. Figure 4 (a) and Fig. 4 (b) show that when q_1 is smaller than 0.1 and close to 0.1, $\overline{u}_j$ and $\overline{W}$ improve. However, as shown in Fig. 4 (c), when $q_1 < 0.1$, the system flow depends on q_1, therefore J with a new bottleneck with q_1 is smaller than that without another bottleneck. Therefore, in order to maximize J and minimize $\overline{u}_j$ and $\overline{W}$, we should select a q_1 which is smaller than 0.1 but close to it.

5   Simulation Results of Unsteady State with Control

In this section, we investigate the effect of a new bottleneck explained in Sect. 4.2 at unsteady state. In Fig. 5 (a) and (b), we plot the simulation results of the number of waiting particles and flow, respectively, at time t for $q \in \{0.05, 0.1, 0.15, 0.2, 1.0\}$. We fix $(\alpha, p, q, l) = (1, 1, 0.1, 25)$ for Fig. 5 (a) and (b). The simulation starts at $t = 0$ and ends at $t = 500$, which is the time when the system reaches steady state. Figure 5 (a) shows that $W(t)$ reaches steady State A rapidly when $q_1 \leq 0.1$. On the other hand, $W(t)$ reaches steady State B rapidly when $q_1 \geq 0.2$. When $0.1 < q_1 < 0.2$, $W(t)$ reaches steady State B slowly. Figure 5 (b) shows that the larger q_1, the larger J. For example, at time $t = 400$, W with $q_1 = 0.15$ is smaller than that of $q_1 = 0.2$, because W increases more gradually with $q_1 = 0.15$. However, J with $q_1 = 0.15$ is same as that of $q_1 = 0.2$. Thus, we can say that putting a bottleneck with $0.1 < q_1 < 0.2$ in order to reduce congestion levels.

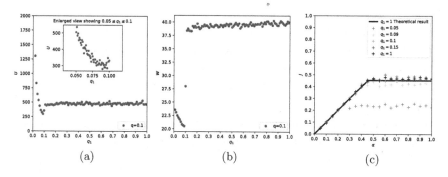

Fig. 4. (a) Simulation results of $\overline{u}_j$ as functions of p for various q_1. (b) Simulation results of $\overline{W}$ as functions of p for various q_1. (c) Simulation results of J as functions of α for various $q \in \{0.05, 0.09, 0.1, 0.15, 1.0\}$.

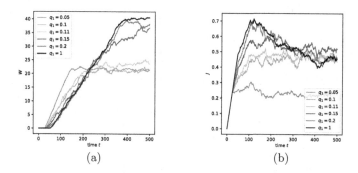

Fig. 5. Simulation results of (a) W and (b) J as functions of time.

6   Conclusion

Our proposed model along with theoretical and simulation results, provides us with more insight into the influence of bottlenecks that cause heavy congestion in large-scale museums and aquariums. We also have introduced a new indicator of congestion level that can be used in a system where moving fast is not the preferred behavior, as is peculiar in museums or aquariums. The modified TASEP model allowed us to propose the implementation of a new bottleneck in front of an existing bottleneck in a different way in steady and unsteady state. We also used simulated data to verify that this method is effective against congestion. This control method can be used in real-life settings in Kaiyukan by arranging attractive exhibitions or narrowing the walking area to encourage visitors to walk slowly before the bottleneck area. For future work, we intend to create a more accurate model for Kaiyukan using trajectory data obtained from Bluetooth sensors.

References

1. Mygind, L., Bentsen, P.: Reviewing automated sensor-based visitor tracking studies: beyond traditional observational methods? Visit Stud. **20**(2), 202–217 (2017)
2. Yoshimura, Y., Sobolevsky, S., Ratti, C., et al.: An analysis of visitors' behaviour in The Louvre Museum: a study using Bluetooth data. Environ. Plan B Plan Des. **416**, 1113–1131 (2014)
3. Piccialli, F., Benedusi, P., Carratore, L., Colecchia, G.: An IoT data analytics approach for cultural heritage. Pers. Ubiquit. Comput. **24**(3), 429–436 (2020). https://doi.org/10.1007/s00779-019-01323-z
4. Yoshimura, Y., de la Torre - Arenas, I., Park, S., Santi, P., Seer, S., Ratti, C.: Paris-Gare-de-Lyon's DNA: analysis of passengers' behaviors through Wi-Fi access points. In: Zuriguel, I., Garcimartín, A., Hidalgo, R.C. (eds.) Traffic and Granular Flow 2019. SPP, vol. 252, pp. 589–596. Springer, Cham (2020). https://doi.org/10.1007/978-3-030-55973-1_72
5. Yoshimura, Y., Amini, A., Sobolevsky, S., Blat, J., Ratti, C.: Analysis of pedestrian behaviors through non-invasive bluetooth monitoring. Appl. Geogr. **81**, 43–51 (2017)
6. Centorrino, P., Corbetta, A., Cristiani, E., Onofri, E.: Managing crowded museums: visitors flow measurement, analysis, modeling, and optimization. J. Comput. Sci. **53**, 1877–7503 (2021)
7. Krebs, A., Petr, C., Surbled, C.: La gestion de l'hyper fréquetation du patrimoine: d'une problématique grandissante à ses réponses indifférenciées et segmentées. In: 9th International Conference on Arts and Culture Management (2007)
8. Ezaki, T., Yanagisawa, D., Nishinari, K.: Dynamics of assembly production flow. Physica A Stat. Mech. Appl. **427**, 62–73 (2015)
9. Chowdhury, D., Santen, L., Schadschneider, A.: Statistical physics of vehicular traffic and some related systems. Phys. Rep. **3294–6**, 199–329 (2000)
10. Appert-Rolland, C., Ebbinghaus, M., Santen, L.: Intracellular transport driven by cytoskeletal motors: general mechanisms and defects. Phys. Rep. **593**, 1–59 (2015)
11. Yanagisawa, D., Tomoeda, A., Jiang, R., Nishinari, K.: Excluded volume effect in queueing theory. JSIAM Lett. **2**, 61–64 (2010)
12. Feliciani, C., Nishinari, K.: Measurement of congestion and intrinsic risk in pedestrian crowds. Transp. Res. Part C Emerg. Technol. **91**, 124–155 (2018)
13. Hoogendoorn, S.P., Daamen, W., Knoop, V.L., Steenbakkers, J., Sarvi, M.: Macroscopic fundamental diagram for pedestrian networks: theory and applications. Transp. Res. Procedia **23**, 480–496 (2017)
14. Seyfried, A., Steffen, B., Klingsch, W., Boltes, M.: The fundamental diagram of pedestrian movement revisited. J. Stat. Mech. **10**, 10002 (2005)
15. Tsiftsis, A., Georgoudas, I.G., Sirakoulis, G.C.: Real data evaluation of a crowd supervising system for stadium evacuation and its hardware implementation. IEEE Syst. J. **10**(2), 649–660 (2016)
16. Fruin, J.: Pedestrian Planning and Design. Metropolitan Association of Urban Designers and Environmental Planners, New York (1971)
17. Yoshimura, Y., Krebs, A., Ratti, C.: Noninvasive bluetooth monitoring of visitors' length of stay at the Louvre. IEEE Pervasive Comput. **16**(2), 26–34 (2017)
18. Liu, M., Wang, R., Jiang, R., Hu, M., Gao, Y.: Defect-induced transitions in synchronous asymmetric exclusion processes. Phys. Lett. A **273**(2), 195–200 (2009)
19. Spitzer, F.: Interaction of Markov processes. Adv. Math. **5**(2), 246–290 (1970)

20. Levine, E., Mukamel, D., Schütz, G.M.: Zero-range process with open boundaries. J. Stat. Phys. **120**(5), 759–778 (2005)
21. Rajewsky, N., Santen, L., Schadschneider, A., Schreckenberg, M.: The asymmetric exclusion process: comparison of update procedures. J. Stat. Phys. **92**, 151–194 (1998)

Pedestrian Movement: An Analysis of Transition Regime the Real-Life Experiment, a Comparison with a Simulation Data at an Example of the "SigmaEva" Software

Ekaterina Kirik$^{(\boxtimes)}$ ⓘ and Tat'yana Vitova ⓘ

Institute of Computational Modelling of the Siberian Branch of the Russian Academy of Sciences, Akademgorodok 50/44, Krasnoyarsk 660036, Russia
{kirik,vitova}@icm.krasn.ru
http://3ksigma.ru

Abstract. The video record with a real-life experiment of the pedestrian movement in a straight corridor is analyzed. Open boundary conditions are realized in the experiment, and it is unusual for known data sets. The aim of the investigation is to determine data from the experiment (initial and in dynamics): initial positions of people, an average movement speed and a density for different moments, a free movement speed. These data are necessary to make a simulation experiment reproducing the real-life experiment and to compare results in order to investigate ability of a software to simulate real process correctly. The data obtained have been applied to test the SigmaEva software which is based on the discrete-continuous pedestrian dynamics model. Some unexpected and discussional findings were derived concerning free movement speed.

Keywords: Pedestrian movement · Real-life experiment · Open boundary conditions · Validation of the model

1 Introduction

Issues of data collection that can be used for validation of computer programs for modeling pedestrian movement [1,18], and, in fact, the development of validation methods [2,3,9,11,14], are engaged all over the world. The most popular is to observe people movement in periodic boundary conditions, when the time-spatial density is approximately constant, and there are no conditions for transformations of the flow. So the steady-state regime is realized. People are uniformly distributed over the entire area (e.g., in an extended corridor without narrowing) and move in one direction. Under these limitations, the speed of each person decreases with increasing density. In terms of a specific flow, the fundamental diagram looks as follows. As the density increases, the specific flow grows, attains its maximum, and then decreases.

B. Chopard et al. (Eds.): ACRI 2022, LNCS 13402, pp. 314–323, 2022.
https://doi.org/10.1007/978-3-031-14926-9_28

The flow spreading is caused by the fact that people tend to move under comfortable local density conditions. If there is an opportunity to keep distance from others, people use it. In this case, the front line has a place to move. Those people who are behind gradually start moving, and their speed is controlled by the local density in front of them. These effects are observed in a transition regime, which can be realized under so-called open boundary conditions. Unfortunately, there is a lack of real-life data which fix this phenomenon.

In this paper we attempted to investigate experiment where transition regime is realized (https://youtu.be/5fbd4kexrzw, Test 1-1/1). Twenty people move in the straight corridor of 20 m in length and 2 m in width. Initially people are placed in a area 5 m in length. The important features of these experiments are:

1. the experiment was carried out on a short section of a path (20 m), which gave small values of the observed times;
2. there is a single implementation of the experiment, while pedestrian movement is a random process with pronounced repeatability of results on average [6,13].

The scientific value of such single experiment is the possibility of a detailed study of a specific instance of a random process. In this case result has a high sensitivity to the initial data. In this situation a comparative analysis of real-life and computational experiments requires the maximum possible proximity of the initial conditions of both experiments. Therefore, first of all, the analysis of the video of the experiment was performed and the initial data were extracted.

To obtain the data of the computational experiment we used the SigmaEva model. The SigmaEva model considered [7,9,12] is designed in a way that a fundamental diagram [5,6,13,16] is an input for the model. The fundamental diagram is used to calculate speed according to the local density for each person. This property of the model is very convenient for practical applications because we omit a step to tune parameters to correspond to desired flow-density dependence. In this article, we investigate the ability of the model to reproduce the certain process under some uncertainties in initial data. Good agreement between the results of the real-life and computational experiments is shown under the proximity of the initial conditions.

In the next section an analysis and results of the real-life experiment is presented. Then we shortly presented the SigmaEva model. And in the Sect. 4 simulation results are discussed.

2   The Analysis of the Real-Life Experiment

The experiments were carried out in the gym. The shooting was conducted from one point, but the camera is not rigidly fixed. During the experiments boundaries of the area were marked on the floor. To measure lengths of the sectors we used markings of playcourts (volleyball, basketball, tennis), Fig. 1.

Movement occurs under open boundary conditions. 20 students (12 male, 8 female) participate in the experiment. In the initial moment of time they were located in their initial places 5 m in length, they started moving along the

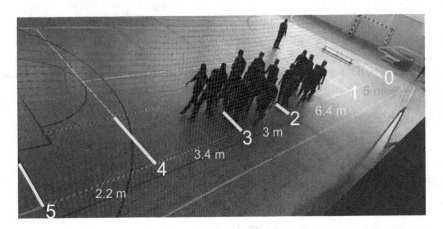

Fig. 1. Control areas and lengths.

observing area 20 m in length and 2 m in width. The experiment is considered finished when the last person leaves the area.

To analyze the real life experiment, methods of visual observation of the participants of the movement are used according to the available video recording. A notable person is selected from the stream and the travel time of the selected section of the path is measured.

In the theory of pedestrian movement, two speeds are distinguished: the speed of movement and the speed of free movement. The first reflects the current speed of movement of a person, the second reflects the speed at which a person can move if other people do not interfere with him. It is known that the speed of human movement in the stream is determined by the current density, and this dependence has an analytical expression [5,6,13,16]. At low densities, the speed of movement is equal to the free movement speed, but when moving in a stream, as a rule, only the first one is realized. As a result of numerous experiments, it was determined that the person's speed is a random variable with a variance decreasing with increasing density. Different categories of people's movement have been identified, characterized on average by different average speeds of free movement (comfortable, quiet, active, increased activity) [6,13]. The graphs of the speed-density relationship for these categories are presented in Fig. 2 (0.96 $[m/s]$ – quiet, 1.3 $[m/s]$ – active, 1.66 $[m/s]$ – increased activity).

In mathematical simulation of pedestrian movement using an individual flow model, perhaps the most important element of the initial data is the free movement speed v^0, which is assigned to each person. Obviously, the value of v^0 determines the evacuation time. Especially it has an impact in the case of short observation areas as in the experiments under consideration.

The purpose of analyzing video recording of the experiment is to determine a free movement speed.

In considered experiment 20 people were located in the area 5 m×2 m (the control area 0–1, Fig. 1). After start, as described in [13], the front part of the

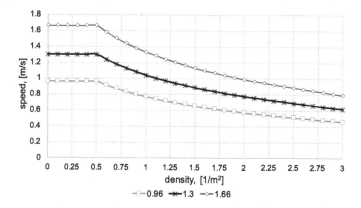

Fig. 2. Speed-density relationship for different free flow speeds {0.96, 1.18, 1.3, 1.66} $[m/s]$ [6].

flow began to move earlier and at a higher speed due to the availability of free space than the middle and tail, the flow began to spread – the distance between people increases.

Table 1 shows the results of the analysis of the flow movement in the control areas 0–5. The density in Table 1 was estimated only for the tail section and calculated as the ratio of the number of people[1] to the size of the area occupied by these people at the moment. We fixed the time when front line (the first person) or tail (the last person) crosses the line which is the beginning of the observed section and then we fixed the time when the end line of the observed section is crossed.

As it can be seen from Table 1, by the beginning of the movement along the control section 1–3, the flow had spread, and the density decreased to 1.4 $[1/m^2]$, by the end of the movement along the section 0–2, the density decreased to 1.25 $[1/m^2]$, by the end of the tail movement along the section 1–3, the density was 1.09 $[1/m^2]$. Figure 3 shows the moment when the front reaches the boundary of the observation area. The length of this area is approximately 8.6 m, there are 20 people in this area, the density for the tail section can be estimated as $20/(8.6 * 2) = 1.16$ $[1/m^2]$.

Thus, the analysis of the video recording of the experiment allowed us to establish:

1. the initial density (2 $[1/m^2]$) decreases as a result of the flow spreading;
2. during the experiment, the density is not constant (which corresponds to the descriptions of the flow behavior in [13], the observed range is [1.09–1.4] $[1/m^2]$, for further analysis we will use the middle of this interval – 1.25 $[1/m^2]$;

---

[1] This value was not always equal to 20, due to the location of control sections 1–3 and 2–4, some participants had already left the experimental area.

Table 1. Flow characteristics in control areas.

Control sections	Characteristic	Front	Tail
0–2	Length, m	6.4	$6.4 + 5 = 11.4$
	Travel time, [s]	5.5	11.78
	Speed, [m/s]	1.16	0.97
	Instantaneous density at the beginning of movement along the control area ρ_{begin}, $[1/m^2]$		$20/(5*2) = 2$
	Instantaneous density at the end of movement along the control area ρ_{end}, $[1/m^2]$		$20/(8*2) = 1.25$
1–3	Length, m	9.4	9.4
	Travel time, [s]	8.08	8.58
	Speed, [m/s]	1.16	1.1
	ρ_{begin}, $[1/m^2]$		$20/(7*2) = 1.4$
	ρ_{end}, $[1/m^2]$		$12/(5.5*2) = 1.09$
2–4	Length, m	6.4	6.4
	Travel time, [s]	5.31	5.81
	Speed, [m/s]	1.21	1.1
	ρ_{begin}, $[1/m^2]$		$20/(8*2) = 1.25$
	ρ_{end}, $[1/m^2]$		$3/(2.2*2) = 0.68$
2–5	Length, m	8.6	8.6
	Travel time, [s]	7.21	8.14
	Speed, [m/s]	1.19	1.06
	ρ_{begin}, $[1/m^2]$		$20/(8*2) = 1.25$
0–5	Length, m	15	20
	Travel time, [s]	12.71	20.1
	Speed, [m/s]	1.18	0.99

3. the estimate of the tail speed varies in the range $[0.97\text{–}1.1]$ $[m/s]$, for further analysis we will use the mean of this interval – 1.035 $[m/s]$;

4. the estimate of the free movement speed of the front varies in the range $[1.16\text{–}1.21]$ $[m/s]$, for further analysis we will use the mean of this interval – 1.185 $[m/s]$.

The movement speed of the front part is the free movement speed, and it can be estimated as the ratio $15/12.71 = 1.18$ $[m/s]$.

Now it is necessary to determine a free movement speed of the tail. We used the estimates of the density, the current speed, and the known the speed-density dependence [6]. So we are interesting in the pair $(1.25; 1.035)$. The closest value 0.98 $[m/s]$ is given by the curve "1.3" (Fig. 2). This value falls within the obtained velocity range $[0.97\text{–}1.1]$ $[m/s]$. This curve corresponds to the free movement speed of 1.3 $[m/s]$.

Thus, as estimates of the free movement speed, we have: $v_0^{front} = 1.18$ $[m/s]$ for front part; $v_0^{tail} = 1.3$ $[m/s]$ for tail part.

These results give rise to the following conclusion: the free movement speed of the front part is lower than the free movement speed of the tail. Is this particular phenomenon or result, claiming to be a pattern? The answer could come from

Fig. 3. Positions of the people when the front line reaches control lines "2" (left) and "5" (right).

the fact that the distance of the tail path is only 20 m, and this distance is not enough to finish transition period when flow transfers to a steady-state regime, and comfortable distance between people is reached. So by our findings we state a new question for further investigations.

Remark. It is necessary to note there is some inaccuracy in fixing the time presented in Table 1, but the adjustment is possible within 0.1–0.2 [s].

3   Description of the Model

A discrete-continuous approach is applied [4,7,12,15,17]. Below we shortly considered the SigmaEva model [7,9,12]. We will use the word "particle" speaking about a person.

A continuous modelling space $\Omega \in \mathbb{R}^2$ is considered. A border $\partial\Omega$ (including an open part $\partial\Omega'$ which is the exit) is known.

We consider flat projections of persons on Ω. A shape of each particle is a disk with diameter d_i, initial positions of particles are given inside Ω by coordinates of disk centers $x_i(0) = (x_i^1(0), x_i^2(0))$, $i = \overline{1, N}$, N – number of particles. Each particle is attributed with the free movement speed v_i^0 [m/s], the particle size f_{0i} [m^2] (which is the area of the disk with diameter d_i).

At each time step t each particle i may move in one of the predetermined directions $e_i(t) \in \{e^\alpha(t), \alpha = \overline{1, q}\}$, q – the number of directions (a model parameter, $q = 16$ in our investigation). Particles that cross the target line ($\partial\Omega'$) leave the modeling space.

A person movement equation is derived from the finite-difference expression $v(t)e(t) \approx \frac{x(t) - x(t - \Delta t)}{\Delta t}$ that is given by a velocity definition. This expression allows us to present a new position of the particle as a function of a previous position and the local particle velocity. Thus for each time t coordinates of each particle i are given by the following formula:

$$x_i(t) = x_i(t - \Delta t) + v_i(t)e_i(t)\Delta t, \ i = \overline{1, N}, \tag{1}$$

where $x_i(t - \Delta t)$ is the coordinate in previous moment; $v_i(t)$, [m/s] is the current particle speed; $e_i(t)$ is the unit direction vector, $\Delta t = 0.25$ [s] is the time step.

It is assumed that the speed of each particle $v_i(t)$ is controlled in accordance with the local density and does not exceed the maximal value (the free movement speed). The local density is estimated along the movement direction. Then the density is substituted to some the speed-density relationship (for example, [5,6, 13,16]). Here, we use the following relationship [6], Fig. 2:

$$v^{Kh}(\rho) = \begin{cases} v^0(1 - 0.295 \ln \frac{\rho}{0.51}), \rho > 0.51; \\ v^0, \qquad\qquad\qquad \rho \le 0.51, \end{cases} \qquad (2)$$

where values 0.295 and 0.51 are parameters for horizontal way; v^0 is the free flow speed.

All predetermined directions for each particle for each time step $e_i(t)$ are assigned with some probabilities to move, and the direction is chosen according to the probability distribution obtained. In this discrete-continuous model we took inspiration from our previously presented stochastic CA FF model [8,10].

Probabilities in the model are not static and vary dynamically. The personal probabilities to move in each direction at each time step depends on: (a) the main driving force (given by a destination point), (b) interaction with other pedestrians, (c) interaction with an infrastructure (non-movable obstacles). The highest probability[2] is given to a direction that has the most preferable conditions for movement considering other particles and obstacles and a strategy of the people movement (the shortest path and/or the shortest time).

Parallel update is applied.

4   Simulation

The initial data for computational experiments are as follows. The same geometry of the modeling area and the number of people are as in the real-life experiment. Figure 4 shows the initial positions of particles in the computational experiment, as close as possible to the location of people in the real-life experiment. The particle size was assumed to be 0.1 $[m^2]$ (the people size in summer clothing [6,13]). Since there is no narrowing in the finish line and after it, we assume that people who cross the finish line (number 5 in Fig. 1), do not affect the process inside the area. Therefore in a computational experiment the computational area coincides with the observation area in the real-life experiment.

According to our findings presented in the previous section two variants ("a" and "b") were considered:

a) 5 particles at the front were assigned the free movement speed $v_0^{front} = 1.16 \ [m/s]$, the others were assigned with $v_0^{tail} = 1.3 \ [m/s]$, Fig. 4a);
b) all the people were assigned with $v_0 = 1.3 \ [m/s]$.

For each variant 20 runs were conducted. The results are presented in Table 2. The histograms for the evacuation time are shown in Fig. 5. One can see that

---

[2] Mainly with value > 0.9.

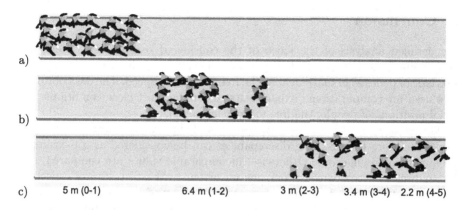

c)   5 m (0-1)   6.4 m (1-2)   3 m (2-3)   3.4 m (3-4)   2.2 m (4-5)

Fig. 4. Positions of particles in the simulation with $v_0^{front} = 1.16$ $[m/s]$ and $v_0^{tail} = 1.3$ $[m/s]$: a) initial positions; b) the front line riches the line "2"; c) the front line riches the line "5" (finish).

the discrepancy for the variant "a" is smaller then for variant "b". The Fig. 4 shows spread of the flow which is comparable with real-life experiment, Fig. 3.

The obtained intervals of exit (evacuation) times in the model include the time value of the real-life experiment for each case. A small standard deviation indicates the stability of the simulation results.

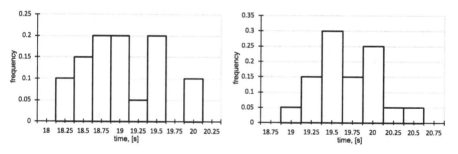

Fig. 5. Evacuation time histograms: $v_0^{front} = 1.16$ $[m/s]$ and $v_0^{tail} = 1.3$ $[m/s]$ (left), $v_0 = 1.3$ $[m/s]$ (right).

Table 2. Statistics over 20 runs and experimental data.

Characteristic		
Free flow speed in simulations, $[m/s]$	Front 1.16; tail 1.3	1.3
Mean T_{mod}, $[s]$	19.69	19.01
Standard deviation, $[s]$	0.38	0.52
Evacuation time in real experiment T_{exp}, $[s]$	20.1	20.1
Free flow speed according to analysis of video, $[m/s]$	Front 1.18; tail 1.3	Front 1.18; tail 1.3
Discrepancy $\delta = 100 \times \frac{T_{exp} - T_{mod}}{T_{exp}}$, $\%$	2.04	5.42

5 Conclusion

The detailed analysis of the video of the considered real-life experiment was carried out. This analysis made it possible to evaluate such an important characteristic of pedestrian movement as the free movement speed. The data obtained were used for computational experiments under the most close conditions (the initial positions of people, the free movement speed).

The closer the conditions of a computational experiment to a real-life experiment, the more the resulting discrepancies can be considered as a measure of the quality of simulations. Otherwise, incomparable values are compared, and the analysis of discrepancies does not make sense. "Fast" tests are especially sensitive to the initial data when the process is observed in a transitional stage.

We tested combinations of initial data which were not determined directly (the free movement speed of the middle part and tail of the flow is different from the front line). Simulations show that "two-speed" variant gives the lower discrepancies with real-life result then "one-speed" variant (Table 2). The spread of the flow is observed in the simulation in variant "a". So we can state a good coincidence of final result (evacuation time) and dynamic of the process (spread of the flow) of the simulation and real-life experiments. But at the moment the question if the free movement speeds of the front part and people how are behind are different in the open boundary conditions is open.

References

1. Data archive of experimental data from studies about pedestrian. http://ped.fz-juelich.de/database/. Accessed 23 Mar 2022
2. International maritime organization/msc.1/circ 1533 – revised guidelines on evacuation analysis for new and existing passenger. https://www.traffgo-ht.com/en/pedestrians/downloads/index.html. Accessed 18 Mar 2022
3. Guideline for microscopic evacuation analysis, version: 3.0.0 (2016). https://rimea.de/de/rimea-projekt/. Accessed 18 Mar 2022
4. Baglietto, G., Parisi, D.R.: Continuous-space automaton model for pedestrian dynamics. Phys. Rev. E **83**, 056117 (2011). https://doi.org/10.1103/PhysRevE.83.056117
5. Gwynne, S.M.V., Rosenbaum, E.R.: Employing the hydraulic model in assessing emergency movement. In: Hurley, M.J., et al. (eds.) SFPE Handbook of Fire Protection Engineering, pp. 2115–2151. Springer, New York (2016). https://doi.org/10.1007/978-1-4939-2565-0_59
6. Kholshevnikov, V., Shields, T., Boyce, K., Samoshin, D.: Recent developments in pedestrian flow theory and research in Russia. Fire Safety J. **43**(2), 108–118 (2008). https://doi.org/10.1016/j.firesaf.2007.05.005
7. Kirik, E., Malyshev, A., Popel, E.: Fundamental diagram as a model input: direct movement equation of pedestrian dynamics. In: Weidmann, U., Kirsch, U., Schreckenberg, M. (eds.) Pedestrian and Evacuation Dynamics 2012, pp. 691–702. Springer, Cham (2014). https://doi.org/10.1007/978-3-319-02447-9_58
8. Kirik, E., Yurgel'Yan, T., Krouglov, D.: On realizing the shortest time strategy in a CA FF pedestrian dynamics model. Cybern. Syst. **42**(1), 1–15 (2011). https://doi.org/10.1080/01969722.2011.532636

9. Kirik, E., Malyshev, A., Senashova, M.: On the evacuation module SigmaEva based on a discrete-continuous pedestrian dynamics model. In: Wyrzykowski, R., Deelman, E., Dongarra, J., Karczewski, K., Kitowski, J., Wiatr, K. (eds.) PPAM 2015. LNCS, vol. 9574, pp. 539–549. Springer, Cham (2016). https://doi.org/10.1007/978-3-319-32152-3_50

10. Kirik, E., Vitova, T.: On formal presentation of update rules, density estimate and using floor fields in CA FF pedestrian dynamics model SIgMA.CA. In: El Yacoubi, S., et al. (eds.) ACRI 2016. LNCS, vol. 9863, pp. 435–445. Springer, Cham (2016). https://doi.org/10.1007/978-3-319-44365-2_43

11. Kirik, E., Vitova, T., Malyshev, A., Popel, E.: On the validation of pedestrian movement models under transition and steady-state conditions. In: Snegirev, A. (ed.) The Ninth International Seminar on Fire and Explosion Hazards, pp. 1271–1280. SPb Polytechnic University (2019). https://doi.org/10.18720/SPBPU/2/k19-67

12. Kirik, E., Vitova, T., Malyshev, A.: Turns of different angles and discrete-continuous pedestrian dynamics model. Natural Comput. 18(4), 875–884 (2019). https://doi.org/10.1007/s11047-019-09764-4

13. Predtechenskii, V.M., Milinskii, A.I.: Planning for Foot Traffic Flow in Buildings. Amerind Publishing, New Dehli (1978)

14. Ronchi, E., Kuligowski, E., Reneke, P., Peacock, R., Nilsson, D.: The process of verification and validation of building fire evacuation models. Tech. rep., National Institute of Standards and Technology (2013). https://doi.org/10.6028/NIST.TN.1822

15. Seitz, M.J., Köster, G.: Natural discretization of pedestrian movement in continuous space. Phys. Rev. E 86, 046108 (2012). https://doi.org/10.1103/PhysRevE.86.046108

16. Weidmann, U.: Transporttechnik der fussgänger. Transporttechnische eigenschaften des fussgängerverkehrs (literaturauswertung). Tech. rep. Institut für Verkehrsplanung, Zürich (1992–2001). https://doi.org/10.3929/ethz-a-000687810

17. Zeng, Y., Song, W., Huo, F., Vizzari, G.: Modeling evacuation dynamics on stairs by an extended optimal steps model. Simulat. Model. Pract. Theory 84, 177–189 (2018). https://doi.org/10.1016/j.simpat.2018.02.001

18. Zhang, J., Klingsch, W., Schadschneider, A., Seyfried, A.: Transitions in pedestrian fundamental diagrams of straight corridors and t-junctions. J. Statist. Mech. Theory Exp. 2011(06), P06004 (2011). https://doi.org/10.1088/1742-5468/2011/06/p06004

Cluster Motion of Multiple Elevators and Indices Related to the Transportation Efficiency Studied in a Discrete Model Simulation

Sakurako Tanida[✉][ID]

Research Center for Advanced Science and Technology, The University of Tokyo,
4-6-1 Komaba, Meguro-ku, Tokyo, Japan
u-tanida@g.ecc.u-tokyo.ac.jp

Abstract. Elevators are familiar transporting systems exhibiting non-trivial out-of-equilibrium behaviors like the cluster motion in which multiple elevators arrive without much time between them. In this study, especially focusing on the interaction which occurs between elevators unintentionally and spontaneously and causes the cluster motion, we investigated the dynamic behavior of elevators during the down peak period by using a discrete model. We introduced a control parameter that changes the proportion of passengers who can get in an earlier-arriving elevator and numerically simulated the dynamics of the elevators. We examined the order parameter, the round-trip time, and the number of passengers transported in a single round trip. The cluster motion emerges when both the proportion of passengers who can get in an earlier-arriving elevator and the inflow rate are not small. In this condition, the round-trip time is short, and the number of passengers transported in a single round trip is small. Those results indicate that arriving without much time between elevators does not directly reduce the efficiency contrary to our intuition. In addition, we also investigated the response of an elevator to the external force by performing the control operation of one of the elevators.

Keywords: Elevators · Transportation system · Out-of-equilibrium · Oscillators

1 Introduction

As the urban population in the world is still increasing, the efficient usage of land has been more required. Building higher tower blocks can supply more space in limited areas, while it can take a longer time to move in such tower blocks. As the major system of transportation in high buildings is elevators, it is important to increase the efficiency of elevator transportation in the higher building for the urban economy. To increase the efficiency of transportation, improving directly the machine performance such as operating systems and hardware is one

ⓒ The Author(s), under exclusive license to Springer Nature Switzerland AG 2022
B. Chopard et al. (Eds.): ACRI 2022, LNCS 13402, pp. 324–331, 2022.
https://doi.org/10.1007/978-3-031-14926-9_29

method, however, investigating and understanding the phenomena that emerge unintentionally is also worthwhile because it can lead to coming up with a future breakthrough. A phenomenon popularly emerging in elevator systems is the cluster motion in that multiple elevator cars arrive on each floor almost at the same time. Pöschel et al. [1] demonstrated that elevators tend to synchronize their motion in down-peak, and Nagatani et al. [2] addressed elevators in up-peak also show synchronization. Also, behaviors in various conditions have been studied extensively in recent years [3–10]. However, the coupling interaction between elevators is not sufficiently discussed. One possible coupling interaction causing the cluster motion was the capacity of the elevator car, however, a previous study demonstrated that elevators with extremely large capacities also show the cluster motion [11]. In other words, the cluster motion occurs irrespective of the capacity of the elevator cars, which suggests that there are other factors that play a role in the coupling interaction.

In this study, we focus on the existence of passengers who can get in the elevator which arrives earlier as an interaction between elevators. Generally, the multiple elevators in the elevator hall adjoin each other, and passengers can move in the elevator hall to ride the earlier-arriving elevator. However, in the case that passengers cannot select the earlier-arriving elevators, for example, in the case that the distance to the elevator is too far for the passenger, the effect of arrivals of other elevators on the arrival timing of an elevator can become weaker. Thus, we introduced the proportion of the passengers who can ride the early-arriving elevator as a control parameter. We numerically simulated the time development of two elevators in a down peak period for the various value of the control parameter and investigated an order parameter characterizing the cluster motion, the round-trip time, and the transported number.

Furthermore, we investigated the entrainment, which is a phenomenon that the oscillators match their periods. As an external force for the elevator, we prepared a controlled elevator that stops on every floor and stays there for a given period of time. We examined the ratio of the round trip time of two elevators for the various round-trip time of the controlled elevator.

2   Problem Formulation

The elevator system consists of two elevators,elevators A and B, serving K floors (Fig. 1 and $K = 10$ in this study). The elevators take a time step to move one floor up or down and γ time steps for the passengers to enter or exit. We set the coefficients of the model as $\gamma = 10$. Consistent with previous studies [1,3,11,12], all calls are from passengers waiting for the elevators at k-th floor ($1 \leq k \leq K$) in order to move to the ground floor and exit the building. The elevators can simultaneously carry not more than Λ passengers.

The capacity of elevators is set to be large enough to accommodate any number of passengers, which is based on the results of a previous study showing that elevators move as a cluster even if the capacity is hugely large [11].

In this study, we consider a downward elevator system motion during peak loads. We assumed that the arrival of new passengers at each floor is a Poisson process. Thus, the number of new passengers on each floor and at every time steps, n, is distributed according to Poisson law:

$$P_\lambda(n) = \frac{\lambda^n}{n!}e^{-\lambda} , \tag{1}$$

where $\lambda = \mu/K$ is the Poisson parameter and μ stands for the passenger inflow rate for the entire building. We set η as the proportion of passengers who can ride an earlier-arriving elevator; Other passengers can ride in only the predetermined elevator.

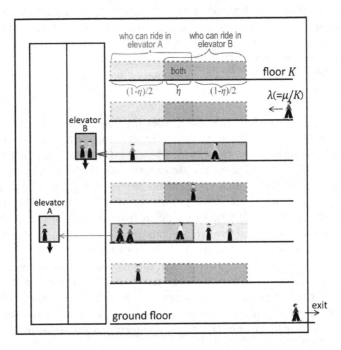

Fig. 1. Schematic of the model. We consider two elevators in a building with K floors except for the ground floor. The passengers arrive in front of elevators on the upper floors to move down to the ground floor. The proportion of η can ride in an elevator that arrives earlier; Others can ride in only the predetermined elevator.

The elevators do not necessarily move to the highest floor during each round trip in this study. Once an elevator goes down, it does not go up again until it arrives at the ground floor. If there are no passengers in neither the elevator nor floors, the elevators stay on the floor where they stopped until the next call. In case of no waiting calls and no passengers in the elevators, the next call will be accepted by the elevator closest to the calling floor. If the two elevators stay on the same floor without any passengers with a single new call, only one of the elevators moves. If there is more than one unresolved call and both elevators are free, the elevator which stops at a higher floor (the upper elevator) moves upward to the top floor. Simultaneously, the lower elevator starts moving if there are some calls it can reach faster compared to the upper one.

In order to estimate the time to go to the target floor k_t from the floor k, we make the following assumptions:

- If the elevator is going up or on the ground floor, it will stop at the highest floor among those having unresolved calls, k_h, and then will switch to going down and will stop at all floors with unresolved calls between k_h and k_t.
- If the elevator is going down and $k > k_t$, it will stop at all the floors with unsolved calls between k and k_t.

The estimated time is also employed to decide whether the lower elevator goes up or stops at a floor with unresolved calls when the upper elevator has passengers and goes down. Note that the actual time to arrive at the target floor is different from the estimated one because the number of waiting passengers is updated at every time step. As an initial condition, we set two elevators at random floor numbers and zero passengers on all floors. The elevators are not smart enough to identify the number of carrying passengers and possibly stop even if they are full.

3   Results

First of all, we investigated the dynamics of the two elevators for the various η and μ. To characterize the cluster motion, we use the order parameter of two elevators, which is defined as

$$S = \left| \frac{1}{N} \sum_{j=1}^{N} \exp\left(2\pi i \frac{\tau_j}{T}\right) \right| , \tag{2}$$

where τ_j is the time between j-th and $(j+1)$-th departures of either elevator on the ground floor, as used in previous studies [11,12]. T is a mean of the time of a round trip, which is defined as the time from the departure to the next arrival of each elevator. N is the total number of departures irrespective of which elevator is. This order parameter S represents the regularity of the time interval of the elevators arriving at the ground floor. S would be one when the two elevators arrive simultaneously, while it would be zero when the time interval differs for every arrival. Figure 2(a) shows S for various η and μ. S is small for small μ and increases with μ as consistent with the previous study [11]. Similarly, S tends to increase as η increases as shown in the previous study [12]. It indicates that the elevators show the cluster motion in the high η and μ regions. In contrast to the order parameter, the typical round-trip time and the number of passengers transported in a single round trip decrease with η [Fig. 2(b) and 2(c)].

To compare the efficiency when we change η at the same μ, we normalized the round trip time and the number of passengers transported in a single round-trip at each μ with the value at $\eta = 0$ [Fig. 3(a) and 3(b)]. Both measurements

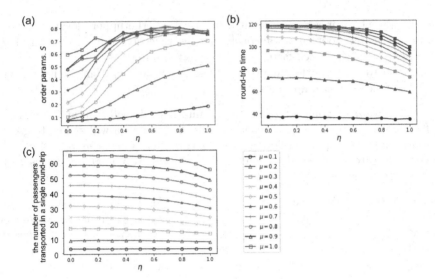

Fig. 2. (a) The order parameters for various η and μ. (b) The mean round-trip time for various η and μ. (c) The mean number of passengers transported in a single round trip for various η and μ.

decrease with η, which indicates that the average number of passengers transported per unit time will increase as η increases irrespective of μ. Although γ is constant in our model, however, the average number of passengers transported per unit time will increase more if γ increases linearly with the number of passengers riding on the elevator car. Those results indicate that the round-trip is short and the congestion in an elevator is reduced when the elevators move together.

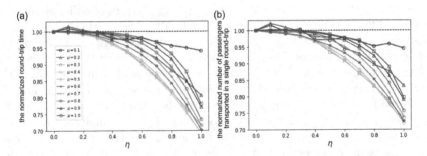

Fig. 3. (a) The round-trip time normalized by the value at $\eta = 0$ for each μ. (b) The number of passengers transported in a single round trip, which is normalized by the value at $\eta = 0$ for each μ.

Next, we examine the waiting time of each passenger, which is defined as the time since they arrive in front of the elevators until they get in an elevator. Figure 4 displays the distribution of the waiting time for various η at $\mu = 0.4$. As η increases, the maximum waiting time decreases, and the proportion of the number of passengers waiting less than 10 time steps time increases. It indicates that the waiting time when the elevators move together tends to be shorter.

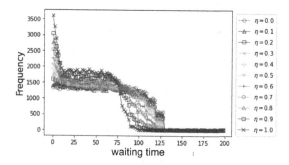

Fig. 4. The distribution of waiting time of each passengers at $\mu = 0.4$.

Finally, we examine the response of an elevator to the external force by performing the control operation. In the control operation, elevator A stops on all floors. We vary the round-trip time of elevator A, T_A, as a control parameter by changing the stopping time γ to satisfy $T_A = 2K + \gamma(K + 1)$. For the discrete simulation, γ is rounded to be an integer. Elevator B moves as follows the previous rules. Figure 5 displays the ratio of the round-trip time of elevators A and B, T_A/T_B, for various T_A, where T_B is the mean round-trip time of elevator B. At around $T_A = 100$, T_A/T_B is almost equal to one, which suggests that the entrainment occurs in this range of T_A. As shown in Fig. 5, the arriving timing of the two elevators are close typically, which suggests synchronization. At around

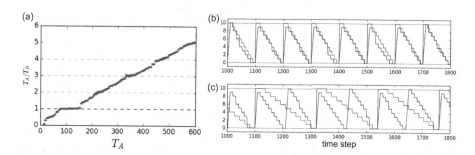

Fig. 5. (a) The ratio of the round-trip time of elevators A and B when elevator A is in the control operation. [(b) and (c)] Examples of the time evolution of the positions of elevators A and B. Red and blue lines represent the positions of elevators A and B, respectively. (b) $T_A = 100$ and (c) $T_A = 210$. (Color figure online)

$T_A = 210$, T_A/T_B is about two. However, it is not sure to be the entrainment because the range of $T_A/T_B = 2$ is small. Figure 5 shows the example of the time evolution of two elevators at $T_A = 210$. When elevator A arrives on the ground floor, elevator B tends to arrive on the ground floor also. To confirm the entrainment with different periods of elevators, further research is needed.

4   Discussion and Conclusion

In this study, we investigated the dynamics of two elevators in a down peak, focusing on the coupling interaction between the elevators which induces the synchronization of elevators. We introduced a control parameter, η, which change the proportion of passengers who can get in an earlier-arriving elevator and examined the order parameter, the round-trip time, and the number of passengers transported in a single round trip for various control parameter η and the inflow rate μ. The results showed that the elevators show disordered motion at small η whereas cluster motion is displayed at an enormous η. At the same time, the behaviors when μ increases are consistent with the previous studies; The elevators tended to exhibit the cluster motion in a large μ region. Next, we investigated the typical round trip time and the mean number of passengers transported per round trip. As η increased, the round trip time, T, became shorter, and the number of passengers transported in a single round trip, m, became smaller. The reduction rate of T when η increased was more significant than that of m, which indicates that the typical number of passengers transported per unit time would increase when η increased. Furthermore, we examined the distribution of waiting time of each passenger. As η increased, passengers who waited for an elevator for a short time increased while those who waited for a long time decreased.

Those results suggest the intuition that synchronization phenomena always reduce efficiency is not correct. A factor that this counterintuitive phenomenon occurs would be the rule that an elevator does not stop on a floor where passengers have just ridden other elevators and new passengers have not appeared until the elevator arrives. Moreover, the number of passengers in an elevator can be reduced at the same time that the number of passengers transported in unit time increases, which results in providing a comfortable ride during the synchronization of elevators occurs. We want to note that those results do not indicate that if synchronization occurs, then efficiency and comfort always increase. For example, when an operation rule that elevators always stop on a floor where other elevators are staying is employed, the round trip time does not improve even if the elevators show synchronization. In addition, we employed an extremely large capacity of an elevator car because we are interested in synchronization, which occurs irrespective of the capacity. For applications of these results to real scenarios, future studies that employ elevators with an appropriate capacity are needed.

Finally, we also investigated the ratio of the round trip time of two elevators when one of the elevators is in the control operation, in which the round-trip time of the elevator is set. When the round trip time of the controlled elevator is close to the natural round-trip time of elevator B, the entrainment occurs. It suggests that elevators can synchronize their motion to a so-call external force.

Acknowledgement. We are grateful to Katsuhiro Nishinari, Daichi Yanagisawa, Yuki Koyano, Kaori Sugimura, Jia Xiaolu, and Claudio Feliciani for helpful discussions and for their kind interest in this work. Part of this work was supported by JST [grant number JPMJMI20D1].

References

1. Pöschel, T., Gallas, J.A.C.: Synchronization effects in the dynamical behavior of elevators. Phys. Rev. E **50**(4), 2654–2659 (1994)
2. Nagatani, T.: Complex motion in nonlinear-map model of elevators in energy-saving traffic. Phys. Lett. A **375**(20), 2047–2050 (2011)
3. Hikihara, T., Ueshima, S.: Emergent synchronization in multi-elevator system and dispatching control. In: IEICE Transactions on Fundamentals of Electronics, Communications and Computer Sciences E80-A(9), pp. 1548–1553 (1997)
4. Nagatani, T.: Dynamical behavior in the nonlinear-map model of an elevator. Phys. A: Statist. Mech. Appl. **310**(1–2), 67–77 (2002)
5. Nagatani, T.: Complex behavior of elevators in peak traffic. Phys. A: Statist. Mech. Appl. **326**(3–4), 556–566 (2003)
6. Nagatani, T.: Dynamical transitions in peak elevator traffic. Phys. A: Statist. Mech. Appl. **333**, 441–452 (2004)
7. Nagatani, T., Tobita, K.: Effect of periodic inflow on elevator traffic. Phys. A: Statist. Mech. Appl. **391**(18), 4397–4405 (2012)
8. Nagatani, T.: Complex motion induced by elevator choice in peak traffic. Phys. A: Statist. Mech. Appl. **436**, 159–169 (2015)
9. Nagatani, T.: Effect of stopover on motion of two competing elevators in peak traffic. Phys. A: Statist. Mech. Appl. **444**, 613–621 (2016)
10. Feng, Z., Redner, S.: When will an elevator arrive? J. Statist. Mech. Theory Exp. **2021**(4), 043403 (2021)
11. Tanida, S.: Dynamic behavior of elevators under random inflow of passengers. Phys. Rev. E **103**(4), 042305 (2021)
12. Tanida, S.: Passengers' selections of early-arrival elevators induce the synchronization of elevators. arXiv preprint arXiv:2203.12854v1 (2022)

Other Studies on Cellular Automata

A Simple Model of Knowledge Percolation

Franco Bagnoli[1,2]([✉])[iD] and Guido de Bonfioli Cavalcabo'[1]

[1] Department of Physics and Astronomy and CSDC, University of Florence,
via G. Sansone 1, 50019 Sesto Fiorentino, Italy
`franco.bagnoli@unifi.it`, `guido.debonfiolicavalcabo@stud.unifi.it`
[2] INFN, sez. Firenze, Firenze, Italy

Abstract. We investigate how knowledge percolates and clusters in a given knowledge space. We introduce a simple model of knowledge organization in which each contribution spans a certain number of items. If this contribution overlaps with others above a certain threshold, they form a cluster. A contribution can also merge clusters together. We study the growth of global knowledge and the cluster dynamics, both showing a nontrivial behavior.

Keywords: Knowledge modelling · Knowledge visualization · Percolation model · Cluster dynamics · Agent based-model

1 Introduction

Knowledge is the set of ideas, emotions, beliefs and experiences, such as facts (descriptive knowledge), skills (procedural knowledge), or objects (acquaintance knowledge) owned by an individual or shared across collaborating individuals [7, 11]. It can be roughly seen as a set of concepts linked by some relationship (e.g. derivations linked to prerequisites or axioms to form theorems). The set of knowledge items that are connected by a path of links can be denoted as a cluster of knowledge.

A good representation of this description is a network [2] where the single knowledge items are the nodes and the links represent connections among items. A connected cluster is a corpus of knowledge. By adding knowledge three things can happen: the new knowledge item is isolated and forms an isolated cluster, it might join an existing cluster, or it may act as a connection between two clusters, fusing them together.

Since percolation describes the patterns of linked elements under a stochastic or semi-stochastic connection mechanisms [8,10], the process of filling the vector is analogous to a percolation process, and we can refer to it as the knowledge percolation problem [4,14].

The reference scenario is that of reconstructing the process that has led to the accumulation of a given corpus of knowledge, and, more important, the underlying cluster dynamics. There are many models that interpret the formation of a

B. Chopard et al. (Eds.): ACRI 2022, LNCS 13402, pp. 335–345, 2022.
https://doi.org/10.1007/978-3-031-14926-9_30

collaboration network by the random joining of individuals or contributions, i.e., the formation of a giant component by the establishment of random links. Our model is first of all bipartite, contributions contribute to the knowledge corpus, and the contribution overlaps gives the link among them. Moreover, we require a minimum overlap for establishing the link.

The whole corpus of knowledge can be spanned by several clusters separated by unknown elements of the corpus, or organized in a single cluster where all pieces of knowledge are connected by established relations, the process of acquiring knowledge has many similarity with the formation of a giant components in a random graph [3].

However, in a real case, redundant links are needed for considering concepts as belonging to the same cluster or discipline. So, we assume that a new knowledge item has to have minimum overlap with at least one of the members already belonging to the cluster to be inserted.

Alternatively, this model can be seen also as a collaboration model, in which every agent knows a certain number of concepts, but is able to collaborate with others (i.e. belong to the same group), only if they have a minimum overlap (like speaking the same language and having a shared background [5]), evaluating therefore the possibility of agents to collaborate or to communicate with others, that could be seen as the cooperation of individuals, research groups or societies, to solve a given problem represented by the knowledge vector.

Our model can serve as an interpretation tool for examining, ex-post, how a given corpus assembled and the relative cluster dynamics. For instance, one could study how authors cluster by measuring the overlaps between citations of their papers [9], or compare the evolution of customers of a supermarket by studying the overlap among their buying habits [13]. Our model is however still too rough to be compared with real data.

We study how the number and size of knowledge clusters evolve when adding new items. This can be considered as a k-core growth percolation problem, although normally k-core models are studied by pruning an existing network [6].

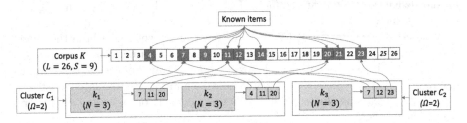

Fig. 1. Schematic representation of the system in the case of a knowledge space with $L = 26$ items, $N = 3$ and $\Omega = 2$ divided into two clusters $C_1 = \{k_1, k_2\}$ of size $c_1 = 2$ and $C_2 = \{k_3\}$ of size $c_2 = 1$.

2   The Model

We represented the corpus of knowledge K as a numbered set of L items, where $K(n) = 1$ if the knowledge item n is present in the corpus and $K(n) = 0$ if it is absent. Each contribution k_i is given by a set of N random items $k_i^{(n)}$, $n = 1, \ldots, N$ among the available ones $(k_i^{(n)} \in \{1, \ldots, L\})$,. When k_i is added to the corpus, we set $K(k_i^{(n)}) = 1$ for $n = 1, \ldots, N$.

The new contribution is added to a group if it has at least an overlap of Ω to one of the elements of the group. A new contribution can also cause the fusion of two separated groups. This process is illustrated in Fig. 1.

Once fixed the values of L, N and Ω, the algorithm proceeds as follows:

- Randomly generate a contribution k_i with N random items $k_i^{(n)}$ among the L available $(1 \leq k_i^{(n)} \leq L)$ without repetitions;
- Add this contribution to the knowledge corpus $K(k_i^{(n)}) = 1$ for $n = 1, \ldots, N$;
- Check if there is any overlap with all previous contributions k_j $(\forall j < i)$.
  By denoting this overlap $\omega_{ij} = \sum_{nl} \delta_{k_i^{(n)}, k_j^{(l)}}$ (where δ is the Kronecker delta), we can have three cases:
  1. $\omega_{ij} \geq \Omega$ and k_i not belonging to any group: k_i is added to the cluster C_m of k_j;
  2. $\omega_{ij} \geq \Omega$ and k_i already belonging to a group: merge the cluster C_m of k_i and C_q of k_j;
  3. $\omega_{ij} < \Omega$: create a new group C_q and assign k_i to it.

There are two different dynamics occurring in our model: how the knowledge corpus size grows, and how clusters are formed or merged together. The first one is a representation of how knowledge grows in a single individual or in a group/society, while the second one could be seen as the representation of how different branches of knowledge are intertwined [12].

2.1   Knowledge Corpus Dynamics

Let us denote the corpus size by $S = \sum_n K(n)$. In the case $L \gg N$, at the beginning contributions do not overlap because the probability to have overlapping items is too low. Therefore the corpus size S grows linearly with time.

The population dynamics of the corpus is an independent stochastic process, with the probability of adding an original contribution decreasing in time (t), while the number of those already present in the corpus (x) increases.

Let us examine the case with $N = 1$ for simplicity. The probability $(P(S, t))$ of having S items already present at time t is

$$P(S, t+1) = \frac{L - (S - 1)}{L} P(S - 1, t) + \frac{S}{L} P(S, t). \tag{1}$$

In the limit of continuous time and space, we have

$$\frac{\partial P}{\partial t} = -\frac{L - S}{L} \frac{\partial P}{\partial S} \tag{2}$$

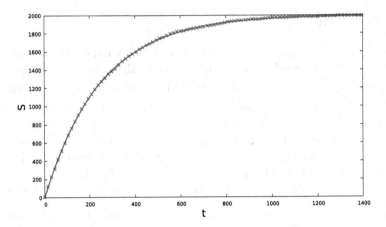

Fig. 2. Knowledge size S vs. time t for $L = 2000$, $N = 8$, $\Omega = 3$ (crosses) confronted with Eq. 4 (continuous line) with the same values of N.

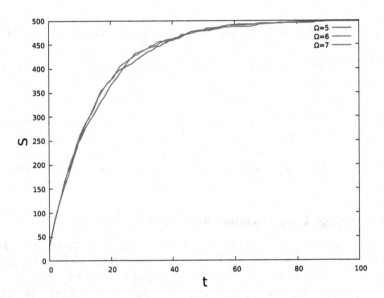

Fig. 3. Knowledge S vs. time t with $L = 500$ and $N = 31$ for several values of Ω.

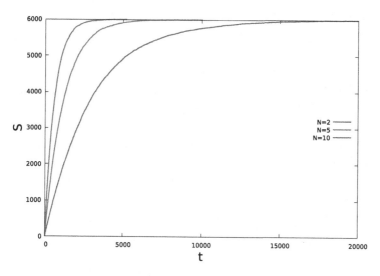

Fig. 4. Knowledge S vs. time t with $L = 6000$ and $\Omega = 1$ for several values of N.

And using the method of characteristics [1] we obtain that: $P = f\left((L-S)\exp(\frac{t}{L})\right)$ and therefore the average knowledge $(\overline{S})$ grows as $\overline{S} = L(1 - C\exp(-\frac{t}{L})$, where C is an integration constant, fixed by the initial condition $\overline{S}(0) = 0$, so that $C = 1$,

$$\overline{S} = L(1 - e^{-\frac{t}{L}}) \tag{3}$$

Since the addition of knowledge is an independent process we can write Eq. (3) with arbitrary N

$$\overline{S} = L(1 - e^{-\frac{Nt}{L}}). \tag{4}$$

Confronting Eq. (4) with the results of simulations we get an almost complete overlap as shown in Fig. 2, even though in simulations $\Omega > 1$.

Indeed, it seems that the knowledge size S does not depend much on the value of Ω, as shown in Fig. 3.

The knowledge size S grows faster for larger values of N, as shown in Fig. 4 and consistently with Eq. (4).

2.2   Cluster Dynamics

The number of clusters A at first grows with time, reaches a maximum and then decreases, ending with a single cluster, as reported in Fig. 5.

We can distinguish three phases:

- An initial almost linear growth of A, where new contributions mostly form a new cluster;
- An intermediate phase with, in which new contributions are mostly added to an existing cluster;

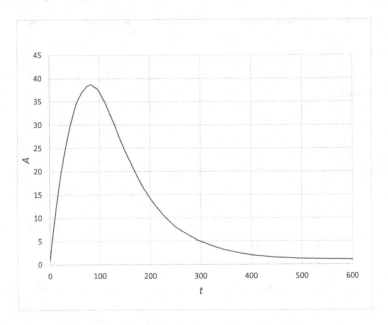

Fig. 5. Number of clusters A vs. time t for $L = 600$, $N = 2$ and $\Omega = 1$.

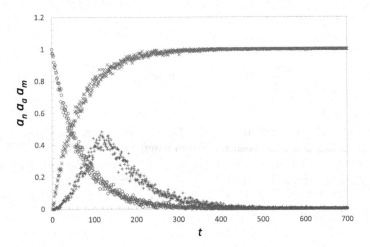

Fig. 6. Number of new clusters $a_n(t)$ (red circles), number of additions $a_a(t)$ (green times signs) and number of merging $a_m(t)$ (blue pluses) vs. time for $L = 600$, $N = 2$ and $\Omega = 1$. (Color figure online)

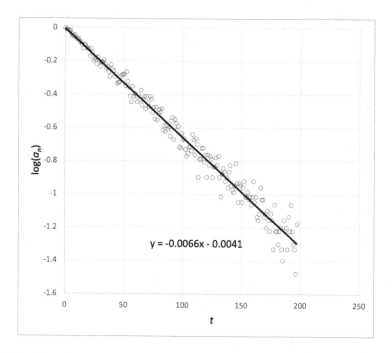

Fig. 7. Number of new clusters a_n vs. time t in log-log scale for $L = 600$, $N = 2$ and $\Omega = 1$. The exponential decreasing factor is $(3N - 4)/L$.

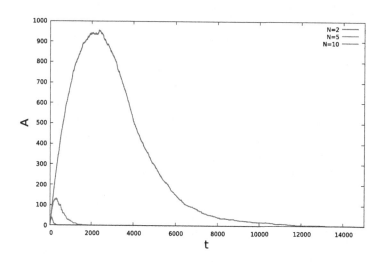

Fig. 8. Number of clusters A vs. time t for $L = 6000$, $\Omega = 1$ and varying N.

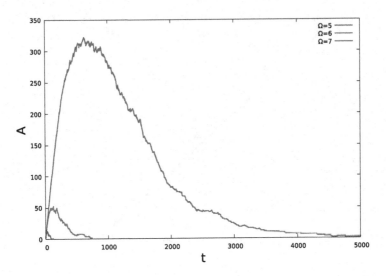

Fig. 9. Number of cluster A vs. time t for $L = 500$, $N = 31$ and varying Ω.

– A decreasing behavior dominated by cluster merging.

We measured the formation of a new cluster (number of new clusters $a_n(t)$), the addition to an existing cluster (number of additions $a_a(t)$) and the merging of two clusters (number of merging $a_m(t)$), as shown in Fig. 6.

The actions of forming new clusters or adding it to an existing one (whether or not it causes a merging) are mutually exclusive, therefore $a_n + a_a = 1$ and the total number of clusters $A(t)$ is given by

$$A(t) = \sum_{\tau=1}^{t} a_n(\tau) - a_m(\tau) \tag{5}$$

We can develop a simple approximation for a_n in the case $N = 1$, $\Omega = 1$, for which we have either the formation of a new cluster (of size one) or the addition of another cluster, and no cluster merging.

By denoting with $P(A, t)$ the probability of having A clusters at time t, we have

$$P(A, t+1) = \frac{L - A + 1}{L} P(A - 1, t) + \frac{A}{L} P(A, t)$$

which can be approximated by

$$\frac{\partial P}{\partial t} = \frac{A - L}{L} \frac{\partial P}{\partial A}$$

and therefore

$$P = f\left((A - L) \exp\left(\frac{t}{L} \right) \right)$$

so that, for large A and small t, we have

$$a_n(t) = \frac{d\overline{A}}{dt} \propto \exp\left(-\frac{t}{L}\right)$$

which, for $N > 1$ corresponds to

$$a_n(t) \propto \exp\left(-\frac{g(N)t}{L}\right)$$

and numerically, as shown in Fig. 7, we have roughly

$$g(N) = 3N - 4.$$

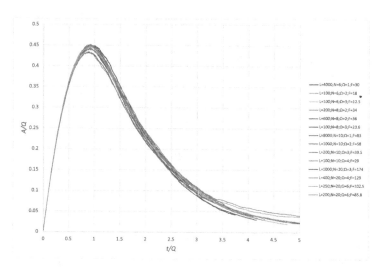

Fig. 10. Scaled A/Q vs t/Q with $Q = (L/F)^{\Omega}$.

The time distribution of the numbers of clusters $A(t)$ depends on N and Ω. In particular with a smaller number of items in each contribution (smaller value of N) is less probable to get items have an Ω overlap and therefore a larger number of clusters A will form before merging, as shown in Fig. 8.

On the contrary, having a smaller number of elements needed to match for merging (smaller values of Ω), means that the dynamics will reach the final state much faster, and the maximum number of clusters reached will be much smaller, as shown in Fig. 9.

It is therefore expected that $A(t)$ scales with N and Ω. Numerically, we found that all numerical curves overlap, as shown in Fig. 10, by rescaling A/Q and t/Q, with

$$Q = \left(\frac{L}{F}\right)^{\Omega}$$

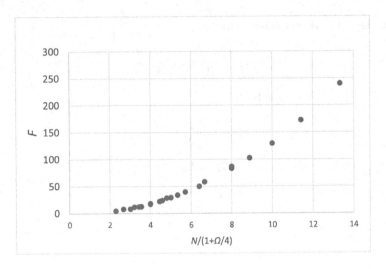

Fig. 11. Scaling factor F vs. $X = \frac{N}{1+\Omega/4}$.

and

$$F = aX^2 + bX + c$$

with

$$X = \frac{4K}{4 + \Omega}$$

as shown in Fig. 11. We have not found a valid approximation for this behavior.

3 Conclusions

We investigate a problem related to knowledge percolation, clustering and formation of a giant component, somewhat related to k-core percolation problems.

We studied a simple model in which each contribution is constituted by a certain number of items, joining a cluster or even fusing two of them when the overlap exceeds a given threshold. We showed that the growth of global knowledge and the cluster dynamics has a nontrivial time behavior, providing some analytical approximations.

References

1. Abbott, M.B.: An Introduction to the Method of Characteristics. American Elsevier (1966)
2. Barabási, A.L.: Network science: luck or reason. Nature **489**(7417), 507–508 (2012). https://doi.org/10.1038/nature11486
3. Ding, J., Kim, J.H., Lubetzky, E., Peres, Y.: Anatomy of a young giant component in the random graph. Rand. Struct. Algorithm. **39**(2), 139–178 (2010). https://doi.org/10.1002/rsa.20342

4. Essam, J.W.: Percolation theory. Rep. Progr. Phys.**43**(7), 833–912 (1980). https://doi.org/10.1088/0034-4885/43/7/001

5. Fleming, L., Frenken, K.: The evolution of inventor networks in the silicon valley and boston regions. Adv. Complex Syst. **10**(1), 53–71 (2007). https://doi.org/10.1142/s0219525907000921

6. Kong, Y.X., Shi, G.Y., Wu, R.J., Zhang, Y.C.: k-core: theories and applications. Phys. Rep. **832**, 1–32 (2019). https://doi.org/10.1016/j.physrep.2019.10.004

7. Kumbhar, R.: Knowledge organisation and knowledge organisation systems. In: Library Classification Trends in the 21st Century, pp. 1–6. Elsevier (2012). https://doi.org/10.1016/b978-1-84334-660-9.50001-1

8. Lee, D., Kahng, B., Cho, Y.S., Goh, K.I., Lee, D.S.: Recent advances of percolation theory in complex networks. J. Korean Phys. Soc. **73**(2), 152–164 (2018). https://doi.org/10.3938/jkps.73.152

9. Leicht, E.A., Clarkson, G., Shedden, K., Newman, M.E.: Large-scale structure of time evolving citation networks. Eur. Phys. J. B **59**(1), 75–83 (2007). https://doi.org/10.1140/epjb/e2007-00271-7

10. Li, M., Liu, R.R., Lü, L., Hu, M.B., Xu, S., Zhang, Y.C.: Percolation on complex networks: Theory and application. Phys. Rep. **907**, 1–68 (2021). https://doi.org/10.1016/j.physrep.2020.12.003

11. Renn, J.: The Evolution of Knowledge: Rethinking Science for the Anthropocene. Princeton University Press, Princeton (2020). https://press.princeton.edu/books/hardcover/9780691171982/the-evolution-of-knowledge

12. Shen, Z., et al.: Interrelations among scientific fields and their relative influences revealed by an input–output analysis. J. Informet. **10**(1), 82–97 (2016). https://doi.org/10.1016/j.joi.2015.11.002

13. Stassen, R.E., Mittelstaedt, J.D., Mittelstaedt, R.A.: Assortment overlap: its effect on shopping patterns in a retail market when the distributions of prices and goods are known. J. Retail. **75**(3), 371–386 (1999). https://doi.org/10.1016/s0022-4359(99)00013-5

14. Stauffer, D., Aharony, A.: Introduction to Percolation Theory. Taylor & Francis (1985). https://doi.org/10.4324/9780203211595

Cellular Automata Enhanced Machine Learning Model for Toxic Text Classification

M. J. Elizabeth⬤, Shekhat Meet Parsotambhai, and Raju Hazari⁽✉⁾⬤

Department of Computer Science and Engineering, National Institute of Technology, Calicut, Kerala, India
hazariraju0201@gmail.com

Abstract. As we know internet and social media usages are increasing day by day. Sometimes users take social media as a medium to use hateful and abusive comments that may rude and dis-respectful for others. So it is important to detect the toxicity and remove it from the social media. As social media users are in millions so it is impossible for filtering out the toxic comments manually, and hence there is a need for a method to filter out the toxic comments and make social media cleaner and safer to use. This paper aims to detect toxic comments in social media using cellular automata based LSTM (Long Short-Term Memory) model. Our approach produces 97.43% of F1_score without using any kind of pre-trained word embeddings or language models.

Keywords: Cellular automata (CA) · Toxic text classification · Machine learning · Long Short-Term Memory (LSTM)

1 Introduction

Social media has grown in popularity over time. People nowadays utilise social media to express themselves and their thoughts, as well as to talk with others. However, due to differences in opinion, conversations can sometimes devolve into ugly confrontations on social media, with toxic comments being utilised by one side. Comment can be classified as a toxic comment if users face issues like harassment, dis-respectful comments, insults, threats, abuse words and hate speeches. Detecting such toxic comments is important for prevent this type of attack from one user to another user and from one group to another group, and for discouraging associated wrongful activities. Because, this type of attack mentally affect to the person. Toxicity in social media is a serious problem for today's world as millions of people have been using social media. According to the pew poll on online harassment, every four out of ten internet users are victims of online harassment. It impacts many people. So it is important to solve this problem. Nowadays, social media platforms are attempting to eliminate toxic comments from their platforms. A few of the social media platforms gives access to their users to turn off comment section for safe online environment. Thus, such a task is inefficient and unscalable.

In the past, many deep learning based techniques have been designed for toxic comments detection in social media for English language. Abusive comment classification work started with Yin's work. Yin et al. [11] applied Term Frequency-Inverse Document Frequency (TF-IDF) and Support Vector Machine (SVM) features on a chat-style database. Georgeakopoulos [4] proposed a CNN model for toxicity classification and compared the results to K-nearest neighbours, SVM, Nave Bayes, and Linear discriminated analysis. This comparative study reveals that CNN is the best model with 92.7% accuracy score. Chu and Jue [3] also proposed a CNN model, in which they used word embeddings and character embeddings. CNN with character embedding performs better than CNN with word embedding with an accuracy of 94% is shown in their paper. Akash et al. [1] proposed a BERT - Transformer model with a RoBERTa weights which gives an accuracy of 95.15%. Transformers is a multi-head attention system that learns contextual relationships between words in a text. After identifying this, Facebook AI Research released RoBERTa (Robustly Optimized BERT Pre-training Approach), a robust and optimised version of BERT. A hybrid Deep Learning model with an accuracy of 98.39% presented by Beniwal et al. [2] using Jigsaw's dataset. But this model less performed with other datasets. Ameya and Feng [8] proposed a multi-task learning model with an attention layer gives AUC score of 0.9709. Kunnupudi et al. [6] used LSTM and LSTM with hyperbolic embeddings with an accuracy of 0.87% and 0.89% respectively.

In paper [3], Chu et al. tested word-level embeddings on the LSTM model which produces 93% of accuracy. But they did not test character-level enbeddings on LSTM. Our proposed approach uses character embedding on LSTM model. This characher embeddings are generated using cellular automata (CA) which produces cycle length (CL) sequences for text vectorization. These sequences are used as input for LSTM model. CA records the text information in the form of cycle length (CL) values. The classification is done by the LSTM model. In other papers, the classification is done using a machine learning model with some kind of pre-trained tools for language modeling such as Glove, BERT or word vectors etc. But our model does not use any pre-trained language models. CA with the LSTM model also works fine for this classification task.

The rest of the paper will proceed as follows. Section 2 describes the basics of cellular automata. The proposed CA based LSTM model design techniques are explained in Sect. 3. The performance analysis of the model is done in Sect. 4. Section 5, concludes the paper with recommended instructions for future work.

2   Basics of Cellular Automata

The journey of Cellular Automata has started with Von Neuman [7] for the purpose of modelling a biological self reproduction system. A cellular automaton (CA) is a discrete, spatially-extended dynamical system that has been studied extensively as a model of physical system. It evolves in discrete space and time.

A CA consists of a lattice of cells, each of which stores a discrete variable at time t that refers to the present state of the cell. The next state of a cell is affected by its present state and the present states of its neighbors at time t. In other words, a cellular automaton is made up of a regular grid of cells, each of which can be in one of a finite number of states. Each site or cell evolves with a finite set of values in discrete time by using a set of rules and the states of neighbourhood of sites around it. Elementary cellular automata (ECA) is the simplest form of CA, proposed by Wolfram [10]. In case of ECA, the next state of a cell is affected by its present state and the present states of its two nearest neighbors, and each of the CA cell store a binary state at time t. The next state of a cell is determined as :

$$S_i^{t+1} = f(S_{i-1}^t, S_i^t, S_{i+1}^t) \tag{1}$$

where f is the next state function, and S_{i-1}^t, S_i^t and S_{i+1}^t are the present states of the left, self, and right neighbor of the ith cell at time t. The function f : $\{0,1\}^3 \mapsto \{0,1\}$ can be expressed as a look-up table (see Table 1). The decimal equivalent of the 8 outputs is called 'rule' [10]. There are total $2^8 (= 256)$ ECA rules. Two such rules 90 and 150 are shown in Table 1.

Table 1. Look-up table for rule 90 and 150

Present State:	111 (7)	110 (6)	101 (5)	100 (4)	011 (3)	010 (2)	001 (1)	000 (0)	Rule
(i) Next State:	0	1	0	1	1	0	1	0	90
(ii) Next State:	1	0	0	1	0	1	1	0	150

Traditionally, each of the cells of a CA follows same next state function. Such a CA is called as *uniform* CA. On the other hand, if the CA cells are allowed to follow different next state functions (rules), the CA is a *non-uniform* (or *hybrid*) CA. In this work we used non-uniform ECA under periodic boundary condition where first and last cells are neighbors of each other.

3   Proposed CA Based LSTM Model Design

Long short term memory (LSTM) is one of the deep learning approach used for time-series data. LSTM architecture employs a recurrent neural network. Unlike traditional feed forward neural networks, LSTM has feedback connections. It's a special kind of recurrent neural network that can figure out long-term data dependencies. We have used LSTM for the processing of CL sequences because CL sequences are also a kind of time series data. The design of cellular automata based LSTM model for toxic comments detection can be categorized into three modules as shown in Fig. 1, which are listed below:

- Module-I : Text to rule vector conversion
- Module-II : CL Value generation
- Module-III : Implementation of LSTM model

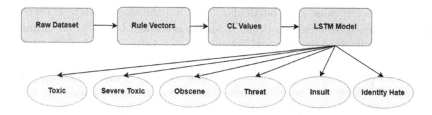

Fig. 1. Design of our model

Module-I : Text to Rule Vector Conversion

First of all, rule vectors are to be generated for the text vectorization process for each text in the dataset. These rule vectors are inputs to the CA machine. So, those vectors are created based on corresponding ASCII values of the characters in the text of the dataset as in the examples given below.

Text-1:
"You, sir, are my hero. Any chance you remember what page that's on?"
Rule Vectors for Text-1: [89, 111, 117, 44, 32, 115, 105, 114, 44, 32, 97, 114, 101, 32, 109, 121, 32, 104, 101, 114, 111, 46, 32, 65, 110, 121, 32, 99, 104, 97, 110, 99, 101, 32, 121, 111, 117, 32, 114, 101, 109, 101, 109, 98, 101, 114, 32, 119, 104, 97, 116, 32, 112, 97, 103, 101, 32, 116, 104, 97, 116, 39, 115, 32, 111, 110, 63].

Text-2:
"I would appreciate an apology from both of you but I can see that is unlikely."
Rule Vectors for Text-2: [73, 32, 119, 111, 117, 108, 100, 32, 97, 112, 112, 114, 101, 99, 105, 97, 116, 101, 32, 97, 110, 32, 97, 112, 111, 108, 111, 103, 121, 32, 102, 114, 111, 109, 32, 98, 111, 116, 104, 32, 111, 102, 32, 121, 111, 117, 32, 98, 117, 116, 32, 73, 32, 99, 97, 110, 32, 115, 101, 101, 32, 116, 104, 97, 116, 32, 105, 115, 32, 117, 110, 108, 105, 107, 101, 108, 121, 46].

Module-II : CL Value Generation

The rule vectors obtained from the Module-I are given as input to CA machine. For generating CL values, the CA is initialized with alternate 0's and 1's (Random initialization does not affect the results because the initial condition is the same for all the sentences. If we change the initial condition then it will change for all the sentences in the dataset. So it does not affect the results). After that based on the state of the neighbours cells in CA, the next state of the current cell is obtained using the rule number in the rule vectors. CA machine evolves 2000 times. This step value is considered based on the length of the text. (The maximum length of the text in the dataset we consider is approximately equals to 5000 and we saw that there is no change in the CL values after 2000 times of evolution.) After certain iterations on a particular cell, the pattern starts repeating. The length of the pattern is called Cycle Length (CL) value. We consider this value as a CL value for a particular CA cell if the same pattern is repeating at-least 32 times. The length of the CL values are taken based on the minimum 32 times repetition of the pattern. We can use any value instead of 32, that will not affect the performance because CL values are the length of the repeated pattern. If there is no repeated pattern found in the CA cell, we assign the CL value of the cell is '0'. The evolution of CA shown in Fig. 2. The CL sequences of Text-1 and Text-2 are given below:

CL Values of Text-1: [6, 2, 1, 1, 1, 2, 2, 2, 1, 1, 3, 9, 9, 9, 9, 9, 1, 1, 2, 2, 1, 1, 1, 1, 1, 3, 3, 3, 1, 1, 1, 1, 1, 1, 1, 1, 1, 1, 1, 1, 1, 1, 1, 3, 3, 3, 3, 3, 6, 2, 1, 2, 1, 1, 1, 1, 1, 1, 1, 1, 1, 3, 3, 3, 3, 3, 3, 3, 3].

CL Values of Text-2: [1, 1, 2, 2, 1, 1, 1, 1, 3, 3, 3, 3, 6, 2, 1, 2, 1, 1, 1, 2, 1, 1, 3, 3, 3, 3, 24, 8, 8, 8, 4, 2, 1, 1, 1, 3, 3, 6, 6, 2, 1, 1, 1, 1, 1, 6, 6, 6, 6, 6, 6, 3, 3, 3, 3, 1, 1, 2, 2, 1, 1, 1, 1, 13, 13, 13, 13, 13, 13, 1, 1, 1, 1, 1, 1, 1, 1, 1].

	1	0	0	0	0	0	1	
	0	0	1	0	1	1	1	
	0	0	0	1	0	1	1	
	0	1	1	0	0	1	0	
	1	0	1	1	0	0	0	
	0	0	1	0	1	1	1	
	0	1	0	1	0	1	1	
	1	0	0	0	0	0	1	
	0	1	1	1	1	1	0	
	0	1	1	0	1	1	0	
	1	0	0	1	0	0	1	
	0	1	1	0	1	1	1	
	0	0	0	1	0	0	1	
	1	0	0	0	0	0	0	
	0	1	0	1	0	0	0	
	0	0	0	0	0	0	1	
	1	1	0	1	1	0	1	
	0	1	0	0	1	0	1	

Fig. 2. CA evolution

Module-III : Implementation of LSTM Model

The CL sequences obtained from Module-II are converted to numpy array or tensors, then used as an input to the LSTM model. This prediction model is one of the deep learning method, so no need to extract features manually. The feature set needed for the prediction process are automatically extracted from the CL sequences. In CA evolution the entire text is considered as it is, in the form of rule vectors are evolving for finite amount of time. Therefore, the model does not require any pre-trained knowledge for extracting information. To record extra information, LSTM introduces a memory cell that has the same shape as the hidden state as well as a number of gates for memory cell control. The cell's entries are read out using the output gate. An input gate is required to determine when data should be read into the cell. Finally, we need a forget gate-controlled mechanism to reset the cell's content. We have used sequential model of keras for building the LSTM model. Sequential model allows us to build model, layer by layer and each layer has its own input and output tensors.

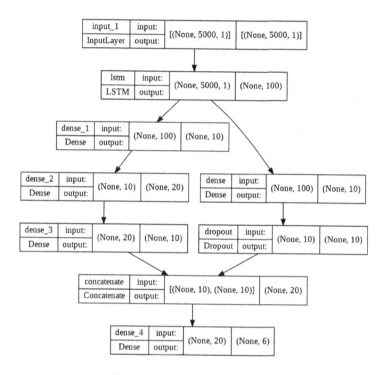

Fig. 3. Layers of LSTM model

In our model, the input is given to the input layer with maximum CL sequence length (For *Jigsaw* dataset [5], the maximum sequence length is 5000) and number of neurons (we used 100 neurons here) and the other four layers used here are LSTM layer, dense layer, concatenate layer and dropout layer. We used *ReLU* activation function in all the layers except dropout layer and output layer. In a neural system, a dense is simply a typical layer of neurons, receives the output of all previous layers neurons and helps with gradient flow refinement. The over-fitting problem is fixed by using dropout layers because dropout is a regularization strategy for minimizing over-fitting in neural networks by eliminating or ignoring a number of layer outputs. In other words, it sets input units to '0' at random with a rate frequency at each step throughout the training period. The output layer is dense layer with *Sigmoid* activation function for getting comment labels of six classes such as toxic, obscene, severe toxic, insult, threat and identity hate. The number of layers and neurons used in our model is shown in the Fig. 3 and the proposed step by step procedure is explained in the algorithm 1.

Algorithm 1 Algorithm for toxic text classification using CA based LSTM model

---

INPUT: Textual Comments
OUTPUT: Predicted labels for each comments.

1: Pre-process each comments in the dataset for generating rule vectors.
  – Removal of long repeated patterns.
  – Removal of non ASCII characters.
  – Removal of blank rows from the dataset.
2: Convert pre-processed data into CA rule vectors using ASCII values.
3: Find out the CL sequences using CA rule vectors.
4: Implement a sequential LSTM model for toxic text classification using *adam* optimiser and *Relu or sigmoid* activation function.
5: With the aid of a specified threshold value, predict the labels for toxic comments.
6: Performance analysis of our model is done by calculating precision, recall, accuracy and F1_Score using the formulae:

$$Precision = TP/(TP + FP) \tag{2}$$

$$Recall = TP/(TP + FN) \tag{3}$$

$$Accuracy = (TP + TN)/total \ \# \ of \ comments \tag{4}$$

$$F1\_Score = (2 * precision * recall)/(precision + recall) \tag{5}$$

7: Calculate Error rate or Mis-classification rate of proposed model using the following equation:

$$Error \ rate = (FP + FN)/total \ \# \ of \ comments \tag{6}$$

In toxic text classification, '0' represents positive comments (non toxic) and '1' represents negative or toxic comments. So the terms used in the equations (2) – (4) and (6) are defined as follows:

– True Positives (TP): These are correctly predicted positive comments (non toxic)
– True Negatives (TN): These are correctly predicted negative comments (toxic comments)
– False Positives (FP): These are incorrectly predicted positive comments (Also known as a "Type I error.")
– False Negatives (FN): These are incorrectly predicted negative comments (Also known as a "Type II error.")

Jigsaw Dataset: The dataset [5] is collected from the Kaggle website which contains two set of files. The training set contains 1,59,572 comments that they have divided into 6 toxicity labels: toxic, obscene, severe toxic, insult, threat and identity hate. The testing set contains 1,53,165 comments with same labels. The difference what we analysed in the dataset is that, each class of the training set contains only binary values: 0 and 1. The following percentages of toxicity were found in the training dataset: toxic (10%), severe toxic (1%), obscene (5%), threat (0.3%), insult (5%), identity hate (1%). But in the testing set there are three values : 0, 1 and -1. So all the entries of -1 are removed from the test set. Now the size of the testing dataset is 63,479.

4   Results and Performance Analysis

The proposed model is cross validated using the training set of Jigsaw dataset. In the cross-validation approach the model is validated using subsets of input data; that is to train the model, a subset of input data is used and then testing process is done on previously unknown subset of the same input. So, we used a function **train_test_split** of sklearn python module for spliting training data into random train and test subsets. The first experiment is done on 5 subsets of 90:10 splitting of the input dataset. We got an accuracy as per Table 2. Finally, the same process is repeated for 80:20 splitting of input data. The results are shown in Table 3. The overall accuracy of the cross validation process is calculated by taking the average of toxic score, severe_toxic score, obscene, threat, insult and identity_hate score of the above experiment results, which is of 96.31%.

Table 2. Accuracy calculation (when train and test-data ratio is 90:10)

Dataset	Toxic	Severe_toxic	Obscene	Threat	Insult	Identity_hate
Set-1	92.35	98.4	95.02	99.54	94.78	98.97
Set-2	91.08	98.72	94.61	99.24	95.02	99.26
Set-3	90.71	98.46	94.03	99.36	94.16	98.74
Set-4	93.06	98.33	94.92	99.14	95.26	98.07
Set-5	92.14	98.61	94.24	99.48	94.48	99.13
Avg.	**91.86**	**98.5**	**94.56**	**99.35**	**94.74**	**98.83**

Table 3. Accuracy calculation (when train and test-data ratio is 80:20)

Dataset	Toxic	Severe_toxic	Obscene	Threat	Insult	Identity_hate
Set-1	90.65	98.03	94.79	99.04	94.98	98.46
Set-2	91.76	99.04	95.04	99.23	95.11	99.02
Set-3	90.49	98.47	95.69	99.37	95.74	99.14
Set-4	92.34	98.63	94.36	99.03	95.34	98.84
Set-5	90.52	99.04	94.65	99.16	94.96	99.09
Avg.	**91.15**	**98.64**	**94.9**	**99.16**	**95.22**	**98.91**

The entire Jigsaw dataset [5] is used for training and testing in our model and the results are shown in Table 4. The overall training accuracy and validation accuracy of the Jigsaw dataset are 99.42% and 99.41% respectively. Testing results such as accuracy, precision, recall and F1_score for each category are given in the Table 4. The average misclassification rate of the proposed model is 4.95%, calculated using Eq. 6. The overall accuracy and F1_score for testing dataset is 95.03% and 97.33% respectively.

Table 4. Results obtained with Jigsaw dataset

Metrics	Toxic	Severe_toxic	Obscene	Threat	Insult	Identity_hate	Average
Accuracy	90.07	96.15	92.73	98.20	94.17	98.87	**95.03**
Precision	99.51	96.67	98.23	98.52	99.49	100	**98.73**
Recall	90.45	99.43	94.29	99.66	94.62	98	**96.08**
F1_Score	94.77	98.03	96.24	99.09	96.99	99.43	**97.43**

There are no baseline articles available to compare the outcomes of the proposed model more closely. So we have done a comparative study with other techniques as per Table 5.

Table 5. Different models and their results in terms of F1_score for Jigsaw dataset

Authors	Techniques used	F1_score
Wang et al. (2021) [9]	CNN with GloVe	99.5%
Zhao et al. (2021) [12]	RoBERTa	78.22%
Akash et al.(2021) [1]	BERT	95.15%
Georgakopoulos et al.(2018) [4]	CNN	91.2%
Our model	**CA based LSTM**	**97.43%**

5   Conclusion

Toxicity in social media is a serious problem for today's world and have many negative impacts on the mental health of people in society. So it is important for us to detect the toxicity and remove those harmful comments from the social media. We designed a model for toxic comments detection based on cellular automata without using any pre-trained word embeddings. We explored cellular automata based technique to detect and classify toxic comments on social media platforms. Our model is giving a good accuracy score of 95.03% for the jigsaw dataset.

We can improve the efficiency of the model by reducing the false positive and the false negative rates. The improvement can be accomplished further through fine-tuning the LSTM parameters such as the number of neurons, epochs, and batch size. It is also necessary to assess the presence of over-fitting and under-fitting concerns. In future, we will explore different tasks in this direction. We will develop a similar CA based model to classify toxic comments in dialects and will focus on performance and error analysis of the model.

References

1. Akash, G., Kumar, H., Bharathi, D.: Toxic comment classification using transformers. In: Proceedings of the 11th Annual International Conference on Industrial Engineering and Operations Management Singapore, pp. 1895–1905 (2021)
2. Beniwal, R., Maurya, A.: Toxic comment classification using hybrid deep learning model. In: Karuppusamy, P., Perikos, I., Shi, F., Nguyen, T.N. (eds.) Sustainable Communication Networks and Application. LNDECT, vol. 55, pp. 461–473. Springer, Singapore (2021). https://doi.org/10.1007/978-981-15-8677-4_38
3. Chu, T., Jue, K., Wang, M.: Comment abuse classification with deep learning. https://web.stanford.edu/class/archive/cs/cs224n/cs224n.1174/reports/2762092
4. Georgakopoulos, S.V., Tasoulis, S.K., Vrahatis, A.G., Plagianakos, V.P.: Convolutional neural networks for toxic comment classification. In: Proceedings of the 10th Hellenic Conference on Artificial Intelligence, pp. 1–6 (2018)
5. Jigsaw (2018). https://www.kaggle.com/competitions/jigsaw-toxic-comment-classification-challenge/data
6. Kunupudi, D., Godbole, S., Kumar, P., Pai, S.: Toxic language detection using robust filters. SMU Data Sci. Rev. **3**(2), 12 (2020)
7. von Neumann, J.: The Theory of Self-Reproducing Automata. Burks, A.W. (ed.) University of Illinois Press, Urbana, London (1966)
8. Vaidya, A., Mai, F., Ning, Y.: Empirical analysis of multi-task learning for reducing identity bias in toxic comment detection. In: Proceedings of the International AAAI Conference on Web and Social Media, vol. 14, pp. 683–693 (2020)
9. Wang, K., Yang, J., Wu, H.: A Survey of Toxic Comment Classification Methods. arXiv preprint arXiv:2112.06412 (2021)
10. Wolfram, S.: Theory and Applications of Cellular Automata. World Scientific, Singapore (1986)
11. Yin, D., Xue, Z., Hong, L., Davison, B.D., Kontostathis, A., Edwards, L.: Detection of harassment on web 2.0. In: Proceedings of the Content Analysis in the WEB, vol. 2, pp. 1–7 (2009)
12. Zhao, Z., Zhang, Z., Hopfgartner, F.: A Comparative Study of Using Pre-trained Language Models for Toxic Comment Classification, pp. 500–507. Association for Computing Machinery, Inc. (2021). https://doi.org/10.1145/3442442.3452313

Irregular Learning Cellular Automata for the Resolution of Complex Logic Puzzles

Theodoros Panagiotis Chatzinikolaou⊙, Rafailia-Eleni Karamani⊙, and Georgios Ch. Sirakoulis(✉)⊙

Department of Electrical and Computer Engineering,
Democritus University of Thrace, Xanthi 67100, Greece
{tchatzin,rkaraman,gsirak}@ee.duth.gr
http://gsirak.ee.duth.gr

Abstract. Learning Automata (LA) in combination with Cellular Automata (CA) have been proven to be viable candidates as a mean to deal with problems of high complexity. Their ability to learn and adapt combined with their inherit parallelism can speed-up the solution process of various problems, including complex logic puzzles. A well-known logic puzzle is the Sudoku, which is a combinatorial optimization problem of increased difficulty and complexity. In this work, the representation of a Sudoku puzzle as a Irregular Learning Cellular Automaton (ILCA) has been explored, incorporating the necessary rules of a reward and penalty algorithm as a resolution process. The results prove the successful operation of the proposed algorithm, highlighting the concurrent and learning capabilities of the ILCA structure.

Keywords: Complex logic puzzles · Sudoku · Cellular Automata · Learning Cellular Automata

1 Introduction

Since their introduction [2], Learning Cellular Automata (LCA) have sparked the interest of the research community as a promising architecture for the resolution of a wide variety of problems. The combination of the parallel processing computational capabilities of Cellular Automata (CA) with the learning capabilities of Learning Automata (LA) has introduced the principles of Learning Cellular Automata (LCA) modeling tool. LCA is a distributed computational model [1] where, through the spatial interaction of simple identical units, global complex phenomena can emerge. The characteristic that differentiates LCA from traditional CA is the adaptation of the decision process. LCA improves the behavior of its cells based on the overall system's response, in an effort to provide optimal results [2].

The Sudoku is a combinatorial optimization problem whose roots connect it to the ancient magic square problem (Latin squares). A common property of

B. Chopard et al. (Eds.): ACRI 2022, LNCS 13402, pp. 356–367, 2022.
https://doi.org/10.1007/978-3-031-14926-9_32

many complex logic puzzles (including Sudoku) is that the solver is challenged not to only find the solution but this must be realized under the constraint that a unique solution exists. This solution should be delivered following the puzzle's specific rules and not only by using search in the space of all possible solutions [16]. The LCA's adaptivity and ability to learn and correcting itself, make it an appropriate candidate for the resolution of logic puzzles that can benefit from these characteristics. In this work, we will explore the adequacy of Irregular Learning Cellular Automata (ILCA) to challenge the Sudoku puzzle. This architecture was selected as the LCA's spatial characteristics reveal appropriate fitting towards modeling of the Sudoku's configuration. They can also adapt during their evolution to Sudoku's set of rules which are closely related to its spatial connections.

2   Basics of the Employed Computational Models

2.1   Learning Automata

One model of Automata, capable of operating in abstract and random environments, are the Learning Automata (LA) [13]. A LA performs an action guided by its past actions and responses and its environment responds to this action, either favorably or not. The system's goal is to learn how to choose the optimal action to perform. In detail, a LA selects one action from a set of L available actions $T = \{T_1, T_2, ..., T_L\}$ based on this action's occurrence probability; therefore, there is an action probability vector $P = \{p_1, p_2, ..., p_L\}$ that characterizes the LA. Initially, all actions have the same probability to be selected by the LA. During its time evolution, the LA receives feedback from its environment through a reinforcement signal that updates the action probability vector. As a result, the LA favors the desired actions by increasing their probabilities and, at the same time, penalizes the undesired ones by decreasing their corresponding probabilities. This process is repeated for a predefined number of time-steps until the LA has learned how to choose the optimal action depending on the application [13].

2.2   Learning Cellular Automata

Combining the properties of CA and LA results in the introduction of a hybrid model, called Learning Cellular Automata (LCA). LCA are a distributed learning model that effectively combines the parallel processing capabilities of CA with the learning capabilities in unknown environments of LA. A LCA is a CA grid where each cell utilizes a finite number of LA as learning modules. Therefore, LCA aims to improve "classical" CA by enhancing them with learning abilities and, thus, making them suitable for a wider range of applications that may require probabilistic behavior. At the same time, LCA can be considered superior to LA as they exploit local interactions of CA to achieve learning and, moreover, receive feedback from neighboring cells to adjust the action probability vector.

■ Irregular Learning Cellular Automata

The LCA's structure can be either regular or irregular depending on the restrictions applied at its connectivity. In the case of Irregular Learning Cellular Automata (ILCA) the restriction for a regularly structured grid is removed. The connections among the cells of the ILCA are undirected and update of the cells' states is affected by the selected rule. On the contrary, in "classical" CA, the cell state update in this case is determined through the action probability vector which is updated considering actions selected by the LAs. During the ILCA's time evolution, the action probability vectors of neighboring LAs vary making the local environment of each LA, non-stationary.

In detail, the ILCA's operation in time can be described by the following. Consider an ILCA consisting of N cells where each cell c_i contains a LA, namely, LA_i whose action set A_i is finite (for $i = 1, 2, ..., N$). Initially, every cell's state is specified through the action probability vector of the LA that resides within that particular cell. At every following iteration k, each LA, LA_i selects an action a_i. Based on the selected action a_i, a reinforcement signal b_i, computed using the ILCA's rule, is applied to the LA. This reinforcement signal will either favor or penalize the specific action and serve as the basis to update the action probability vector for the next time-step of the ILCA's evolution in time. This process is repeated for a sufficient number of time-steps, until the system reaches the desired behavior. Figure 1 presents a 4×4 ILCA grid, and the respective connections among its cells, providing a more detailed insight in the red circle.

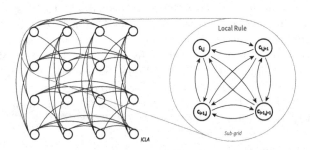

Fig. 1. 4×4 ILCA structure.

In general, the CA getting also inspiration by variations of LCA and ILCA have been properly utilized to solve a variety of complex problems like the shortest path [18], the collision avoidance [6,11], the graph coloring [17], logic design [4], edge detection [7], as well as the bin-packing and the maximum-cut ones [12]. Their adaptivity along with their inherit parallelism can provide viable and scalable solutions to computationally-heavy problems and, thus, the resolution of complex logic puzzles could be a perfect-fit. Having all these in mind, along with the irregularity of ILCA, solving a Sudoku puzzle could be dealt accordingly as it is a well-known NP-hard problem, i.e. its solution can not be found in polynomial time.

3   Complex Logic Puzzles: The Sudoku Paradigm

A complex logic puzzle is defined as a problem that, following specific steps, leads to the extraction of one or more definite solutions. They differentiate from games on the basis that puzzles are solved whereas games are won. The typical characteristics of logic puzzles include: single player, simple rules that dictate their evolution, language independency and solution by deduction [5].

One of the most popular logic puzzles available is the Sudoku. It became popular in Japan in 1986 and also gained international popularity in 2005. It is often described as "the Rubik's cube of the 21st century" [9]. It derives its attraction from its characteristic of following very simple rules that lead to its solution, yet the course of reasoning that is required for its completion can turn out to be of high difficulty and complexity. Each puzzle configuration leads to a unique solution and does not require the search of the solution, meaning it is based merely on reasoning.

In detail, a typical Sudoku puzzle is represented as a 9 × 9 grid (although other variations also exist), divided in nine 3 × 3 sub-grids. Each one of the Sudoku's 81 cells is assigned a value from 1 up to 9. Initially, only some of the cells are filled with their assigned number. A partially filled 9 × 9 Sudoku grid that specifies a unique cell with its unique column, unique row and unique sub-grid is shown in Fig. 2. The puzzle's goal is to fill the entire grid with the appropriate values such that the following rule is satisfied [15]:

- Each row contains exactly once every integer from 1 to 9.
- Each column contains exactly once every integer from 1 to 9.
- Each 3 × 3 sub-grid contains exactly once every integer from 1 to 9.

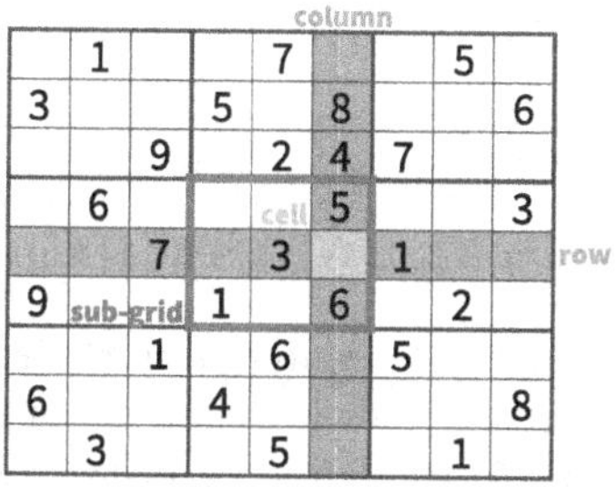

Fig. 2. 9 × 9 Sudoku grid with initial predefined cells specifying a cell with yellow, a column with blue, a row with brown and a sub-grid with green. (Color figure online)

4   Solving Sudoku Puzzles

Several approximate optimization methods have been explored for the resolution of the Sudoku problem. In [10], it is proposed solving of Sudoku puzzles by using a combinatorial genetic algorithm. Other efforts include a metaheuristic technique [8] to be applied on a large number of problem instances and to provide a robust method, especially for lower order puzzles. Deep learning methods have also been successfully applied [19], where an input image is utilized to further detect the largest area contour and extract the digits from the Sudoku image using Optical Character Recognition (OCR). These digits are inserted in a neural network which ultimately outputs the solution of the puzzle. Hardware-based solutions are also presented in literature including FPGA-based implementations performing genetic and/or heuristic algorithms [20] as well as unconventional and novel nano-devices like memristors emerging to the solution due to the circuit dynamics [3]. Furthermore, Artificial Bee Colony algorithm has been used [14] as an alternative method to find the optimal solution in Sudoku puzzles.

4.1   Solving Process Using Irregular Learning Cellular Automata

As already mentioned, a Sudoku puzzle consists of a grid divided in 81 cells. Representing a Sudoku puzzle using CA can be realized considering the Sudoku as a graph, where each node corresponds to a cell of the puzzle. Therefore, the CA is a 81-node graph (9×9) with undirected connections among the cells and 9 possible cell states. Two cells are neighboring, thus affect each others state evolution, when they are adjacent. For the case of Sudoku there is a 9×9 grid where every cell $C_{i,j}$, $1 \leq i \leq 9$ and $1 \leq j \leq 9$, is connected to all the cells in the same column ($N_{i,j}^c$), all the cells in the same row ($N_{i,j}^r$) as well as all the cells in the same 3×3 sub-grid ($N_{i,j}^{sg}$). Therefore, each cell will have 20 neighbors ($N_{i,j}$) excluding itself. The rule that dictates the ILCA's evolution considers the states of all the neighbors. These neighboring connections are described as follows:

$$N_{i,j}^c = \{C_{1,j}, C_{2,j}, ..., C_{9,j}\} \tag{1}$$

$$N_{i,j}^r = \{C_{i,1}, C_{i,2}, ..., C_{i,9}\} \tag{2}$$

$$N_{i,j}^{sg} = \{C_{i-1,j-1}, C_{i-1,j}, C_{i-1,j+1}, C_{i,j-1}, C_{i,j}, C_{i,j+1}, C_{i+1,j-1}, C_{i+1,j}, C_{i+1,j+1}\} \tag{3}$$

$$N_{i,j} = N_{i,j}^c \cup N_{i,j}^r \cup N_{i,j}^{sg} \cap C_{i,j} \tag{4}$$

Solving a Sudoku puzzle can be benefited from incorporating learning characteristics to the resolution process, allowing the system to adapt to every unique puzzle configuration. This leads to equipping every cell of the CA with a LA, resulting to LCA. Due to the irregular connectivity among the cells, the grid can be considered a graph, and solving the puzzle is translated to the use of ILCA. With given initially predefined cells, every Sudoku puzzle has a unique solution.

The action probability vector of each cell's LA is updated in every time-step following a reward and penalty algorithm until the ILCA chooses a valid solution for the given grid configuration. The criterion that dictates the action selection of the ILCA is the degree of the cell ($d_{i,j}$). To enhance the algorithm's operation, the neighboring cells also affect directly the probability vector for every possible cell state in order to boost the initial function but not to overpass it. Degree of a cell $d_{i,j}$ is defined as the number of neighboring cells whose selected action is different (i.e. the number of cells that did not choose the same action):

$$d_{i,j} = |C_{k,l}, \text{ for each } C_{k,l} \in N_{i,j} \text{ where } c_{k,l} \neq c_{i,j}| \tag{5}$$

```
 1  FinalizedCells = 0
 2  for each cell C_{i,j}
 3      if d_{i,j} == |N_{i,j}|
 4          P^{t+1}_{i,j}(c^t_{i,j}) = P^t_{i,j}(c^t_{i,j}) · a(d_{i,j})
 5          FinalizedCells++
 6      elseif d_{i,j} > max[d_{k,l}, for each C_{k,l} ∈ N_{i,j} where c_{k,l} = c_{i,j}]
 7          P^{t+1}_{i,j}(c^t_{i,j}) = P^t_{i,j}(c^t_{i,j}) · a(d_{i,j})
 8      else
 9          P^{t+1}_{i,j}(c^t_{i,j}) = P^t_{i,j}(c^t_{i,j}) · p(d_{i,j})
10      end
11      for each neighbor C_{k,l} ∈ N_{i,j} and each number n ∈ [1,9]
12          if P^t_{k,l}(n) > 1/9 :
13              P^{t+1}_{i,j}(n) = P^{t+1}_{i,j}(n) · p(P^t_{k,l}(n))
14          else
15              P^{t+1}_{i,j}(n) = P^{t+1}_{i,j}(n) · a(P^t_{k,l}(n))
16          end
17      end
18  end
19  if FinalizedCells < 81
20      t++
21      goto line 1
22  end
```

Pseudo code of the proposed ILCA sudoku resolution algorithm.

4.2 Irregular Learning Cellular Automata Algorithm

The resolution process to solve Sudoku by ILCA indicates that each Sudoku cell is mapped to a cell of the ILCA where each cell's variables are the chosen action/cell's state ($c_{i,j}$) and its action probability vector ($P_{i,j}(n)$). The ILCA receives the initialized Sudoku graph, with some predefined numbers, as input. Initially, the predefined numbers probability is considered as 100%, while their neighbors as 0%. Thus, for the remaining cells and numbers, all states have equal probabilities to be selected.

The generated output of the ILCA is the solved puzzle. For the ILCA evolution every cell is characterized by its degree. The chosen action which depicts the cell's state is considered as the number (n) with the highest probability.

$$c^t_{i,j} = n, \text{ where } P^t_{i,j}(n) = \max[P^t_{i,j}(k)], k \in [1,9] \tag{6}$$

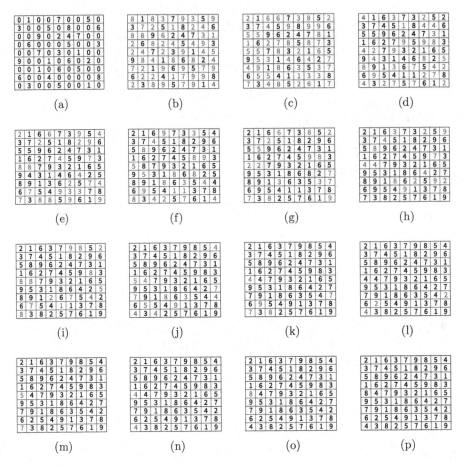

Fig. 3. Step-by-step solving of a 9×9 Sudoku using the proposed algorithm. (a) Initial configuration. (b–o) Intermediate steps presenting updated numbers in red. (p) Final solved puzzle. (Color figure online)

In each step, the probability vector is awarded or penalized multiplying the respective probability of the number by a factor a (award) or p (penalty):

$$P_{i,j}^{t+1}(n) = P_{i,j}^{t}(n) \cdot (a(\bullet) \mid p(\bullet)), \text{where } a(\bullet) > 1 \text{ and } p(\bullet) < 1 \quad (7)$$

After the ILCA has been initialized, the presented algorithm occurs to reach the generated output, where the cell state assignments are evaluated so as to achieve the necessary conditions for the resolution of the puzzle.

In detail, if the cell has selected an action that is different from the actions selected by all its neighbors, i.e. the cell's degree is equal to number of neighbors, then it is rewarded resulting its probability to get increased (lines 3–4). In case the cell selects an action that has been selected by some of its neighbors, then this action will only be rewarded under the condition that this cell's degree is greater than the degrees of all its neighbors that have selected the same action (lines 6–7). Otherwise, the selected action is penalized, so its occurrence probability decreases (lines 8–9). Regarding the direct effect from neighboring cells, for each possible cell state, if neighbor's probability to be in this state is greater than the average, then the corresponding probability of the cell is penalized (lines 12–13). If not, it will be rewarded (lines 14–15). Each cell will choose the action with the highest probability from its available action set. The above process is repeated until all cells' actions are different from their neighboring ones, i.e. FinalizedCells is equal to the total number of ILCA cells (lines 19–21).

5   Results and Discussion

The described algorithm was simulated using the MATLAB® R2020a software. As a proof of concept, Fig. 3 presents the results obtained after the simulation of a 9×9 Sudoku grid. Initially the values of the predefined cells are given, and the evolution of the ILCA is provided focusing on the changed numbers of each time-step. After 10 time-steps, the changes are limited to just a few cells driving to the solution of the 9×9 Sudoku on 15 time-steps. This proves the inherit parallelism of CA in combination with the stochastic and learning capabilities of LA can lead to the successful resolution of Sudoku in limited time-steps showcasing the proposed ILCA ability over other implementations.

The action probability vector evolution for each cell is presented in Figs. 4 and 5. Predefined cells can be easily spotted as the probability of the predefined cell state remains 100% (e.g. $c_{1,2}, c_{2,6}, c_{3,3}, ...$). Also, cells that have ruled off all numbers except from one due to the initialization phase can be spotted with the remaining cell state to have 100% probability throughout the ILCA's evolution (e.g. $c_{3,9}$). For the rest cells, the probabilities vary in each time-step resulting to changes on the cell state which leads to different chosen actions. In some cases the successful selection of the cell state took place at the beginning of the evolution (e.g. $c_{2,2}, c_{5,8}, ...$), while on other cases the selection needed more time-steps to end up to the final cell state selection (e.g. $c_{5,1}, c_{9,1}, ...$). It should be noted that on some cells there was an overturn on the cell state even if there was a divergence between these numbers (e.g. $c_{1,6}, c_{7,1}, ...$) verifying the learning and adaptive capabilities of the proposed algorithm.

Considering the generalization of the proposed algorithm in various Sudoku puzzles, the required time-steps to achieve a solution is 4 for easy puzzles, 6 for medium ones, and 16 for hard ones. These time-steps are derived as the mean time-steps from a set of 30 different randomly-generated Sudoku puzzles.

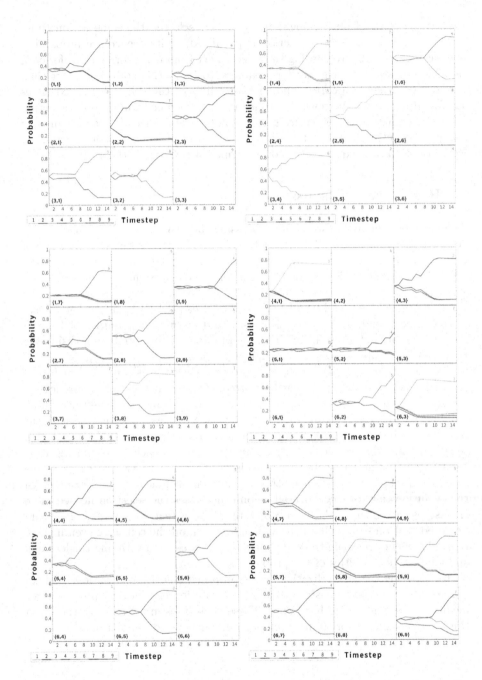

Fig. 4. Action probability vector evolution in time-steps for each possible cell state for every cell of the 9 × 9 Sudoku. For clarity, the Figure has been split in two parts and this part is depicting cells from (1,1) up to (1,9), (2,1) up to (2,9), (3,1) up to (3,9), (4,1) up to (4,9), (5,1) up to (5,9) and (6,1) up to (6,9).

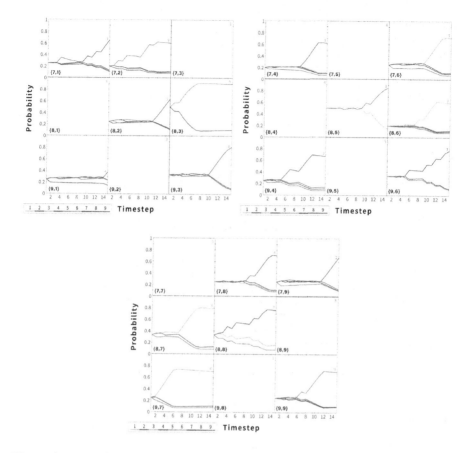

Fig. 5. Action probability vector evolution in time-steps for each possible cell state for every cell of the 9 × 9 Sudoku. For clarity, the Figure has been split in two parts and this part is depicting cells from (7,1) up to (7,9), (8,1) up to (8,9) and (9,1) up to (9,9).

6   Conclusions

In this work, we have presented an ILCA algorithm for the resolution of Sudoku puzzles. The process that is followed exploits successfully the CA's spatial and temporal evolution enriched with learning capabilities. The ILCA's ability to solve the Sudoku in only a few time-steps proves that this can be a promising architecture for several problems that have analogous characteristics. As future work, a more extensive testing of the proposed algorithm with larger number of Sudoku puzzles will be investigated in order to quantitatively compare its results with other methods.

Acknowledgments. The work of Rafailia-Eleni Karamani was supported by the Hellenic Foundation for Research and Innovation (HFRI) under the HFRI PhD Fellowship grant (Fellowship Number: 1333).

References

1. Ahangaran, M., Taghizadeh, N., Beigy, H.: Associative cellular learning automata and its applications. Appl. Soft Comput. **53**, 1–18 (2017)
2. Beigy, H., Meybodi, M.R.: A mathematical framework for cellular learning automata. Adv. Compl. Syst. **7**(3–4), 295–319 (2004)
3. Chatzinikolaou, T.P., et al.: Memristive oscillatory circuits for resolution of np-complete logic puzzles: sudoku case. In: 2020 ISCAS, pp. 1–5 (2020)
4. Floros, T., Tsakalos, K.A., Dourvas, N., Tsompanas, M.A., Sirakoulis, G.C.: Unconventional bio-inspired model for design of logic gates. Int. J. Unconvent. Comput. **15**(3), 141–156 (2020)
5. Hufkens, L.V., Browne, C.: A functional taxonomy of logic puzzles. In: 2019 IEEE Conference on Games (CoG), pp. 1–4. IEEE (2019)
6. Ioannidis, K., Sirakoulis, G.C., Andreadis, I.: A cellular automaton collision-free path planner suitable for cooperative robots. In: 2008 Panhellenic Conference on Informatics, pp. 256–260 (2008)
7. Karamani, R.E., Fyrigos, I.A., Tsakalos, K.A., Ntinas, V., Tsompanas, M.A., Sirakoulis, G.C.: Memristive learning cellular automata for edge detection. Chaos Solitons Fractals **145**, 110700 (2021)
8. Lewis, R.: Metaheuristics can solve sudoku puzzles. J. Heurist. **13**(4), 387–401 (2007)
9. Lynce, I., Ouaknine, J.: Sudoku as a sat problem. ISAIM **11**(1), 6–13 (2006)
10. Mantere, T., Koljonen, J.: Solving, rating and generating sudoku puzzles with GA. In: 2007 IEEE Congress on Evolutionary Computation, pp. 1382–1389 (2007)
11. Mitsopoulou, M., Dourvas, N.I., Sirakoulis, G.C., Nishinari, K.: Spatial games and memory effects on crowd evacuation behavior with cellular automata. J. Comput. Sci. **32**, 87–98 (2019)
12. Mozafari, M., Shiri, M.E., Beigy, H.: A cooperative learning method based on cellular learning automata and its application in optimization problems. J. Comput. Sci. **11**, 279–288 (2015)
13. Narendra, K.S., Thathachar, M.A.L.: Learning automata - a survey. IEEE Trans. Syst. Man Cybern. SMC **4**(4), 323–334 (1974)
14. Pacurib, J.A., Seno, G.M.M., Yusiong, J.P.T.: Solving sudoku puzzles using improved artificial bee colony algorithm. In: ICICIC 2009, pp. 885–888. IEEE (2009)
15. Russell, E., Jarvis, F.: Mathematics of Sudoku II. Math. Spect. **39**(2), 54–58 (2006)
16. Simonis, H.: Sudoku as a constraint problem. In: CP Workshop on Modeling and Reformulating Constraint Satisfaction Problems, vol. 12, pp. 13–27. Citeseer (2005)
17. Torkestani, J.A., Meybodi, M.R.: A cellular learning automata-based algorithm for solving the vertex coloring problem. Exp. Syst. Appl. **38**(8), 9237–9247 (2011)
18. Tsompanas, M.-A.I., Dourvas, N.I., Ioannidis, K., Sirakoulis, G.Ch., Hoffmann, R., Adamatzky, A.: Cellular automata applications in shortest path problem. In: Adamatzky, A. (ed.) Shortest Path Solvers. From Software to Wetware. ECC, vol. 32, pp. 199–237. Springer, Cham (2018). https://doi.org/10.1007/978-3-319-77510-4_8

19. Vamsi, K.S., Gangadharabhotla, S., Sai, V.S.H.: A deep learning approach to solve sudoku puzzle. In: 2021 ICICCS, pp. 1175–1179. IEEE (2021)
20. Van Der Bok, K., Taouil, M., Afratis, P., Sourdis, I.: The TU Delft sudoku solver on FPGA. In: 2009 International Conference on Field-Programmable Technology, pp. 526–529. IEEE (2009)

Author Index

Printed in the United States
by Baker & Taylor Publisher Services